Ernie Shepherd

THE MIDLAND
GREAT WESTERN RAILWAY
OF IRELAND

An Illustrated History

Midland Publishing
Limited

This book is dedicated to
Joy, Lynda and Alan for their patience
and understanding

© 1994
W Ernest Shepherd

Published by
Midland Publishing Limited
24 The Hollow, Earl Shilton
Leicester, LE9 7NA
England

ISBN 1-85780-008-7

Printed and bound by
Woolnough Bookbinding Limited
Irthlingborough, Northants.
NN9 5SE

Designed by
Midland Publishing
and Stephen Thompson Associates.

Typeset in
ITC Garamond and Gill Sans

Title page:
'Lm' 0-6-0 No.84 'Dunkellen'.
Built at Broadstone in 1891, the 'Lm' class
was similar in many respects to the
'L' class of 1885, but incorporated
improvements introduced on the '7-12'
and 'E' classes. The main difference was
the use of steel rather than wrought iron
for the frames and boiler. This locomotive
was withdrawn in 1925.
The late H Fayle, courtesy IRRS.

Front cover:
Trains hauled by two 'E' class 0-6-0
tank locomotives pause at Mallaranny on
the Westport to Achill branch.
The MGWR branches to Achill, Clifden
and Killala were largely financed by
public money advanced under the terms
of the Light Railways (Ireland) Act of
1889. Built at a cost of £131,400, the 27
mile line was opened in 1895 and
closed in 1937.
Courtesy John Kennedy.

CONTENTS

The illustration on this page is of Galway station, taken from an early woodcut.

PREFACE

IN A SERIES of articles published in the *Railway Magazine* in 1926, and subsequently published in book form in 1954, E L Ahrons made the following opening remarks in relation to the Midland Great Western Railway of Ireland. 'The Midland Great Western Railway was, perhaps, the most Irish of the large main line railways on this side of the water'. This is true, for the Great Southern & Western Railway had close affinities with the London & North Western Railway, the Waterford & Limerick Railway was closely influenced by the Great Western Railway (of England), while the Great Northern Railway showed many similarities with its English namesake and of course the Belfast & Northern Counties Railway was in later years annexed by the Midland Railway of England. Rumours did occasionally surface of possible alliances between the MGW and either the L&NW or the Lancashire & Yorkshire Railway, but nothing came of them.

The Midland, as it was generally known in Ireland, had a character all of its own. The locomotives and coaching stock designed by Martin Atock had a very distinctive appearance as had the later coaching stock built under Edward Cusack. One reason why the MGWR was not so well known outside of Ireland, surmised Ahrons, was that fewer English people travelled on Midland trains since the line travelled through wild country: 'Travelling companions, other than those disciples of Isaak Walton, consisted chiefly of politicians, priests, farmers and people who had a horse to sell'. The system served a mainly agricultural area of the country, much of which, particularly west of the River Shannon, suffered from extreme poverty. Changing fortunes in agriculture affected the railway company's prosperity more than most other lines. The only towns of note between Dublin and Galway were Mullingar, Athlone and Ballinasloe.

As the 150th anniversary of the Company's Act of Incorporation approaches, it is a fitting time to record the history of this fascinating railway. It is hoped that the reader will receive as much enjoyment as did the author in researching it. Any errors or omissions are the fault of the author.

ACKNOWLEDGEMENTS

IT WOULD have been impossible to have written a history of this nature without assistance from many sources. First of all, the author owes a great debt of gratitude to the Secretary of CIE and the staff of his office for allowing access to the various Minute books, not only of the MGWR, but also of other lines whose history overlapped that of the Midland. This research provided the basic skeleton onto which the finished product was moulded. The Director and staff of the National Library of Ireland provided free access to newspaper files, Ordnance Survey maps, Parliamentary papers and manuscript sources, all of which helped to add flesh to the skeleton. The Librarian and the Archivist of the Irish Railway Record Society have allowed access to the vast store of material in the Society's care, much of which is no longer available elsewhere.

Many individual members of the Irish Railway Record Society have assisted in many and varied ways, and whilst there is a danger in naming individuals of omitting somebody's name, the following must receive special mention. The late Robin 'Bob' Clements spent a lifetime studying the Midland, and gave freely of his time and knowledge. In addition, he read the draft manuscript, made corrections, and suggested alterations. Michael Conlon, son of a railwayman, kindly provided extracts from Westmeath and Longford papers which he has been researching for some years. Padraig O'Cuimin likewise has researched aspects of the Midland and graciously provided the author with locomotive and rolling stock drawings. Other IRRS members who contributed included John Kennedy, Kevin Murray, the late Jim O'Dea, and Peter Rowledge. The section on tickets is the result of researches by the late Charles R Gordon Stuart and Eugene Field, acknowledged experts in this specialised subject.

In compiling the photographic content of the book, I am deeply indebted to my good friend John Kennedy of the Green Studios, as witnessed by the many illustrations attributed to him. John has been active in restoring the fine glass plate negatives taken by the late Harold Fayle. These photographs are now in the care of the Irish Railway Record Society and have been made available through the kindness of the committee of the Society. The historic photograph of Sligo around 1870 comes from the collection of Mr H Fraser of Sligo, via Mr Leslie Matson of Cork. The photographs of Jim O'Dea, who had the foresight to record stations at a time when other enthusiasts were concentrating on locomotives, are now in the care of the National Library of Ireland, and I am grateful to the Director and staff of the library for access to this material. Other illustrative material came from either the cameras or the collections of Athlone Public Library, W H Butler, Des Coakham, L Daly, Des McGlynn, K A Murray and H Richards. Pictures from other sources as well as those from the Fayle collection, were supplied by the IRRS.

Thanks are due to H Richards and the London area of the Irish Railway Record Society for permission to reproduce the layout of Broadstone. Other station drawings are courtesy CIE. Tom Ferris of Midland Publishing also requires a special mention.

In the event that I have omitted anyone, please accept my apologies and my gratitude for assistance.

AUTHOR'S NOTE

AS MENTIONED in the Preface, the Midland Great Western Railway was generally referred to in Ireland as 'the Midland'; only in official circles was it known by its full title. The Midland Railway of England also operated and controlled a railway system in Ireland, but as it was generally known in its earlier years as the Northern Counties Railway and later simply as the Northern Counties Committee, the author uses the term 'Midland' in the context by which it was familiarly known in Ireland. English readers should appreciate that the Midland Great Western Railway had no connection with the English Midland Railway, my use of the term 'Midland' always refers to the Midland Great Western Railway and never to the synonymous Derby based owners of lines in Ulster.

Some thought has been given to the spellings of place names. In general, the spellings used by the railway company have been adopted although they do not in all cases agree with those used by the Ordnance Survey. For example, the latter refer to Innfield, Moyvally and Ballysadare, whereas the railway used Enfield (the name by which the village is signposted), Moyvalley and Ballysodare. Since this work deals with the history of the railway, it was felt more appropriate to adopt its spellings.

The 24-hour clock has been used throughout, except in direct quotations from other sources.

Reference to monetary values have been expressed in the currency of the period. Prior to 1970, the pound (£) was divided into 20 shillings, each of 12 pence – there being 240 old pennies to the £. The abbreviations used were 's' for shillings and 'd' for pence.

The acknowledged expert on the MGWR and especially its locomotives, was 'Bob' Clements of Celbridge in County Kildare. Just before this book went to press we had the sad news of Bob's death. Though he did not live to see his work in print in this book, Chapter Fourteen in particular owes much to his research over the years.

SOURCES

DURING my researches, many documents have been consulted and the following is a list of the more important sources: The board and traffic minutes of the following railway companies – Athenry & Ennis Junction, Dublin & Meath, Dublin & South Eastern (and its predecessors, including the City of Dublin Junction), Great Northern & Western, Great Southern & Western, Midland Great Western and the Waterford, Limerick & Western. In addition, in respect of the MGW, some further minute books have survived for some periods, relating to locomotives and officers' conferences. Other MGWR sources which have been used are working timetables and their appendices, weekly circulars, rule books, carriage and wagon drawings, the carriage and wagon register of 1891 which is still extant, the notebooks of W H Morton and station layout and signalling diagrams. Much useful information is contained in Ordnance Survey maps, Parliamentary papers and railway companies Acts of Parliament, also in arbitration proceedings and the Board of Trade's reports on accidents. Many of the makers' drawings of MGWR carriages and wagons are held on microfilm in the Birmingham Public Library.

Newspapers referred to:
Connaught Telegraph,
Galway Vindicator, Irish Independent,
Irish Press, Irish Times,
Longford Independent,
Mayo Constitution, Meath Herald,
Roscommon Journal,
Saunders Newsletter, Sligo Champion,
Westmeath Independent.

Railway periodicals:
The Engineer, Engineering,
Herepath's Railway Journal,
Irish Railfans' News,
Irish Railway Bulletins,
Irish Railway Gazette,
Journals of the IRRS, The Locomotive,
Railway Gazette, Railway Magazine,
Railway News, Railway Times.

Other printed sources referred to:
The Baronial Lines of the MGWR:
    O'Cuimin, P; Transport Research Ass.
The Cavan & Leitrim Railway:
    Flanagan, P; David & Charles, 1966.
The Dublin & South Eastern Railway:
    Shepherd, E; David & Charles, 1974.

Fifty Years of Railway Life:
    Tatlow, J; Railway Gazette, 1920.
A Fortnight in Ireland:
    Head, Sir F; 1852.
The Great Northern Railway:
    Murray, K; GNR, 1944.
The Great Northern Railway:
    Patterson, E; Oakwood Press, 1962.
The Great Southern & Western Railway:
    McNeill, D & Murray, K; IRRS, 1976.
A Guide to the MGWR:
    Measom, G; MGWR, 1866.
History of Railways in Ireland:
    Conroy, J; 1927.
Irish Railways since 1916:
    Baker, M; Ian Allan Limited, 1972.
Irish Railways Today:
    Pender, B & Richards, H;
    Transport Research Association, 1967.
Irish Steam Locomotive Register:
    Rowledge, P; Irish Traction Group, 1993.
Locomotive & Train Working in the 19th Century: Ahrons, E; Heffer & Sons, 1954.
MGWR 1847-1947 - A Locomotive History:
    Clements, R; unpublished, 1947.
Railways in Ireland, 1834-1984:
    Doyle, O & Hirsch, S; Signal Press, 1983.

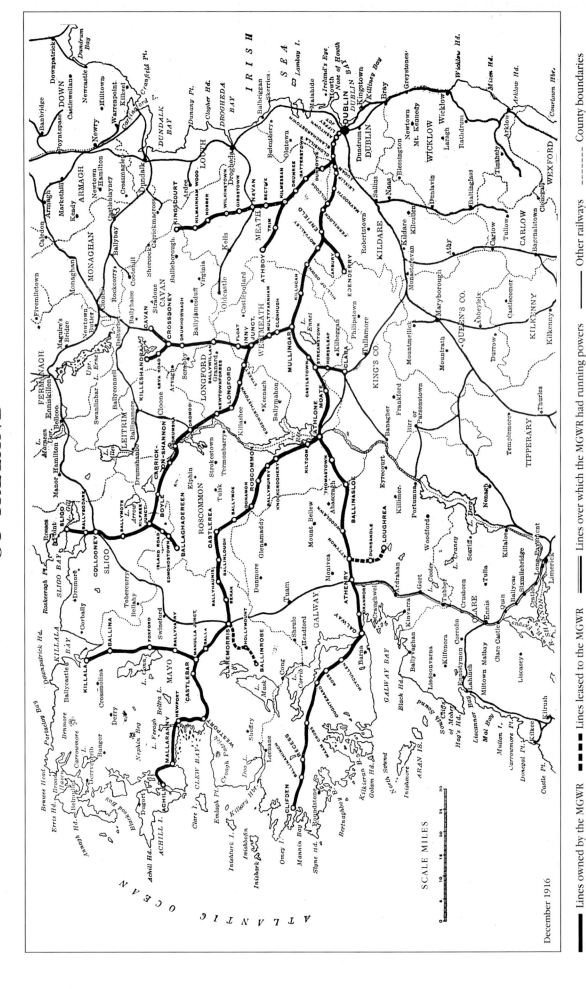

MAP OF THE
MIDLAND GREAT WESTERN RAILWAY
OF IRELAND

December 1916

Lines owned by the MGWR ▬▬▬ Lines leased to the MGWR ▰▰▰ Lines over which the MGWR had running powers ▬▬▬ Other railways ─── County boundaries ------

SCALE MILES

Chapter One

THE FORMATIVE YEARS

THE Midland Great Western Railway, running right across the centre of the country from east to west and serving 13 of the 32 counties of Ireland, passed through almost as many variations of landscape as it did counties. Much of the area through which the line was constructed was impoverished and sparsely populated and even today there are few centres of population, Mullingar and Athlone being notable exceptions. The counties of Meath, Westmeath and Kildare comprise excellent pasture; Meath was a centre for fattening cattle transported from the cattle rearing lands of East Galway. Counties Longford, Westmeath and Cavan are situated in the heart of the central lowland and all three have numerous lakes. Longford in particular lies wholly in the basin of the River Shannon, which forms the boundary between the provinces of Leinster and Connaught. A characteristic of Longford is the succession of drumlins or hump-backed hills dating from the last ice-age.

The famous phrase 'to Hell or Connaught' dating from the time of Cromwell's sojourn in Ireland in the middle of the seventeenth century was apt, particularly in the years of famine. Much of the land in the province of Connaught is of poor quality providing a bare subsistence for many smallholders. Population density is low – the county of Galway with an area of 2,293 square miles had a population of around 150,000 in 1980, of whom some 35,000 lived in Galway city itself. Galway is a county of extremes – to the east of the city is the lush cattle rearing area which includes Ballinasloe, noted for its large livestock fair held in the first week of October. In 1853, some 20,000 cattle and 100,000 sheep were offered for sale. This fair still continues but is now considerably smaller. The western portion of the county is sparsely populated and dominated by the Maamturk and Twelve Bens or Twelve Pins mountains. It is an area of outstanding natural beauty and is therefore a major destination for tourists.

The more northerly counties of Leitrim, Roscommon and Mayo, particularly the former, have land of poor quality. Most of the emigration immediately after the disastrous famine years of 1845 to 1848 took place

from the counties west of the Shannon and it was to remain a feature of life in this part of Ireland ever since that time. In addition, many young people travelled to England and Scotland to take part in the potato harvest. Special fares were arranged for these travellers.

Amongst the first railways proposed for connecting Dublin with the west coast was the Grand Atlantic Railway & Steam Packet Company whose prospectus was published in 1835. This company hoped to construct a line from Dublin via Mullingar, Foxford, Ballina and Crossmolina to Blacksod Bay; from where it planned to operate a steamer service to Halifax and New York. Another early contender was the Great Central Irish Railway, the route of which bore strong similarities to that later followed by the Midland. Before the scheme could get off the ground however, the Government appointed a Royal Commission to consider the country's future transport needs. This effectively put a brake on railway speculation for the moment.

A searching enquiry was carried out and a report issued in 1838. It should be remembered that the population of the country at this time was calculated to be somewhat in excess of eight and a half million, with the largest concentration in the north-eastern counties. Whilst the northern, southern and midland counties were reasonably prosperous, the commission found the inhabitants of Connaught 'decidedly inferior both in condition and appearance'. Their cabins were wretched hovels with beds of straw and the staple diet consisted only of potatoes. The report said that 'poverty and misery (had) deprived them of all energy'.

When one considers that it was this area which was to be principally served by the Midland one can perhaps understand the problems encountered. Furthermore, these comments were made before the disastrous famine years between 1845 and 1850 decimated the population. It is reckoned that at least one million people died and a further million emigrated, setting a pattern for the future.

Lord Lucan, who was the power behind the later Great Northern & Western Railway, was said to have done more to assist emigra-

tion with the building of the railway into Mayo than any other agency. In this context, it is perhaps hardly surprising to find that the commission felt there was no necessity for railway communication to the west; in any event it was already well served by the two great canals, one of which should never have been constructed in the first instance. The report found serious flaws in the figures put forward by the GCI, which were likely to ruin its investors. The commission also looked at the western harbours to see if they offered any particular facilities for communication with America. A harbour survey had been carried out in 1835 by the Royal Navy which had concluded that Galway offered no special advantages.

Within three months of the second report of the commissioners being published, an influential and well attended meeting was held condemning the treatment given to the west. The canals, although entitled to fair protection, should not be a bar to railways to the west. May 1843 saw a meeting convened in London to consider the expediency of reviving the project for a railway between Dublin and Cork. At about this time also, the *Galway Vindicator* was saying that a line from Dublin to Ballinasloe was once again being seriously considered. In September 1843, Sir John Macneill submitted plans and estimates for a line from Dublin to Cashel which were considered by the provisional committee of the Great Southern & Western Railway. At its meeting on 3rd September it was recommended that plans should also be drawn up for a line to Carlow and a report prepared on the 'great capabilities of railway communication to', *inter alia*, Galway.

At this time the provisional committee of the GS&WR included John Ennis, Robert Guinness, Alderman Joseph Boyce, Charles Williams and James Perry. Within a year the GS&W board minutes refer to the resignation of one of its number, John Ennis, following disagreements over the construction of a line to the west; it was obvious however that moves had been made as early as March 1844 to break away and form a separate company. Ennis and the other aforementioned gentleman were, by that time, members of a provisional committee, to further the construction of such a line to the west. The company that they formed was the Midland Great Western Railway.

Macneill produced preliminary surveys for a line to Athlone at a meeting held on 4th May, at which the above mentioned gentlemen were present. This line would diverge from the GS&WR near Sallins and run through Edenderry from whence a branch would run to Mullingar. Considerable discussion followed as to the likely traffic, some of those present being of opinion that much of this route would be devoid of population. An alternative suggestion was to go via Maynooth, Kilcock, Kinnegad and Mullingar to Athlone, Macneill being requested to report on this route. This latter was in due course agreed to be superior, particularly as an extension could be made to Longford and the western counties. In July, for the first time, consideration was given to the practicability of purchasing the Royal Canal.

Mr Fitzsimon, a director of the canal company, stated that he was sure that the proposed purchase would be favourably received by the canal's court of directors and he undertook to confer with them and report back. There still appeared to be some doubts as to the best route to follow as Lord Castlemaine and others favoured the Edenderry route. Macneill however persuaded the doubters that it would be much quicker and cheaper to build the line along the canal bank. A meeting was held on 21st August with the canal directors who

expressed their willingness to sell, considerable discussion ensuing as to its value. The *Westmeath Guardian* for 25th July 1844 referred to a meeting having taken place for the purpose of taking effective steps to form a railway from Dublin to Athlone and Longford. However, pending some arrangement with the canal company, the meeting had reached no firm conclusions.

At a meeting on 9th September it was agreed to issue the prospectus for the new company despite lack of an agreement. An offer of £34 for every £100-worth of canal stock had been made but the canal authorities wanted £40. This figure was finally acceded to towards the end of October but the canal people went back on their earlier figure and demanded £45. The provisional committee resolved 'that all idea of further negotiations with the canal company be given up and the engineer be requested to submit alternative plans'. Within a week however, the canal proprietors realised their position was not as good as they had at first thought and came back to say they would accept £298,059, this representing 40% of the capital holdings. One-tenth was to be paid over when the conveyance was executed, with one tenth every three months, bearing interest at four per cent per annum.

A rival scheme.
Hardly had the prospectus been issued than

there was a defection in the camp. Richard More O'Ferrall, one of two MPs on the provisional committee, was discovered to be involved in the promotion of a rival company, the Irish Great Western Railway, which was planning a line to Galway. This line was initially proposed to leave the GS&W line near Sallins and run through Athlone and Ballinasloe to Galway. It soon became obvious that the GS&W was closely associated with the new company's affairs, although not approving of it deviating so close to Dublin as Sallins on the grounds that it would receive insufficient receipts on the western traffic. The promoters were persuaded to make their junction at Portarlington, in return for unqualified support from the GS&W board.

The reaction of the Midland people to this incursion into what they clearly saw as their territory was predictable. They said they could not sanction such a proceeding and would strenuously oppose it and would bring out a prospectus for an extension to Galway. They would be happy if the rival company restricted its extension to Banagher or any other town south of it to the

The MGWR terminus in Dublin was Broadstone; this is the view seen by the prospective passenger, and remains largely unaltered today. The late J P O'Dea, courtesy National Library of Ireland.

The down mail running alongside the Royal Canal between Leixlip and Lucan. The train is hauled by a 'C' class 4-4-0 and comprises sections for Galway, Mayo and Sligo. This photograph illustrates the close proximity of the canal and the railway. For much of the way from Dublin to Mullingar they ran next to each other.
Courtesy J Kennedy.

east of the Shannon. The stage was now set for an exchange of acrimonious correspondence in the newly published *Irish Railway Gazette* and an expensive and rather futile parliamentary battle. From this time right up to 1860, the MGW directors were in dispute with their opposite numbers on the GS&WR. In the very first issue of the *Gazette*, the Irish Great Western fired the opening salvo, stating that it had heretofore scrupulously abstained from making any allusion to a company brought before the public projecting a railway under the title of the Great Western Railway for a line from Dublin to Athlone (this was the MGWR). It did this on the basis that the line would stand or hopefully fall on its own merits. Within the past week however the Mullingar company had been calling itself the Irish Great Western, but the genuine IGW was far superior as regards route and gradients.

A numerously attended meeting at the great Ballinasloe fair gave impetus to the Mullingar company in its thoughts on a Galway extension and it was agreed that it would construct a bridge over the Shannon

at its own expense and place six or eight of its number on a provisional committee of a separate company to be formed to construct such an extension; it further agreed to work such a line if built. Highly influential meetings were also held at Mullingar in December and at Longford in January 1845. The Mullingar meeting was of the opinion 'that the Great Western from Dublin to Athlone is eminently deserving of our hearty and cordial support, as being the company which has given the most sterling proofs of speedily carrying into effect a work of undeniable public utility'.

The Longford meeting looked to the Mullingar company 'to carry our cattle and butter to the Dublin market in a few hours and to carry our corn at a far cheaper rate than is possible by the canal or by the Shannon'. Other meetings were held at Loughrea, Clara, Edenderry and Tullamore, all in support of the rival Galway company. At the GS&W half-yearly meeting in March 1845, the chairman announced that 'the next branch that is proposed is that from Portarlington to Galway. It is a line sanctioned and approved by the Board of Trade. It is a line that we have from the earliest stage of our proceedings in the formation of our company held in contemplation . . . it is a portion of traffic we have always calculated upon'. Some behind the scenes discussions had obviously been taking place as on 14th April it was announced that the Mullingar company had agreed to abandon its branch to Athlone in the hope of obtaining an Act

for its line as far as Mullingar. At the same time, the GS&W agreed not to oppose it if it abandoned its Athlone branch and all opposition to the Portarlington branch was also withdrawn.

It was now left to the BoT and ultimately to Parliament to decide. In the interim, the Grand Canal Company had sent a deputation to the BoT asking that a decision in relation to the competing lines be deferred in order to enable it to construct a line of rails along the canal bank. Mr Pim, one of the canal directors, had a business agreement with the Samuda brothers and hoped to lay an atmospheric line to Ballinasloe. The BoT did delay its decision, not at the canal company's request, but in the hope that the two railway companies might come to an agreement to amalgamate their resources.

The above mentioned announcement of 14th April was embodied in a memorandum of agreement signed in London on 5th May 1845, by James Perry on behalf of the Mullingar company and by Fitzstephen French for the Galway company 'and other petitioners', the latter obviously referring to the GS&W. The Midland Great Western Railway Company of Ireland's Act of Incorporation received the Royal Assent in July 1845 and gave the new company powers to construct a railway from Dublin to Mullingar and Longford and also to purchase the Royal Canal. It was stipulated that navigation was to be maintained on the canal and tolls were not to be altered without the prior consent of the canal authorities. The company was authorised to raise capital of £1 million. Its title was altered in 1850 to the more familiar Midland Great Western Railway of Ireland Company.

Towards the end of June the London correspondent of the *Irish Railway Gazette* advised that the IGW Bill was in a very dangerous position before Parliament, due to alleged defects in the line's engineering details. Calculating on the bill's defeat, the MGW prepared a prospectus for an Athlone extension. Despite concerted opposition, the IGW bill passed through the House of Commons but by the end of July had been rejected by the Lords. In evidence, allegations were made of forged and fictitious names placed on the contract deeds and it transpired that the directors made no checks as to the references or characters of parties applying for shares. Allotments had been made under forged signatures to paupers and other undesirables.

Undaunted by its failure, it was announced in August that a further bill would be presented in the 1846 session. Coincidental with this announcement, a Midland board minute of 2nd August states that 'it is the opinion of the board that with the rejection of the Galway Bill, nothing contained in the memorial of last April precludes this company from extending the railway to Galway'. It was therefore resolved to proceed in the next session. At the time this debate was going on in Parliament, the country was in the grip of the railway mania, numerous schemes being put forward to provide railway accommodation to the western and north-western districts. Among these were the Galway & Kilkenny and the Irish North Western, this latter planning a line from Dublin to Sligo with branches to Kells, Cavan and Boyle. In May 1845, the INW amalgamated with the Great Northern & Western Trunk (Dublin to Cavan and Enniskillen). The title of the combined company was the Irish North Midland Railway.

The IGW determined to adopt the line already sanctioned by the Commons and called in Sir John Macneill, who now resigned his position as consulting engineer to the MGW, to be replaced by George Willoughby Hemans. The Midland meanwhile was busy making an agreement with the Galway & Kilkenny Railway, whereby the Midland would extend its line to Galway while the Kilkenny company would make a line from Kilkenny to Ballinasloe, the Midland working its Ballinasloe to Galway traffic on equitable terms.

Work commences.
About this time, the first general meeting of the Midland scripholders was held at the Company's offices at 23 College Green, Dublin, to appoint fifteen directors as specified under the Act. Lord Dunsandle was appointed chairman and John Ennis deputy chairman. The *Railway Times* for 15th November 1845 carried a notice to contractors seeking tenders for the construction of a 26½ mile stretch of line from Dublin to Innfield, either as one or two lots. The whole contract was awarded to Messrs Jeffs from Scotland. The ceremony of turning the first sod was performed on 12th January 1846 by the Lord Lieutenant before a 'numerous, influential and fashionable assemblage, which comprised some of the most distinguished members of the nobility, the bar, the army and the merchants of Dublin'. Two or three platforms had been erected at the Broadstone, on one of which the band of the 41st Regiment performed some admirable airs. His Excellency performed the ceremony with a spade handed to him by Hemans and trundled off with a wheelbarrow to deposit the contents amid the cheers of the assembled multitude.

This operation was repeated by Lord Dunsandle, Ennis, Hemans and Thomas Jeffs, following which the invited dignitaries were conducted to the Board Room of the Canal House where a splendid *déjeuner* had been arranged. Following this a number of speeches were made: His Excellency said the new railway would have a great and direct influence on the portion of the country through which it would pass. The loss of the potato crop might produce a scarcity of food and the present work was necessary. People had it in their power to protect themselves from the threatened distress by exertion and energy. No doubt there would be employment for thousands of men.

Tenders were soon invited for locomotives and rolling stock and the directors decided to let a third division from Innfield Bridge to the western boundary of County Meath, a further 11 miles. In fact tenders were accepted at the board meeting on 29th April 1846 for two divisions, number three to Champ & Malone as above and number four, a further 16 miles to Belmont in the parish of Mullingar was given to Daniel Desmond. A Mr Cockburn was appointed in June as contractor for the erection of offices at the Dublin terminus; later he was awarded the contract to build the intermediate stations to Enfield, at £600 for first and £380 for second class stations.

The *Irish Railway Gazette* referred in its issue of 16th March to what it described as 'a very unfair attempt (being) made by the political press to prejudice the Messrs Jeffs in the public estimation'. The charge was that the men were not paid in cash on Saturdays as per their agreement, but by note payable a month after date, thus causing the navvies to obtain credit for goods. Futhermore, it would restrict them in their choice of shops. This system, known as truck, was fairly widespread in England at the time, enabling contractors to make enormous profits from their navvies.

On the parliamentary front, the rival companies' Bills came up before the committees, the Midland in respect of its Athlone extension and the IGW as per the previous year's bill. The latter was taken first and reference was made to the agreement between the two companies which was now being broken by the Midland; the latter's counsel contended that it was intended to apply only for the duration of the 1845 session and in any event its line was the more direct and likely to be more productive of traffic. The *Railway Times* referred to the contest as being like the Battle of the Gauges in the previous year. The Midland was not of course alone in its opposition to the IGW as the Grand Canal was also strenuously opposed to the scheme.

A meeting of IGW scripholders was held in London to rally support and it was suggested that the line might be restricted initially to the section from Portarlington to Tullamore. The committee mentioned that it had received the most cordial support from the London & Birmingham Railway. Suggestions were made that the line might be leased to the GS&W. This time the IGW Bill got safely through the Lords but was defeated in the Commons and within a month a meeting was held in Dublin to consider the propriety of dissolving the company, the voting being unanimously in favour of dissolution. Another company which suffered defeat in the 1846 session was the Irish North Midland. The GS&W half-yearly report in August said the directors regretted the loss of the branch from Portarlington to Galway, but that after the strong opinion expressed by the BoT in its favour, it would not be long before such a line was built. In fact, the GS&W obtained an Act in 1847 for a branch from Portarlington to Tullamore as part of this connection.

Flushed with its success, the Midland announced plans for a Galway extension, although it was aware it would most likely have severe opposition in Parliament. The Grand Canal still had notions of its atmospheric line while a new company, the Western Counties Railway, proposed a line from Mountmellick to Galway with a branch to Ballinasloe. The seriously depressed financial state of the country at the height of the famine in fact meant that the Galway extension had a comparatively easy ride through Parliament in 1847.

At the half-yearly shareholders' meeting in September 1846, the directors of the Midland were understandably in jubilant mood and it was announced that with the demise of the INM, instructions had been issued to Hemans to carry out a survey of the district in the direction of Kells. Hemans was able to report good progress on the section of line to Enfield, two-thirds of the earth-works having been excavated. Approximately 15 out of the 26½ miles were formed and ballasted with some permanent way laid, while the Dublin terminus was in a forward state. As regards the third division, Messrs Champ & Malone had only recently obtained possession of the land. Operations on the fourth division commenced early in August 1846 at Saunders Bridge, close to the town of Mullingar, under Daniel Desmond. Difficulties were being encountered in coming to agreement with landowners and only some 40 labourers were initially employed. They were reported to be receiving 12s.0d per week for first class labourers and 9s.0d for second class.

By October, this contract was causing severe embarrassment, many complaints being made against Desmond for alleged non-payment of wages. At one point the police had to intervene to escort Desmond safely out of Mullingar. The *Westmeath Guardian* for 15th October referred to an unpleasant occurrence when a party of

A 2-4-0 departing Broadstone with a mainline train which includes sections for the Sligo and Mayo lines, which will be dropped respectively at Mullingar and Athlone. Immediately behind the train is the signal cabin, while on the left is one of the three 2-2-2WTs. Author's collection.

about 100 men, some armed with sticks, visited a portion of line sub-contracted by Desmond where 54 labourers were at work and ordered them to cease their labours until their wages were raised. A ganger was struck and two men shoved into a boghole. Other gangs working along the line were subjected to the same intimidatory treatment. Desmond in fact subsequently attended the Petty Sessions Court in connection with non-payment of wages by the sub-contractor who had absconded. He (Desmond) was found not to be liable but very generously agreed to pay the workmen an amount totalling £53.

Work appeared to return to normal in November, when 1,900 men were actively engaged. It was short-lived however for by mid-December work had been brought to a halt by a strike. It seemed that wages had been reduced for the duration of the winter months when there were fewer hours of daylight available. The strike only lasted a week and the men returned to the lower wage, each class being reduced by 2s.0d per week.

A sad event of March 1847 gives an indication of the poverty existing among the labouring classes at the time. An inquest was held in Mullingar on Michael Kelly, a labourer employed on the railway works and who had died of starvation. His widow said they had arrived about nine months previously from Offaly expecting work on the railway. He received 11s.0d per week in

summer but only 9s.0d in Winter. They had five children to support, and since Christmas 1846, as the result of bad weather and want of employment, Kelly had only received 10s.0d. It was reported that he had eaten nothing since Sunday evening when he had taken a little gruel. He worked all day Monday without eating anything and apparently died in his sleep on Monday night. The doctor who performed the post-mortem said the deceased's stomach and intestines 'were perfectly empty' and he had the appearance of a man who had not had food for a length of time.

Tenders were invited in the autumn of 1846 for the 24 mile extension to Athlone. As it might be required to go to work on the whole section simultaneously and as the earthworks were of considerable magnitude, the advertisement called on contractors with large railway plant only to apply.

Builders' plate from No.3, a 30ft first class 6-wheel carriage. Courtesy Stephen Mourton

Chapter Two

EXTENSION TO GALWAY

THE *Irish Railway Gazette* for 3rd May 1847 announced that a single line of rails having been completed between Dublin and Enfield, an experimental trip was made on the previous Friday with a Grendon locomotive and a further trip on the Saturday with the directors. Details of this latter appeared in the next week's issue. It was made in sixty-one minutes and a very elegant *déjeuner* was served under the arches of the bridge over which the high road passed near Lucan, which had been fitted up for the occasion. The train was drawn by the Grendon locomotive *Dunsandle* which was reported to have been constructed in a substantial and durable manner. During the following week, the *Gazette's* correspondent had the opportunity of accompanying Mr Hemans down the line, departing Broadstone at 10.30. On arrival at Enfield the party transferred to a fly-boat for Hill of Down, the greater part of the extension being ready for the laying of rails. Some details of the general character of the line were given. Leaving Broadstone, the line took a straight run through a deep cutting for about half a mile when it swept by a gentle curve to reach the left bank of the Royal Canal along which it ran until entering on an embankment at the rear of Morgan's School. This was the only embankment on the line and was due to the fact of the line leaving the canal bank in order to serve Blanchards-town. Proceeding through the Deep Sinkings, it followed the canal with only minor deviations all the way to Enfield. The works struck the correspondent as being 'peculiarly well designed'.

The curves were of an unobjectionable nature despite apparent comments to the contrary; there was no curve on the line which might not with perfect safety be passed at the rate of 50 miles an hour. The permanent way was laid in 15ft lengths on longitudinal bearers, 12in by 6in, these being secured at every joint by two oak dowels with cross-ties under the joints of each pair of rails. Rail weight was quoted as 74½ lbs per yard. The stations were designed by Mulvany, architect to the company and were described as being highly creditable to his taste and judgement. Mulvany was also architect to the Dublin & Kingstown, the station at the latter point being to his design. The Dublin terminus at the Broadstone when completed would be an elegant, substantial and commodious building, while the remainder of the stations were to be in an unpretending style but admirably designed to accommodate the traffic and convenience passengers. On the return journey, the train ran over some portions of the line at 50mph and completed the journey at an average of 36mph with perfect ease and steadiness.

Saunders Newsletter congratulated the company on having their line ready as promised by 1st May. Opening however would have to be postponed at least until the Queen's birthday on 23rd May due to the delay in delivering the Grendon locomotives.

Meanwhile, in March, the directors had been giving consideration to matters of staff. At the board meeting on 23rd March three candidates were interviewed for the post of Locomotive Superintendent: John Dewrance of the Great Southern & Western, William Robertson of Grendons and Robert Anderson of the Edinburgh & Glasgow. A decision was deferred, the position being granted in April to Dewrance of the GS&WR at £300 per annum plus rent of one of the company's houses on Cabra Road. Dewrance was immediately dispatched to Fairbairns to learn of the progress of locomotives under construction. It was also agreed in March that a ticket clerk be appointed at £1.10s.0d per week, two first class Station-masters at £5 per month plus house, four second class at £4 plus house and 25 policemen at 13s.0d per week plus clothing. It was stated that no person over the age of 40 was to be appointed to any position and nobody with any bodily infirmity or defect would be considered. At the meeting on 21st May a Mr Nugent was appointed cashier at Broadstone and on 22nd July Peter Roe was appointed to the office of ticket issuers. Roe was to quickly

A view from Broadstone looking towards Liffey Junction with the carriage shed and signal cabin to the left. IRRS collection.

rise to become traffic manager and is perhaps best remembered for the introduction of fourth class travel to Irish railways.

Also at the May meeting, a schedule of proposed fares was discussed and approved. Broadstone to Blanchardstown was to be 8d, 6d and 4d for 1st, 2nd and 3rd class respectively; Broadstone to Enfield was 4s.0d, 3s.0d and 2s.0d with 9s.0d for 2-wheeled carriages and 13s.6d for 4-wheeled carriages. In July the board announced that return tickets would be issued to and from all stations at single fare plus 50%. Ticket printing machines, ticket cases and tickets were ordered from Edmondsons in March. Some problems were being encountered with Grendons, the secretary being requested to write in May for an explanation as to why one of their engines intended for the MGWR had been delivered to the Dublin & Drogheda. Despite this rejoinder, doubts were expressed in July that they were about to dispose of another engine. That apart, the company was obviously happy with the Grendon engines as a further six were ordered in August, along with six more from Fairbairns at £2,400 each.

On Tuesday, 14th June, Hemans reported to the board that Captain Coddington, the Government inspector of railways, had travelled over and examined the line as far as Enfield on the previous Friday. Apart from some further ballasting required and the provision of a turntable at Enfield, Captain Coddington expressed himself duly satisfied and saw no reason why the line should not be opened on 1st July. This was to be one of the last inspections on behalf of the Board of Trade by Coddington as he was shortly afterwards appointed as Manager of the Caledonian Railway.

So to *Saunders Newsletter* of 24th June 1847; when an advertisement appeared announcing the opening of the line as from Monday 28th June, from its terminus at the Broadstone, Upper Dominick Street, to Enfield in connection with the Royal Canal to Mullingar and Longford. Down trains would leave at 06.00, 07.00, 12.00 and 17.00 with up trains at 08.30, 10.00, 15.00 and 19.00; the first trains in each direction not running on Sundays. Details were also given of the passage boat arrangements. Fly boats would proceed to Mullingar on the arrival of the 07.00 and 12.00 down trains at Enfield, corresponding up services connecting with the 10.00 and 19.00 up trains (these boats departed Mullingar at 06.15 and 15.15 respectively). Boats departed for Longford on arrival of the 17.00 down and from Longford a night boat departed at 19.00, arriving at Enfield in time for the first up train next morning. The advertisement over the signature of Henry Beausire, secretary to the company, went on to state that coaches and other conveyances for Galway, Sligo,

Edenderry, Kells and intermediate points would run in connection with trains.

The line was opened apparently without ceremony. Within a week of the opening, a special additional train was advertised to run on Sunday 4th July in connection with Mullingar fair on the following day. This was to depart from Broadstone at 06.00, a train which was normally scheduled to run on weekdays only. No doubt additional carriages and wagons were added to the other trains on that day, if they were available. Three months later a special was run for Lucan Races: this is the only year this special was advertised and as the GS&W also ran specials it seems likely that it was left to them for the future. Fares on both lines were the same although the MGW provided third class accommodation.

The first recorded accident occurred on 21st July when Thomas McGrath was killed at Coolmines level crossing as the result of the ballast engine coming in contact with the gates. McGrath, who was seated in the wagon next to the engine, was struck on the head by a splinter of wood and was reported to be dead on admission to Dr Steven's Hospital. The board minute makes it clear that the road and ballast train were under the control of the contractors at the time. An inquest was held and the county coroner was called on to give evidence. It appeared that for some time past, an engine and several wagons had been engaged in ballasting after the company's trains had ceased to run each evening. For the purpose of ensuring safety, the contractors had placed men to act as watchmen at all level crossings. David Cuffe, one of the railway company's policemen, reported having seen the Coolmines watchman, Patrick Nevins, on duty on several occasions during the night. Cuffe was on the footplate of the ballast engine which reached Coolmines at about 05.00. The train consisted of the engine and eight or nine ballast wagons. When only about 150 yards from the crossing it was realised that the gates were closed across the line, the driver braked but was unable to stop in time. Nevins was found on the floor of the lodge with all the appearance of a person who had just awakened from sleep and he was taken into custody to Kilmainham Jail.

Ennis becomes chairman.

A decision was taken in July to have stations at Ferns or Ferran's Lock and Reilly's Bridge; the former to be similar to that at Clonsilla. A special train was run in August to accommodate those persons attending Daniel O'Connell's funeral. Also in August, Lord Dunsandle the chairman of the board, died of fever and in his stead the deputy chairman John Ennis was appointed. This appointment was to have far-reaching consequences for the company in later years. At

the shareholders' meeting on 24th September it was reported that trains had kept time with great regularity and that the arrangement of the different classes of carriage and rates of fares appeared to have met general approval from the travelling public. Receipts for the first twelve weeks amounted to £4,822.5s.2d from the railway and £6,244.8s.1d from the canal, a most satisfying result. It was confidently expected that the line would soon be opened to Hill of Down and an agreement had been arrived at with the Postmaster General for the conveyance of the Galway and Sligo mails. This, along with the Galway Extension Bill passed in July, meant that the future prospects of the company looked promising.

At this time the carriage stock numbered fifty-three, there were twenty goods wagons and a goodly supply of ballast wagons. The *Railway Times* in October made reference to the second class carriages being provided with cushions and lights in addition to plate glass windows. Furthermore, the harvestmen and reapers from the province of Connaught had not been over-looked, as fourth class carriages had been provided in the shape of open wagons, the fare in which scarcely exceeded a farthing per mile. The article went on to say that with such traffic arrangements a favourable result might be expected and hopefully the Government would look favourably on the Midland by advancing funds on the same terms as had recently been granted to the GS&W.

In June, Lord Bentinck called the attention of the House of Lords to a petition from the company seeking a loan. In the petition the company said that employment had been given to some 4,000 labourers, which represented upwards of 20,000 people being kept from the public famine relief works. The company wished to continue and in fact extend these good works. The extension of the line to Galway represented one of the most advantageous lines in Ireland, particularly as regards the west coast. Due to the current state of the money markets and the country, it might however prove necessary to suspend some of these works. It was therefore hoped that the Government would look favourably on the Midland's request – as far as security was concerned it could compete with any line in Ireland. Success finally came in June 1849 when the Chancellor of the Exchequer agreed to an advance of £500,000 at 3½% towards the construction of the Galway extension. The Act giving effect to this received Royal Assent on 28th July 1849. Tied in to this loan was a proviso that the whole of the county and city of Galway and two baronies in Co Roscommon were to be accountable for payment of interest should the net profits of the extension line be insufficient to pay interest.

Moyvalley looking west, 30¼ miles from Broadstone as indicated by the nameboard. Moyvalley House, behind the station building, was at one time a hotel on the adjoining Royal Canal and for a short period was operated by R W Switzer as a hydropathic establishment. The buildings have all been demolished. The original MGW platforms were lower than the extensions subsequently added, hence the two levels apparent in the photograph.
The late J P O'Dea, courtesy National Library of Ireland.

Extension to Hill of Down.

The second section of line from Enfield to Hill of Down, or Kinnegad & Ballivor as it was initially called, was opened on Monday 6th December 1847, following the customary Board of Trade inspection by Captain Laffan on 5th November. This necessitated a recasting of the timetable. Ten days after the opening, the *Westmeath Guardian* reported that passengers by the 11.00 train had taken two hours longer than scheduled to reach their destination. 'The engine could not get up some of the ascents and the labouring men on the line had to apply their force to help it up'. The *Guardian* referred to this as an indifferent mode of railway travelling and hoped that the company would either dismiss the engine or the engineer. The company now had some 37 miles of line open for traffic and work was proceeding with the Mullingar extension, which was to cause considerable difficulties, constructed as it was, across the bog. Hemans had decided rightly or wrongly to deviate from the line of the canal for this last section to avoid many of the severe curves. He persuaded the directors of the necessity of this move and a deviation Act was obtained in 1847.

The principal difficulty encountered was that the line now had to traverse a long line of bogs, which on examination proved to vary in depth from 25 to 70 feet. Some of these were termed swell bogs, consisting of soft pulpy material which had gradually risen above the level of the surrounding country and held vast quantities of water.

The excavation or embankment of this substance proved almost impossible and at one point Hemans seriously considered returning to the canal bank. One of the main causes of so much water being held in the bog was believed to be the canal embankment which prevented proper drainage along the general fall of the country towards the River Deal. Hemans commented that one 1,500 acre area of wet bog had only a 9" square wooden shoot passing under the canal to drain it. He decided therefore to open up sufficient outlets to form a system of drains.

The banks and the bottom of the canal consisted of clay imposed on the bog lying on fine gravel, which later proved treacherous in the context of introducing culverts up to 3ft in diameter under the canal. An added problem was that navigation was not to be suspended while the works were being carried out. A breach of the canal in this area would have proved a serious matter as the locks on either side were some 20 miles apart at this point. A coffer dam was driven into the bed of the canal allowing half its width to be closed off at a time, water was then pumped out of the enclosed section allowing excavation of the tunnel in comparative safety. This work progressed in lengths of about 3ft at a time. Gradually the summit of the bog subsided, in turn causing subsidence of the drains which required constant attention. The next process was to lay two courses of heather sods over the whole surface of the seat of the rails to a width of 30ft, care being taken to lay this on a curved cross-section, rising about 18in in the middle. In some areas clean gravel ballast was laid on top of this, the latter being conveyed in light wagons pushed by hand.

The permanent way consisted of half baulks of red pine 20 to 25 feet long with 12in by 6in scantling laid transversely at 3ft intervals all along the summits and softer sections, surmounted by longitudinal timbers to which the 75lb flat-bottomed rails were fixed. Problems arose with subsidence, in part due to the fact that the contractors were under pressure to have the line ready for opening at the earliest opportunity. Three times the line on the summit of Croboy Bog was lifted and under packed to keep it above the drains. After a heavy fall of rain the rails would be under water for a considerable distance. One particular hole about 200 yards long in Annaskiernan Bog, which was probably originally a lake, required the rails to be lifted by as much as 12in per day and repacked. This section was visited by Captain George Wynne on 20th September 1848 and he was initially reported to be staggered by the rolling motion of the locomotives. He ordered two locomotives to be coupled together and run up and down; he was quite pleasantly surprised to discover that the greatest deflection was less than 2in and in due course passed the line for traffic.

Opening to Mullingar.

The directors made an experimental trip to Mullingar two days before the line was opened to the public. For the opening on 2nd October 1848, down trains left Broadstone at 07.00, 11.00, 16.30 and 19.15 (mail) with corresponding up workings. It appears that scarcely any curiosity was exhibited by the local people at the arrival of the first train, nor was any welcome extended to the directors. Business was apparently good and within a month the number of trains was increased to five each way. The original terminus at Mullingar was only temporary, plans being drawn up eight years later for a new station to the designs of the company's architect, George Wilkinson. The contract went to Messrs Crowe in the sum of £7,240.

Following on the taking over of the chairmanship by John Ennis the company entered on a period of change. In April 1848 the decision was taken to reduce the num-ber of staff at some stations, and in June wage reductions were made. Porters' wages were reduced from 12s.0d. to 10s.6d. and policemen from 13s.0d. to 11s.6d. Stationmasters, class one, i.e. Maynooth, Kilcock, Enfield and Hill of Down, were reduced to £4 per month, second class to £3 with a coal and candles allowance from 1st October to 1st April. In August it was announced that Dewrance had dispensed with the services of a number of staff in the locomotive department. The ultimate in savings was when roof lamps were no longer lit in third class carriages, a decision which led to some adverse and lengthy correspondence in the *Galway Vindicator*, a newspaper which was consistently anti-MGWR.

Also in August, Dewrance was authorised to obtain a boat-load of black turf for use in the new engine, probably one of the Fairbairns. Nothing is known of the experiments carried out in this regard, but it would not seem to have been a success bearing in mind the decision only six months later to erect coke ovens at Broadstone.

Two items from the board minutes for October 1848 are of interest. Moyvalley House was to be advertised for letting. This building, originally constructed by the Royal Canal as a hotel for overnight stops between Dublin and Mullingar had been opened on 20th October 1807 and was reported to be 'the best of its kind and the best kept of any in Ireland'. In the 1820s, when members of the agrarian secret society, the Ribbonmen, were active in the area, and attacks were being made on boats, a local police force was raised and stationed there. When the railway first opened, it was temporarily converted into a station house. In November 1847 the governors of Stackallen College, later St Columba's in Rathfarnham, were reported to be interested in the advantages of this commodious building. In May 1849 the Edenderry Union Workhouse briefly considered it for use as a female school but considered the asking price of £75 for a six months lease too high.

The house was subsequently leased to a Mr Switzer in May 1851. Reference is made in the journals of the Irish Railway Record Society to the Hydropathic Establishment of the MGWR – this was Moyvalley House, although no reference to its use as such has been found in the board minutes at this time. In January 1891 a letter was received from John Switzer to the effect that he contemplated forming a company and establishing a Hydro-sanatorium at Moyvalley House. This was expected to cost £10,000 and he requested an extension of his lease. A 250 year extension was granted but we do not know if he proceeded with his plans. The building was finally demolished in 1977 in connection with the construction of a new road bridge, having lain disused since the 1930s.

The second item refers to an accident at Kilcock on 30th October 1848 when a cattle special ran into a wagon loaded with rails, sixty-two cattle being injured and the engine 'disabled and rendered useless'. The engine in question was quite probably *Saturn*, as Fairbairns were requested to put it in the same repair as before the accident. They replied in November asking to be allowed to repair it without fixing a price, but the Directors were not however prepared to take such a risk and ordered Dewrance to fix a screw patch over the fractured part of the firebox.

We have already seen in the first chapter

Below: **An early view inside the station at Galway. Note the ladder used to light the oil lamps in the carriages, which had no end steps as found on other lines. The carriage next to the buffer stops on the left includes a dog compartment in the centre. The company-owned hotel was directly beyond the end wall of the station.** Courtesy John Kennedy.

The Shannon bridge at Athlone completed in 1851. It is 542 feet long and had an opening span. In Midland days there was double track across the bridge.
The late H Fayle, courtesy IRRS.

Floor plan of Mullingar based on a CIE drawing.

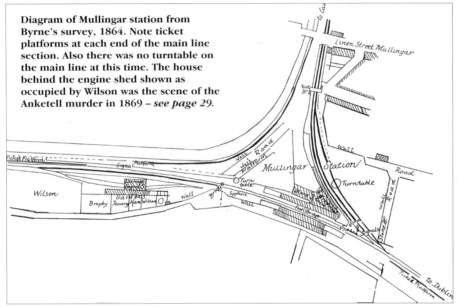

Diagram of Mullingar station from Byrne's survey, 1864. Note ticket platforms at each end of the main line section. Also there was no turntable on the main line at this time. The house behind the engine shed shown as occupied by Wilson was the scene of the Anketell murder in 1869 – *see page 29*.

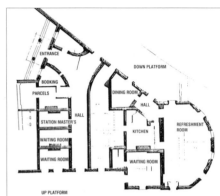

Mullingar from the Dublin end, with the main line to Galway on the left and Sligo lines diverging to the right. On the extreme right is the Cavan bay, now lifted. The curved building behind the signal cabin is the refreshment room. Prior to 1900 a footbridge joined the two Galway platforms. IRRS collection.

how Acts were obtained in successive years for the Athlone and Galway extensions. Reporting on the latter, *Saunders Newsletter* wished the company all the success 'which their persevering and finally successful efforts justly entitled them to'. The editorial went on to call the attention of the noblemen and gentry of the province of Connaught to the great importance to Connaught, to Ireland, the British Empire, Europe and America of assuring that Galway was established as a packet station. Hardly had the Act been passed when a deputation waited on the Lord Lieutenant urging on him the necessity of a Government loan to construct the extension. His Excellency visited Ballinasloe Fair in October, an opportunity taken by the directors to lay on a special train in each direction, a gesture apparently much appreciated. A large meeting attended by a number of directors was held in Galway when the Government was called upon to advance a sum of £500,000 to save the people of the western counties from starvation by creating employment on the railway.

The Government showed a reluctance to become involved in private enterprise, pressure being maintained throughout the following year to bring about change. The main thrust of the argument centred around the extreme deprivation in the west of Ireland resulting from the famine. The Government had already committed money to improving the Shannon navigation and military works in Galway.

The first signs of success came in 1849 when it was admitted that the circumstances of urgent distress in the west might warrant special consideration and it was announced that a plan would be laid before Parliament to promote the completion of the railway to Galway. Early in June the directors announced they had been successful in obtaining a Government loan of £500,000 at 3½%. They now lost no time, and even before the Galway Extension Act had been formally put on the statute books the directors entered into a contract with William Dargan for the construction of the entire line from Mullingar to Galway. By mid-August some 600 men were employed with an expectation of considerably more finding work on the railway as soon as the harvest was completed. At the end of August arrangements were made for the ceremonial turning of the first sod in the neighbourhood of Galway, permission being given for the band of the 68th Regiment to head the procession. The ceremony was performed by the Reverend Mr Daly who alluded to the great benefits which would accrue to the city. About this time Beausire wrote to the Loan Commissioners requesting the first installment of the loan, which was paid over on 3rd November.

The *Westmeath Independent* reported in November that a row had broken out near Athlone amongst unemployed labourers in the district who were of opinion that the contractor was giving undue preference to strangers who were crowding into the area. The contractor explained that initially men acquainted with preparing land for railway purposes were being employed and it was hoped within a few weeks to have an abundance of employment for the local people. His explanations were in vain and the police had to be called to restore peace. Despite this apparent setback work was proceeding well and it was confidently expected to have the line opened within two years. January 1850 saw the third vessel arrive in Galway laden with plant and materials. January also saw the arrival of Ennis, Hemans and Dargan to inspect the works and to finalise plans for the terminus which was to be built at Renmore, thus subjecting the travelling public to much inconvenience, particularly in winter, situated as it was half a mile from the city.

Further labour problems surfaced early in the new year at Moate and Mullingar. In the latter town it was announced that an arrangement had been arrived at with the contractor to employ paupers from the workhouse. On the occasion of the half-yearly shareholders' meeting on 28th March, Ennis was able to record that upwards of 6,000 men were employed on the earthworks, a figure which would now increase daily as the weather improved. The *Westmeath Independent* complained however that the Ordnance Board had been slow in giving up possession of lands around Athlone, but for which even more employment would have been available. By September the employment figure had topped 9,000 with the works in a most satisfactory state. The large bridge over the Shannon at Athlone which had been contracted to Fox Henderson & Company was in a forward state as were the bridges over the River Suck and Lough Atalia. In December the directors announced their intention of erecting an extensive hotel adjoining the terminus at Galway to the designs of Mr Mulvany. The *Galway Mercury* gave details of the viaduct over Lough Atalia. It consisted of five spans, two of 60ft and three of 40ft, the masonry being of local stone quarried and wrought at Merlinpark.

The line was completed on 20th July 1851 with the laying of the last rail on the Shannon bridge, supervised by Hemans, who then proceeded to drive the locomotive *Venus* over the viaduct. It had been decided in June that the line should be opened for traffic on 1st August but there was to be no public ceremony. There would be down trains at 07.30, 10.30 and 19.15 (mail) with

up trains at 00.30 (mail), 09.00 and 16.00 plus an extra train each way to and from Ballinasloe. The BoT inspection was carried out on 28th July when a train ran from Dublin double-headed by *Juno* and *Pelican*. The Shannon bridge was tested by running a train of ballast wagons across with the two locomotives. The *Western Star* reported that there was 'not the slightest vibration and the ponderous mass passed over it as it would have done if that part of the line had been a deeply embedded rock'. The station houses at Galway and Woodlawn were incomplete but would soon be ready; at the latter place a Mr Craig intended establishing a hotel. To enable the shareholders to see the new line, free return tickets were granted to them during the week commencing 1st August.

Great credit was due to Dargan who had completed the works five months ahead of the time specified in the Act. True, not all of the stations were complete but Galway had now been brought within five hours of Dublin. Apart altogether from the necessity of connecting Galway with the metropolis, it was seen by the railway directors as the future transatlantic packet station. During 1850 Hemans was ordered to prepare a report for the board on its suitability or otherwise. He put forward a number of arguments in its favour, the principal one being that it would require considerably less expenditure to upgrade it to the necessary standards than the other places under consideration.

Two of the other likely contenders, Castletown Berehaven and Valentia, would require a vast expenditure to effect railway communication while the Shannon Estuary was unsuitable from a nautical point of view. As we know, Galway was destined never to achieve success as a transatlantic packet station although the Midland directors did make every effort to achieve this. In May 1850 the *Galway Vindicator* had reported that the railway directors had very generously donated £400 towards the placing of a first rate steam packet at Galway. This would enable experimental trips to be made between Halifax and Galway.

The paddle steamer *Viceroy* built at Govan in 1846 and used by the Dublin & Glasgow Steamship Company was chartered for a first trip on 1st June. Under the command of Commander Robert Ewing, she was described as being of 800 tons with only first class accommodation at a fare of £25 which included steward's fees and provisions but not wines or liquors. Passengers would be conveyed free from Liverpool, Glasgow, Bristol, Belfast or Dublin to Galway, courtesy of the MGW. The vessel in fact sailed with thirty-three passengers and 1,120 letters on board and reached Halifax at 17.00 on 11th June. Her success was shortlived for she was lost at sea on the return crossing.

Chapter Three

FURTHER EXPANSION

THE TOWNS of Longford and Cavan both featured in the plans of the Great Central Irish Railway as proposed in 1836, but as we have already seen these plans were shelved pending the outcome of the Commissioners' deliberations. Longford of course was also included in the Midland's first Act but problems associated with the Irish Great Western and perhaps more importantly the depressed state of the money market due to the famine, saw Longford deprived of railway accommodation at that time. Another company, the Great Northern & Western Trunk – not to be confused with Lord Lucan's later line (see chapter nine) – put forward the concept of a line from Dublin to Cavan with a possible extension to Enniskillen. The prospectus issued in November 1844 showed Lord Farnham of Cavan on the provisional committee, which also included three MGW directors, James Digges LaTouche, Captain Hatton and John McDonnell.

It was proposed to share 'the central site on the north side of Dublin for its station and the first five miles of track with the company now proposing to construct a line to Mullingar'. Leaving the MGW it would strike north-westwards through Castleknock, Dunboyne, Kilmessan, Trim, Navan and Kells to Cavan. The BoT reported on the GN&WT in March 1845 and expressed grave reservations as to the likely traffic. Furthermore, if this direct line were constructed the towns of Navan and Kells would be debarred from railway access to their nearest port, Drogheda. The GN&WT scheme was rejected but two months later it was announced that it was to unite with another proposed line, the Irish North Western, which was planning a line from Dublin to Sligo with branches to Cavan, Mullingar, Athlone and Banagher at which point it would join the Galway & Kilkenny Railway. The INW would change its name to the Irish North Midland.

This company approached the MGW suggesting the use of its line for about 20 miles out of Dublin to a point beyond Kilcock from whence the INM would run via Trim and Kells to Longford. It proposed that construction of and revenue from the Longford to Sligo section should be mutually arranged. A further proposal from the INM was that it would construct a line from Edgeworthstown to Cavan and abandon the Kells to Longford section over which it would presumably have sought running powers. In any event when the prospectus was issued in September it mentioned that it had acceded to the request of the Dublin & Belfast Junction that the construction of the Navan to Kells line should be left to the latter company. It also announced that as the MGW was about to apply for a Longford to Sligo extension, it (the INM) would also abandon this line.

Yet another company had appeared on the scene at this time – the Dublin & Enniskillen, which was also going to serve much the same territory. It wished to run over the Midland as far as the Rye Water Aqueduct, the Midland preferring Kilcock. When the prospectus appeared it showed the point of deviation as Celbridge, presumably Rye Water, which brought an angry reaction from the INM which wrote to the Midland in January 1846 requesting it to confirm that it would oppose the D&E. This it did but within four months the INM had been rejected by the House of Lords Committee. A North Midland letter book still extant shows that it persuaded not only the MGW to oppose the D&E but also the D&D, D&BJ and the Dundalk & Enniskillen, who all contributed financially to the costs of the parliamentary contest.

With the opening of the Midland to Mullingar in October 1848 arrangements were made with a Mr Boyd to provide a coach service to Cavan and Killeshandra. As a result of local pressure, Hemans was instructed in August 1851 to survey and report on a line from Mullingar through Granard to Cavan and onwards to either Newtownbutler or Clones. A deputation from County Cavan waited on the board in September and urged a Cavan extension, the result being that the deputation agreed to call a meeting of the gentry and landowners of counties Cavan, Longford and Westmeath to discuss means of raising funds. The *Railway Times* reporting in October said that the proposed line would be injurious to the port of Drogheda; cattle for export would henceforth go by the new line to Dublin. It went on to suggest that the speedy formation of the proposed Kells to Cavan line of the D&D might persuade the MGW directorate and the Cavan gentry to have second thoughts.

The Cavan meeting was attended by Hemans and three of the Midland directors together with James Murland of the D&D. The meeting convened by the High Sheriff of Cavan was told of the merits of the rival schemes. The Drogheda proposal was proposed by Murland but was unable to even find a seconder and was thus defeated. Undeterred by this apparent setback the D&D pressed ahead and saw its Bill passed on 7th February 1852 on the back of guarantees from Counties Meath and Cavan; four months later it announced its intention not to proceed. The Midland for its part decided in December 1851 to proceed with the Longford and Cavan extensions and the necessary notices of intention were duly lodged. At their half-yearly meeting on 11th March 1852, the shareholders were told that steps had been taken to bring Belfast into direct communication with Galway which was now poised to become the port for trans-atlantic operations.

The Act duly received Royal Assent in May although it was to be the following February before advertisements were placed seeking tenders for construction. About a dozen contractors attended on the board on the afternoon of 7th April 1853, at which time two, Dargan and the partners Killen & Moore, were asked for further information. The successful candidate was Dargan at £146,751, of which he agreed to accept 5,000 shares of £20 each in part payment. The original contract in respect of the Cavan branch included nine bridges and a tunnel 153 yards long, the latter in the Crossdoney to Cavan section. This was later substituted by a deep cutting at Drumleny.

The *Westmeath Guardian* reporting in May hoped the works would commence early in the following month, employment being therefore afforded to many labourers who had previously entered the poorhouse when the spring work was completed and remained there until the beginning of the harvest. Advertisements were placed in August seeking the services of a civil engineer to oversee the works. It was estimated that the engagement would be for about two years and it was imperative that only those who could devote their entire time to the work should apply. Edward Wilson from the York & North Midland met with the board's approval and it was agreed that he be offered the post at a salary of £400 per annum. Hemans however objected referring to the terms of his contract as 'Consulting and Parliamentary Engineer'. The board felt that he was being unreasonable as he was being paid £1,600 a year, a very large sum in those days. At the end of August, a Mr Butler offered to undertake the work for a one-off payment of £3,500 and this was accepted on condition that he provide his own staff.

When the first sod was ceremonially turned by Lord Farnham in September, it was reported that most of the landowners had provided land in a fair and liberal spirit. Work was commenced immediately and it was confidently expected to complete the lines within 18 months. At the half-yearly shareholders' meeting it was announced that the line to Cavan would form a junction with the proposed line from Armagh to Cavan which when completed would form a through route to Belfast, the Midland agreeing to subscribe £33,000 towards it.

Longford looking towards Sligo with locomotive and carriage sheds on the left. In recent years, this area has been altered to deal with container traffic.
IRRS collection.

A watery grave.
On 19th January 1854 the contractors suffered a severe setback when some 60ft of the recently constructed embankment across the end of Lough Owel, on which sleepers and rails had been laid for the movement of wagons, disappeared into the bed of the lake. It was fortunate that no workmen were engaged there at the time. It was later discovered that the foundation on which the embankment rested was no more than a deposit of sand and marl which had formed several feet above the true bed of the lake and appeared to be quite solid. Dargan's foreman, Connolly, had a large drag constructed and succeeded in recovering most of the rail and sleepers. Further damage occurred here in February and it was to be six months before this problem was finally overcome. At about the same time as these wash-outs occurred, some silver coins of ancient date were found by a labourer engaged in making fences.

Hemans was obliged to take over as engineer in July due to Butler's ill health and he was given authority to alter the orders for sleepers and rails. By this time some 400 men were employed in the immediate vicinity of Mullingar while in September 2,500 men and 400 horses were engaged on the entire works. The *Westmeath Guardian* stated that the works were progressing in a most satisfactory manner and were 'giving good and permanent employment to a large number of sturdy labourers'. By December, the *Longford Journal* was reporting a rather different state of affairs at its end of the line, namely a spirit of combination which had

broken out among the workmen, and more particularly among the better classes whose horses were employed on the line. One or two who had apparently expressed a desire to work had the shafts of their carts sawn off. The *Journal* hoped the perpetrators would be severely punished so as to deter others.

Early in the following year there was considerable discussion about the location of stations and it was resolved that they should be at the Float Road and Ballywillan rather than Abbeylara and Dundavan; the location of stations north of Ballywillan was to be postponed for further consideration. In December, Wilkinson submitted plans to the board for a smaller type of station for the Cavan branch and these were approved for Crossdoney and Float. Further plans for the latter were presented to the board on 24th April 1856 and tenders based on these were to be obtained at a cost not exceeding £700, the single platform to be reduced in length to 200ft.

We have jumped ahead a little and must return to April 1855 when a progress report was given by the *Longford Journal*. The crossing of the Royal Canal at Mullingar had been completed by a handsome cast iron girder bridge embracing a span of nearly 70ft. Another engineering feature which had been completed was a very substantial wooden bridge over the River Inny; some of the piles had to be driven down from 40 to 70 feet to find a firm foundation. The *Journal* was of opinion that the line should be open from Longford to Mullingar in time for the Ballinasloe fair traffic early in October. By June the junction at Mullingar

was fast approaching completion, while in August Cockburn's tender was accepted for the engine, carriage and coke sheds and platforms at Longford, where it was agreed there should be separate waiting rooms for third class passengers.

In September, the chairman made further reference to the station at Mullingar which he described as being 'never more than an inconvenient accumulation of temporary arrangements' which ought to be rebuilt into a good new junction station. There was ample room on the company's lands without disturbing the existing buildings until they could be removed. The decision to rebuild was taken in 1856 and the present station to Wilkinson's design was built. As early as October 1848, the *Westmeath Guardian* had referred to Mullingar station as 'a very commodious but temporary station house'.

The *Longford Journal* proved to be only a month out in its predictions and the line to Longford was inspected by Colonel Wynne on 2nd November. Its condition was pronounced to be highly satisfactory and notice of opening was given for Thursday, 8th November, with two trains daily in each direction calling at Multyfarnham, Edgeworthstown and Longford.

The *Westmeath Gazette* saw the new line as a great convenience to the people of Boyle and Sligo who would have their journey time to Dublin cut by three hours.

Within a week however *Saunders Newsletter* was rather more critical – instead of proving a boon to travellers, it was the reverse as the directors had only condescended to favour the public with two trains daily 'and with singular absurdity – they chose to start them during this cold wintry season in the darkness of night rather than the light of day'. There is 'no alternative between a start in the dark mists of 7.15am and the darker shades of 6pm'. Goods traffic

Cavan looking north. The right-hand platform road is in two halves separated by a pedestrian bridge and buffer stops on both sides. The portion nearest the camera was used by MGW trains, that on the far side by the GNR. The road to the left of the island platform was the through connection between the two companies. The lines on the extreme left led to the locomotive shed and turntable. The late J.P.O'Dea, courtesy National Library of Ireland.

Cavan showing the unusual platform arrangement. Also of note is the signal cabin situated between the station building and the goods store. The GNR had a separate cabin out beyond the MGW station, but there was no interlocking between the two. The late J.P.O'Dea, courtesy National Library of Ireland.

commenced from 1st January 1856 and at the same time the passenger service was improved by the addition of a daytime train.

In December a letter was received from the BoT requiring the immediate construction of bridges in lieu of three unauthorised level crossings on the branch and a strong reminder was sent two months later. Despite an order being given for their construction it would seem that it took a further two years for anything to be done as tenders were sought for the construction of a bridge at the Poor House crossing near Mullingar in June 1858.

Notice of opening for the Cavan branch for passengers only appeared in the press on Saturday, 5th July 1856, the opening to take place from the following Tuesday with the usual two trains. It was also announced that a well appointed four-horse coach would run daily, Sundays excepted, between Cavan and Enniskillen, thus making it possible to reach Londonderry from Dublin in one day. Within two months of the opening, consideration was being given to the doubling of the section between Mullingar and Cavan Junction – the initial name for what later became known as Inny Junction. Work commenced on the doubling in 1857 and whilst completed by April 1858 it was not brought into use until June due to difficulties with the BoT, principally relating to signalling. It was recommended that suitable 'stages' be erected at Mullingar and Cavan Junction for the reception of distant signal levers.

Traffic on the Cavan branch proved disappointing with trains often running empty. The directors however saw the line as a 'gateway to a more extended district' and were hoping to extend northwards. Hemans had been requested to undertake a survey of the country towards Clones and in fact notice of application for a Bill for such an extension appeared in December 1858. The various station buildings on both lines were incomplete at the time of the lines' respective openings and in the case of the Cavan branch it was to be some time before these were fully completed.

Good news for the Midland came in March 1859 with the incorporation of the Atlantic Royal Steam Navigation Company to establish a direct communication between Galway and America. The Cavan branch could now be seriously promoted as part of a through route from Belfast. The shipping company was reported in September 1860 to have entered into a contract with the postal authorities for the conveyance of mails. These great hopes were dashed before too long with the early demise of the ARSN Company. To complete the picture as regards the Cavan branch we must take a brief look at railway communication from Belfast.

Northern connections.
The Ulster Railway had originally been incorporated in May 1836 to join Belfast with Armagh but in the event only got as far as Portadown by September 1842. Built to the 6ft 2in gauge that had been recommended by the Irish Railway Commissioners in their report, the line was regauged to 5ft 3in in 1846-7 and extended to Armagh by March 1848. As early as October 1852 consideration was given to extending the line to Clones or Cavan but the proposal was defeated and the matter postponed, although it briefly resurfaced as a means of connecting Belfast directly with the west. The Ulster directors were also firmly convinced that a transatlantic packet station would be established at either Galway or Blacksod Bay. Another scheme which emerged briefly in January 1853 was the Belfast & West of Ireland Junction Railway, proposing a line from Armagh to Clones where it would join the line then under construction to Enniskillen. To return however to the Ulster Railway, a further Act of June 1855 authorised a 16½ mile extension to Monaghan which was opened on 25th May 1858. Clones, 12 miles from Monaghan, was reached by the Dundalk & Enniskillen on 2nd February 1859 and the UR directors now saw a prospect of increasing their traffic if they extended to Clones and Cavan.

The D&E was not however prepared to allow this incursion so deep into its territory and the Ulster had to be content with getting as far as Clones. A separate company, the Clones & Cavan Extension Railway, was incorporated by Act of Parliament on 1st August 1859, the extension being built by the Dundalk company with subscriptions from the UR, D&D and the D&BJ companies. The Clones to Cavan section was opened on 7th April 1862, three months before the D&E changed its name to the Irish North Western Railway. The INW had running powers into the Midland station at Cavan. The remaining section of the route, that from Monaghan to Clones, was opened on 2nd March 1863.

Over the years there were numerous disagreements between the Midland and its northern neighbours which at times led to strained relations. The only other point of contact between the two companies was at Navan. In September 1887 the Midland decided that the Great Northern as successor to the INW should be asked to pay £500 per annum for the use of the facilities at Cavan. The GNR responded with the view that £300 was a more reasonable figure and this was accepted for the time being by the Midland. It appears to have been left unaltered as this amount was still being paid in 1896. Passengers from Cavan to Dublin could travel one way by GNR or MGW and return via the alternative route.

Chapter Four

THE TROUBLED YEARS

WHILE the various extensions were being actively pursued the company became involved in a dispute with its arch-rival, the Great Southern & Western, a dispute which was to last right up to 1860 and which was to leave the company in a severely weakened condition, financially and otherwise. The GS&W still saw the west of Ireland as being rightfully part of its territory. In 1847 when the Midland was busy obtaining its Act for the Galway extension, the GS&W obtained an Act for a line from Portarlington to Tullamore but due to the famine and the subsequent depression in the money market no work was carried out and it became necessary to seek an extension of time in 1852. The line was finally opened in October 1854. Meanwhile the Midland directors, not content with ownership of the Royal Canal, turned their attentions to the second of the great east-west waterways, the Grand Canal. This had been opened to Shannon Harbour in April 1804 and followed a more southerly course than the Royal Canal.

The Ballinasloe branch of the Grand Canal had proved to be one of its most successful routes until the opening of the Midland's line to Galway. A rates agreement was negotiated between the canal company and the GS&W in 1852 and some interest was shown in its possible purchase.

The Midland also confessed to having an interest in the traffic on the Grand Canal and in November 1852 the two railway boards met ostensibly to discuss the possibility of the GS&W constructing a line from Tullamore to join the Midland, a possibility which the former company stated was remote.

During the course of discussion it was agreed that any negotiations or arrangements with the Grand Canal Company should be considered as being on behalf of the two railway companies. It was agreed also that if the GS&W were to obtain possession of the canal no traffic should be carried over it between Dublin and Athlone, the MGW being entitled to the business from the Kilbeggan and Ballinasloe branches at a fair proportion of the terms. Additionally, the MGW should be at liberty to construct a line from any point on its line between Mullingar and Athlone to join the GS&W Tullamore extension without any opposition or interference from the latter company.

One can but imagine the surprise and anger in the Kingsbridge boardroom when only a month later news broke that the Midland had made an offer for the purchase of the canal which had been accepted. Needless to say the GS&W strenuously opposed the purchase, so much so that the Bill giving effect to it failed in Parliament and the MGW had to be content with leasing the tolls and duties for a period of seven years. Despite earlier assurances to the contrary, the GS&W realised that steps had to be taken to protect its interests and looked at the possibility of extensions into Midland territory. Public meetings were held both in Sligo and Mayo to consider how best to effect railway communication to these counties. Initially, as far as Sligo was concerned, a northern connection was being contemplated.

The Londonderry & Enniskillen Railway had been incorporated in 1845 to link the points named in its title. Even before the line reached Enniskillen in August 1854, plans were put forward for an extension via Manorhamilton to Sligo. In December 1853 it became clear that the GS&W was involved in a new scheme for a line running from Tullamore through Athlone to Sligo, Ballina and Westport.

At a largely attended meeting held in Roscommon in January 1854, presided over by Lord Crofton, it was clear that the G&SW supported scheme, the Grand Junction Railway, had a large measure of support from the Grand Juries of the counties through which it would pass. At this meeting Sir Percy Nugent attempted to speak on behalf of the Midland but he was shouted down. The Bill passed standing orders early in February but was thrown out in May – an action described by the *Mayo Constitution* as a 'heavy blow and a deep discourtesy to the west of Ireland and in particular to Mayo'.

The Midland meanwhile had lodged a bill for a line to run from Streamstown to Tullamore, and thus effect a junction between the two lines 'at that point which promises to be most conducive to the interests of the public'. In truth, it is doubtful that either board of directors had the public interest at heart at this time. Lord Talbot de Malahide was a shareholder in both companies and endeavoured at both half-yearly shareholders' meetings to bring about a cessation of hostilities, but to no avail.

Ennis, the Midland chairman, stated that his board had made every exertion to avert the present state of things but at the same time everything must be done to defend their position. At a board meeting early in June, Hemans reported on various plans prepared by him for further extensions. For the first time it became clear that the Midland was considering extensions from Longford to Strokestown and from Athenry to Tuam, these to be constructed at its own expense. While these matters were being considered, no agreement was in sight in relation to the proposed connection between the GS&W and the Midland companies. The GS&W was firmly of opinion that the junction should be at Athlone, the Midland believing Streamstown to be more suitable.

Following a good deal of correspondence, during which Moate was suggested as an alternative by the GS&W, the Midland's view was accepted. In December the Midland shareholders expressed reservations about further extensions bearing in mind the state of the money market. As a result it was decided to shelve plans for the Tuam and Strokestown extensions, at least until the Grand Juries of the counties concerned decided on the best route for these lines. In any event, the Galway gentry were strongly opposed to the Strokestown extension on the basis that every pound earned would be so much deducted from the Galway extension receipts.

In August, the MGWR (Baronies Contribution) Act received Royal Assent. This Act came into being because although the company had borrowed £500,000, and all of that amount had been expended, not all had been used on works from which the baronies might be considered to derive advantage.

This latter referred to the building of the company's hotel in Galway – *see pages 28 and 29*. As a result, the amount for which the baronies should be liable for interest was reduced to £470,000.

An efficient traffic manager.

On 10th March 1855 it was announced that Peter Roe, the efficient and popular superintendent of the traffic department, was resigning his appointment. Roe had joined the company in July 1847 as a ticket issuer at Broadstone at a salary of £62 per annum and within a month was promoted to the position of station superintendent, and superintendent of all stations in January 1849. Roe was very much in favour of low fares and was responsible for the introduction of fourth class travel on the Midland. Apparently some complaints were made against him, as in December 1854, the committee appointed to inquire into the charges against him reported to the board. What the charges were is unknown but in the following March the company advertised for a traffic superintendent, the position being given to William Forbes at a salary of £350 plus a rent-free house and travelling expenses. Roe was granted a year's salary and the board agreed to forego an advance to him of £60 on his guidebooks on the understanding that the books and engraving blocks were handed over to the company.

Roe left the company's service in June to go to the Londonderry & Coleraine Railway in a similar position. Despite the complaint against him, a service of silver plate was presented to him by his colleagues and the principal officers of the company as a token of their respect for his high character and abilities as well as their appreciation of his kindness and courtesy in the discharge of the weighty and responsible duties of his position. Roe moved on to become manager of the Newry, Warrenpoint & Rostrevor Railway in January 1866. In the following year he gave evidence before the Royal Commission on railways, once again advocating low fares, quoting by way of example how the Londonderry & Coleraine had been brought from a virtually bankrupt concern in 1855, to a profitable undertaking.

By September 1855 further agitation was becoming evident from Mayo at the lack of any railway communication. It was pointed out that the Midland had pledged in 1854 to introduce a Bill for a line from Athenry to Tuam. If the Midland would undertake to construct such a line, then the Mayo people would consent to a fair guarantee for its extension into the county. In desperation they even stated their intention to carry out part of the works themselves if any enterprising contractor would come forward. In contradiction of this, the Midland directors found the Mayo gentlemen to be apathetic and lukewarm to the project; despite this they requested Hemans to survey a line from Longford through Strokestown and Ballaghaderreen to Castlebar, indicating some interest on their part. This proposal was not favoured in Galway and a meeting was held in December to oppose it, as was a similar meeting in Sligo. Further matters in relation to the Tuam connection are dealt with in Chapter Ten, while the full story of railway communication in County Mayo is dealt with in Chapter Nine.

In July 1856 the Midland directors had their attention drawn to the setting up of an independent company with English financial backing for a line from Athlone to Sligo, a route apparently favoured by the Sligo Grand Jury. Leaving Athlone, the line would run through Roscommon, Strokestown, Elphin and Boyle to Sligo. The Grand Jury gave it their unanimous approval and guaranteed sixpence in the pound on the county at large. No doubt spurred on by these proposals, the MGW brought out its own plans for an extension of its Longford branch by much the same route to Sligo. Doubts were still being expressed with regard to the state of the money market but it was realised that it had to protect its territorial rights. Two branches were proposed – to Ballysodare and an extension to the Ballast Quay at Sligo. The necessary plans were submitted in December, along with those for the Tullamore line. As regards the latter, the GS&W had written again in October suggesting that the two companies should desist from applying to Parliament for any line between the two railways but the MGW board felt it inexpedient to postpone the matter any longer.

Obviously in an attempt to swing matters in its favour, the GS&W sent a deputation to the Broadstone in November proposing that the Athlone to Sligo line be allowed to proceed in return for both companies abandoning their several extensions. The suggestion was that the Midland should work the Sligo to Athlone section, the South Western that from Athlone to Tullamore, a suggestion found wholly inadmissible by the Midland board.

Murder at Broadstone.

The year 1856 came to a sad close with the murder of the cashier at Broadstone. George Little had only been appointed to

Streamstown Junction, looking east. Clara branch trains used the rear face of the down island platform. The photograph was taken a few days before the station closed in 1963. Although the junction for the Clara branch, the station nameboard did not indicate the fact at this period.
The late J P O'Dea, courtesy National Library of Ireland.

the position of cashier in May 1856, having joined the company some three years earlier as a special clerk to the secretary. The circumstances surrounding the murder were unusual in that Little was found with his throat cut in his office, which was locked. An amount in excess of £300 was found to be missing from the day's takings and it seemed that the crime was an inside job as the culprit obviously had a knowledge of the station layout. One of the curious aspects of the case was that the murderer left a large amount of paper money, taking instead coin. Initially, some suspicion fell on a few employees but nothing came of this and it was not until seven months later that a Mrs Spollin went to the police, telling them that her husband was the murderer. Spollin, a railway employee, was duly arrested and brought to trial but was acquitted for lack of sufficient evidence. At this time a wife could not testify against her husband, nor could she be a witness or be cross-examined. Based on Mrs Spollin's statement to the police a total of £230 was recovered from various hiding places in and around the station. The directors donated £200 towards a fund for the support of Little's widow and sister.

The year 1857 commenced with a board resolution that whatever rate reductions were made by the GS&W would be met by a 10% reduction on the Grand Canal. At the GS&W's half-yearly shareholders' meeting in March an animated and personal discussion took place between the Chairman and Richard Perry, representing the Midland. As the *Railway Times* put it – 'the two companies having renewed their old inveterate

warfare'. The GS&W was once again talking about Athlone as the proper point of junction, even going as far as allowing the Midland to construct the line, the latter company being equally determined that Streamstown was the right and proper place.

So it was left to Parliament to decide between the rival schemes. In due course they conceded that the GS&W should go to Athlone, but tempered this decision by preventing it from crossing the Shannon, a decision not wholly pleasing to the GS&W. The Midland proposal for a Streamstown to Tullamore line was restricted to run from the former point to Clara where a junction would be effected with the GS&W line. There is little doubt that the Athlone extension was seen by the GS&W as a means of putting pressure on the Midland to hand over the Grand Canal. The Midland on the other hand saw possession of the canal as of the utmost value and was not prepared to relinquish it.

The Sligo Extension Bill also received Royal Assent in August, despite determined opposition from the Great Northern & Western which obtained its Act for the Castlerea extension. Resulting however from the formation of this company, the Midland directors agreed to alter the course of their Sligo extension as between Boyle and Longford, a decision which met a lot of opposition and was to deprive the town of Ballaghaderreen of railway communication for some years. A Bill putting these changes into effect was given Royal Assent in 1858. Meanwhile, the Sligo Grand Jury, still not happy with the new line, insisted that work

should begin simultaneously at both ends and that the entire line from Longford to Sligo be opened at once.

The additional capital approved by the Act was £580,000 with borrowing powers for £193,000. Tenders were eventually invited in September 1858 for the Boyle to Sligo section, the contract being awarded to Messrs Smith & Knight, work commencing at Boyle early in the following year. Difficulties were encountered at the Sligo end resulting from considerable opposition regarding the acquisition of land. The contract for the southern portion of the line was also awarded to Smith & Knight. With work on the Sligo line now under way, we must return to 1857 to consider some other events.

As part of its hostilities towards the GS&W, the Midland advertised through fares between Limerick and Dublin via Athlone and the Shannon. In October 1857 it was announced that two additional steamers had been put into service on the Shannon, putting it in a position to compete for the Limerick traffic. Third class rail with a fore cabin cost as little as 7s.0d, second class with a state cabin 11s.6d and first class 14s.0d. The service operated on three days a week, shortly to be increased to a daily service. A goods service was also offered by this route, a matter referred to in the GS&W's half-yearly report for the second half of 1857. Whilst the GS&W used to charge 42s.0d per ton from Limerick to Liverpool, the MGW was now charging 28s.6d of which it got only 1s.0d. For this latter sum it had to move the goods by canal to Killaloe, thence by Shannon steamer to Athlone where it was once again trans-shipped to rail for the trip to Dublin. Passenger rates were less than 1d per mile first class.

The Midland penetrated further into GS&W territory in 1858 with excursions to Killarney at 20s.0d return, second class and available for 28 days; this was exactly half of the GS&W's excursion fare. Opposition to the Limerick fares and rates also came from the Waterford & Limerick which saw its traffic to England being poached. In 1856 the Limerick & Castleconnell Railway had been incorporated for a line from Killonan to Castleconnell, being opened in August 1858. An extension to Killaloe was also planned and the MGW agreed to invest

Athlone East Junction with the crew of a down cattle special in the charge of an 'F' class cattle engine, handing up the staff for the section from Moate. The line trailing in on the right is the GS&W branch from Portarlington, now used by Galway and Westport trains. This photograph was taken during the 1950s.
The late J P O'Dea, courtesy National Library of Ireland.

£10,000 in the undertaking. Ennis referred to this subscription in the following terms – 'arising out of the Grand Canal contest, a contest that I shall ever deplore, has been a subscription to the L&CR . . . this line is not in our district but we were hurried into a subscription in the general principle of offence and defence'. Killaloe was of course the southern terminus of the Shannon steamer service.

In the wider context, Ennis referred to the unsatisfactory state of the accounts for the half year ended June 1858, a direct result of the competition, low rates and fares and a desire to do business at any cost. In contrast to the depressed state of the country generally, a quite different picture of events was portrayed when a presentation of a service of plate was made to the company secretary, Henry Beausire. At the commencement of his service with the company in 1845, Ireland was one widespread scene of want and desolation with but nominal property values. People were unable to obtain subsistence and were perishing in their thousands. Since the railway was opened to Galway an uninterrupted stream of prosperity and happiness flowed over the land and no quarter of the empire exhibited a higher spectacle of agricultural improvement than the western areas of Ireland traversed by the railway. There were many people who would not have agreed with these sentiments.

Also in June 1858 the GS&W submitted proposals to end hostilities All opposition rates between the two companies and the Grand Canal should cease, the latter to be worked by both companies on a joint account. Likewise, all opposition rates on the Shannon should cease. The Midland board did not disagree with these proposals but insisted that the proposed junction at Athlone and the traffic from there to Dublin should also be included in the discussions. The GS&W would not accede to the latter and suggested arbitration which was in turn declined by the Midland. When the latter company proposed arbitration later in the year, common sense at last began to prevail. Edward Watkin of the Manchester, Sheffield & Lincolnshire Railway agreed to act as arbitrator for the Midland, Captain Mark Huish, recently retired from the London & North Western for the GS&W. Their award was finally announced in August 1860 but before considering its provisions we must bring some other matters up to date.

In 1859 the incorporation of the Atlantic Royal Steam Navigation Company was welcomed by the Midland directors. The prospect of Galway becoming a transatlantic packet station came closer in September 1860 when the new company was granted the Government mail contract. The *Galway Vindicator* referred to the new company as 'a harbinger of prosperity of the Liverpool of Ireland'. Notice was published in November 1859 for the Galway Pier Junction Railway, a line 7 furlongs and 5 chains in length to commence by a junction with the MGW at or near the north-western end of the Lough Atalia bridge and to run alongside the new docks across the Corrib, through the Claddagh to terminate near the high-water mark at Fairhill, opposite to Mutton Island. The GPJR was in fact a Midland sponsored undertaking. As we have already seen this euphoria was to be shortlived as the shipping line was out of business within five years, being financially weak and using small underpowered vessels. In all, sixteen steamers were employed which between them made a total of only 50 round trips; six of these vessels were involved in serious accidents, two foundering on their first voyages. The Pier Extension Bill was in fact withdrawn later in 1860.

The GS&W's Athlone branch was opened for traffic on 3rd October 1859, the junction with the Midland being finally completed the following September. In the interim, the MGW directors had been giving thought to the abandonment of the Clara branch, an idea which was not without strong opposition from local landowners, including a Mr Goodbody who had a number of mills in that town. The company for its part said this was the first line it had sought to abandon; the only reason it had proposed such a line in the first place was the GS&W's rival scheme. Its appeal was unsuccessful and the line finally opened in 1863. Another request for abandonment, that of the line to Sligo Quay, was confirmed.

Arbitration.

So to the arbitration award. As far as the two companies were concerned, the arbitrators laid down a line of demarcation beyond which neither company was to encroach. This line basically joined Dublin to Athlone via Clara; from Athlone it followed the centre line of the Shannon to Scariff, and thence by Scariff Bay to Ennis and terminating in the centre of the mouth of the Shannon equidistant between Loop and Kerry Heads. The Midland was bound to remain to the north, north-west and north-east of the line, the GS&W to the south, south-west and south-east. Neither company was to construct or to give any assistance to any company promoted outside its boundary.

In view of the fact that the two companies were already competing for traffic between Dublin and Athlone and between Dublin and Ennis, special arrangements were necessary. Equal rates and fares were to be charged in respect of the latter, whilst in the case of Athlone the receipts were to be thrown into a common fund and divided in the following proportions. In respect of the years 1860 to 1865 the Midland would receive 65% of passenger and 55% of goods and cattle, the GS&W 35% and 45% respectively. After 1865, the Midland proportion of passenger traffic would reduce to 60%, with goods remaining unaltered. Neither company was to endeavour to evade these provisions by resorting to rebooking or charging lower proportional rates at intermediate stations.

As regards the Clara branch, provision was also made for a division of receipts. During the first five years after opening, the Midland would receive 35% of passenger and 45% of goods receipts. The passenger proportion would increase to 40% after five years. The arbitrators were firmly of the opinion that the new system of working effected by the award would lead to greatly increased accommodation, and to this end they laid down that there should be interchange of through rates and fares where convenient between all non-competitive towns.

The arbitrators next turned their attention to the traffic on the Shannon between Athlone and Killaloe which they wished to see efficiently worked under the direction of a joint committee. The steamboats and other vessels were to be worked by the joint committee with a rent or payment to be allowed to the MGW. An equal number of between four and ten directors from the two boards were to be appointed to this committee. The chair was to rotate annually. One further railway matter was dealt with, namely the Limerick & Castleconnell. Here it was arranged that the GS&W would take over the Midland's shareholding.

The arbitrators finally dealt with the matter which more than any other had been the main cause of friction between the two companies, namely the Grand Canal. Having carefully considered the position, they were of the opinion that the canal could more efficiently be worked by the two companies and laid down that they should mutually agree to make an application to Parliament for its joint purchase at a cost of £330,000. If no such Act was obtained, the canal was to revert to the Grand Canal Company and this is in fact what actually happened. It carried on as an independent organisation until 1st June 1950 when it finally became part of Coras Iompair Eireann.

So came to an end a costly and at times an extremely bitter dispute which had, one way or another, affected the Midland company since its inception fifteen years earlier. As we shall see later, the GS&W did eventually realise its ambitions of obtaining access to the west and north-west of the country with its absorption of the Waterford Limerick & Western Railway as from 1st January 1901. One of the protagonists in this rather sordid affair, Sir Edward McDonnell, chairman of the GS&W, died on 22nd November 1860, shortly after peace was restored between the two companies.

End of an era.
A most unusual case came before the Mullingar Petty Sessions in May 1861. A man named Patrick Conway aged about 22 or 23 was charged with having jumped out of a second class carriage on the previous day. The statement he gave in justification of his action was strange to say the least. In the compartment were a priest, two ladies and another gentleman. Shortly after the train left Mullingar, the gentleman took out a kind of spear and fixed it to the end of his stick, at which the ladies, perhaps understandably, became terrified and clung to the priest. Conway was afraid he was going to be murdered and jumped from the carriage to save his life, luckily sustaining no injuries. On his person he had a ticket to Athenry, a common silver watch and an amount of £2.15s.3d. He said he had been a servant to a Lieutenant Cheevers of the 5th Royal Lancers in Aldershot and was returning home after leaving his master's service. He was remanded for a week pending reports from his father and his employer.

In August 1861 Smith & Knight offered to open the Sligo line throughout in June of the following year for a consideration of £5,000 over and above the contract price, an offer which was declined. They were however urged to use their best endeavours to have it ready by 1st September. Smith wrote to the Chief Secretary for Ireland in December stating that 'there appears to be unwillingness on the part of the labouring classes to leave their houses for employment'. He went on to say that he could employ at least 1,500 men between Longford and Boyle, but want of men had led to the suspension of work for six weeks between Carrick-on-Shannon and Boyle. These claims were denied by the local press which stated that the men had to walk up to 5 miles to work before daylight and frequently in inclement weather. If the day was wet, the men were sent home after a quarter of a day with a paltry 5d. The works ran through a district principally comprised of large grass farms with few houses and it was suggested that the situation would be much improved if the contractors were to erect some shanties for the men.

The extension was inspected by some of the directors early in September 1862 and they expressed themselves well pleased with the works. Some time was spent examining the substantial bridge over the Shannon at Drumsna, some detail being given in the press. It was 800ft long, of metal girders on

Athlone West Junction showing the main line to Galway on the left and the Mayo line diverging to the right. The only remaining evidence of the locomotive shed in the centre is the turntable pit. In the foreground is the mechanical staff exchanging apparatus, installed by the GSR.
The late J P O'Dea, courtesy of the National Library of Ireland.

cut-stone piers. There were six arches, two of which were 75ft long, the remainder of 30ft span. One of these opened as required by the Board of Works for admitting sailing vessels of large size. The line was inspected by Captain Rich early in November but was found wanting; it was finally passed after a second inspection on 24th November, being opened on Wednesday, 3rd December.

There were intermediate stations at Dromod, Carrick-on-Shannon, Boyle, Ballymote, Collooney and Ballysodare. Even before the line was opened, consideration was given to doubling the Ballysodare to Sligo and Street to Longford sections. Following a report from Hemans, it was decided that only the former section should be doubled.

Hints of trouble to come began to surface in 1862 with poor half year figures reported in September, reportedly due to two successive bad harvests and the social state of the country. One of the shareholders, a Mr Dixon, suggested reducing the number of directors by half which would effect some saving. The second half year results were also bad with receipts down almost £6,000 and a deficit on the Galway extension of £2,557. The number of passengers carried was down some 50,000 to 180,000. In September 1863 Ennis reported that the previous 3½ years had brought about a deficit of some £8,000 against the western baronies. At the shareholders' meeting Ralph Cusack was appointed one of the auditors following the death of William Geoghegan. At a board meeting in November it was resolved that no legal proceedings were to be taken against the baronies for monies owing as the result of the deficit on the Galway extension, but a week later Lord Clancarty gave notice that he would move at the next board meeting that the suspended proceedings be resumed immediately.

In view of this threat the board agreed to the action being resumed. The *Galway Vindicator* for 7th November referred to a proposal to withdraw all passenger trains between Athlone and Galway except for the mail trains, which had been put into effect from the previous Monday. In lieu, passenger carriages were now being attached to goods trains, which were of little or no value to the public. This action led to the wholesale indignation of the people of Galway and drew a complaint from the Galway Town Commissioners who were told that the reductions were made to reduce the claims against the baronies.

A lengthy editorial in the *Vindicator* for 12th March 1864 gave some hint of the problem, referring to gross mismanagement by the railway directors. It went on to state that the Chairman had done everything in his power to inconvenience the people of Galway. Reference was made to an agreement made between the baronies and the Chairman and some of the directors on 18th June 1858. No mention was made of this agreement at the shareholders' meeting by Ennis during the course of a lengthy speech until he was specifically questioned on the point, and it seemed as if he had no intention of referring to it as he stated it was hoped that with due economy and an expected increase in traffic there would be no necessity to call on the baronies.

What had happened was that at the time of incorporation of the GN&WR there had been strong opposition to the new company from the Galway baronies who foresaw losses on their line in the future. In return for withdrawing that opposition, Ennis and two of his fellow directors, G A Boyd and Sir Percy Nugent, agreed with the baronies that they would be released from any contribution which they might become liable to pay for deficiency of interest. One of the provisions of that agreement was that it was to be referred to the Midland shareholders within a reasonable period of time for ratification. What was a reasonable period? Certainly not six years, but then for the first three years or so there had been no losses and therefore no call on the baronies. Ennis had tried to repudiate the agreement, saying it had been made on the spur of the moment. The truth was of course that Ennis had little choice in 1858 – it was either this agreement or the GN&W would have formed an alliance with the GS&W, disastrous for the Midland.

By September the *Vindicator* was referring to the 'dictator of Broadstone' and to the fact that there were unmistakable proofs that his reign was drawing to a close. The half-yearly meeting in September turned into a marathon session of recrimination and uproar, being adjourned on three separate occasions and totalling 23 hours of heated discussion. The upshot of the meeting was that the 1858 agreement was formally repudiated and it was decided to bring the matter before Parliament. Significantly, Ralph Cusack was elected to the board at this meeting. Ennis survived as chairman but it was now obvious that he could not remain for much longer.

In the midst of the furore, the company suffered the worst accident of its entire history when a train was derailed at Ballinasloe resulting in the deaths of two passengers. It was to lead to very heavy expenditure on permanent way renewal in the coming years and was another indication of the unsatisfactory state of things in the company. At a special board meeting on 1st February 1865 attended by a deputation from Galway, consideration was given to the best course of action and it was agreed that there should be an unconditional release of liabilities in 1870, all arrears of interest being paid over.

The Act giving effect to this agreement received Royal Assent on 5th July. Another Act, passed through in May, redefined the capital of the company and enabled it to create preference shares.

Also in February, William Forbes resigned as traffic superintendent on his appointment to the management of the Metropolitan Junction Railway. In March he was presented with a valedictory address and a splendid service of plate in recognition of his ten years service with the company. He was replaced by William Skipworth at a salary of £500 per annum plus house, coal and light. At the same meeting at which his appointment was confirmed, it was moved by Mr Bayley and seconded by Cusack that so long as the dividend was below 4%, the directors should relinquish £1,000 per annum of their remuneration.

The shareholders intervene.

Like the September 1864 meeting, that of 1865 was also adjourned, this time because a committee of inquiry had been set up to examine the affairs and management of the company. The meeting was adjourned to 9th November to receive this report. Included on the committee were the Honourable George Gough, David McBirney and James Malley. During the course of the adjournment, William Maunsell was appointed chairman at a board meeting on 26th September, and although he expressed his unwillingness to accept the position, he had to submit his formal resignation in writing, which he did at a further meeting two days later, Ralph Cusack being elected in his stead. It has been said that Cusack only accepted the position on the clear understanding that he be given a free hand. With the change at the top, the *Mayo Constitution* looked forward to a brighter future for the railway and for the people in the west.

When the shareholders' meeting was reconvened in November it was clear that the committee, despite the comparatively short time at its disposal, had been busy. It had most carefully inspected every portion of the system with the exception of the Clara branch, and it had some scathing comments to make in this regard. Major expenditure and losses had arisen out of the leasing of the Grand Canal. Midland involvement with the Grand Canal had also, it was believed, been a factor in the construction by the GS&W of the Portarlington to Athlone line, which in turn had led to the Clara branch which served no useful purpose and was unprofitable. Furthermore, in an attempt to halt the GS&WR's advance into Connaught, the MGW had found themselves having to contribute substantial sums to the GN&W.

The committee was of opinion that the Cavan branch had been undertaken without due regard to the interests of the shareholders at a time when monies might have been more judiciously expended in developing traffic on the existing lines. Adverse comment was made as to the construction of bridges on the Cavan branch, some of which had already required to be renewed. The committee next turned its attention to the Sligo extension which again had been carried out without due consideration. There were only eight stations between Longford and Sligo, some possessing limited accommodation. These eight stations together with Sligo station itself had cost £60,000, the station house at Sligo had been built in such a sunken situation that foundations of huge thickness were required. It was felt that a more convenient site might have been selected.

Turning to rolling stock and permanent way materials, very expensive contracts had been let without sufficient competition prior to 1862 which had given rise to charges of official corruption, leading to the resignation of one of the company's leading officers and the transfer of the stores department to the charge of the secretary. This latter move did not improve matters as it was clear that there had been no proper stock taking for many years. Two specific matters were next considered – receipts and expenditure and traffic. Under the first head, it was calculated that increased yearly profits in the

region of £21,500 would be required to increase dividends by 1%. This extra revenue could be expected from two sources, a reduction of expenditure and an increase in traffic.

Of these, the former was more clearly under the directors' control and there was considerable room for improvement. During the previous four years there had been increases under every heading with the exception of advertising and locomotive expenses. Increases in staff, salaries and office expenses were disproportionate to the additional working mileage, while station maintenance rose without any apparent causes – in fact several stations were not at all well maintained. An example of gross expenditure under this latter heading was cited. On 24th October, the committee found a painter sent from Dublin at 24s.0d a week plus allowances, working on palings at Mullingar, when this work could have been undertaken by a porter or labourer at 8s.0d per week.

The Ballinasloe accident of the previous October had considerably increased permanent way expenditure, although 'watchful, skilful and well distributed repairs and more gradual relaying would have avoided this sudden expenditure'. Under the heading of traffic and general suggestions, the committee came up with some useful and constructive ideas. As regards passenger

fares, general reductions should be considered, although the committee conceded that this was perhaps not an opportune time for such a change. However in the interim, the validity of return tickets should be extended as distances increased, third class returns should be at a fare and a half, and third and fourth should be amalgamated. Season tickets should be issued at 10s.0d per mile per annum for all stations beyond Enfield.

In other areas, there was also room for improvement. The purchase of all materials and stores should only follow public advertising for same. The final major recommendation was that the committee was of opinion that the company's affairs might be more effectively managed by a smaller number of directors. It was suggested that powers be sought to reduce the number to nine. The report was put to and approved by the shareholders who now requested that the directors carry out the various recommendations as far as practicable in the interests of the company.

Sligo station around 1870. This photograph is of historical interest as it is the only known illustration of a Grendon engine in original condition. No.2 was named *Jupiter* **between 1868 and 1870. The smokebox door is unusual in being hinged from the left. H Fraser collection, courtesy L Matson.**

Chapter Five

THE CUSACK ERA 1865-1904

IT WILL BE obvious to the reader that matters were far from well with the management of the company by the time Cusack was elected to the office of Chairman. Much happened during this 40 year period and some events are dealt with as separate issues. The shareholders had clearly identified many of the problems and made suggestions for improvements. One of the early changes was a considerable reduction in third class fares – up to 50% in some instances – in an attempt to attract those of the poorer classes whom Cusack commented were in the habit of walking up to 20 miles to a market. More excursion trains were run and more comfort provided for harvestmen who no longer had to stand in open wagons. In March 1867 the directors agreed to play their part by taking a reduction of £500 in their remuneration: their number had already been reduced from fifteen to nine in May of the previous year. At the half-yearly meeting in September, Captain Gough said he had sought a reduction in the number of directors, not in their fees.

Fluctuations in the company's receipts from one half-year to another clearly demonstrate how outside factors such as adverse weather, or diseases in cattle could affect its fortunes. For example, the half-year ended December 1868 was 'cause for satisfaction, although not devoid of trouble and anxiety due to a very great depression in the cattle trade'. Six months later Cusack reported that some 4,000 less harvestmen had travelled due to the prospect of there being plenty of work at home – the summer of 1869 was a fine one weatherwise and the crops were expected to be good. Such a summer also meant a good turf harvest, the result being a drop of as much as 8,000 tons in coal carried during the ensuing winter.

A system of cheap stamped parcels was introduced in March 1870, the first of its kind in Ireland. Irrespective of distance carried, set charges were made in various weight groupings up to a maximum of 21lb. Rates included collection and/or delivery within the area bounded by the Circular Roads in Dublin. Within six months it was obvious that this had been a good move and this branch of traffic continued to grow for some years until the postal authorities

agreed a scheme with the Irish railway companies in 1882. A measure of its success was the fact that parcels traffic increased from 30,000 to 120,000 items during its first five years of operation.

In March 1869, Thomas Anketell, the Mullingar Station-master, was murdered, allegedly as the result of the dismissal of a railway policeman by the name of Moran. Feelings ran high in the town as Moran's dismissal was generally believed to be on religious grounds. Furthermore, the atrocity was widely regarded as being connected with the Ribbon Society, a secret brotherhood seeking agrarian reform, which was particularly active in County Westmeath at this time. So highly was Anketell regarded by his employers at the time that on the night of his shooting a special train was laid on to transport the traffic manager, William Skipworth, from Dublin accompanied by an eminent military surgeon, Mr Jolliffe Tufnel.

On the following day, no less a personage than Cusack himself travelled to Mullingar and £200 reward was offered for information. Two men were arrested in May 1869 on suspicion of being implicated but were subsequently released. This outrage was later referred to when a select committee of the House of Commons sat to report on unlawful combinations in Westmeath in March 1871.

At the shareholders' meeting in September 1870 the Chairman referred to the unfinished state of the Ballina branch, ending as it did at a very large double ditch at Foxford. In its current state this branch could hardly be expected to make a worthwhile contribution to the company's receipts. On the other hand, if the GN&W was not prepared to complete the line, the Midland was certainly not prepared to put up the money. Cusack commented that he had a dread of branch lines and he hoped he would never see another extension. It is fortunate that this hope was not put into effect as the western lines would never have been built, although it has to be said that later additions were constructed on the back of baronial guarantees or direct government grants.

By 1870 the facilities for repairing rolling stock at Broadstone had outgrown the traffic requirements and the decision was taken to obtain more land. An approach was made to

the Board of Superintendence for a plot of ground within the walls of the Grangegorman prison garden. Thus began the process of extending the works, which was to continue for the next thirty years. The hope was expressed that it would no longer be necessary to go outside for rolling stock. The year 1870 saw a serious downturn in the number of cattle carried due to an outbreak of foot and mouth disease in the grazing districts. This outbreak did not extend west of the Shannon but it effectively stopped the movement of cattle. Despite this, receipts were up during the second half-year, but against this, expenditure was rising, as another track relaying programme got under way, with longitudinal sleepers being replaced with those of the conventional type. Another event of 1870, already alluded to, was the relieving from further liability, of the Galway and Roscommon baronies in relation to the Galway extension.

Whilst on the subject of Galway, one of the shareholders, referring to capital expenditure, brought up 'the building of a gazebo of a hotel which he believed was not paying more than £100 per annum although it had cost £30,000 to build'. Cusack pointed out that it was unreasonable to hold the present board of directors liable for the actions of their predecessors. Extensive works got under way to improve the facilities at North Wall, which it was hoped would not only be of value to the shareholders but would be of great advantage to the city of Dublin. If ever the country was not to be so adversely affected by bad weather and cattle disease, it would be necessary to increase industry in Dublin, and more docks at the North Wall would play a vital part.

On 1st May 1872 the company began conveying third class passengers on all passenger trains, a move welcomed by the press. The Midland was the first company in Ireland to do this. This had the effect of steadily reducing the number of second class passengers and increasing third class. In the first half of 1875 third class passengers increased from 266,000 to 348,000, second class reducing from 68,000 to 44,000. By the end of 1872, working expenses were 54%, a figure which compared very favourably with the 23 largest companies in England and

Wales. Expenditure still continued to rise however, not only due to relaying but also to increasing coal prices. In 1869, coal had cost 13s.0d per ton, but by 1873 had increased to 25s.6d. Thanks to economies pursued by the locomotive engineer consumption was 2,574 tons less in the same period despite a mileage 29,619 greater.

Tuesday, 15th April 1873 was a momentous day for both the company and for Ralph Cusack, namely the opening of the new docks complex at the North Wall. These extended from Sheriff Street bridge, at which the old canal dock terminated, to the lattice bridge over the Dublin & Drogheda Railway. It measured 1,800ft on the east side, 1,800ft on the west, providing a depth of 15ft. In all, accommodation was provided for between 70 and 80 vessels. The *Dublin Evening Mail* gave an extended account of the day's events, beginning with praise for the company. It referred to its chequered career, of difficulties surmounted and errors acknowledged and repaired in a laudable spirit of hopefulness and determination. This successful turnaround was principally due to Ralph Cusack's determined leadership. The public ceremony of opening the new dock was performed by the Lord Lieutenant who had kindly consented to the new complex being named after him.

Following this ceremony, the party proceeded to partake of the usual *déjeuner* after which a knighthood was conferred on Cusack in recognition of his long and distinguished service. Modestly, in reply, Sir Ralph commented that he was not vain enough to suppose that the honour was being bestowed on him personally, but as the result of his position as Chairman of the

Sir Ralph Cusack was chairman of the board from 1865 to 1904 when he retired at the age of 84. Under his leadership the company progressed from a situation of making losses to relative prosperity. Although autocratic, he was fair-minded and generally liked by all ranks.
Author's collection.

company. From the company's point of view, with an annual requirement for upwards of 30,000 tons of coal for locomotive purposes, the cost of transport from the port to Broadstone would be substantially reduced.

Another important decision was taken early in 1875, namely to extend the time limit on all return tickets for journeys under 50 miles to seven days, and over 50 miles to

one month, a system which had previously been introduced by the London & North Western Railway. At the half-yearly meeting in March 1876, Cusack looked back on his first ten years in office, and reflected on the more important achievements – the leasing of the D&M and the GN&W, opening of the Spencer Docks and the various other improvements. Reference was made to rumours circulating that discussions had been taking place with a large English company regarding a possible merger, a rumour strongly denied. Mr Wilson, a shareholder, complained about the lateness of trains but was put down by the Chairman as he had only become a shareholder on 17th January.

The year 1876 saw the death of Henry Beausire, company secretary since its formation 30 years earlier. Tributes were paid both by the chairman and by Mr McBirney who referred to Beausire's dedication and guidance during a trying period. His successor was George Greene who received a salary of £600 per annum. Foot and mouth disease caused a considerable reduction in livestock traffic with hardly any sheep sales at Ballinasloe fair. This was counterbalanced by the highest carryings of goods to date, coupled with good passenger figures enabling a 5% dividend. During the year a dispute arose with the engineer, James Price, in relation to figures to be included in the annual report. Price had been appointed to the position of civil engineer in October 1862 at the age of 31, having previously been engaged in surveying the route of the Banbridge Junction Railway. His major undertaking on the Midland had undoubtedly been the works associated with the Spencer Docks, for which he received the sum of 500 guineas in April 1873.

The upshot of these differences was that Price tendered his resignation in March 1878 allegedly on the grounds of ill-health. Correspondence in the *Irish Banker* in the latter half of the year indicated that Price left because he was not prepared to be a party to the inclusion of figures relating to steel rails allegedly in store but which had in fact been used. He was granted a figure of £2,100 on his departure, part salary and part in respect of extra works, including the Edenderry branch and doubling on the Sligo and Mayo lines. His replacement was Robert Rowan

Galway's The Railway Hotel . . . 'a gazebo of a hotel which . . . was not paying more than £100 per annum although it had cost £30,000 to build'. An unattractive but utilitarian building overlooking Eyre Square in the centre of the 'City of the Tribes'. Designed by J.S.Mulvany, certainly not one of his better works, and built by William Dargan, it had 44 bedrooms, 8 sitting rooms and 3 coffee rooms.
The late H Fayle, courtesy of the IRRS.

Greene at a salary of £700 plus house, gas and light and £20 per annum for coal. Price later went into general practice in Dublin, carrying out works on the new Galway docks and the Lough Erne drainage scheme. He also acted as consulting engineer to other railway companies. He remained in good health up until a week before his death, which took place in Greystones on 4th April 1895 from the effects of influenza. Following his resignation, Cusack made a scathing attack on him at the half-yearly meeting in March 1879, referring to him as 'an incompetent engineer and a spiteful and malicious liar'.

A programme of relaying with steel rails began in 1877 and was to prove a serious drain on the company's resources during the ensuing years. This coupled with a drop in passenger and livestock traffic due to a series of bad harvests saw the dividends fall back to 3% although they did temporarily recover during the 1890s. Unlike other companies, the Midland was heavily dependent on agriculture for its success so poor weather and the attendant bad harvests played a greater role in its affairs. At the shareholders' meeting in September 1880, a Mr Hayes criticised the financial management of the company and also made a strong attack on the running of Sunday excursion trains.

Robert Greene died in 1882 and was replaced by George Newenham Kelly as civil engineer, a position he was to hold for eight years. The stamped parcels scheme was abandoned in April 1883 when a new agreement was completed with the postal authorities which was to benefit the company to the extent of £1,800 per annum. Passenger traffic showed a steady decline during this period, due in no small measure to continuing emigration; the chairman referring to this matter in March 1885 stated that upwards of 100,000 people had left the west of Ireland. Commenting again in February 1889, Sir Ralph referred to signs of improvement after a ten year decline resulting from bad weather, poor harvests, cattle disease, political disturbances and the almost total destruction of the milling industry, the latter due to the almost unrestricted importation of foreign flour. One good factor was the reduction of working expenses to a very healthy 46.5%, a reduction of more than 10% in 10 years. All but 50 miles of line had been relaid with steel rails. The Armagh accident on the GNR was to result in the requirement for the fitting of automatic brakes to all passenger rolling stock and this coupled with the necessity for interlocking pushed up expenditure.

A notable event of 1890 was the appointment of Joseph Tatlow as manager in succession to J E Ward who had held the position since August 1869. Little reference is made in the company records to Ward until November 1889 when certain irregularities in the discharge of his duties were brought to the board's attention. Some hint of the problem was given when it was reported that Ward and the chief engineer would not speak to one another. Both men were called before the board as the result of which they were threatened with dismissal if some positive assurance of cordial relations being established between them was not quickly given. Kelly, the engineer, was asked to resign in September 1890 which he refused to do and he was discharged, to be replaced by Arthur Smythe. Ward tendered his resignation in October on the grounds of ill-health and was granted a pension of £200 per annum. He died at his brother's residence in August 1891.

Tatlow was born in Sheffield in 1851 where his father was employed on the Midland Railway. Most of his childhood and youth was spent in Derby where he entered railway service in 1867 at a salary of £15 per annum. He was appointed general manager of the Belfast & County Down Railway in May 1885 at the early age of 34, having in the interim seen service on two Scottish railways. In the course of a holiday in Paris in October 1890 he was informed of the MGW vacancy and returned home via Dublin, where he obviously made an impact on

Cusack. The two men were to make a formidable team over the next fifteen years. Hardly had he arrived at Broadstone than he became involved in the Battle of Newcomen – *see chapter six*. He became a director of the D&K in 1911 and of the Midland in November 1912 after his resignation from the post of General Manager. He was succeeded by Michael Keogh from the D&SER. Tatlow was very highly regarded in railway circles and among his many achievements was his appointment as Chairman of the General Managers' Conference in London in 1910.

The nineteenth century came to a close with dividends back to 4%. At the shareholders' meeting in August 1901, a Mr Reigh enquired why the company was not manufacturing all its own rolling stock and thus provide employment at home; a subject to which he returned six months later. He compared the cost of purchasing wagons outside with those produced by the GNR in their own shops; similar comparisons were made with locomotives produced by the GS&W at Inchicore, after which he moved on to the question of directors' fees. The Midland directors each received £428 odd as against £250 on the GNR. Furthermore, 'the board was composed of high class city gentlemen, professional men and gallant military men, but no businessmen like the Pims, Jamesons and Gouldings who were on other railway boards'. The chairman in reply said there was no comparison between the GNR and themselves and never would be until gold was found in Connemara. As regards directors' fees, had Mr Reigh forgotten that it was the shareholders themselves who had voted an increase!

The closing years of Cusack's chairmanship were characterised by a further decline in receipts, a phenomenon not restricted to the Midland. This did not satisfy Mr Reigh who once again attacked the directorate in August 1904, commenting that the majority of the shareholders were opposed to Cusack's re-election as chairman. Cusack was by now almost 84 years of age and his health was beginning to fail. He was re-elected but at a special board meeting on 24th November he announced that he was stepping down. A resolution was unanimously passed putting on record the high esteem and warm feelings towards Sir Ralph for his unfailing courtesy, impartiality and sympathetic advice and guidance during his thirty-nine years as Chairman. During this period, the company had been brought from a depressed state to a large and successful undertaking. Cusack was replaced by the Honorable Richard Nugent, who had been a board member since 1881. For the first time in thirty-nine years a Deputy Chairman was appointed – Major Cusack, the late chairman's nephew.

Joseph Tatlow, who joined the company as manager in 1890 at the age of 39. On his retirement in 1912 he became a director, having been elected as Chairman of the General Managers' Conference at the Railway Clearing House in November 1909. Author's collection.

Further extensions.

Apart from the western extensions which are dealt with in a separate chapter, two further branches were opened, from Enfield to Edenderry and from Crossdoney on the Cavan branch to Killeshandra. The former line had been proposed as early as November 1864 when an influential meeting was held in Edenderry courthouse. Nothing came of this nor of proposals for a line from Maynooth in 1873. The company did however agree to guarantee monies towards a survey and the cost of an Act. Luck was on the side of the inhabitants of Edenderry when a local landowner, a Miss Nesbitt, came forward with an offer of £10,000 towards the proposed line, not seeking any security in return. Early in March 1875, tenders were sought for construction of a line from a point on the main line between Enfield and Moyvalley to the town of Edenderry; that of Edwards & Bagnell at £20,500 being accepted.

Work was commenced six months later, much of the land having been taken by then. Bagnell also tendered for the station works at Edenderry as well as an intermediate station at Carbury. In recognition of her generosity, Miss Nesbitt was asked if the point of junction might be named after her, a request to which she readily agreed. The line was completed early in 1877 and following a BoT inspection was opened for traffic on Tuesday 10th April, the first train leaving Edenderry at 07.50. Initial receipts were encouraging with an average of £10 per mile per week in the first six months. Livestock formed an important element of traffic,

Cusack reporting at the shareholders' meeting on 8th September that a train of 44 loaded cattle wagons had been worked off the branch on the previous day. A line was proposed from Edenderry to Limerick in 1898 but never got beyond the proposal stage.

Further north, a memorial from the residents of Killeshandra for the construction of a branch line to the town in October 1880 received a favourable response, so much so that Cusack met a deputation and agreed to a bill being lodged in Parliament. Tenders were sought for construction in January 1883, that of Walter Scott & Company at £51,459 being accepted. Work commenced on 17th April at which stage all necessary land had been acquired, but it was reported in the local press that the men struck three weeks later for higher wages. It is not clear how long this stoppage lasted but when Scott was queried in December 1884 as to the delay in completion, he informed the board that it was due to a combination of strikes and the boggy nature of the ground which required a considerable amount of extra work than initially envisaged.

Objections from the county surveyor to some of the road bridges resulted in the BoT being requested to arbitrate; Major Marindin carried out an inspection and expressed himself happy with what he saw. It was eventually to be 24th May 1886 before the BoT finally inspected the completed line and gave their approval to opening from 1st June. Services on the branch normally operated through from Cavan. A number of schemes for extension northwards from

Crossdoney Junction with a Killeshandra branch train in the charge of an 'E' class 0-6-0T with its original tall chimney. The branch trailed in on the down side.
Courtesy K A Murray.

Killeshandra were proposed in the following years, including proposals for a line to connect with the SL&NCR. A station was provided at Arva Road, two miles from the village of Arva with the opening of the branch.

Proposed extensions.

In July 1861, Parliament passed an Act authorising the Parsonstown & Portumna Bridge Railway Company to construct a line between those two points. In due course the GS&W agreed to work the line for a period of ten years. When this agreement expired in 1878 the GS&W announced that it would not renew the agreement as it had been losing upwards of £2,000 per annum and as a consequence the line closed to all traffic in December of that year. The Public Works Loan Commissioners who had put up money for the project took possession of the line but made no attempt to work it, making a half-hearted attempt to sell it. It lay derelict for five years during which time it was regularly patrolled by five caretakers. In 1883 the PWLC relinquished any responsibility for it and some rails were taken up to cover unpaid rates and taxes. This was the signal for a free for all and over a very short period of time everything movable was stolen. The station buildings at Portumna Bridge disappeared overnight and an attempt to steal the

Kilfree Junction looking west from the footbridge. The turntable is just beyond the signal cabin, while the Ballaghaderreen branch trailed in on the left behind the camera. There is virtually no trace today of a station having existed at this location. The late J P O'Dea, courtesy of the National Library of Ireland.

Kilfree Junction, with an ex-MGW 'K' class 2-4-0 leaving on a branch train. In the background is the branch goods.
The late J P O'Dea, courtesy of the National Library of Ireland.

Edmondstown, an intermediate station on the Ballaghaderreen branch, with a period piece in the form of a double arm signal post operated from the adjoining groundframe: note the position of the spectacles. The signal remained in situ until the closure of the branch but escaped preservation. The engine is a 'K' class 2-4-0. The late J P O'Dea, courtesy of the National Library of Ireland.

girders of the six span bridge over the River Brosna was only foiled by the intervention of the police. Ever after it was known as the stolen railway.

An attempt was made to reopen the line in 1889 when the GS&W agreed to work it if it was handed over free and they were paid the £24,000 estimated to be the cost of restoring the track. A similar attempt was made in 1907. At various times between 1879 and 1900 a Mr Denis Baldwin of Weybridge in Surrey approached the Midland for its support in working the line and even extending it across the Shannon to Loughrea. On each occasion the Midland declined to become involved.

Another project dating from 1861 was the Midland Counties & Shannon Junction Railway (Clara via Banagher to Meelick, some 21 miles). Beset with financial difficulties, the line eventually terminated at Banagher, only being opened on 29th May 1884. Once again, unsuccessful approaches were made to the Midland to work the line and it became part of the GS&W system in 1896.

During the 1870s various tramway projects were put forward, one such being a line to connect Galway with the nearby seaside resort of Salthill. This short tramway was opened for traffic on 1st October 1879 and shortly afterwards the chairman announced that it was intended to project the line into the MGW terminus as soon as arrangements were completed. The Midland had other ideas and duly informed the tramway directors that the station premises at Galway would not permit of the company affording accommodation for tramcars. A similar request in September 1881 elicited much the same reply. No connection was ever made and the tramway survived until January 1918 when the Galway & Salthill Tramway Company was wound up. It seems

unlikely that access to the station would have prolonged the life of the tramway.

Away to the south the Waterford & Kilkenny Railway had been opened to traffic in 1848. Eighteen years later, the Kilkenny Junction Railway was promoted as a northerly extension, being opened to Maryborough (Portlaoise) in 1867. In the previous year the two companies jointly obtained an Act for the Central Ireland Railways, a line from Maryborough to Mullingar, the W&K altering its name to the Waterford & Central Ireland. In the event the CIR only got as far as Mountmellick, being opened in 1885, having been absorbed into the W&CI in 1877. In 1895, the W&CI again promoted an extension to Mullingar and sought running powers over the MGW to Cavan. The Midland strongly petitioned against the proposed line on the grounds that it would 'seriously injure, inconvenience and interfere with the efficient working of traffic'. At the very least it would be necessary to provide an additional block post and second platforms at some stations and might even involve the doubling of the Cavan branch. One cannot escape the conclusion that the Midland over-reacted to the threat. The line was also petitioned against by the GS&W, W&L and the GW (of England) despite which the Act was passed in 1896. No construction was

ever carried out and the W&CI became a part of the GS&W in 1900.

To the north of the Midland, 'a very bold and enterprising project' was put forward in 1888 for a line from Dromod on the Sligo branch to Clifden via Strokestown, Roscommon, Mount Bellew and Tuam. The Ulster & Connaught Light Railway (3ft gauge) was in fact intended as an extension of the Cavan & Leitrim Railway. Nothing further was heard of the scheme for fifteen years when it resurfaced as an even more ambitious scheme to connect the east and west coasts, taking in such existing lines as the C&L, the Clogher Valley and the Bessbrook Tramway. Branches would have run to Galway and Tuam and had it been built it would have been the largest narrow gauge system in the British Isles with a route mileage of 234 miles.

Towards Cookstown.

Long before the Kingscourt line was completed – *see chapter eight* – consideration was being given to northern extensions. As early as February 1866, powers were being sought to construct a line from Kingscourt to join the INW at Castleblayney. The bill was withdrawn for examination but reappeared the following November with Carrickmacross as the suggested terminus. Various proposals were put forward in the ensuing years and by 1878 these had culminated in a grand trunk line to the north of Ireland which was to terminate at Coleraine. Sir Ralph Cusack's comments were that the Navan & Kingscourt could go to Coleraine if they so wished but not with Midland money. It is perhaps surprising that it was March 1883 before the GNR entered the arena with plans of their own for a line from Inniskeen to Carrickmacross.

Once again the project was resurrected in 1889 when a memorial was received from the inhabitants and traders of Carrickmacross requesting the Midland directors to consider the advisability of extending from Kingscourt. The feeling was however that the traffic of the district would not be sufficient to pay for a second line. Four years later an inspection was made for a line to run through Armagh and Dungannon to a proposed junction with the Belfast & Northern Counties Railway at Cookstown. This time the GNR reacted, considering the MGW action to be 'destructive of all good relationships between the two companies' and they suggested a comprehensive agreement as to pooling of traffic, each company confining themselves to their own legitimate districts. Undeterred by this response, the MGW announced plans for the line in November 1893.

There was unexpected opposition to the project however from the Midland shareholders and the scheme was withdrawn and an agreement was entered into with the GNR. Four years later an independent company, the Kingscourt, Keady & Armagh Railway was promoted but subsequently the Kingscourt to Castleblayney section was abandoned and yet another company, the Castleblayney, Keady & Armagh Railway was proposed to which the GNR subscribed £50,000. The line from Armagh to Keady was opened on 31st May 1909 and the remaining section on 10 November of the following year.

Ballaghaderreen.

In October 1862 a meeting of the Sligo Town and Harbour Commissioners was held to consider connecting the thriving town of Ballaghaderreen with the MGW and with Sligo. The produce of the town previously exported through Sligo now went to Dublin via Castlerea over the GN&W, but a line to the Sligo branch would be of great benefit. The ground had already been surveyed by Hemans who was confident that the line could be constructed for a sum not exceeding £40,000. In view of the agreement between the MGW and the GN&W not to construct lines within each others territories, it would be preferable if the line were independently constructed. Notice of intention to apply for an act was published for a line joining the Sligo branch at Kilfree. The Midland directors attended a banquet in connection with the opening of their Sligo extension on 3rd December and during the course of the speeches, no opportunity was

Ballaghaderreen was unusual in that there was never a signal cabin here, the ETS instrument being housed in the Stationmaster's office. The cattle bank could accommodate 24 wagons but shunting was severely restricted by the head-shunt which could only hold 8 wagons. IRRS collection.

lost to further the proposed line, although this fell largely on deaf ears.

The prospectus for the new company, the Sligo & Ballaghaderreen Junction, appeared three days later and the *Railway Times* referred to it as 'a small affair and yet well and influentially supported'. The Act of Incorporation received Royal Assent on 13th July 1863 but thereafter the project appears to have gone into a state of suspended animation and it was necessary to apply to Parliament in 1865 for an extension of time. Work eventually got under way towards the end of 1869 but came to an abrupt halt at the end of the following January when the company's plant was seized by the subsheriff to meet the demand of Mr Martin, a Dublin timber merchant. Following an intervention by Mr Kernaghan, the company's solicitor, the proposed sale of the property was postponed. A further extension of time was sought in 1871, in which year the company was taken over by the Consett Iron Company, presumably against a debt for rails. The original board was dismissed, David Dale of the CIC becoming Chairman and Rod Mackey, Secretary.

Although work proceeded throughout the year 1872 there was no sign of the line being opened and in fact it was 31st October 1874 before an advertisement appeared announcing the intended opening from 2nd November. Colonel Hutchinson had inspected the line in July 1873 but had found it wanting in many respects. During the summer of 1874 there was much correspondence regarding rates to be charged for working the line. The new line failed to live up to expectations and when the S&BJ directors requested a reduction in the working charges in July 1875 this was refused. For the Midland's part, constant demands were made for prompt payment of their accounts, demands which tended to go unheeded. So in October notice was given that the MGW

would cease to work the line from the end of the year, prompting Mackey to propose, not for the first time, a sale of the line to the Midland. In desperation in December, the line was offered to the Midland for three years, the latter company to retain all the receipts; this request to the Broadstone went unheeded as did a last minute appeal for a two months extension and the line closed on 31st December 1875.

Following a meeting between Mackey and Cusack in London early in March 1876 it was agreed that the line be reopened as from 24th March on the same terms as before. Later in the year Cusack met Dale and agreed to purchase the line for £24,000, the necessary Act receiving Royal Assent in 1877 and so came to an end the independent existence of the S&BJ. Subsequently, various proposals were put forward for extensions, including one to Castlerea.

Further northern connections.

A railway to join Enniskillen and Sligo was first mooted in 1845 but it was not until 1872 that this began to become a reality with the promotion of the Sligo Leitrim & Northern Counties Railway in that year. Authorised by Parliament in 1875 its Act gave the SL&NCR running powers over a portion of the MGWR Sligo branch and the provision of facilities at the latter terminus.

The point of junction was at Carrignagat near Collooney. The SL&NC, opened throughout on 7th November 1882, was never financially strong and at one point during the 1890s consideration was given to the joint purchase of the line by the GNR and MGW companies. However the SL&NC managed to clear its debts and maintained its independent existence. With the opening of the W&L line, some fifteen years later, the tiny village of Collooney boasted three separate stations which must be something of a record for a village of 600 or so inhabitants.

Chapter Six

THE DUBLIN RAILWAYS

THE VARIOUS companies serving the city of Dublin opened their termini over a 25 year period from 1834 to 1859 and for some years no attempt was made to connect up these various points around the city. The first move in this direction came from the Midland in 1859 with the passing of its Act for the Liffey branch. Powers for such a line had originally been obtained in 1846. In May of that year the chairman commented that the importance of such a branch must have been evident to every proprietor. These powers were allowed to lapse and it was not until December 1858 that the matter was raised again.

The *Dublin Builder* reporting on the proposed line in February 1859 noted the utility and advantage of such a line. The article went on to say however that the proposed railway would necessitate a steep arched bridge for the road in Sheriff Street and this would present some difficulties, particularly to the Seville Iron Works in the movement of heavy machinery. So strong were the residents in the area in their views that they met with Hemans, the upshot of which was that he recommended a swivel or pontoon bridge. A memorial to this effect was put to the Corporation who demanded two such bridges, at Mayor Street and on the North Wall Quay.

Advertisements for tenders for construction were published in October 1860, the contract being awarded to the Moore Brothers. In June 1861 the contractors asked the Corporation to consent to the diversion of public traffic from Newcomen Bridge to Summerhill during the erection of the new bridge. This was readily agreed to, subject to a wooden bridge being provided for pedestrians. In December, plans were approved for the new goods store at the North Wall, while at the same meeting Mr Malley wrote with an application for assistance towards the proposed cattle markets there. This request was declined on the grounds that the board had no powers to contribute, despite which a sum of £5,000 was subscribed in the following October.

In February 1861, Hemans had submitted a report on the feasibility of connecting the GS&W into the new Midland line, the course of which connection largely corresponded with the line later built. *Saunders Newsletter* for 25th February 1864 included a notice of the opening of the Liffey branch for cattle and goods traffic with effect from Tuesday 1st March. From that date, all goods and cattle traffic would be handled at the North Wall with the exception of livestock specials on Tuesdays and Wednesdays which would continue to run to Broadstone for the Dublin cattle markets. Within a fortnight of opening, the newspapers were referring to braking experiments being conducted on the new branch. These consisted of stopping loaded wagons of 20 tons gross weight from speeds varying from 7 to 20 miles per hour in less than nine feet. What were referred to as 'unparalleled results' were obtained by placing buffer stops connected with a long iron bar on the rails. When struck by the wagons, the iron bar was sheared by being driven between sharp cutters and 'the force was thus expended in this innocuous manner'. No further mention is made of this experiment which was witnessed by a number of eminent engineers and a Reverend Professor Galbraith.

In November 1866, Skipworth was requested to provide space for storing of Richey's *(sic)* ore and a month later was ordered to provide a siding for same. At the same board meeting a sub-committee was appointed to consult as to the proposed swivel bridge and the new approach to the company's premises at Sheriff Street. In connection with the excavation works at the canal docks, Price was ordered to hire a steam dredger from the Ballast Board. The contract for the new bridge was awarded to Messrs Courtney & Stephens of Dublin at £735.10s.0d, to be completed by 20th January 1873 under penalty of £15 per week.

The *Irish Builder,* referring to the new works in September 1872, stated that the MGW 'will possess superior advantages for carrying on the great inland traffic for the east and west of Ireland and in conjunction with steamers'. The west quay would be for the use of the public, that on the east side being intended solely for the railway. The two docks were to be connected by a very fine swivel bridge. The work was completed by the end of March 1873 and as we have seen in chapter five the new docks complex was opened by the Lord Lieutenant, at which time a knighthood was conferred on Cusack.

Connection with the GS&W.
With the opening of the Liffey branch, the GS&W now saw the means of reaching the Liffey and made plans to make a junction with the MGW branch. It seems clear that Hemans' report of 1861 played a large part in deciding the route which was designed to be as simple and inexpensive as possible. Although the Bill for the new line did not come before Parliament until 1872, various meetings were being held towards the end of 1870 between the two chairmen, with representatives from the L&NW also being actively involved. At a meeting in Chester in October 1870, it was said that the line would cost £120,000, of which amount the GS&W were to contribute £50,000, the remainder coming from the L&NW. The latter also had extensive facilities at the North Wall in connection with their cross-channel shipping services and a further connection with the Irish rail network was of prime importance to them. Central to this was the London to Dublin mail route, for many years the sole preserve of the City of Dublin Steampacket Company as far as the sea crossing was concerned.

A postal service to Ireland dated right back to the year 1572 when post stages were set up for a weekly mail service via Chester and Liverpool, changed four years later to Holyhead. There was also a second route via Reading, Bristol, Swansea and Milford Haven with a sailing to Waterford. The Holyhead route obviously had the major advantage of having the shortest sea crossing. Steamers first began operating out of Holyhead in 1819 with the Admiralty running the service from 1837 to 1850, by which time the Chester & Holyhead Railway had been opened, introducing through rail communication with London. At one stage it was not clear whether Holyhead would remain as the cross-channel port due in no small measure to the difficulties encountered by travellers in crossing the Menai Straits and in 1836 plans were put forward for a line to Port Dynllaen, much further south in

Caernarvon Bay. From 1st May 1850 right up to 27th November 1920, the Holyhead mails were in the charge of the CofDSP company, a fact which annoyed the C&H and later the L&NW who always maintained they were entitled to the contract. In the intervening years no opportunity was lost to further the cause of the L&NW and the subscription to the GS&W can be seen as an example of this.

Let us now return to the GS&W project in November 1870 when the Midland board decided on charges to be levied on the GS&W for carriage of goods and livestock. Passenger fares were also quoted although of course up to this time no passenger traffic operated over the branch. It had never been the intention to carry passengers although as we shall see, in later years, there was to be a thriving traffic in harvestmen journeying to and from England.

Both the GS&W and the L&NW objected to the proposed rates and there were many discussions on the subject before agreement was finally reached at the end of 1871. The Act for enabling the GS&W to effect a communication between their railway and the North Wall and the works of the L&NW received Royal Assent on 25th July 1872. The agreed tolls to be paid for the use of the Liffey branch were listed in Schedule 'A' to the Act.

Construction of the new line was slow and it was not opened for traffic until 2nd September 1877. Briefly, the line diverged from the GS&W at Islandbridge Junction, just outside Kingsbridge, and after crossing the River Liffey tunnelled under the Phoenix Park, emerging near Cabra where the company built extensive siding accommodation at the nearest point to the Dublin cattle markets. The line joined the Midland about a mile further on at Glasnevin Junction, from which point running powers were exercised to Church Road Junction. From here, the GS&W built another short line to its new installations at the North Wall, as well as a connection into the L&NW passenger station; the latter was conveniently situated just across the road from its steamer berths and adjacent to a hotel also built by that company.

It should be mentioned at this point that another piece of the jig-saw forming the Dublin railways fitted into place at this time with the opening of the short line diverging from the D&D just outside its Amiens Street terminus at East Wall Junction and curving around to join the North Wall complex at Church Road Junction. Thus by 1877, three of the four companies serving Dublin had been joined up and it now only remained for the Dublin, Wicklow & Wexford to form a connection, a subject which is separately treated later in this chapter. In November 1877, boat trains commenced running between Kingsbridge and North Wall in con-

nection with the L&NW steamers. Two trains connected with the early morning arrival, leaving North Wall at 08.30 and 09.55. The MGW also began to operate passenger services from Broadstone, as from 1st December, connecting with main line trains.

Other connecting services.
It would not be possible to mention all of the schemes proposed, many of which in any event had no relevance to the Midland. Some of the schemes did propose connections with the MGW while others were strongly opposed by the Midland directors. In November 1861, notice of application appeared in the press for powers to construct a central station in Dublin, to be supported on piers and arches over the Liffey between the Carlisle and Metal bridges. A circular railway was intended to form a junction with all railways having termini in Dublin, tramways also being proposed on either side of the quays. This was the Dublin Metropolitan Railway which was strenuously opposed by the Midland and was in due course withdrawn.

Another scheme which survived somewhat longer was the Dublin Trunk Connecting Railway, notice for which appeared in November 1863. It was to run from Kingsbridge to connect with the DW&W and was to make connections with and assume running powers over other

companies' lines. Although a deputation from the DTC met the Midland directors in May 1864, the latter were not prepared to give their support, preferring instead a scheme promoted by a Mr Bolton under the simple title of the Dublin Railway. This latter failed to get off the ground, while the DTC Bill successfully passed through the legislature in June 1864.

In the following February, a letter was received from Mr Mulvany, Deputy-Chairman of the DTC suggesting a meeting of traffic managers, Forbes being requested to attend on behalf of the Midland. Three months later, Forbes' name appears as General Manager of the new company. During the 1865 session, powers were sought to extend the DTC from Amiens Street into Sackville Street (now O'Connell Street) and for the building of a hotel. A similar and equally unsuccessful application was made in 1866, and the company was still making attempts to obtain these powers in 1870.

City of Dublin Junction Railways.
We must now move to the boardroom of the DW&W at Westland Row on 23rd August 1883 when a report was put before the directors by their engineer, Mr Smith, in relation to a proposed railway to connect Westland Row with the lines north of the Liffey. It was decided to send copies of the report to the GN, GS&W and MGW, inviting

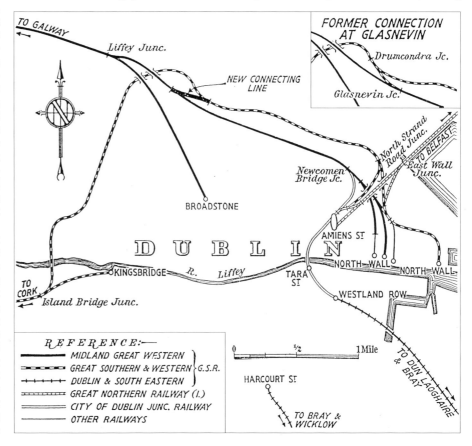

their co-operation in applying to Parliament. The GNR replied within a week pledging its support, at which time it was decided to approach additionally the Dublin Port & Docks Board, Dublin Corporation, the Chamber of Commerce and the City of Dublin Steampacket Company. The latter approved of the scheme as did the GS&W which was not prepared however to offer any pecuniary support. The GS&W was of course allied to the L&NW and there is little doubt that the Euston directors would not have wished to see the GS&W involved.

A letter was sent by the DW&W to the Chief Secretary seeking a Government loan of £300,000 towards the project. By November, the DW&W felt it had sufficient support to make application to Parliament for the City of Dublin Junction Railways. Railway no.1 was to run from Westland Row to cross the Liffey near Tara Street by a viaduct and join up with the GNR at Amiens Street. From the termination of this line at the latter point, railway no.2 would run steeply downhill to connect with the MGW Liffey branch near Newcomen Bridge. Powers were also sought enabling the various companies to subscribe to the undertaking. Another scheme proposed at the same time was to run from the GS&W at Inchicore to join the DW&W at Lansdowne Road.

The Inchicore scheme was strenuously opposed by the DW&W and also by the MGW and whilst the GS&W preferred it to the CofDJ or 'Loop Line' scheme as it gave a faster time for the American mails from Kingstown, nevertheless, if the DW&W and the MGW were prepared to co-operate in the running of the mails over the loop line, then it (the GS&W) would regard it as satisfactory. At their half-yearly shareholders' meeting on 18th February 1884, the DW&W Chairman said he felt justified in stating that the Midland, which must benefit from the

new line, would afford every reasonable facility with regard to traffic arrangements and also that it might see its way to providing material assistance. Two weeks later, at their shareholders' meeting, Cusack said he could see no reason to recommend a subscription to the undertaking. The GNR and GS&W saw advantages in it, the DW&W and the CofDSP needed it if they were to retain the mail contract, but the Midland gained no advantage from it. In any event, the citizens of Dublin were just as well pleased to have their letters at 08.30 as at 07.30 'as it is not pleasant to read business letters by candle light'. In June, the *Railway Times* commented that opposition to the loop line appeared to be gaining strength in spite of strong support received from commercial interests. Dublin Corporation was reported to be strongly opposed to the concept of the viaduct over Beresford Place which would disfigure the city. Apart from the disfigurement, its arches would harbour criminals and others of ill repute. Despite this opposition, the CofDJR Act received Royal Assent on 28th July 1884.

On the next day, a conference of the delegates of the guaranteeing companies was held and the MGW engineer requested to prepare plans and estimates for a double line junction at Newcomen Bridge as well as a separate bridge to serve local traffic to the west side of the Spencer Dock. The plans for the junction were produced by Kelly on 15th October and within a fortnight the line received a serious setback when the GS&W announced its intention not to remain a supporter of the project. The reason given was that its engineer had expressed an unfavourable opinion of the proposed junction. This was the official reason given although within a month yet another line was being projected, the Kingstown & Kingsbridge Junction Railway.

Briefly, a third line of rails was to be laid

from Kingstown to Booterstown, at which latter point a flying junction would take the line over the DW&W tracks. It would pass through Milltown, where it would communicate with the Harcourt Street line and terminate by a junction with the GS&W near Inchicore. Another line would join the North Wall branch of the GS&W with the Midland at Fassaugh Bridge, near Liffey Junction. The Midland strongly opposed this line due to sharp curves and a gradient of 1 in 75. Initially, the GS&W declined to become involved, although it later offered to take up £100,000 of the capital, an offer most likely made in an endeavour to defeat the loop line. With the GS&W now opposing the proposed junction at Newcomen, the Midland directors thought about their position and in February 1885 informed the DW&W that they could not see their way to join in the guarantee to the CofDJ.

At the half-yearly meeting of the DW&W shareholders in August, the chairman said that without the support of these two companies it had been decided that there was no point in proceeding with the project at this time. The matter was raised in the House of Commons in February 1887 when, in reply to a question, Mr Raikes said that the Government was not in a position to give any pledge regarding postal contracts. However, the non-performance of the loop line undertaking by the various companies, had operated very strongly to counterbalance the advantages of Queenstown and if the loop line was not constructed without delay it must tend to prejudice the line whenever future contracts were under consideration.

By the following February steps had been taken to obtain land, the arbitrator appointed by the Board of Works having completed his draft award in respect of land values on the south side of the Liffey. Plans for the Liffey viaduct were agreed in April and were submitted to the DP&DB for its approval. These plans were agreed and tenders invited in May, that of Arroll Brothers of Glasgow being accepted at £14,639; Messrs Meade's tender was accepted for the earthworks.

By October 1890, most of the line was ready for tracklaying and in fact a trial run was made from Kingstown through to Amiens Street on 12th December with the Belfast mails. Unable to resolve the impasse in relation to the Midland's objections to the proposed junction at Newcomen, the CofDJ referred the matter to the BoT who sent over Captain, Sir Douglas Galton. This eminent

Liffey Junction looking east, the main line to Broadstone to the right with the Liffey branch diverging to the left. This photograph was taken in the 1970s.
H Richards.

gentleman duly set out the necessary details for the junction and went back to London, believing the problem solved. Hardly had the good captain returned home but the Midland refused to accept his findings. Despite this, and believing that right was on its side, the CofDJ notified its intention of proceeding with the necessary works, the Midland in turn serving a writ for an injunction and damages.

The ensuing battle between the two companies' employees became known as the Battle of Newcomen as the boundary wall was repeatedly breached and rebuilt by the opposing sides. In due course, the matter was referred to the Master of the Rolls in March 1891, at which point the Midland announced that it did not wish to proceed with litigation although still making it clear that its overall view was unaltered. So the junction was finished and the City of Dublin Junction Railways opened throughout as from 1st May 1891 but as we shall see the problem was far from being resolved. An engine was derailed on 12th August, and then again on 7th October MGW No. 112 *Hornet* was derailed at the junction effectively stopping all traffic on the west side of the canal. In the interim, on 1st September, the DW&W engineer complained of obstruction by the Midland on the previous Sunday when 22 up and 18 down trains passed the site of the junction. Many of these were reported to be empty wagon trains. The Midland engineer, for his part, complained

of the want of bolts in rails. Following two further derailments in December, the matter was referred to the BoT.

Also in December, it was reported that the DW&W had brought two of its carriages out of the North Wall hauled by horse as far as the lift bridge and thence by its own engine over the loop line. This led in due course to the DW&W being advised that the Midland would refuse to allow traffic to be worked over Newcomen Bridge Junction. By now, Major General Hutchinson had inspected the works and reported to the BoT. Approval was given for use of the junction subject to it being very carefully maintained and engines and trains being strictly limited to 5 miles per hour. The Midland was still not happy and advised the CofDJ that despite the line having been passed by the BoT, it would still refuse to receive, forward and deliver the CofDJ traffic at or by means of the said junction.

It had in mind a complete reconstruction of the layout at the junction and was prepared to contribute towards the cost. The DW&W now applied to the railway commissioners to compel the MGW to afford all reasonable facilities at the junction in accordance with Sir Douglas Galton's award and the BoT approval. The case was heard at the Four Courts in Dublin early in May. In evidence, the MGW endeavoured to persuade the commissioners that no driver would be able to restrict his engine to 5 miles per hour. The commissioners found in favour of the DW&W and so this dispute finally came to an end.

Drumcondra link line.

As far as the Dublin railways were concerned, it remains only to briefly outline the history of the Drumcondra Link line. The first tentative proposals for a line leaving the GNR near Amiens Street and running via Clonliffe and Drumcondra to connect up

with the GS&W and touching the Liffey branch were put to the Midland board in September 1891. The latter saw the line as being of no advantage to it and declined to become involved. The Drumcondra & North Dublin Link Railway Company's Bill received Royal Assent in August 1894 and authorised a line from the GS&W's North Wall extension near Glasnevin to the same line at Church Road Junction, thus by-passing the MGW line. Provision was also made for a connection into the DW&W at Amiens Street.

The GS&W was asked to give financial support and also guarantee traffic, both of which it was reluctant to provide. We have already seen how it had ideas of a direct line to the DW&W in the shape of the K&KJ, a project in which it was still interested. It was unlikely however to provide much if any local traffic whereas the Drumcondra line might be expected to do so. In due course the GS&W took over the link line's powers. The MGW was not happy with the prospect of losing the GS&W traffic over the Liffey branch and belatedly offered to reconstruct Newcomen Bridge Junction to make it safer if the GS&W would continue to send its traffic over that route; additionally it offered to reduce its tolls. The GS&W would not agree and the link line was duly opened for traffic on 1st April 1901 between Glasnevin and Church Road, but it was 1st December 1906 before the final portion between Amiens Street and North Strand Junction was brought into use.

The delay in opening the final portion resulted from the length of time it took for the DW&W engineer to approve the GS&W's plans. This dispute in its turn had to be referred to the railway commissioners, the actual trackwork having been completed in August 1903. The local passenger traffic hoped for was shortlived. Seven steam railmotor trains operated from Kingsbridge and

A long cattle train at Liffey Junction around 1920 in the charge of one of the 'P' class 0-6-0Ts. These locomotives were used to bank heavy goods trains from North Wall to either Liffey Junction or Clonsilla. Liffey Junction was the closest station to the Dublin cattle markets and therefore handled considerable traffic in livestock.
Courtesy John Kennedy.

Arrangements for the Working of Goods Traffic

TO AND FROM DUBLIN & SOUTH EASTERN RAILWAY CO.'S SYSTEM

AND

MIDLAND GREAT WESTERN & GREAT SOUTHERN & WESTERN RAILWAYS,

Via

NEWCOMEN BRIDGE JUNCTION.

The following are the arrangements for transfer of Goods Traffic between Dublin and South Eastern Railway ; Midland Great Western Railway (North Wall) ; and Great Southern and Western Station (North Wall), *via* Newcomen Bridge Junction.

Traffic between D. & S. E. Railway and G. S. & W. Railway to be worked by Dublin and South Eastern Company as follows :—

I. Wagons from Dublin and South Eastern Railway for G. S. & W. Station (North Wall) on arrival at Newcomen Junction are to be backed on to the West Dock (Loop Siding) where the Engine will run round the wagons, push them over the Lift Bridge to No. 11 points, and then cross to Up Line proceeding to destination, Engine in front. Should there be more wagons than the Loop Siding can accommodate, then the Train is to be divided on west side of Spencer Dock, one part left on Main Line under G. N. overhead Bridge, and the other part pulled on to the Loop Siding, when the Engine will run round the wagons, join up both portions, push the Train to No. 11 Points, and then cross to Up Road for destination, Engine in front.

II. Wagons from G. S. & W. Station, North Wall, for Dublin and South Eastern Stations are to be taken to No. 10 points Main Down Line, pushed to West Dock Loop Siding, where D.S.E.R. Engine will get round the wagons, clear Exchange Siding (if necessary), push back to No. 11 points, cross over, and proceed to Amiens-street.

If any wagons with B. and I. S. P. Co.'s traffic are displaced on West Dock Loop Siding by the D. & S. E. Engine, they are to be replaced by it as soon as shunting is completed.

Traffic between Dublin and South Eastern Co.'s Stations (other than Dublin), and Midland Great Western Stations (other than Dublin) to be worked as follows :—

III. Wagons from D. & S. E. Stations for Stations on M. G. W. Railway to be delivered in Exchange Siding, West Dock, by D. & S. E. Engines.

IV. Wagons from Stations on M. G. W. Railway for D. & S. E. Railway to be delivered by M. G. W. Co.'s Engines at Exchange Siding, West Dock.

Hours of Transfer.

V. D. & S. E. Engine to leave Newcomen Junction at 9.20 a.m. for G. S. & W. Station, North Wall, return without delay, and clear West Dock Siding at 11.20 a.m. for Amiens-street.

VI. D. S. & E. Co. to send an Engine to G. S. & W. Station, North Wall, at 11.25 a.m. from Amiens-street, to return at 1.15 p.m., and clear West Dock Siding (M. G. W.) not later than 2.0 p.m. for Amiens-street.

VII. D. & S. E. Co. to send an Engine to G. S. & W. Station, North Wall, at 3.30 p.m. from Amiens-street, and return with wagons at 6.0 p.m. for D. & S. E. Line.

VIII. Exceptional Traffic from D. & S. E. Line for G, S. & W. Line, by 2.0 p.m. Train from Bray, is to be worked specially to North Wall (G. S. & W.) by D. & S. E. Co.'s Engine, eight in the opposite direction for the opening, but were gradually withdrawn, the last such operating on 31st December 1907. As far as the Midland was concerned, the new line saw the transfer of the mail service away from its Liffey branch. There were two intermediate stations at Drumcondra and Glasnevin, which like the local service, were shortlived. Glasnevin Junction was closed during December 1906 at the suggestion of the GS&W, the Midland agreeing subject to it being re-opened at any time at their request.

Tramway connections.
In October 1902, the Secretary of the Dublin United Tramways Company wrote in connection with a proposed tramway extension to the Broadstone. The tramway company was prepared to provide a service from College Green but the Midland was unable to agree to the proposed terms. Further correspondence followed in April 1905, the DUTC being of opinion that traffic would not pay its way for some time, but would be prepared to promote an Order in Council and if authorised, build and equip a line if the railway company agreed to contribute two thirds of the cost of a double line from Findlater's Church to the front entrance of the station; additionally the MGW was to persuade the Corporation to forego the wayleave of £500 per mile per annum.

A meeting was in due course arranged with the Paving Committee of the Corporation but it declined to forego the wayleave. The MGW promoted a Bill in 1909 to construct its own tramways but the Bill failed to comply with standing orders in this regard and was passed with the tramway clauses deleted. A final approach was made by the DUTC in November 1911 offering to work a line from Rutland Square or Mountjoy Street if the MGW obtained the necessary powers and constructed the line. So the Midland terminus remained isolated from the city centre, this being one of the reasons for its early closure under the Great Southern.

Midland Great Western Railway
OF IRELAND.
NOTICE.
The Directors hereby give Notice that Stone throwing is strictly Prohibited on the Company's premises, and any persons detected committing this Offence will be Prosecuted. Should the Offenders be residents of any of the Company's houses, they will not be allowed to continue as such, and Parents will be held responsible for the conduct of their children.

BY ORDER,
GEO. WM. GREENE,
Broadstone,
April, 1892.
Secretary.

Photographs on the following page:

One of the last movements from Broadstone. A 'Woolwich' Mogul lifts an assorted collection of permanent way vehicles and goods stock. In the background are signs of the new order – the area encompassed by this photograph was levelled and tarmacadamed for use by CIE's provincial bus operation. The engine shed in the right background has been demolished. Courtesy IRRS.

'J5' 0-6-0 No.642 after arrival at Amiens Street, Dublin, from the West in the early 1950s. Originally MGWR No.45, built by Armstrong Whitworth (works No.176) in 1922 and withdrawn in October 1961. Although intended as a mixed traffic engine with their 5ft 8in wheels, they were universally known as the 'cattle engines'. They were regarded as poor steamers although on occasions were credited with a good turn of speed. One is reputed to have run the 43 miles from Mullingar to a stop in Clonsilla in 50 minutes on a stock special in 1924. John Kennedy.

Below: 'Woolwich' 2-6-0 arriving at Amiens Street on a West of Ireland train in the early 1950s. Behind the train is the GNR signal cabin. No.396 was one of the 'K1A' class built by the GSR at Inchicore in 1930, with 6ft driving wheels. She was withdrawn in October 1959. John Kennedy.

Chapter Seven

WESTERN EXTENSIONS

THE AFTERMATH of the Famine years of 1845 to 1850 and the country's heavy reliance on agriculture left it in a different financial situation to the remainder of the British Isles. Extreme poverty led to massive emigration, particularly from the western counties. A number of Acts were passed between 1860 and 1889 with a view to opening up the country by means of improved internal communication. The first of these was the Tramways (Ireland) Act of 1860; its principal drawback was the fact that approval had to be obtained from each of the grand juries through whose territories the lines were proposed to be built. In addition, the Act also limited working of these lines to animal power. This latter limitation was altered by the 1871 Tramways Act, subject to severe speed restrictions.

The short title of the Tramways (Ireland) Act of 1883 stated that it was an 'Act for promoting the extension of Tramway communication in Ireland and for assisting Emigration'. For the first time in a general Act, the idea of a baronial guarantee on the paid-up share capital was fostered. At this point, a brief description of the baronial system would not go amiss. The barony system has its origins in Anglo-Norman times. During the eighteenth century, the grand jury system had been introduced as an early form of local administration, with membership mainly comprised of landed gentry and members of the legal profession. The grand juries were responsible for the development and maintenance of the local road system and for the administration of hospitals and gaols. County rates were levied by the grand jury and were paid on a barony basis. The Grand Jury Act of 1836 authorised the holding of presentment sessions in each barony, this latter being for the purpose of allocating county funds to particular baronies.

The end of the barony system in this form came with the passing of the Local Government Act of 1898 which brought about the present administrative county system. It should however be pointed out that the concept of the county system in Ireland developed from the English shire system, the last such county created being Wicklow in 1606. To return to the 1883 Act, default by the promoters to complete or maintain a tramway left the baronies through which it ran with powers to acquire the undertaking. The Act was still not entirely satisfactory and so far as the MGWR was concerned, only the Loughrea and Ballinrobe branches were constructed under its auspices, neither of which served districts intended to benefit from the Act. The Light Railways (Ireland) Act of 1889 specifically targeted districts where the development of fishing or other industries would benefit, but circumstances of distress in those districts necessitated State assistance. The idea of the baronial guarantee was of course not new to the MGW as the Galway extension had been constructed on the strength of such guarantees from the counties of Galway and Roscommon by Act of 1849.

The extension of the company's network in the west falls under two distinct headings – the Loughrea and Ballinrobe lines, constructed under the auspices of the Tramways and Public Companies (Ireland) Act of 1883, and the Clifden, Achill and Killala branches under the Light Railways (Ireland) Act of 1889 – otherwise known as the Balfour Act after its author. Balfour was at this time Chief Secretary for Ireland. Shortly after the 1883 Act became law, a royal commission was set up to investigate Irish public works, railways being included within its brief. The result of the Allport Commission as far as railways was concerned was the passing of the Balfour Act of 1889. For the first time, the principle of direct state aid by free monetary grants was put forward. It also represented the first attempt to induce existing railway companies to maintain and work light railways. The 1883 Act had been a failure in the sense that the lines constructed did not serve the poorer districts which it had been desired to reach.

The baronial lines.

This title has been used in connection with the two lines constructed under the 1883 Act, namely the Loughrea and Ballinrobe branches. Unlike the later Balfour lines, both were promoted by local interests and were independent companies worked by the MGW. There was a close affinity between the two lines in that they were built by the same contractor and used the same offices and accountant. The town of Loughrea lies on the northern shore of the lake of the same name, some 9 miles due south of the mainline from Dublin to Galway. In the second half of the nineteenth century, it had a population of about 2,500 and was an important market town by-passed by the railway but on the main Dublin to Galway road.

Loughrea had formed part of the plans of the IGW in 1845 for its Portarlington to Galway line. It also featured in proposals put forward by a number of companies, including the Parsonstown & Portumna Bridge Railway. Ballinrobe is situated about 13 miles south-west of Claremorris and 27 miles north of Galway. Like Loughrea, it was a fairly prosperous town, with a population of about 1,800 serving an agricultural district. The earliest scheme for a railway to serve Ballinrobe was the South Mayo Railway, originally intended to connect Claremorris with Cong via Ballinrobe. In November 1863, the promoters' plans were altered with the line to terminate at Ballinrobe.

Although the Midland had no plans to connect either of these towns with its existing system, it did establish a cartage service in the early 1870s which appears to have thrived in both cases. Apart from the larger enterprises already mentioned, the local people of Loughrea made attempts of their own to bring the railway to the town in 1856 and again in 1866. In the latter year, consideration was given to a line to either Attymon or Craughwell. The latter was again considered in 1872 but had been ousted by Attymon in the following year when a deputation from the Loughrea & Attymon Light Railway met the Midland directors. They informed the Midland board that the gentlemen of County Galway would subscribe £20,000 towards construction and guaranteed the necessary land. The Midland expressed some interest, being of course aware of the not inconsiderable traffic from the town to its Ballinasloe and Woodlawn stations. The *Roscommon Journal* for 27th December however stated with regret that the matter was being shelved.

There the matter rested for another five

Claremorris, looking West, photographed prior to the rebuilding of the station from 1942 onwards which resulted in the provision of one signal cabin in replacement for three, including the one in the photograph. The W&L line from Athenry trailed in on the left hand side behind the photographer, as did the Ballinrobe branch. The branch locomotive shed is on the left. Courtesy John Kennedy.

years until the Bishop of Clonfert, the Reverend Dr Duggan entered the scene. There was an intention to apply to the Government for £50,000: if this loan was forthcoming, would the Midland construct the line? Consideration was postponed until the Government decided, a similar reply being given to the Loughrea Union. Once again nothing happened until the passing of the 1883 Act when the project was revived. The Loughrea & Attymon Light Railway Company Limited was incorporated with a capital of £70,000. A deputation waited on the Midland board on 1st April 1885 when a considerable measure of agreement was reached.

The Midland would contribute a sum not exceeding £4,800. The line was to be constructed to Midland standards and it would provide a station and the necessary signalling at Attymon. It would work and maintain the line under a 50 year lease for 55% of gross receipts, providing two trains each way daily on weekdays; and it would bear the cost of the Act. At a second meeting in June, the question of accommodation at Loughrea station was discussed and it was agreed that Longford should serve as the standard. Due to difficulties in obtaining a suitable contractor, construction did not commence until May 1889 under Robert Worthington. One of the first tasks was the provision of the junction at Attymon to facilitate movement of plant and ballasting materials. Construction was comparatively easy and the BoT inspection was carried out in October of the following year. The line was officially opened on 1st December 1890, with one intermediate station at Carrowkeel, named Dunsandle after the residence of the Daly family.

The first mention of a railway involving the town of Ballinrobe has already been

alluded to, namely the South Mayo Railway of 1863. Twelve years later, the MGW engineer, Price, was requested to report on the cost of a line from Claremorris to the town. It is not known whether this survey was ever completed, but in March 1876 a public meeting was held in Ballinrobe, the result of which was a resolution calling on the Midland directors to make a branch from Claremorris. Nothing came of this but following a second meeting when the barony of Kilmaine was called upon to guarantee interest on monies if the MGW would construct the line, some interest was shown.

It was to be June 1884 before the Claremorris, Ballinrobe & District Light Railway Company (later the Ballinrobe & Claremorris Light Railway) was proposed with a capital of £70,000. The Midland directors expressed themselves in favour of a connection being formed with Ballinrobe, and agreed to recommend a subscription to their shareholders. So in June 1885, we find a deputation from the B&CLR agreeing to a ten year lease at 50% of gross receipts, the MGW to provide suitable station accommodation for both passengers and goods at Claremorris. Construction got under way on this line in May 1890, the work also being contracted to Worthington. This line proved rather more difficult to build, with rock cuttings and a bridge over the River Robe. An

inspection of the entire line was carried out by the MGW engineer, Kelly, in September 1891. There was adverse criticism of the proposed layout at the intermediate station of Hollymount, which the MGW wanted as a crossing place. In February 1892, Worthington requested the Midland to have one or two engines in readiness for the BoT inspection which did not in fact take place until June, the line being eventually opened on 1st November 1892.

The two lines were worked by the Midland until 1st January 1925, when they became an integral part of the newly formed GSR. The two companies had maintained their independence up to this time and held their last board meeting at the joint offices in Dame Street, Dublin on 30th December 1924.

The Allport Commission.

During the course of the Allport Commission's enquiries, much evidence was given in favour of alternative lines in the west. As far as Clifden was concerned, two routes were put forward, one direct from Galway via Oughterard and Recess and one via Headford, Cong and Killary, some 70¾ miles. The former had advantages in being some 20 miles shorter with easier gradients; comparative costs were £187,000 and £325,000. The plans for the direct route included a branch to Roundstone in connection with the fish traffic. The advantage of the longer route was that the land was generally superior and there was a larger population, although the towns of Headford and Cong might be better served by the construction of a line from either Tuam or Claremorris. The works between Cong and Killary would be very heavy with steep gradients. In any event, a comparatively inexpensive line could be run from Recess to Killary, which latter was acknowledged to have remarkable advantages for fishing.

As far as Ballina was concerned, two general areas were considered. One was for a line to Belmullet via Crossmolina, a distance of 39¾ miles with an estimated construction cost of £152,000. This figure was to include the provision of a deep water extension at Blacksod Bay. Traffic would, apart from the fish traffic from Belmullet itself, be purely agricultural and trifling in amount, inasmuch as a large portion of the line would run through bog.

The alternative was a coast line via Killala and Ballycastle, some seven miles longer, this being the line favoured by the commissioners. Evidence was given in favour of a line only as far as Killala, on which a guarantee had already been given by the barony of Tyrawley. If Mayo was to get some 50 miles of railway, it would be preferable to see a 16 mile line from Westport to Mallaranny which would help to meet the needs of the

Achill islanders. Strangely enough, nobody seems to have considered constructing a line any closer to Achill. So much for the Allport Commission and the Balfour Act and we must now take a look at some earlier schemes for extending rail communication within Counties Galway and Mayo.

The Clifden line.

The county of Galway, stretching as it does from the River Shannon right across to the Atlantic Ocean represents an area of remarkable contrasts. To the east of the city of Galway is good, fertile, land which produces large numbers of livestock and in this context, the annual Ballinasloe Fair in October was for many years a very important event in the Midland's calendar. To the west, the main features are the mountain ranges and considerable areas of bogland, with the Twelve Pins and the Maamturks dominating the skyline; it also is an area of many lakes. The population of Connemara in 1860 was in the region of 55,000, many of whom lived in the coastal districts and thus were employed in fishing. Poverty was widespread and famines in 1821, 1841 and 1845-8 had done little to improve the lot of the peasant population.

John D'Arcy of Kiltulla in East Galway visited the area in the early years of the nineteenth century and was so taken with the landscape and with the plight of the people that he came up with the idea of setting up a town on the west coast. So came about the founding of the town of Clifden in 1812.

The Corrib Bridge on the Clifden branch consisted of three spans, each of 150 ft and a lifting span of 21ft on the bascule principle. The bridge was electrically locked from Galway station signal cabin although it had its own five lever cabin at the western end of the bridge, which is visible to the left of the picture.
The late H Fayle, courtesy IRRS.

The pier at Clifden was improved under D'Arcy's guidance and by 1840 quite a good road connected the town with Galway. At this time there was a reasonably good sea trade with Liverpool. The various famines however had a severe effect on the far west of Ireland and led to massive emigration.

The first reference to a railway to connect Galway with the capital of Connemara was a report in the *Galway Vindicator* of a public meeting held in Clifden courthouse on 12th December 1860 to consider the formation of a tramway. It would not be possible in the confines of this history to list the many schemes put forward for railways to Clifden over the next thirty years but suffice to say that they were all doomed to failure. In some instances, this was due to lack of support from the absentee landlords, but the underlying fact was that the district through which the line would run was sparsely populated. A coastal line, whilst running through a more populated district, would have been considerably longer in view of the long sea inlets.

We have already reviewed the various schemes brought before the Allport Commission and the passage of the Act in 1889. At the MGWR shareholders' meeting in February 1890, reference was made by the Chairman to the proposed lines and the fact that the company was in negotiation with the Government with a view to working the various lines. In April, a question was asked of the Attorney General for Ireland in the House of Commons concerning the doubts being expressed as to whether the MGW would ever in fact take over the working of the various lines. Further debates followed in May and June with memorials being presented from the Connemara clergy requesting that urgent steps be taken by the Government to ensure early construction of the Clifden line. The West had been slow to recover from the effects of the famine years and needed urgent assistance. The Clifden

workhouse found itself struggling to cope with the distress in the locality. In one week during 1886, relief was issued to a total of 18,828 in a Union with only 24,259 recorded inhabitants.

The *Railway Times* was able to announce in September that arrangements had been concluded for the construction of the Clifden and Killala lines, with agreement not quite settled on the Mallaranny line. It went on to state that there would be no undue delay as the Midland directors had decided not to wait for local assistance but would proceed at once with advances made by the Treasury. The agreement made with the Government was that the company would construct, maintain and work the three lines in return for a free grant of £264,000 for the Clifden line, £131,400 for the Mallaranny line and £44,000 for that to Killala, the company to finance the balance.

Late in October 1890, Balfour paid a visit to the distressed districts of counties Galway and Mayo to see for himself the extent of the problem. The party arrived at Westport and after spending a night at Kylemore Abbey, arrived in Clifden. There, Balfour told a deputation that the railway should be looked at from two aspects, first as a source of employment and secondly it would give the people of Connemara access to every market, irrespective of weather. This would bring to an end unstable prices. The building of a railway to Carraroe on the coast was suggested to him but turned down.

Pending the completion of the plans by the engineers, Messrs Ryan and Townsend, a provisional contract was entered into with Robert Worthington and by 7th January 1891 about 100 men were reported to be at work near Clifden, with about 500 employed along the line. This early work was confined to the preliminary drainage of bogland and towards the end of the month the Clifden Board of Guardians complained of the comparatively small number of men

employed on the works, Worthington in reply stating that he would double the numbers employed if the engineers' plans were given to him. He in fact threatened to reduce the numbers and ultimately cease work altogether if he did not receive these plans. Some doubts were by now being cast on the quality of Worthington's work.

The board meeting on 8th April, tenders were opened from four contractors, of which Worthington's at £231,804.9s.9d was the highest. A week later, Charles Braddock of Moot Hall Chambers, Wigan was given the contract at £204,800.3s.1d. As however some changes were envisaged in the plans for the Corrib bridge, this work was removed from the contract, reducing it by £18,715.17s.0d. The changes in design most likely resulted from negotiations with the Corrib Navigation Trustees as a board minute of 29th April refers to the necessity to submit plans to this body for approval. Braddock promised full employment to all and notices were posted throughout Connemara to this effect, work being resumed on 4th May near Galway; two weeks later, 854 men and 35 horses were employed.

Towards the end of May, plans were submitted for station layouts at Galway, Moycullen, Ross, Oughterard, Maam Cross, Recess, Ballynahinch and Clifden, all being approved with the exception of Galway. There was a proviso that no expense was to be incurred on stations without board approval. Braddock was apparently quite prepared to employ every able-bodied man

who applied for work but it was quite a different matter when it came to paying them. In August, it was reported that 200 men had struck for an increase in wages from 12s.0d to 15s.0d and payment for wet days. The strikers had organised themselves in Galway and great indignation was expressed at the number of strange hands employed, to the apparent exclusion of local men. Some of the parish priests portrayed a different story. One priest had written to the Chief Secretary stating that free lodging, free cooking and 12s.0d per week had been offered to any who cared to take work. Only nine in his parish had accepted the offer, and of those, five were so drunk as to be incapable of work, while the remaining four soon abandoned it as 'not good enough'.

In accordance with a new BoT requirement regarding the crossing of mixed trains, it was decided to make the stations at Oughterard, Maam Cross and Recess suitable for crossing trains. In August, Braddock secured the contract for the Corrib bridge, the work to be completed in 15 months. Further troubles surfaced during 1892 due to non-payment of wages, the company refusing to interfere. In June, the engineers reported that Braddock was indebted to various traders in Galway and wages had not been paid for about four weeks, no work had been done on the Corrib bridge and the tunnel at Prospect Hill was stopped for want of bricks. Matters came to a head in July when Braddock's contract was terminated, the company taking possession of all plant and machinery. Appeals from Braddock's

Clifden, with 'D' class 2-4-0 No.33 *Arrow* on the up Tourist Express. The third vehicle is a Cusack bogie coach with its distinctive roof profile. Next to this is the 12-wheeled diner No.3. The train is in the short lived blue and white livery. Note the lack of a spectacle in the clear position of the signal – white signified all clear at this time. The photograph was taken in the early years of the twentieth century.
Courtesy John Kennedy.

creditors went unheeded. In the following month, the contractor commenced proceedings in the Chancery Court against the company but the action was dismissed.

In September, proposals were submitted from T H Falkiner for completing the works and these were approved. Although originally intended to be opened for traffic on 1st December 1892, this was no longer possible and extensions of time had to be obtained. By August 1893, Cusack was able to report that 14 miles of line to Oughterard had been laid. Further complaints were still being made as to the non-employment of local men, this matter being taken up by the Congested Districts Board. This board had been set up in 1891 to help people in the western seaboard counties, where a combination of small farms, poor soil and climatic conditions coupled with distance from their markets left farmers too poor to avail of land purchase schemes.

The first section of line, as far as Oughterard, was finally opened on Tuesday, 1st January 1895, the remainder of the line then being in a forward state of completion. The first train to reach Clifden arrived there on 3rd May when the directors carried out an inspection of their new line and found it to their satisfaction, it being duly opened to the public on 1st July. At this time, Maam Cross and Ballynahinch stations were not sufficiently far advanced to be opened. Major Marindin also approved the opening of an additional station at Ross. The Congested Districts Board wrote in March 1900 requesting additional accommodation for mackerel traffic at Ballynahinch, the upshot of which was the provision of an additional siding there. There had at one stage been plans for a line to Roundstone Quay but this never materialised.

The Killala branch.
The Midland was approached in December 1882 seeking support for a proposed railway from Ballina to Killala, but declined to become involved despite a guarantee being given by the Tyrawley Presentment Sessions. This scheme also envisaged alterations to the pier at Killala. No further mention is made of the scheme until June 1887 when a letter was sent to the Midland asking for a working agreement 'for a considerable period if not in perpetuity and based on the lowest percentage of gross receipts'. This was not to the board's liking until a definite guarantee was forthcoming that work would actually be carried out.

Mallaranny on the Achill branch with the passenger train hauled by an 'E' class 0-6-0T. On the left is a short goods, also in the charge of an 'E' class. Courtesy John Kennedy.

In June 1889, a meeting was held in Crossmolina and a resolution passed in favour of a direct inland line from Ballina to Belmullet, the Midland's support being once again requested. This time the MGW decided to await the outcome of the Light Railways Bill. By August 1890, agreement had been reached with the Government for a line restricted to Killala. Samuel Fraser was requested to prepare the necessary plans and estimates ready for letting the contract. In October, the Company agreed to work a Ballycastle extension if constructed by the Government. December 1890 saw a provisional contract being entered into with Thomas Falkiner so as to give immediate employment to the distressed able-bodied men of the district. In March 1891, Falkiner's tender for £29,000 was accepted, this to exclude the widening of the station yard at Killala, signals, stations and the like.

It was decided that there would be no intermediate stations on the line, although one had been considered at Ballysokeary, but rejected until such time as the traffic on the line was studied. Work proceeded quickly and by the following February it was reported that rails had been laid over the entire line, with a ballast engine working. This latter had been hired from the MGW at a figure of £3.10s.0d per day exclusive of crew who were to be provided by Falkiner. Major General Hutchinson carried out his inspection at the end of October, but he was not entirely satisfied and had to return on 23rd December when approval was given for an opening to traffic on Monday, 2nd January 1893.

February 1893 saw yet another project for a line from Ballina to Belmullet, the Midland being asked to enter a working agreement at a percentage of gross receipts. It refused to entertain the proposal but was prepared to work a line from Killala to Ballycastle at either 60% or £5 per mile per week. Over the years up to 1907 various proposals were put forward for providing communication with Belmullet but nothing came of these.

Westport to Achill.
This line falls into two distinct sections, that from Westport to Mallaranny and thence to Achill. The former section was constructed by the MGW, the latter by the Board of Works. The decision to extend to Achill was apparently taken at the time of Balfour's visit in October 1890. At this point, it should be mentioned that the spelling of Mallaranny varies in different documents and at different times, being also known as Mulranny. The presentment for the section from Westport to Mallaranny was passed by the Grand Jury of the county on 24th November, with work commencing almost immediately under Worthington. Messrs. McCrea & McFarland submitted the lowest tender but subsequently advised that they had made an error in their calculations and asked to be allowed to withdraw, Worthington getting the contract at £110,000.

Plans for the Achill Extension railway were submitted to the Summer Assizes in July 1891 and were unanimously approved; the line would be a boon to the impoverished and densely populated district through which it would pass. The estimated cost of construction of the 8 mile 2 furlong line was £56,000. An intermediate station was pro-

posed at Tonregee, the BoW's engineer proposing a siding there for fish traffic. In October, Worthington wrote proposing alterations to the bridge beyond Newport. The MGW engineer agreed that the alterations would be desirable; a second letter offered to allow the company £750 in return for substituting a cutting for the proposed Barley Hill tunnel. In regard to Newport tunnel, the company agreed to it being shortened by 100ft at the south end, thus enabling the contractor to obtain more materials for embankments. In April 1892, James Barton wrote on behalf of the BoW enclosing a draft agreement for the working of the Achill extension when completed. It was suggested that the MGW should provide the station buildings, water supply, turntable and signals at Achill, for which the BoW were prepared to pay. This suggestion was turned down and it was requested that the line be completed by the BoW.

Three months later, correspondence was received in relation to the location of Mallaranny station, the Midland replying that no decision had been taken pending an agreement over the extension. As a direct result of the lack of an agreement in this regard, the MGW found it necessary to open its line in two stages, as far as Newport on 1st February 1894 and to Mallaranny on 16th July. A request for an intermediate station at Roskeen level crossing was declined. An inspection of the Achill extension in August by the Midland directors was combined with a visit to Keel and Dugort to ascertain their eligibility as hotel sites.

At the end of April 1895, Major Addison inspected the extension and gave his approval subject to the issue of special instructions concerning the long 1 in 70 gradient facing down trains on leaving Mallaranny station. The line was finally opened throughout as from 13th May with

Two memorials at Achill, the first in respect of the tragedy in 1894 when a number of islanders en route to the potato picking in Scotland were drowned. The second was for those who died in a fire in Scotland in 1937. The branch was virtually opened and closed by funeral trains, bringing to mind the prophesy by an islander made long before the advent of railways. Both courtesy John Kennedy.

the usual two trains each way. Early in 1897, the Congested Districts Board proposed the introduction of a steamer service between Westport and Achill, a proposal vigorously opposed by the Midland. During these early years, further extensions were mooted, from Westport to Louisburgh and from Achill to Gubbardletter but none of these came to fruition although in the latter case agreement had been reached with the BoW.

A tragic accident occurred on 16th June 1894 which saw the Achill extension being used by a special train before it was fully completed. Emigration had been a normal event in the lives of the Achill islanders, with large numbers of young people travelling annually to Scotland for the potato harvest. On the morning of 16th June, several hundred islanders left Achill aboard a hooker bound for Westport Quay where they intended embarking on the Laird steamer *The Elm* for Glasgow. Approaching Westport the captain of the hooker proceeded to jibe the mainsail without slackening the sheet or lowering the sail. This action had the effect of causing the sail to change over suddenly, capsizing the vessel. Tragically, 30 of the passengers were drowned, 25 of whom were young girls. A special train was run to bring home the bodies of the victims.

Ironically, coincident with the final closure of the line in 1937, another similar train was run following the deaths of ten Achill youths in a fire in their lodgings at Kirkintilloch in Scotland. Once again, these young men were potato diggers, ranging in age from 13 to 23. Many of the victims were related to the victims of the 1894 disaster.

This petrol railcar was introduced in 1911 on the Achill branch. Its introduction enabled additional stops to be made at level crossings to drop and collect mail. It was transferred to the civil engineer's department in 1916 and was finally scrapped in 1933. Author's collection.

Chapter Eight

THE DUBLIN & MEATH RAILWAY

ONE OF the first references to an independent line to serve the county of Meath appeared in *Saunders Newsletter for* 17th September 1857 reporting a meeting on the previous day in Navan courthouse. The crowded meeting was called to give further consideration to a proposed direct line from Navan to Dublin with a branch to Trim and Athboy. Navan was at this time already served by a branch line of the Dublin & Drogheda Railway from Drogheda. Powers for this line had originally been granted in 1845 to the Dublin & Belfast Junction Railway which was promoted to bridge the gap between the D&D and the UR in the north thus providing a through line from Belfast to Dublin. The D&BJ passed the powers to construct the Navan branch to the D&D in 1847. The D&D opened the line in February 1850 having in the meantime obtained powers to extend it to Kells.

Mindful of the roundabout route from Dublin to Kells, Parliament made a proviso in the D&D's Act that should any direct line be made from Dublin to Navan, the latter's owners should have automatic running powers from Navan to Kells. To return however to the meeting at Navan, it was attended by a number of important persons, including the Earl of Fingall, Lord Lieutenant of the county, Lord Dunsany, Sir Benjamin Chapman and the Duke of Leinster.

Sir John Macneill gave evidence of the lack of engineering difficulties, and the expected low cost of construction. The Midland directors had earlier met a deputation from the proposed Dublin & Meath company but nothing had come of this. Matters moved swiftly and notice of intention to lodge a bill in Parliament was issued in November for a line diverging from the MGW at or near Clonsilla and running to a junction with the Kells branch of the D&D at Navan. Running powers were to be sought over both lines. Despite opposition from the D&D and some of the land-owners, the Act of Incorporation received Royal Assent on 23rd July 1858. The D&D had also endeavoured to join the Midland in opposition to the scheme with a suggestion in March that the two companies should go to Parliament for a line from Ferns Lock through Trim to Navan.

The capital of the new company was £230,000, with additional borrowing powers of £75,000. The first shareholders' meeting was held in Dublin on 22nd October with Lord Dunsany in the chair. It was announced that the contract for construction had been awarded to the Moore Brothers of Dublin. The Chairman also stated that the ceremony of turning the first sod had been performed on the previous day at Trim by His Grace, the Duke of Leinster. A newspaper account of the ceremony added that the spade and barrow were specimens of the most tasteful and expensive manufacture. The spade was made of solid silver and engraved with the arms of Trim and of the Duke, the barrow was of Irish oak. The National Anthem was rendered by the 13th Light Dragoons' band brought down specially from Dublin. Afterwards, upwards of 300 of the elite were entertained to the customary *déjeuner* by the directors.

The Chairman also made the point that the population through which the line would pass was composed of a class of comfortable farmers who would furnish a considerable traffic. After all, Meath was the richest grazing county in the Empire! Despite this optimism, there appeared to be some clouds on the horizon. A further Bill was in contemplation to enable the company to extend to join the GS&W at Lucan. In December, the directors agreed not to proceed with this extension, in return for which the Midland board stated that it was prepared to name a mileage rate for working the line. This was not to the liking of the Meath directors, who preferred the idea of the line being worked on a percentage of gross receipts; they also hoped to run over the Midland from Clonsilla to Dublin. These differences were to lead to the D&M applying for powers for its own line into the city with a terminal station 'close to the penitentiary' on the North Circular Road in the parish of St.George's.

Reason eventually prevailed and following an arbitration hearing before Mr C W Eborall, general manager of the South Eastern Railway, it was agreed that the line would join the Midland at Clonsilla. The award required that the Meath traffic be carried between Clonsilla and Broadstone for a period of ten years 'by fit and proper engines and carriages' belonging to the Midland company. The latter was to provide and run four trains each way on weekdays in connection with Meath line trains, to be charged at half the Clonsilla to Broadstone fare. Two trains were required on Sundays but the MGW was at liberty to use its existing trains. Through rates were to be agreed, and the MGW was to submit monthly statements.

While this arbitration hearing was taking place, the D&M directors carried out an inspection of their new line in July and were apparently pleased with what they saw. The contractors had 1,200 men employed and had laid about twelve miles of rails southwards from Navan. A good deal of work had also been carried out on the Athboy branch. Earthworks were sufficiently far advanced for the laying of rails to within four miles of Clonsilla. Contracts were entered into for the delivery of rolling stock by February 1862. The Boyne viaduct was reported to be a bold and massive structure.

Opening to Navan.
A further inspection was carried out by the directors in February 1862, at which time *Saunders Newsletter* was confident of an opening by May. It was however to be 28th August before an advertisement appeared announcing the opening on the following day, with trains scheduled to leave the Broadstone at 07.50, 10.50, 16.50 and 18.40 on weekdays. Up trains were to leave Navan at 08.40, 11.40, 15.00 and 19.25. Captain Rich had inspected the line on behalf of the BoT on 31st July, and required some minor alterations and adjustments. On the opening day, the first down train did not leave Dublin until 08.30, its passengers including the directors, Sir John Macneill and John Broughton, the company's traffic manager. With its line nearly ready for opening in April, the Meath company had notified the D&D that it wished to avail of the provisions in the latter's Act of 1847 to use the Navan to Kells section. The D&D procrastinated and eventually this matter had also to be referred to arbitration.

The D&M obtained its running powers, and also a new platform at Kells, as well as

the use of the engine shed and turntable for £220 per annum. Having notified its intention of opening to Kells with effect from 1st December, it was necessary to insert a notice in the press on Saturday, 29th November, to the effect that 'owing to the non-completion by the Drogheda company of a proper signal at the junction, the trains advertised to be run to Kells on and after 1st December are unavoidably postponed until further notice'. These trains in fact commenced as from 15th December. In the meantime, the D&D began advertising a special fast train to Kells and on 16th December announced fare reductions. Reference was made to this fact at the D&M's half-yearly shareholders' meeting in February. When the Meath trains commenced running in December, their fares to Kells were 6s.6d, 4s.6d and 3s.6d, and to Navan, 5s.0d, 3s.6d and 2s.6d. Within days, the Kells return fares were reduced to 4s.0d, 2s.10d and 2s.0d, those to Navan to 3s.0d, 2s.0d and 1s.4d. The Meath company determined to charge equal or lower fares 'to prevent undue interference with a line which is the natural and proper route between Dublin and Kells'. Within three months, the two companies had reached amicable agreement and by August, the Meath directors were able to report average receipts of £7.6s.0d per mile per week.

The year 1863 saw difficulties in another direction when the contractors, Messrs Moore Brothers, went bankrupt. The creditors wanted assignment of the contract, but the directors preferred dealing with the

Moore Brothers and a scheme was agreed. By April, ballasting had been completed and the trustees arranged an auction of the contractors' plant at Kilmessan. As far as the Athboy branch was concerned, the contract went to John Killeen. By September, line was laid to Trim, enabling a cattle special to operate in connection with Trim fair on 1st October. The BoT inspection of the entire branch was carried out on 26th January 1864, and an opening for passengers approved as soon as an additional passenger platform was completed at Kilmessan. Passenger services to Athboy in fact commenced on 26th February.

By this time, the company was beset by debts of £200,000. Many of the creditors were given Lloyds bonds, shares only being sold at large discounts. Lloyds bonds were described by the *Railway Times* as being at best a means of enabling directors to get into debt. The law recognised two methods of raising money, namely by shares and mortgage. Before resorting to the latter, it was necessary that all the share capital be subscribed and that not less than half be fully paid-up. Lloyds bonds evaded both of these conditions and generally were the precursor of a company's collapse. During 1864, the directors refused to discuss settlement with their creditors, who forced the issue by putting their representatives on the board. The new board solved the debt problem by persuading most of the creditors to take preference shares in lieu of the Lloyds bonds.

Kilmessan Junction looking east with the old D&M locomotive shed on the right. The Athboy branch diverged immediately in front of the signal cabin which remains in situ. The station building is currently occupied as the Railway Hotel.
The late J P O'Dea, courtesy of the National Library of Ireland.

Plans for Kingscourt.

The company's fortunes appeared to be improving, as in March 1865 the Chairman was able to report a 19% increase in traffic, although expenditure remained high. He called for economies to be effected wherever possible. By this time, plans were afoot for the construction of a line from Navan to Kingscourt and even for an extension to Castleblayney, where it was hoped to join up with the INW. The Kingscourt line is separately dealt with later in this chapter. Following a further approach to the Midland board in March 1866, the latter declined to work the Meath line on a percentage basis but was disposed to entertain a proposal for a mileage rate. In June however, the Midland made a definite offer to work the line at 2s.2d per mile for the first 90,000 miles and 1s.2d thereafter. Legal doubts as to the carrying out of this arrangement brought an end to the idea for a further two and a half years. Meanwhile, in April a deputation from the D&D met with the Midland board in regard to the Kells to Navan traffic and it was agreed that neither company would enter negotiation with the D&M without the knowledge of the other.

Agreement on this latter issue was reached towards the end of May when it was proposed that the Navan and Kells to Dublin traffic be divided on a common purse principle. The proportion by each route was to be based on the traffic of the past three years and in the case of surplus passenger traffic, 20% to be allowed to the carrying company. Of all the surplus passenger traffic, the D&D was to receive 80%, the D&M 20%, while goods traffic was to be allocated 66% and 33% respectively. The Midland was to accept as its share of surplus traffic by the D&M route its mileage of the 20 and 33%.

A complaint was made by the Midland in July 1867 that if arrangements were not made by the D&M to supply additional wagons, it (the MGW) would notify the public that D&M goods would only be forwarded as wagons were available. This matter was not quickly resolved, as reference was made to it at the Midland's shareholders' meeting the following March. Although the entire line from North Wall was some 36 miles in length', of which we have nine or one-quarter . . . they think we should supply three-quarters of the stock'. Such was the poor financial state of the D&M, that a further approach was made requesting the Midland to consider working the line at a percentage. This proposal was initially refused, although this was undoubtedly a tactical move as the Midland directors were obviously fully aware of the smaller company's plight. A loan of £13,500 had been arranged with the PWLC and in January 1869 the company had to appeal to the U.K. Rolling Stock Company for a three months extension of a loan on the rolling stock.

A working agreement is signed.

A working agreement was finally signed by the two companies on 10th February 1869 and authorised by Act of Parliament in May. The agreement was for ten years, and could be terminated after that period on twelve months notice. The Midland was obliged to run not less than two passenger trains each way on weekdays, plus one each way on Sundays, the times of such trains to be so fixed as to be convenient for connection with through trains on the Midland. Within six months, the D&M was to erect and provide at its own expense, a proper and convenient permanent station at Navan. It will be recalled that it had been using the D&D station. As regards Athboy, the MGW was at liberty to expend £1,000 on station improvements, in return for which it was to retain annually out of the percentage payable to the D&M, one-tenth of the sum so expended. The Midland was to retain 52% of gross receipts, except that when they exceeded £20,000 in any year, it would retain 40% in excess of £18,000. The D&M

was to sell to the MGW all tools and moveable machinery in its Kilmessan workshops, together with all rolling stock. Locomotives were excluded from the latter, and they could be disposed of as the D&M saw fit.

It was agreed in May that the two companies' locomotive engineers, Ramage and Armitage, should value the rolling stock with John Eaton of the Ulster Railway to act as arbitrator, if required. A figure of £10,519 was agreed in June and this sum, along with £1,350 agreed for locomotive No.7, was paid over to the U.K. Rolling Stock Company. About the same time, the machinery at Kilmessan was valued at £928. The Midland commenced working the line as from 1st June 1869, having unsuccessfully tried to postpone this until July. The question of running powers between Navan and Kells was raised at the end of June, when it was agreed that the service would continue for the present, although notice was given to the D&D in August that it should take over the working from 1st September. The Midland obviously commenced running its own carriages through, as in July it was reported that the Meath line platforms would require alteration to suit the Midland carriages. At this time also, plans and estimates were requested for altering the old engine shed at Clonsilla to accommodate the men at the station.

An approach was made by Dowd, the Traffic Manager, in August to see if the Midland might be interested in purchasing the locomotive stock. It was deemed unsuitable, although No.7 was purchased but would appear to have been little used. About this time, Dowd was appointed Assistant Manager of the Midland and resigned his position on the Meath, having been with it for six years. In March 1870, Samuel Sheppard, who had been Chairman since 1865, announced his resignation from the board and was replaced by John Law. At the same board meeting, it was announced that the directors had foregone any remuneration since 1864, a saving of £2,500 to the company.

Law was only to remain on the board for ten months and he in turn was replaced by David McBirney, a post he was to retain for ten years. The board appointed a Mr Theobold to the post of Company Secretary at a salary of £100 per annum in September. In June 1873, consideration was given to converting the agreement with the Midland into a more permanent arrangement. It was agreed that negotiations be opened accordingly with a view to securing a rate of working expenses not exceeding 48%. The new agreement was finally incorporated in an Act of 1875, under which the Meath line was leased to the Midland for a period of 99 years from 1st July 1875. Clause 10 laid down that the line was to be worked at 48%

as previously proposed. Prior to the conclusion of this agreement, moves had been made to transfer the management of the company from London to Dublin.

A general meeting of shareholders in Dublin on 28th March 1874 had resolved that the existing board should retire, but the directors thought otherwise as they felt duty bound to those shareholders who had extricated the company from its difficulties. Early in May, three months notice was given to Theobold, a Mr Henry Hanson being appointed Secretary for the time being, this appointment being duly confirmed in August. On 27th May, Hanson was authorised to take offices in a central location in Dublin at a rent not exceeding £30 per annum. A board meeting was held at the new offices at 40 Dame Street on 19th June.

Before the railway commissioners.

Evidence of friction between the two companies began to emerge in November 1876, principally relating to the working of trains. The Meath chairman, David McBirney, wrote in October 1877 complaining of delays to trains, the Midland replying to the effect that the delays were mainly caused by the line being single. It was satisfied that at least a portion of the line should be doubled, and when the D&M was willing to join in the expense of this alteration, the delays would cease. The truth of the matter was of course that the Meath directors were not in a position to incur this expenditure. In December, further insult was added by the withdrawal of the mid-day market train on Thursdays, leading to further protests. Matters were sufficiently bad by the following July for a deputation of shareholders to attend on the Midland board in relation to services and traffic arrangements. A further deputation attended about this time to discuss the question of the Midland purchasing the Meath line, a figure of £385,000 being put forward. The Midland directors found themselves unable to entertain this figure. January 1879 saw the deteriorating relations between the two boards discussed by the D&M, resulting in the matter being referred to the railway commissioners in August.

The Meath company referred to the competition from the GNR's Oldcastle branch and asserted that three trains each way daily were required. There had been a third train, run at unsuitable and inconvenient times, as the result of which the MGW claimed a loss on its working and had therefore withdrawn it. Another complaint referred to delays at stations. The commissioners found in favour of the D&M, and the working company was obliged to restore the third train as from 1st January 1880. If it was thought that relations would improve, some people were in for a disappointment. In February, the D&M Secretary was instructed to see the

MGWR Traffic Manager and arrange for the last up train from Navan to leave at 19.50. The 'morning shuttle' between Kilmessan and Navan and vice-versa was to be discontinued and replaced by an evening train to connect with the 19.50. In June 1881, the Midland announced its intention of discontinuing the running of the third train by the end of the month. The Meath board replied by saying that it would take legal action to have the railway commissioners' order enforced.

It was in fact the Midland which went to the commissioners again, in 1882, asking them to review, vary or rescind that part of the earlier order relating to the third train. Its case was based on the fact that the third train did not result in increased receipts and passenger traffic had remained virtually stationary since 1879. The commissioners were sceptical of the figures put forward by the Midland for three reasons. The three year period under review was one of general depression for all railway companies, there had been fare reductions on the D&M in 1880 due to third class fares exceeding the maximum fixed by the company's tolls, and thirdly, part of the increase in train mileage bore no relation to the existence of the third train. The commissioners felt that proper adjustment of the figures should have enabled the Midland to work the line profitably, even with the third train.

At the earlier hearing, the D&M had complained that the GNR had been taking an increasing share of the Navan to Dublin traffic, the former's proportion having been reduced from 74 to 60% in a few years. This reduction, it attributed to the two trains as opposed to three, the unpunctuality and slow speed of trains and the unreasonable delays with connections at Kilmessan for Athboy passengers. In relation to a 40 minute connection at Kilmessan in the mornings, the D&M had suggested running the Athboy train through to Navan and back again. This proposal had been declined by the Midland on the grounds of insufficiency of crossing places, which it had advised should be provided at Batterstown and Trim. The companies could not agree as to who should pay for the work.

Having considered the matter at length, the commissioners decided that they could not rescind the order of 1879, but they did give leave to either company to apply to have the matter again considered at any time after 31st December 1883. The Midland was far from happy with this decision and determined to make life as difficult as possible. Lengthy correspondence passed between the two boards in relation to train delays. The Midland wrote again in January 1886 seeking permission to withdraw the third train, a request which was refused. The result was that both companies made

cross-applications and so for the third time in seven years the commissioners found themselves in the middle of a dispute between the two companies.

Some of the points raised show how ridiculous companies could be in their dealings with each other. One related to disinfecting fees which resulted from an order made by the Privy Council in 1876 for the disinfecting of cattle wagons. The MGW charged 1s.6d per wagon and for a considerable period the whole receipts from that fee were placed to the credit of the Midland. In 1883, the D&M claimed its share and a compromise was reached. Then in April 1884, the D&M wrote to the Midland claiming the same right to share in the fees from cattle conveyed over its line from the Navan & Kingscourt, according to its mileage since 1880. So far so good, the Midland accepted this proposal, but a dispute then arose as to which years accounts the sum so received should be credited, the D&M claiming it should be 1884, the Midland 1883. At this point, no agreement could be reached and the Meath withdrew its offer of not going back prior to 1880. The commissioners took the view that it was immaterial which years accounts were concerned and also thought the Meath wrong on going back on its earlier agreement. Another item concerned expenditure of about £90 by the Midland in 1880 in providing cattle troughs, this figure being deducted from the D&M's share of the total receipts on the grounds that it was a capital expense. The Meath directors did not agree, nor did the commissioners.

The two main points of disagreement were the provision of the third train and the average speed of the trains. Regarding the former, the Midland had offered to provide a third train if either the receipts from it were credited to it in full or else it received 1s.6d per mile for running it. The commissioners thought the first of these options the simplest and postponed any decision for two months in the hope that the companies could reach mutual agreement, in the absence of which they would make an order relieving the Midland from its obligations in this regard. No agreement was forthcoming and the Midland in due course ceased to provide the extra train. In reference to the train speeds, it was directed that they should not occupy a longer journey time than they did in 1879.

The independent life of the Meath company was nearing an end but we must first return some years to recount other events. In April 1881, a Mr James Kelly of Ratoath wrote to the Midland calling attention to the want of a station at Fairyhouse Bridge. The Midland replied that it had no powers as it was only a lessee of the line. The matter was raised again in the following February when a deputation attended from the Ward Hunt

Race Committee, by which time there was a temporary station there. An additional narrow platform was suggested, and this was estimated to cost about £80, utilising old materials. The Meath directors were censured in August 1881 for not having advised the BoT of alterations carried out at Batterstown, Drumree and Dunboyne. This was referred to the Midland which replied that the works related only to lengthening of platforms. Some twelve months earlier however, Drumree station had been altered to allow of the crossing of trains there.

David McBirney, who had had a long connection with the D&M, died in October 1882, an event referred to in the *Railway Times*. Apart from being a director and one-time Chairman of the company, he was at the time of his death, Chairman of four other railway companies and head of one of the leading mercantile firms in Dublin. In July 1885, a memorial was received from the residents of the village of Castletown Kilpatrick, equidistant between Nobber and Wilkinstown for a station, a request which was declined, although a halt was eventually opened here on 1st December 1927 and closed some eight years later. Just before the sale of the line was completed, work commenced in October 1888 on doubling the line between Clonsilla Junction and Fairyhouse Bridge.

Navan & Kingscourt.
In November 1864, the Midland board considered a letter from Messrs D&T Fitzgerald seeking support for a proposed railway from Navan to Kingscourt, but it did not feel in a position to contribute. The D&M however supported the line as it saw a northwards extension as being advantageous to its traffic prospects. The Navan & Kingscourt Railway Act was passed in July 1865 with the D&M empowered to subscribe one-third of the £120,000 capital, in return for which two of the Meath directors would serve on the Kingscourt board. The line was to run from a junction with the D&M at Navan to Corgarry, near Kingscourt; working and traffic arrangements were proposed with the D&M. Hardly had the Act been passed, but proposals were being put forward for a further extension to Castleblayney, negotiations being entered into with the INW which proposed a junction between Culloville and Dundalk. It was necessary to go back to Parliament in 1867 for an extension of time as no work had been carried out in the interim, due in no small measure to the state of the money market. Powers for the extension northwards were not granted.

Later in the year, an agreement was reached with the D&M for the working of the line at 40%. Yet another extension of time was sought in 1870, by which time a contract had been awarded to John Edwards for construction. By August, seven miles had been formed and ballasted, with an opening to Nobber expected in the following Spring, but in the event very little happened in 1871 due to the company's inability to pay for rails and sleepers. A further Act of 1871 authorised an extension to Carrickmacross, with proposals for a Castleblayney extension, the Midland offering to subscribe £10,000. The first section of the N&K as far as Kilmainham Wood was finally opened on 1st November 1872, following three inspections by Lieutenant Colonel Hutchinson on behalf of the BoT.

The company was still in financial difficulties and was unable to complete the remaining four miles to Kingscourt; in June, the Midland was approached for a loan to effect purchase of permanent way materials, including rails. The company's financial position brought it to the Chancery Court in 1873, and in the following year the capital was rearranged, control of the company moving to Dublin. This reorganisation enabled Edwards to resume work and the line was made ready for a BoT inspection by May 1875. It requested further works, Edwards refusing to carry them out as he was owed money. The line was taken over in October by the Chairman, William McBirney, the necessary works were completed, and it opened throughout on 1st November. There were still ideas of a Carrickmacross extension, but in the meantime the company arranged an omnibus service.

With the line now completed, a formal agreement was entered into with the Midland for working. This agreement was embodied in the same Act as that for the D&M. Pending the completion to Kingscourt, the MGW worked the line to Kilmainham Wood on a mileage basis at 2s.3d per train mile. With the opening to Kingscourt, the basis of working was altered to correspond with that for the D&M, that is 52% of receipts up to £11,500 per annum, and when receipts exceeded this figure, 52% on the first £10,000 and 40% on the balance. Provision was also made for working the Carrickmacross extension when completed. Further approaches were made to the Midland in 1877 and 1880 in connection with the latter extension, but on each occasion the MGW refused to become involved. Like the D&M, complaints were made from time to time regarding the service provided by the Midland, although the N&K never got as far as going to the Railway Commissioners.

A railway for sale.

In April 1880, the D&M board approached the Midland asking if it would be disposed to purchase the company. In reply, the Midland said it would recommend this course to its shareholders subject to the N&K agreeing to sell its line at the same time and also to the terms being fixed by arbitration. The Midland had a change of heart in May and declined to proceed with any arbitration, partially due to the GNR's intention of extending its line from Iniskeen to Carrickmacross. It was however prepared to consider any reasonable proposals put forward by the two companies. The matter was put on hold until the following January when the D&M proposed a purchase price of £350,000, the Midland making a counter-offer of £300,000 which was to be withdrawn if not accepted. This figure was regarded as totally unsatisfactory and there matters rested until another offer was made by the MGW in November 1887, for £250,000 to be paid in Midland 4% debenture stock.

Attempts were made in December to have this figure increased so as to enable the Meath board to recommend the sale to its shareholders. No increase was forthcoming and the offer, although agreed to be on the low side, was reluctantly accepted. The payment was made on 1st September 1888 and at the same time, the Kingscourt was sold for £50,000, payable by cheque. The last meeting of the D&M board was held on 20th November, when it was agreed that the Secretary should receive the sum of £800 as compensation for work done on behalf of the directors. So came to an end the independent existence of the two companies.

Kingscourt with the locomotive shed just visible to the right. At one time the station boasted two signal cabins, though both had been closed by October 1930. Principal traffic was bricks from a factory situated near the station. Special instructions were in force to enable wagons from the factory to be left on the running line.
The late J P O'Dea, courtesy of the National Library of Ireland.

Chapter Nine

THE GREAT NORTHERN & WESTERN RAILWAY

WITHIN a year of the line being opened to Galway, proposals were being put forward for a line into County Mayo. A meeting was held early in October 1852 at Castlebar chaired by the Earl of Lucan and attended by *inter alia,* the Marquess of Sligo and Lord Oranmore. A resolution was passed that a committee be formed to propose and carry out the most feasible project for the immediate construction of railway accommodation in County Mayo. The *Mayo Constitution* reporting on the meeting quoted Lord Lucan as saying that 'to jump to the conclusion that we must have a railway in the county whether we can afford it or not is quite absurd and ridiculous'. Lord Oranmore said he was quite willing to grant the land free, as was the Marquess of Sligo. On the other hand, Henry Browne said 'that if you run your railway on ten yards of my land you will pay for it'.

Tennyson's poem describing the charge of the Light Brigade at Balaclava during the Crimean War brings to mind Lord Lucan, for it was he who gave the fateful order to charge in October 1854. He was recalled to England early in February 1855, an action applauded by *Saunders Newsletter* which referred to his every move as being not only 'a great blunder, but productive of awful disasters . . . his Lordship has got the sobriquet in the army of 'Lord Look-on' . . . while his Light Horse Regiment was called 'Bingham's Dandies', Bingham being the family name. About this time his wife left him and for the next few years, he devoted his attentions to bringing railway communication to County Mayo.

At a subsequent meeting, the committee proposed to recommend a guarantee on the county of interest on £300,000, this being the estimated cost of a line from Dublin to Castlebar, Westport and Ballina. The Midland directors suggested that the new line might commence at Longford, powers having recently been obtained for their extension from Mullingar. In December, the Midland board received a letter from Colonel Knox-Gore enclosing a memorial from the inhabitants of Mayo to the effect that they would not guarantee any railway which did not recognise Ballina and Westport as termini.

A much more grandiose scheme was discussed at another meeting in Castlebar in April 1853. A long and ably-worded prospectus read by Mr P B Ryan proposed a railway from Dumfries to Portpatrick in Scotland and then from Clones via Carrick-on-Shannon, Castlebar and Newport to Bellport in Clew Bay, with a branch to Westport. This line was to be known as the British & Irish Atlantic Junction Railway Company. Like many grandiose schemes, this was the last that was heard of it. Meanwhile, the Midland directors were considering an extension from Athenry to Tuam, Hemans being instructed in October to carry out a survey. Also at this time, the GS&W was planning a line from Portarlington to Tullamore and thence to Athenry, Frenchpark and Boyle, to be continued from there into Mayo. This scheme had received the sanction of the Roscommon Grand Jury and the Midland board was asked for its help in assisting those in Roscommon opposed to guaranteeing this project.

Considerable discussion took place regarding the GS&W line at the board meeting on 15th December, Hemans being requested to report on the best line from Longford through north Roscommon to Mayo. The GS&W backed project was in fact the Grand Junction Railway of Ireland, whose notice of application to Parliament had been published in mid-November. On 21st January 1854, the *Roscommon Journal* reported on a large railway meeting at Roscommon which was one of the most respectable and influential meetings held for a number of years. It was presided over by Lord Crofton. The great advantages of a line through the west, connecting up with the GS&W were stressed and the meeting unanimously passed a resolution approving the proposed line. The Grand Junction Railway Bill passed the Commons Standing Orders Committee in February despite strong opposition from the Midland. This caused the *Roscommon Journal* to note, 'many are the ways of killing a dog without hanging him . . . just as numerous are the devices of the MGW directors to defeat the project. So far every act of open or disguised hostility has only served to increase the popularity of the new line of railway'.

Again, in March, the Strokestown Union petitioned Parliament for a quick passage for the Grand Junction Bill, but in May it was thrown out – an act described as a heavy blow and a deep discourtesy to the west of Ireland. It came to light that the scheme had been put up by six contractors and a knot of GS&W directors. Following the issue of the prospectus, no money could be raised and the GS&W stepped in with powers being inserted in the Bill for it to subscribe £260,000. It also came to light that a large part of the Grand Junction's promotional expenses had been paid by the GS&W, an action which did little to endear the GS&W directors to their shareholders. The next scheme to be put forward was the North Western Railway of Ireland, the notice of application for which was published in November 1855. This company proposed a line from Strokestown to Castlebar with a branch to Roscommon. Powers were sought for a subscription by and working arrangements with the MGW.

The Chairman of the provisional committee was Fitzstephen French, other members including the Earl of Lucan and John Ennis. The line was to serve Elphin, Frenchpark, Ballaghaderreen and Swinford. The Midland agreed to construct a line at its own expense from Longford to Strokestown. As the time for lodgement of surveys was limited, it was decided in the first instance to take powers for a Strokestown to Castlebar line. The GJR scheme was meanwhile resurrected in an amended form with a southern extension from Ballybrophy to Athlone. The Midland extension to Strokestown and the NWR schemes came before the Commons in April 1856; whilst the Midland scheme might be good in itself, it should not be permitted to interfere with any larger scheme which might in the future be submitted.

With this setback, the NW promoters, probably wisely, withdrew their scheme and once again it seemed as if the counties of Roscommon and Mayo were to be deprived of railway communication. Yet another scheme made a brief appearance in May 1856, namely the Athlone & Sligo Railway. By now the Midland had formulated its own plans for Sligo by extending its Longford branch, a scheme not finding much favour with the Sligo Grand Jury. Lord Lucan now saw his chance of having a line to Mayo realised and he suggested that his proposal for a Tullamore to Sligo line should be subscribed to and worked jointly by the MGW and GS&W companies, the Midland from Sligo to Athlone and the balance by the GS&W. For once the two companies agreed on something: they did not wish to become involved – having said that, no agreement could be reached as to what they should do, and so three Bills went to Parliament.

After much wrangling, the Midland came to an agreement with Lord Lucan whereby the new line was to commence at Athlone and run as far as Castlerea via Roscommon. The Great Northern & Western (of Ireland) Railway Company was incorporated by Act of Parliament dated 27th July 1857 with a capital of £240,000. The *Roscommon Journal* reported great public rejoicing at the return of Lord Crofton and the happy result of his indefatigable exertions in securing railway accommodation for the north-west. The discussions between the two companies were embodied in an agreement dated 22nd June 1857, whereby the Midland was to work the GN&W on terms to be settled, the latter company to provide railway accommodation to Castlebar, Westport and Ballina as soon as deemed prudent. In the event that for any reason the

MGW failed to obtain sanction for a Sligo extension, the GN&W could apply for such powers. The Midland was to provide one-third of the capital in return for which it could nominate one-third of the directors. The principal provisions of the agreement were embodied in the company's Act of 1858.

At this stage in the proceedings, the Athenry & Tuam Railway appeared on the scene. Early in 1858, the GN&W directors gave consideration to the Tuam company's Bill and came to the conclusion that such a line would be adverse to their interests and they were more than surprised to hear that the Midland was prepared to lend support to and work the new line. This course of action was totally inconsistent with the amicable relations which the GN&W board had hoped would have existed between the two companies. In June, there was a flurry of activity beginning with a meeting between Lucan, Ennis and Boyd on behalf of the MGW and Hemans and Bodkin for the A&T. Ennis stated that it was their intention to press for the withdrawal of the running powers and pecuniary assistance clauses in the A&T Bill.

Ennis went on to state that the Midland desired to be allowed to enter into a working agreement, but would guarantee to render it impossible that there would at any future time be an extension beyond Tuam.

The Earl and his fellow directors were far from happy with this situation and proposed an agreement between the two companies whereby the MGW would not promote or assist in promoting or work any line extending north-west from Tuam. If it did, it was to forfeit all rights in the GN&W and allow the latter to connect its undertaking with the GS&W by means of running powers over the Midland at Athlone. The Earl of Lucan obviously felt he was in a strong position to dictate terms, although the Midland rejected these proposals, counter-proposals from it in turn being rejected. In fact, the Midland directors soon agreed to the above proposals with a ten year exclusion on any extension.

In return, the GN&W withdrew all opposition to the Tuam Bill and the agreement was formally signed on 14th June. When the GN&W Bill came before Parliament in June, it was initially petitioned against by the MGW on the grounds that the proposed line would abstract traffic from its line. The petitioners believed the proposed line was uncalled for and unnecessary, the engineering details were defective and the estimate insufficient. Despite this opposition, the Bill was successful. At the board meeting on 6th July, Messrs Smith & Knight's tender for construction of the line at £179,923 was read, subsequently reduced to £175,000 to include the building of all over-bridges and culverts for a double line of railway. The contractors agreed to take 75% in cash, the balance in company shares.

In October, the board's attention was drawn to a projected line from Elphin to Swinford, a line which appeared 'so visionary and so improbable of realisation' that not much credence was attached to it. Nevertheless it was thought advisable to ascertain the Midland's views on it, and if there appeared any likelihood of success, plans for the Castlerea to Castlebar extension were to be pushed forward with all haste. Ennis advised on the Midland's view that the time did not appear right to proceed with the Castlebar line so long as capital for the building of the portion of line already authorised remained unsubscribed. The GN&W saw it differently, as it would hopefully frustrate any attempt to construct the Swinford line which was in fact a resurrection of the NWR project promoted by French. In the following January, French contacted the GN&W offering to restrict his line to Ballina if the GN&W agreed not to oppose the proposed Enniskillen & Sligo Railway. It declined to become involved and instructed its solicitors to oppose the NWR Bill.

March 1859 saw a draft agreement being discussed as to working arrangements and the provision of trains. In the latter context, at least one composite coach was to run

PROPOSED RAILWAY FROM SLIGO TO ATHLONE.

It is in contemplation to seek for Parliamentary Powers, next Session, for the immediate construction of a Line of Railway from Sligo to Athlone, passing by the Towns of Ballisodare, Collooney, and Ballymote, in the County of Sligo, with divergence to Swineford and Ballina; and the Towns of Boyle, Elphin, Strokestown, and Roscommon, in the County of Roscommon.

For which purpose, Capitalists of ample means, and who are unconnected with Railway enterprize in this province, have been consulted on the subject, and are prepared to advance the necessary funds.

As the parties referred to, desire to be fully informed, relative to the extent of the local support, and countenance which will be given to the undertaking, by an expression of approbation, it is necessary to obtain this information before any further step is taken.

I approve of the object above stated, and will give it my support.

Dated _____ May, 1856.

(Signed.)

_____

Lecarrow, situated between Kiltoom and Knockcroghery, was the Midland's main ballast pit and one of two used in later years by CIE, the other being at Lisduff on the main Cork line. The pit was served by a siding on the up side which was controlled by a ground frame released by the section staff. The late J P O'Dea, courtesy of the National Library of Ireland.

through to Dublin from every train to or from the GN&W at Athlone. As regards the actual services, there were to be four trains each way daily, with goods to be conveyed by one or more of these trains as required. In December, it was decided to go to Parliament for powers to make a deviation at Donamon on the understanding that the contractors would indemnify the company against costs and bind themselves to have the line from Roscommon to Castlerea ready for opening by 1st October 1860 under penalty of £11 per day. The only other parliamentary activity of the year was the passing of the Act for the Castlebar extension which empowered the MGW to subscribe one-third of the cost of construction.

The year closed with a bang for the GN&W. As the *Mayo Constitution* put it 'the great railway enterprise initiated by the Earl of Lucan has terminated in success'. On Wednesday 28th December, a trial trip was made by some of the directors and shareholders from Roscommon to Athlone. Although the day was cold, wet and windy, the weather did nothing to dampen local enthusiasm as a large number of townspeople turned out to cheer the directors. The train was loaned by the Midland, although the engine belonged to the contractors and was reported to have been decorated with bunches of gaily covered evergreens and ribbons.

The train departed from Roscommon at about 12.15 and arrived in Athlone at 13.00 after a short interruption 'occasioned by a trifling defect in the gear of the engine'. On the return journey, about 150 people were invited to travel gratuitously. The train stopped at Moate Park, residence of Lord Crofton, where an address was given by Denis Kirwan. His Lordship was presented with a magnificent candelabra of 24 lights and it was reported that the assembled party partook of a splendid *déjeuner* before separating at 4.00pm.

The BoT inspection was carried out on 27th January by Captain Tyler, everything being found satisfactory, and the line was opened for traffic on Monday 13th February with a service of three trains each way on weekdays and one on Sundays. In January, the decision had been taken that there would only be one intermediate station, at Knockcroghery, and instructions were given to the engineer to suspend works on the other stations. In March, Fowler reported as to the necessity of a station at Lecarrow, as the result of which it was resolved that it be opened, it 'and Knockcroghery to be tried for three months to test the traffic'. The former may in fact have been the platform on the down side at Nine Mile Bridge, used in later years for pilgrimage traffic to the nearby St Johns Well. A memorial in July for a station at Kiltoom was met with the response that stations had been authorised for Kiltoom and Ballymurray, the latter being opened later in the year. The station at Kiltoom was shortlived as a letter was sent to Fowler on 15th October 1860 authorising its closure as from 1st November. Another station was opened there in 1879, subsequently closed in 1963.

The *Mayo Constitution* referred in May 1860 to the traffic on the new line as being most gratifying and encouraging; while the goods traffic was remarkable for the regularity of its receipts, the passenger traffic was not as good as it might have been. *The Galway Vindicator* saw the line's prospects as being good, expressing the hope that the traffic would be lucrative to the shareholders, apart from the obvious advantages to the west of Ireland.

Further extensions.

We have already seen how the company obtained powers of extension to Castlebar under their Act of 1859. In April, it was resolved that the extension should be opened in three sections: from Castlerea to Ballyhaunis by 1st June 1861, to Claremorris by 1st September and the final stretch by 1st May 1862. Early in May, it was decided to seek tenders for the entire 37 mile extension. Two tenders were considered in June but were thought excessive and it was decided to offer a guarantee to Smith & Knight of £5,700 per mile, a figure which was accepted. With this problem out of the way, attention was now turned to further extensions. By 18th July it was announced that a Westport extension would go ahead and the first moves in this direction had in fact been inaugurated by the rapid increase in the subscription list, the Marquess of Sligo being reported to have given a most munificent £10,000. Ballina was also being considered and a meeting was held in the town to further this. The Castlerea extension was inspected by Captain Tyler on 14th November and opened on the following day.

By this time, the Castlebar extension was proceeding vigorously with the bridge over the River Suck being far advanced; great credit was due to Frederick Barry, the able engineer. At the half-yearly meeting of the Midland shareholders in March, the Chairman referred to the inadequate haulage rate of 1s.6⅝d. per mile over the Roscommon to Castlerea section, which resulted in a small operating loss. The hope was expressed that as traffic picked up, the situation would improve. The two companies failed to agree on this matter which was eventually referred to arbitration, an award of 2s.0d per mile between Castlerea and Castlebar being made in November. By early 1861, good progress was reported on the Ballyhaunis extension despite a shortage of men due to it being seed sowing time. Masonry work was virtually complete and the bogs thoroughly dried out. This section was inspected by Captain Tyler on 20th August and found in order, apart from the provision of lodges 'at several boreen roads'.

Despite BoT approval, the Midland failed to give its permission due in part to the impending arbitration. Other, more serious, matters were however surfacing, namely the question of a subscription to the Westport extension and talk of a further extension to Ballina. Ennis endeavoured to have the Westport subscription of £21,000 acceded to but a counter-motion that the matter be postponed, was agreed. Despite the possibility of a setback, the GN&W issued notice of application for a Bill for the Ballina extension which included powers for the Midland to contribute. Lord Lucan was aware of the fact that legislation for extensions and for MGW contributions thereto had to be enacted by the Summer of 1862.

For their part, the Midland directors considered the Ballina extension and agreed it was inexpedient to avail themselves of the proposed powers. So 1861 came to a close with the strong possibility of the Midland being embroiled in yet another dispute. By the third week of January 1862, little work remained to be done on the Claremorris extension; Lord Lucan inspected the new stretch of line early in February and expressed himself much pleased with the works. Captain Rich from the BoT was not quite so pleased when he inspected the line a month later, most probably in part due to pressures from other sources! On 29th April, the *Roscommon Journal* commented that the Midland directors had 'again exercised dictatorial and uncontrolled powers by refusing to open the extension . . . the Broadstone autocrats were unexorable'. The BoT approval came on 8th May and the line was opened on Monday 19th May, with two trains in each direction.

Following an offer from the GN&W for the carriage of the night mails, the postal authorities, agreed to a payment of 1s.10d. per single mile between Athlone and Castlerea, but declined to accept a proposed 1s.0d from there to Castlebar. In March, the company also tendered for the carriage of the day mails. John Rummens successfully tendered for the Westport extension in August, the engineer being instructed at the same time to take all steps to let the Ballina extension as soon as possible. This latter decision was taken despite the fact that cash was still not forthcoming from the Midland, the matter being referred to arbitration. The GN&W, with considerable celerity, served notice on the Midland's London agents on Friday 27th June, to appear before the arbitration on the following Tuesday morning. The latter requested time to consult their directors in Dublin but this was refused. Unhappy with this turn of events, some of the Midland shareholders obtained an injunction in the Court of Chancery to stop the arbitration proceedings. Vice-Chancellor Wood granted the injunction. The Ballina extension Bill passed through Parliament with all reference to the MGW subscription deleted, and work on the Westport extension stopped immediately.

These actions caused severe embarrassment to the GN&W directors, Rummens claiming compensation as the result of the stoppage. Part of the trouble arose due to the fact that whilst the Midland had two representatives on the GN&W board, they seldom attended meetings. Unsuccessful attempts had been made to have the board meetings transferred from London to Dublin; apart from this, it would appear that the notices convening the meetings were never sent to the Midland representatives. Lucan was obviously of opinion that once the Midland paid up, they did not require to have a voice as to how their money was spent.

It is hardly surprising that the GN&W now sought to cancel its agreement with the Midland and to make alternative arrangements with the GS&W. In May 1864, the Midland board proposed an amalgamation between the two companies on the basis of a handover of debenture and preference shares. The completion of the GN&W system, including the Westport and Ballina branches, was to be secured, subject to the approbation of the Midland engineer at a total cost not exceeding £698,000, this offer being declined by the GN&W.

The latter company now proceeded with two Bills, one enabling it to raise additional capital, the second more directly affecting the MGW. Clause 4 required it to book through and to convey and forward traffic in both directions to the GS&W station at Athlone. If it refused to provide this service, then the GN&W would be entitled to running powers. Another important aspect of this Act was that it empowered the MGW to dispose of shares held by it in the GN&W.

Apart altogether from the wranglings at this level, it was obvious from the *Mayo Constitution* that the Midland was 'resorting to every artifice to depreciate the Northern line or divert its legitimate traffic'. Scathing editorials appeared condemning the Midland board in relation to lack of services and attempts to divert traffic. By October 1864, the GN&W Deputy-Chairman, John Parsons, was suggesting the desirability of going to Parliament for a Bill empowering the company to raise additional capital for the purchase of rolling stock and also for running powers over both the MGW and the GS&W to Dublin. The matter was raised again at a board meeting in November but was defeated by a majority of four to one, Parsons resigning after the meeting.

By now, it seemed that common sense was beginning to prevail and we find John Kelly tendering for the completion of the various works. By the beginning of the new year, Kelly had commenced work and by April good progress was reported with an opening anticipated by September. It would appear that somewhat similar problems were encountered at Saleen Lake as had been experienced at Lough Owel – *see page 19* – with the works sinking into the lake. The new extension was inspected in September by the Earl of Lucan when it was announced that a flag station would be provided at the Islandeady road crossing, although it was to be almost 50 years before a station was opened here in May 1914. A

further inspection was carried out by the directors early in January 1865, but the severe winter, which had led to a cessation of work prevented an inspection by Captain Rich until 28th January, with the line being opened on Monday 29th January.

Two sections of line now remained unopened, that from Westport town to the Quay and from Manulla to Ballina. It was necessary to go back to Parliament in 1866 for an extension of time. The Act laid down that the Quay line should be opened for traffic before any portion of the line between Foxford and Ballina. Work had already begun between Manulla and Foxford, and by the time the Act was passed, it was ready for the laying of permanent way as far as Ballyvary. Despite the requirement in the Act, which was favoured by the directors, Lucan decided that the Ballina line should be pushed forward. Due to difficulties with the Moy River bridge and also the poor state of the money markets, work slowed up and it was 1st May 1868 before the line opened to Foxford.

Despite the opening of the line, some matters remained outstanding. In particular, at Manulla Junction, the signal cabin and waiting room were in an unfinished state as was the goods store at Foxford. These were only completed after the MGW threatened to write to the BoT. In the interim, at the shareholders' meeting in August 1867, Lord Lucan stated that the directors were recommending that no further works be constructed owing to the inability to raise further capital. It was no surprise therefore, when an application was made for an abandonment order for the line beyond Foxford and also for the Westport Quay line. The matter was referred to the BoT who gave their approval for the abandonment of the Ballina extension but not for Westport Quay. The warrant was duly issued on 24th September 1869.

It was to be another five years before the Quay line opened for traffic, and in the intervening period work had recommenced on the Ballina line, which was opened in May 1873. This latter work resulted from a new agreement between the two companies. The original agreement dating from 1859 had been for ten years and by 1867, the Midland board was reviewing the situation and giving consideration to whether its representatives should remain on the GN&W board. This matter came to a head in July 1869 when the GN&W was informed that as no notice of any of that company's meetings had been received for some years, the three Midland directors were resigning their positions.

In the previous February, Messrs. Cusack and Waldron had met the GN&W directors in London and put forward proposals for a renewal of the 1859 agreement. The MGW was to have the entire working of the line, with a minimum payment of 45% of gross receipts. Additionally, certain works were to be carried out within a year at the expense of the GN&W. No agreement was reached, the principal sticking point being the percentage payable. The GN&W offered 40% up to £40,000, 38% on the next £5,000 and 37% thereafter. The matter was postponed until February 1870, when the GN&W formally requested a renewal for ten years, the MGW again proposing changes which were totally unacceptable. Obviously in an endeavour to pressurise the Midland board, Lucan reverted to his old tactics by publishing a notice of application to obtain running powers over both the MGW and GS&W between Athlone and Dublin. At no stage did anybody enquire as to where he was going to obtain the rolling stock.

A lease is offered.

In March, Benjamin Room, the GN&W Secretary, wrote suggesting three alternatives: a renewal of the 1859 agreement, a 999 year lease on terms to be settled by arbitration or an amalgamation of the two companies. It was agreed that the line should be leased, the Act giving effect to this receiving Royal Assent on 4th July 1870, the arrangement to be effective from 1st November of that year. The entire concern, including the Westport Quay line when completed, was taken care of in the Act, but it specifically excluded the Foxford to Ballina line, which of course had so recently been the subject of an Abandonment Order.

During the course of the discussions, an attempt had been made to include this section of line. The MGW board opposed this but stated that it was prepared to enter into a separate agreement to work it for three years, after which it would lease it. The leasing Act required the MGW to maintain the railway in good and efficient repair and working order. The annual rent was to increase from £28,500 to £33,500 by 1885, sufficient to allow the GN&W to pay a dividend of from 4.5 to 5.5%. A second Act of 1870 extended the time for completion of the Westport Quay line, it being finally opened for traffic on 1st October 1874. It had been inspected by the BoT in November 1873 and again in June 1874, but the MGW refused to take it over due to 'some of the works being most defective'. In January 1876, the Harbour Commissioners requested the running of passenger trains over the Quay line, a request which was refused. It was renewed in June 1880 when they asked that two trains should be extended to the Quay during the bathing season. This time the MGW agreed.

As regards the Ballina extension, the works were in a forward state by March 1872 with prospects of an opening by the Autumn. It was however 19th May 1873 before the line was opened due to various unfinished works. Relations appear to have improved between the two companies about this time. In November 1876, plans were approved for the doubling of the Athlone to Castlerea section, Price being ordered to obtain the necessary tenders. These were submitted in February 1877 for

Athlone to Roscommon, the contract going to J J Bagnell, but progress was slow and the second line was not brought into use until August 1879, at which time Kiltoom was opened as a blockpost.

June 1885 saw talks taking place on a possible amalgamation of the two companies. Nothing came of these talks, but four years later more serious negotiations took place. By November 1889, it had been agreed that a Bill would be promoted for the purchase of the GN&W, the latter's shareholders to be made secure as regards dividends. To accomplish this, it was intended to issue 4.25% Midland stock amounting to £276,339 for a similar amount of GN&W stock. The Act giving effect to the purchase received Royal Assent on 4th August 1890, and thus came to a close the independent existence of Lord Lucan's line. Lucan himself had died two years earlier in 1888. He will always be remembered for his martial misadventures; his contribution to the extension of the railway system in the west of Ireland has largely been forgotten.

Roscommon on a Fair day with a large number of cattle wagons evident. This was a major railhead for livestock traffic and was one of the most important stations on the Mayo line with extensive siding accommodation. Courtesy John Kennedy.

Chapter Ten

CONNECTIONS AT ATHENRY

LONG before any construction had begun, Martin Blake, MP for Galway, called on the board on 18th October 1845 in relation to railway accommodation for north Galway and Mayo. Failure to put forward plans for such accommodation would meet with the strongest opposition and he urged on the company the necessity to have preliminary surveys carried out between Athenry and Tuam as a lead-up to a line ultimately running to Castlebar and Westport. Nothing further happened at this time and it was to be almost eight years before the *Warden of Galway* reported that the Midland intended to construct a single line between Athenry and Tuam. Furthermore, if the line were built to Tuam it was expected that the Mayo people would soon give a guarantee for securing the interest on the loan similar to the Galway loan. A public meeting was convened on 27th September 1853 in Galway to further the project, the chair being taken by the Reverend Peter Daly. He explained that the meeting was called to induce the Midland to alter its plans for a line from Athlone to Mayo which would take away all the traffic of counties Roscommon, Sligo and Mayo.

In July 1854, a deputation from the Midland met the Galway Grand Jury and stated that the company was anxious to have 'a great and stupendous line of railway through the west of Ireland' and proposed taking a line from Athenry to Tuam at its own expense. It only wanted the good will of the country. Notice of application for the relevant Bill was published in January 1855, but by the following September doubts were being cast on the advisability of proceeding. A month later, there was a *Railway Times* report that the 'gentlemen of Mayo had come to the conclusion that it was unfair to expect either the MGW or the GS&W to construct such a line'. Accordingly, they had determined to perform a portion of the work themselves.

The Midland directors, mindful of agitation, called a meeting of shareholders in January 1856 to gather their sentiments regarding extensions generally. For his part, the Chairman declared himself as opposed to extensions as ever he was, and the shareholders concurred with him. At a shareholders' meeting on 9th October called to consider the Sligo extension, Denis Kirwan made a long and impassioned speech in which he called on the company to take steps to progress a Tuam line. Only a month later, a meeting was held in Castlebar comprising members of the provisional committee and supporters of the Athenry & Tuam Railway. In due course, the Midland agreed to subscribe one-third of the required capital provided the remainder had already been subscribed.

The Bill for the new line was lodged in January 1858 and in due course received Royal Assent despite strenuous opposition from the Great Northern & Western. The latter had written to the Midland board in February 1858 asking what course it intended to take in relation to the Bill. When the MGW directors declared their true intentions, the GN&W expressed much surprise as the Bill was so obviously adverse to their interests. It would have expected the Midland to be its most determined opponent and considered it was placing itself in a position altogether inconsistent with the amicable relations to be expected between the two boards. In due course the MGW undertook to give a guarantee so as to render it impossible that there would be within the first ten years any extension of the line beyond Tuam. In default, the MGW would forfeit all rights in the GN&W.

The proposed line was 15 miles 3 furlongs and 5 chains in length, commencing by a junction with the Midland main line just east of Athenry station. It was reported that there were no particular engineering difficulties and the estimated cost of construction was £90,000. The fledgling company advertised for a Secretary in August 1858, offering a salary of £200 per annum and by October it was announced that John Fowler Nicoll had been duly appointed. At the half-yearly meeting in October a lease for ten years to the Midland was approved at an annual rent of £4,000.

The works were let to William Dargan in November and he promised to have the line open by 1st January 1860. Work was quickly commenced and Dargan soon had a workforce of 750 employed at good wages. Whilst good progress was reported by August 1859 it seemed unlikely that the line would be ready in four months. The ground was rapidly approaching the position when rails and sleepers could be laid. The station buildings and platforms at Tuam, which had been let to a local contractor, Andrew Egan, were also advancing rapidly. Some cargoes of sleepers had arrived in Galway and rails were soon expected. Also in August, Ennis stated that the line would be a valuable feeder to the Midland. In due course the line was completed and inspected on 21st September 1860 by Captain Ross for the BoT, accompanied by Hemans and Forbes. The works were found to be satisfactory and the line was opened for traffic on Thursday 27th September, being worked by the Midland.

In February 1861, an approach was made to the Midland board to see if it would be interested in purchasing the line. Whilst it expressed some interest it was quite unprepared to pay the asking price of £80,000. The official reply from the Broadstone was that its idea of the line's value differed so widely from that of the A&T that it thought it better to decline making any proposal. This was perhaps just as well for the first year's figures were disappointing as they continued to be for the remainder of the lease. This was in part blamed on the opening of the GN&W as far as Claremorris. Looking ahead to 1868 and with a line from Athenry south to Ennis now in course of construction, a special shareholders' meeting was held in Dublin in May to consider a Bill which would enable the Athenry & Ennis to lease the Tuam line after the expiry of the latter's lease to the Midland.

The Midland board again gave consideration to the line's purchase in July 1869, an offer of 20,000 Midland shares being made as well as an undertaking to clear the Government debt of £30,000. An amendment was moved that the time was not right to burden the shareholders with the purchase of a line which was sustaining an annual loss of £1,200; the amendment was in due course adopted.

At the half-yearly meeting in March 1870 Cusack, commenting on the approaching expiry of the lease, said this was a line that should belong to the Midland and he would therefore be most happy to enter negotiations with that company's representatives. The Secretary was instructed to write to the effect that because of the Government debt on the line, the Midland directors could not see their way to purchase it but would be prepared to recommend a lease on terms to be agreed. In due course, the A&T offered a lease of the line for 999 years at £1,250 per annum, a figure equating to less than 2% of the capital; the MGW was to agree to be responsible for the repayment of the Government loan. The latter declined to agree to the proposed terms and expressed surprise that this offer was to be regarded as final as it had hoped the matter might be referred to arbitration. The Tuam directors obviously reconsidered their position as Denis Kirwan wrote in October offering a lease in perpetuity for £2,450 or for ten years at £2,200 per annum. None of these proposals were acceptable. This resulted in an advertisement in the local press to the effect that the Midland would cease to work the line after 27th October.

The A&T's situation was now desperate and Kirwan was sent to the Broadstone to negotiate the hire of rolling stock – he came away with one engine and a carriage and an agreement on through goods and cattle rates. Also about this time, the A&T was requested to name a rent for Athenry station – it suggested £125 which was unacceptable, the Midland in turn saying it would accept £200 to avoid arbitration, provided an arrangement was made with Mr Irwin for the supply of water to the A&T at £5 per annum. Kirwan again contacted the Broadstone in May 1871 offering to lease the line for any period which might be mutually agreed at 46% of gross receipts, the Midland to be responsible for working expenses and maintenance. A counter-offer was made to lease the line for 99 years at £2,000 per annum which in turn was not accepted. The final offer from the MGW came in January 1872 but by now overtures had been made to the Waterford & Limerick and by October it was announced that a working agreement had been arranged with both the Tuam and Ennis companies. The arrangement came into force as from 1st November and heralded the introduction of through trains between Waterford and Tuam.

As early as December 1868, plans were afoot for an extension northwards to Claremorris, it being proposed to give the Midland powers to subscribe. No more was heard of the project until May 1871. An Act was obtained in 1872 although nothing was done towards construction and the powers lapsed, to be revived in 1890. Neither the W&L nor its backer, the Great Western (of England) would offer financial support in 1872, hence its abandonment. In the interim, an opposing scheme was proposed

to the Midland, namely for a line from Tuam to Ballyhaunis. At one point in July 1890, the MGW agreed to lease the line, if built, for 50 years for 55% of gross receipts. By now, the Tuam company's Claremorris extension was set to become a reality.

The W&L had been approached in April 1885 and had agreed to work the extension if a minimum of £8 per mile per week could be guaranteed. The agreement was also dependant on the MGW sanctioning a separate goods and passenger station at Claremorris. When O'Connor & Dudley, solicitors, wrote in February 1892 assuming that the Midland would have no objection to the proposed junction at Claremorris, they assumed incorrectly. The latter was referred to the BoT to be arbitrated upon, Sir Douglas Galton carrying out an inspection in June. The Athenry & Tuam Extension to Claremorris Light Railway, a cumbersome title for a 17 mile long railway, was opened for traffic on 30th April 1894 to a temporary station some ¼ mile south of the Midland station.

Major General Hutchinson had to arbitrate on the plans for alterations and additions to the station accommodation at Claremorris, not only in respect of the traffic to and from Tuam but also in respect of a further extension in course of completion from Claremorris to a junction with the Midland at Collooney from whence running powers would be availed of into Sligo. This latter extension, constructed with the aid of a Government grant of £146,000 provided under the Balfour Act, was also worked by the W&L and opened for traffic on 1st October 1895. It now gave the W&L through running from Waterford to Sligo via Limerick and Athenry and to better reflect the line's extended status, its title was changed to the Waterford, Limerick & Western. So much for activities north of Athenry; we must now take a look at connections to the south.

Towards Athenry.

The line between Limerick and Ennis was opened in stages between January and July 1859 by the independent Limerick & Ennis Railway. Further north, the Galway & Ennis Junction had been promoted during the railway mania of 1845 but had been stillborn. The Athenry & Ennis Junction was proposed in 1859 to connect the two points named in its title, along with a possible branch from Craughwell to Loughrea. A large meeting of A&EJ promoters was held in Gort in September 1859, a sum of £13,000 being subscribed for within half an hour. The meeting was attended by Nicoll, secretary to the A&T, and Hemans as consulting engineer to the new company. Hemans reported on the very easy nature of the proposed works which he estimated would not cost

more than £6,000 per mile for the 35 mile line.

A junction with the Midland was proposed at Athenry, but the latter preferred either Attymon or Woodlawn. The Act incorporating the A&EJ received the Royal Assent on 20th August 1860 and included among the promoters were the Honourable George Gough and Denis Kirwan. The capital was to be £200,000, of which the Midland was empowered to subscribe £100,000 and the A&T £10,000. At the first meeting on 19th September, Nicoll was appointed secretary at a salary of £100, although it is clear from correspondence that he had already been acting in this capacity. The contract for the construction of the line was awarded to William Monroe at a figure of £250,000, only £20,000 of which would be payable in cash, the balance in shares, debentures and Lloyds bonds. The contract was in fact divided in two: Ennis to Gort, to be completed by 1st October 1864 and the balance a year later. At a board meeting on 18th February 1863, Messrs Malcolmson and Stephens, directors of the W&L attended in connection with a proposed working agreement, agreeing to a subscription of £6,000, in return for which two of the A&EJ directors would stand down to allow the W&L representation on the board.

Later in the year, the *Railway Times* reported that Monroe had secured lands and set men to work on the first section. By the following July, Hemans said that about five-sixths of the earthworks were complete with three miles of permanent way laid. Plans were approved for stations at Crusheen, Tubber and Gort. Work stopped however on 6th October 1864 as the contractor had not been paid monies due to him. Work was resumed in the following March but was to be shortlived as five months later, Monroe was declared bankrupt.

Matters now dragged on but some hope came for the ailing company in August 1866 with the news that a loan of £59,000 was forthcoming from the Public Works Loan Commissioners. An approach was made to the Midland in November seeking pecuniary assistance in return for a working agreement but it seemed reluctant to become involved. Construction eventually got under way again in 1867 under a new contracting firm, Messrs Edgeworth & Stanford. Colonel Rich made the first of what were to be five inspections of the new line early in March 1869 and he found little that was good to report upon. Finally, at the end of August 1869, approval was given for the opening.

Not having finalised its agreement with the W&L, the A&EJ announced its intention of operating its own line as from 15th September, an engine and two ballast wagons being obtained from the contractors on one weeks notice. The Midland also agreed to loan three carriages and a van for 14 days, later supplemented by a wagon and locomotive No.8. Some of the latter rolling stock was recalled at short notice in December 1870, despite protests from Nicoll. There is more to this apparently unfriendly gesture than meets the eye. In mid-November, the Sheriff of Clare had seized the company's rolling stock for non-payment of debts. Four days later, the Galway Sheriff did the same, only this time the train was not allowed to proceed. In December, two locomotives were offered for sale, being the only tangible assets of the company. These were in fact bought by the A&T and sold back to the Ennis company.

It was obvious that this state of affairs could not continue and in August 1871 the first of many overtures was made to the Midland suggesting that it should take over the working and maintenance of the line. Offers and counter-offers were made, negotiations were then opened with the W&L which agreed to work the line initially for a ten year period on the back of guarantees from the GWR to underwrite any operating losses. The working agreement, signed in January 1872 gave the A&EJ £5,200 per annum plus 50% of receipts in excess of £11,000; this lease dated from 1st November 1872, coinciding with that of the A&T. One might have thought this was the end of the matter as far as the Midland was concerned but this turned out not to be the case.

It was again approached in 1878 regarding a possible purchase, an offer of £145,000 being made in October which was deemed to be totally inadequate. Nevertheless, a Bill was promoted but was defeated in the House of Lords, mainly due to strong W&L opposition. Over the next few years, both the Midland and the Waterford companies were approached and by 1886 the former had increased its offer to £170,000, increased again in 1889 to £175,000. By this time, the acquisition of the line had almost become a personal affair between Cusack and his opposite number on the W&L, Sir James Speight. At the Midland's half-yearly meeting in February 1890, Cusack said 'if we can help it we shall certainly not let Sir James Speight purchase the A&EJ . . . it is neither for the interest of the A&E or the district through which it passes'. But to the W&L it was sold, the announcement being made in June 1892, the price agreed being £180,000.

As the W&L extended northwards, difficulties ensued in relation to the use of Claremorris station. An agreement between the two companies in April 1893 sought to resolve the matter as regards facilities there and running powers between the two junctions. It also prevented the W&L from carrying local traffic between Ballysodare and Sligo. As has been mentioned else-where, the WL&W merged with the GS&W after a bitter struggle for its possession, the result as far as the Midland was concerned being the obtaining of running powers to Limerick. These powers were exercised for some years from 1901 onwards.

ATHENRY & ENNIS JUNCTION RAILWAY COMPANY.

TIME TABLE
of the ORDINARY and SPECIAL TRAINS for the
BALLINASLOE FAIR WEEK,
Commencing on MONDAY, the 4th OCTOBER, and ending on SATURDAY, the 9th OCTOBER, 1869.

FOR THE USE OF THE COMPANY'S OFFICERS & SERVANTS ONLY.

For ATHENRY, BALLINASLOE, & DUBLIN.—Up Trains.

Distance	STATIONS		Special 1, 2, 3	Ordinary 1, 2, 3	Special 1, 2, 3	Ordinary 1, 2, 3
			A.M.	A.M. TICKET	P.M. TICKET	P.M.
—	Ennis,	Leave	—	10 0	2 0	4 30
8	Crusheen	"	—	10 26	2 26	4 56
			STAFF	STAFF	STAFF	STAFF
18	Gort,	"	5 0	11 0	3 0	5 30
25	Ardrahan	"	5 20	11 23	3 23	6 0
31	Craughwell	"	5 40	11 43	3 43	6 15
36	Athenry,	Arrive	6 15	12 0	4 0	6 30
	Athenry, M.G.W , Lve.		6 30	12 20	4 36	6 43
	Galway,	Arrive	—	1 55	—	7 22
	Ballinasloe,	"	7 40	5 15	5 31	—
	Dublin,	"	—	5 15	10 0	—

From DUBLIN, BALLINASLOE, & ATHENRY.—Down Trains.

Distance	STATIONS		1, 2, 3	1, 2, 3	1, 2, 3	1, 2, 3
			A.M.	A.M.	P.M.	
	Dublin,	Leave	—	8 30	1 0	—
	Ballinasloe,	"	—	12 26	5 40	8 20
	Galway,	"	5 20	11 45	4 0	—
	Athenry,	Arrive	5 50	1 17	6 38	—
			Special to Gort and O-dorny through	Ordinary P.M.	Ordinary to Gort and Special thence P.M.	Special to Gort P.M.
			STAFF	STAFF	TICKET	STAFF
5	Athenry,	Leave	7 0	1 30	7 0	9 0
11	Craughwell	"	7 15	1 46	7 15	9 15
	Ardrahan	"	7 30	2 6	7 30	9 30
			STAFF	STAFF	TICKET	
18	Gort,	"	8 0	3 0	8 0	10 0
28	Crusheen	"	8 35	3 35	8 35	
36	Ennis,	Arrive	9 0	4 0	9 0	

During the week, the 1·30 p.m. Train from Athenry to Ennis will not leave Gort until 3 p.m., in order to permit the 2 p.m. Special from Ennis to pass here.
The 5 a.m. from Gort to Athenry and the 7 a.m. Athenry to Gort will not run on Monday the 4th October.
The 9 p.m. Special Train from Athenry to Gort awaits the arrival of the 8·20 Special from Ballinasloe.
DUBLIN OFFICE, 27th Sept., 1869.

Class 'A' 4-4-0 No.129 *Celtic* at the head of a cattle train at Athenry.
Courtesy John Kennedy.

Chapter Eleven

THE TWENTIETH CENTURY

As we have seen, the railway had reached its maximum extent by the time of Cusack's departure. Further schemes for extension were proposed during the early years of the century, notably two involving the Achill branch. One of these began in 1901 as a suggestion from Messrs J Smith & Son of Birmingham for a jetty at and a rail link to Inishlyre Roads. The Congested Districts Board and the Agriculture Department were prepared jointly to put up £5,000 and enquired if the company would be prepared to construct such a line. Initial reaction was only to work the line although subsequently it agreed to contribute one third of the cost. Correspondence passed back and forth until 1904.

An earlier scheme, for a line to Gubbardletter was mentioned in a previous chapter, as were schemes involving Belmullet which was at one stage envisaged as a deep water port for the Canadian mails. The Congested Districts Board in fact ran a steamer service from Westport and unsuccessfully sought a subsidy from the Midland towards its operation.

One of the rather more far fetched schemes involving Belmullet was the Collooney, Ballina & Belmullet Railways & Pier Company which proposed a 4ft 8½in gauge line and would have provided a third rail over the SL&NC and GN systems to Belfast; a cross-channel tunnel would have connected up with the British rail system, an alternative being a train ferry from Larne to Stranraer.

Three other lines, promoted independently, would have made connection with the MGW. The Mullingar, Kells & Drogheda Railway was first proposed in November 1902 and revived periodically right up to 1914. It was strongly opposed by the Midland as it would have diverted traffic to Drogheda. The Sligo & Arigna Railway was to commence by a junction with the Cavan & Leitrim at Arigna and run thence to Sligo with a terminus at the Ballast Quay. Basically of 3ft gauge, it would have had mixed gauge track where it met the Midland. Initially opposed by the MGW it later received its support and a working agreement was entered into with arrangements made for Nugent and Colonel Cusack to become permanent directors. The Act received Royal

Assent in August 1908 but it proceeded no further. The third line was also centred on Sligo. The Sligo & Bundoran proposed a junction with the MGW at Rathedmond and with the GNR at Bundoran. It was opposed by both companies and was withdrawn in October 1909.

Little happened on the Midland itself in the early years of the twentieth century. New stations were opened at Ashtown and Newbrook (1902), both for race traffic only; Thomastown (1909), Island Road (1909) and Islandeady (1914). The Chairman, Richard Nugent died on 19th January 1912 whilst on a short holiday at Mallaranny Hotel; he had been a board member for twenty-five years and Chairman for eight of these. His replacement was the Deputy Chairman, Colonel Henry Cusack.

The outbreak of the world war in 1914 had little immediate impact on the Midland, although later on the works at the Broadstone were to turn out high explosive shells. Likewise, the Easter Rising of 1916 caused minimal disruption, apart from a brief occupation of Broadstone station and the blowing up of a bridge at Blanchardstown where a cattle train was derailed. In December 1916, it was announced that all the Irish railways would be placed under Government control under the Regulation of Forces Act of 1871. It was agreed that compensation would in due course be paid on the basis of net receipts for the year 1913. This situation lasted until 15th August 1921.

Anti-British feeling ran high after the 1916 Rising, the upshot of which was the employment of the Black and Tans, a volunteer force recruited to quell unrest.

Arising from this, a group of L&NW employees at the North Wall refused in May 1920 to unload a shipment of munitions and were duly suspended. Their action was widely supported by railway men who refused to work trains carrying British forces or munitions, leading to further suspensions and the withdrawal of many services. By November, services on the Midland had been reduced to two trains from Broadstone serving Galway and Sligo plus one each to Cavan and Kingscourt. At the end of December, the railwaymen met and reluctantly lifted their ban.

Civil War.
The leaders of the 1916 Rebellion had been duly courtmartialled and sentenced to death. One of their number however, Eamon De Valera, escaped the firing squad because of his American connections. In December 1918, elections were held, with the Sinn Fein party capturing 73 of the 105 Irish constituencies. They refused to take their seats in the Westminster Parliament and set up their own Parliament in Dublin, with De Valera as Taoiseach or Prime Minister. He was in due course arrested and held in Lincoln Jail from which he escaped to the USA, where he set about raising funds to further the Irish struggle. The period from 1919 onwards was one of much civil strife in Ireland. De Valera returned to Ireland in 1921 and in December a Peace Treaty was signed, whereby Ireland was to have its own Parliament although remaining in the Commonwealth; the six north-eastern counties were to remain part of the United Kingdom. Despite apparent independence, there were dissenting voices with almost half the members of the Irish Parliament voting against the Treaty, causing a split which was to lead to the outbreak of civil war in May 1922.

The first indications of interference with the railway occurred at the end of April 1922 when a travelling clerk was held up by armed men at Leixlip station and £800 taken from him. This money was intended to pay Station-masters' wages between Broadstone and Cavan. By July, services all over the country had been disrupted by the tearing up of rails and the blowing up of bridges. These proved little more than minor irritants and services were quickly restored. As far as the Midland was concerned, passenger trains were running as normal on the mainline between Dublin and Ballinasloe and to Roscommon and Dromod on the Mayo and Sligo lines, the Cavan and Meath branches remaining unaffected. Towards the end of August more serious efforts were made to disrupt services.

On the night of 29th August, apart from the burning down of the signal cabin at Knockcroghery, an attempt was made to derail the down Sligo train between Kilfree Junction and Ballymote. The train was stopped by armed men, the passengers ordered out and some of them searched. The driver was then ordered to send the train forward, but he set the regulator so that it stopped after 50 yards. He was again ordered, at gunpoint, to do the job properly and when it disappeared from view everybody was allowed to go. Once again, the train had stopped further down the line and the journey to Sligo was resumed.

This was to be the first of a number of armed hold-ups, some involving goods trains. These disruptions led to a revised timetable being introduced in October 1922, generally with the intention of running services in daylight as far as possible. The night mails were withdrawn as were all services on the Clifden and Achill branches. The blowing up of the Shannon bridge at Drumsna on the morning of 4th October threatened to seriously disrupt the Sligo line, but it was in fact speedily repaired. The hotel at Recess was burned to the ground four days later after the staff and guests were given half an hour to leave. Its burning was believed to have followed the occupation of Oughterard by Government forces to prevent the Irregulars, as those who took up

arms against the treaty were known, from taking it as a barracks. A limited passenger service was resumed from 17th October between Galway and Maam Cross after a three months closure, the Achill branch remaining closed at this time.

On the evening of 7th November, a party of armed men arrived at Liffey Junction with the intention of setting fire to the station. The arrival of a cattle train caused a change of plan and the train was sent off down the North Wall branch to end up crashing into wagons at the L&NW station, the engine concerned being one of the Avonsides. This was one of a number of incidents involving Liffey Junction, where the signal cabin had already been burnt down. Early in November, the parish priest of Achill urged the necessity of re-opening the branch to prevent severe deprivation during the winter months, but the company declined to assist. Attention was turned to the Meath branch about this time, where virtually every cabin between Clonsilla and Kilmessan had been destroyed in a concerted campaign of arson and robbery.

The new year saw an escalation of the attacks as far as the Midland was concerned. In the early hours of 10th January, the station building at Sligo was destroyed by fire and explosives. Two passenger trains in the station were totally destroyed. Some of the raiders went to the engine shed, where they coupled up six locomotives to a seventh which was in steam, and sent this cavalcade down the Quay branch. They broke through the sea wall, one ending up in the sea and a

second suspended over the wall; five of these engines belonged to the MGW, the remaining two to the SL&NC. Eighteen items of rolling stock belonging to the MGW were totally destroyed. Mid-January saw the first of two wreckings at Streamstown Junction. A down goods train consisting of two locomotives and twenty-five wagons was stopped by armed men at the junction, the crew removed and the train sent off at full speed to a break in the rails where the engines were derailed and the wagons piled up on top.

During the clearing up operations, the permanent way gang were told not to be too particular as the road would soon be broken again. In fact within a few days the engine of the Clara branch train was derailed at the same spot. The second of the Streamstown wreckings occurred on 17th February and was graphically described in the *Midland Reporter* and the *Westmeath Nationalist*. A party of armed men arrived shortly after daylight and blew up the temporary bridge to the west of the station. The first train to arrive was the down limited mail and was sent to its destruction, the engine, 4-4-0 No. 124 being very severely damaged as was much of the coaching stock. A following goods train was then run into the wreckage. The engine of an up Ballina goods was uncoupled and finally run to its destruction.

A breakdown gang from Athlone had a new bridge in place by 14.30 that day, at which time the passengers from the two trains were able to resume their journeys. This proved to be the last of the serious inci-

Two of the locomotives damaged in the malicious derailment at Streamstown on 13th January 1923 were No.52 *Regent* and No.135 *Arran Isles* (in the foreground). In all, six locomotives were damaged or destroyed in three separate incidents at Streamstown between 13th January and 17th February 1923. L Daly collection.

dents involving the Midland. Subsequent to this, military guards were provided at a number of locations which helped to reduce the number and ferocity of the attacks. Additionally, a Railway Defence and Maintenance Corps was set up and a number of armoured trains were fitted out, the Midland providing vehicles for one of these trains. The civil war was now in its final months as in April moves were made towards making peace with the Free State authorities.

Amalgamation.
At the half yearly meeting at the end of February 1923, the chairman referred to the year just closed as being one of most exceptional difficulties, with almost daily interference with and destruction of railway property which had been the cause of very great inconvenience and loss. He went on to speak of the extreme loyalty of the railway staffs who had cheerfully faced hardships and danger in the discharge of their duties. At the end of his speech, he referred to another matter which was causing concern; early in 1922, the newly formed Provisional Government had set up a railway commission to review the Irish railways. Whilst agreed that the railways had generally been well managed, the war years had taken their toll and it concluded that the railways should be nationalised, although a dissenting minority suggested unification.

There were forty-five separate railway companies and it was felt that the only way these could be efficiently run was by putting them all under one management. There was certainly no hope of nationalisation as the new Government did not have the financial resources. The larger companies now suggested a grouping and the Government agreed to give them time to consider the matter. As far back as 1903, there had been

rumours of a possible purchase of the MGW by the L&NW, rumours strongly denied on both sides. It would appear however, that approaches had been made by the Midland board to the Lancashire & Yorkshire enquiring if they might be interested in such a purchase.

The *Irish Independent* for 16th February 1923 carried details of another rumour that merger talks had taken place between the Midland and the Great Northern, once again denied. The chief stumbling block to the merger turned out to be the D&SE who favoured going it alone, despite the fact that they were more in need of assistance than any of the bigger companies as regards rolling stock and motive power. The reason for their reluctance goes back to 1902, when the L&NW subscribed a loan of £100,000 towards the New Ross and Waterford extension, also purchasing guaranteed stock.

One of the provisions of the loan was that the L&NW should have a seat on the D&SE board. The LMS, as successors to the L&NW sought to have a seat on the board of the new amalgamated company or else they would seek repayment of the loan. The GS&W, MGW and the Cork, Bandon & South Coast Railway would not agree to such representation. As from 12th November 1924, these three companies amalgamated to form the Great Southern Railway with the Great Southern Railways (plural) coming in to operation on the following 1st January. Thus came to an end the independent existence of the Midland Great Western Railway.

Under the GSR and CIE.
The headquarters of the new Great Southern Railways undertaking was at Kingsbridge, the Dublin terminus of the GS&W line. At the same time it was decided

This was the first of the new 'Woolwich' class, assembled from kits of parts purchased from Woolwich Arsenal. Completed in April 1925, she was quickly painted in full MGW gloss black livery as No.49. Not even steamed, she was taken back into shops, repainted in light grey and fitted with her GSR numberplate – 410 – for photographic purposes. Immediately afterwards, she was repainted in standard GSR dark grey and renumbered 372. She thus had the distinction of having three liveries and three different numbers in less than a fortnight. It had been intended to number the original twelve 410 to 421 between the last of the '400' class and the commencement of the D&SER engines at 422, but acquisition of six additional Moguls with 6ft driving wheels caused a change of plan. Green Studios collection.

to concentrate locomotive and rolling stock manufacture at Inchicore, although the first batch of 'Woolwich' 2-6-0s were constructed at the Broadstone; No.383 being the last to be turned out in 1927. The Midland had decided to single some sections of line, including Dunboyne to Drumree in 1918 and Inny Junction to Longford in 1924. Under the Great Southern, the decision was taken to single the entire Midland network with the exception of the first seven miles out to Clonsilla and the North Wall branch. So, in 1926, the Clonsilla to Dunboyne and Galway to Oranmore sections were so treated.

As part of the rationalisation, Athlone (Southern) and Clara (Midland) stations were closed in March 1925. At the latter the station and Streamstown Junction, cabins were closed and a new cabin brought into use. At Clonsilla, access to the Meath line was effected by a new set of facing points off the down main line immediately to the west of the passenger platform. The old up line on the branch was slewed into the down line east of the canal bridge. The next section of track to be singled was that between Athenry and Attymon Junction, completed on 15th March 1927. As the Oranmore to Athenry and Attymon to Ballinasloe sections were already single, this meant that the mainline was now single west of the latter point. On the Meath branch, two alterations were made during 1927. One was the introduction from 1st August of regular passenger services to the station at Fairyhouse Bridge, previously only used on race days, the other was the opening from 1st December of Castletown Halt, between Nobber and Wilkinstown.

In September 1928, the GSR announced its intention of singling further sections of the Midland, an announcement greeted with much public opposition on the basis that the alterations would lead to delays. As we now know, with the limited level of services provided on the Midland section, it has never proved a problem. Between September 1928 and March 1931 the remainder of the mainline from Ballinasloe to Clonsilla was singled as well as the remaining sections of the Sligo road and Athlone to Roscommon. The last section to be completed was that from Knockcroghery to Roscommon. Additionally, the short stretch between Amiens Street and Newcomen Bridge Junction was also singled.

Between Clonsilla and Ballinasloe there were seventeen single line sections, with three between Athlone and Roscommon and two between Mullingar and Multyfarnham. The mainline could be reduced to four sections worked by the cabins at Clonsilla, Enfield, Mullingar, Athlone and Ballinasloe. The longest possible section was Athlone East Junction to Mullingar West, a distance of 27 miles 3 chains. Webb & Thompson ETS instruments were provided by the Railway Signal Company with uni-directional staffs. At practically all crossing stations, the layouts allowed non-stop trains to have a straight road, while Whittaker's staff exchanging apparatus enabled trains to run through without reducing speed. In general, the staff exchangers worked well, although problems occasionally arose when the apparatus failed to make a clean pick-up, when it was necessary to resort to pilot working. A further alteration from normal was the facility for permissive working whereby a second goods train could follow a previous one into a section after a fifteen minute interval.

Cabins at Newbrook racecourse platform and at Mullingar crossing were dispensed with. Likewise at Nesbitt Junction, where the Edenderry branch joined the mainline, the cabin and junction were removed and the branch diverted to run on the old down line into Enfield station.

Other plans centred around Broadstone. As we have already seen, all the locomotive and rolling stock work was transferred to Inchicore and so the works at the Broadstone were turned into a maintenance centre for the road fleet. As a station it always suffered from being so far from the city centre with no connecting tramway. Plans were therefore drawn up to run the Midland passenger services to Amiens Street. To begin with, the Meath and Cavan branch services commenced to run to and from Amiens Street in 1929. Before the mainline services were transferred, it would be necessary to provide a suitable connection. It will be recalled that Glasnevin Junction had been removed in Midland days and the only access was via the inconvenient Newcomen Junction and the loop line. It was to be another six years before a new junction was laid down at Glasnevin. Meanwhile, the arrival platform at Broadstone was taken out of use on 18th August 1929.

On the Sligo line, Carrignagat Junction was dispensed with as from 7th September 1930, all up and down traffic between Collooney Junction and Ballysodare and between Collooney (SL&NC) and Ballysodare being worked on two separate single lines. The Midland cabin at Collooney station was closed, the section becoming from the junction to Ballymote; the Collooney Junction cabin was closed in February 1931, the junction points being power operated

from Ballysodare. Similarly at Inny Junction, the points were power operated from Multyfarnham. The down Sligo and Cavan branch platforms were taken out of use, the only platform remaining in use therefore being the up Sligo. As a consequence, passengers from the Cavan branch to stations west of the junction now travelled to Multyfarnham where they made the connection. The cabin at Inny Junction was taken out of use on 27th September 1931.

The weekly circular for 3rd October 1931 announced the closure to all traffic as from Thursday, 1st October of the Ballina to Killala line, a substitute road service being provided. Only a week later, it was announced that it had been decided to run one goods train each way daily from Ballina at 13.45 with a return working at 15.15. The line was in fact closed finally as from 1st July 1934, the first of the Midland branches to be cut off completely. The Edenderry branch was closed to passenger traffic in 1931, remaining open for goods and livestock. As from 1st January 1935 goods services were also discontinued but the line remained open for livestock traffic until final closure in February 1963. Next to go was the Clifden branch on 27th April 1935. Of all the western branches this was the most short sighted closure for it ran through some of the best scenery in Connaught. Whilst these closures were being effected, a large number of stations were reduced to the status of halts, while Blanchardstown was closed as from 1st January 1934. Mount Temple Siding, situated close to milepost 73 was re-opened and traffic worked to and from it by one goods train each way as required. Towards the end of 1935, work commenced on the reinstatement of the junction at Glasnevin,

A typical Midland train near Maynooth, in the early CIE years, photographed in 1946. Note the Bredin coach, third from the engine. John Kennedy.

A 'Woolwich' Mogul, fitted for oil burning as denoted by the large white circle on the tender, passing 73 Mile Box, in the early CIE period. John Kennedy.

which had been closed in December 1906, to allow easier access to Amiens Street. Single line working was instituted between Liffey Junction and the Drumcondra Mills Siding in February 1936 over the down line, remaining thus until 28th April. The cabin at Newcomen Bridge Junction was closed as from 30th August 1936, all points and signals being worked from the new cabin at West Road. The new double line junction at Glasnevin was finally brought into use on Sunday, 22nd November 1936 with the points being operated from West Road, the lines being track-circuited throughout with full colour light signalling.

The opening of the junction left the way clear for the closure of Broadstone station, notices to this effect being posted in the press at the end of December. Opposition to the closure was voiced by traders in the locality. The *Irish Press* for 9th January 1937 announced the transfer of services to Westland Row as from Monday 18th January. The last down train to leave Broadstone was the 19.10 on the Saturday evening with 142 passengers, the last scheduled arrival being the up night mail which was greeted by a large crowd. The last departure of all was a special carrying buyers to Athlone and Edgeworthstown fairs which departed at 15.00hrs on the Sunday. So came to an end a 90 year old tradition. In December 1934, the company had announced the withdrawal of passenger services on the third of the western branches, that from Westport to Achill. This brought a storm of protest resulting in a resumption of services, the weekly circular for 25th April 1935 showing one mixed and one passenger train each way daily. Despite continued and increasing protests, the company was determined to proceed with the withdrawal of services. In November 1936, Mayo County Council threw its weight behind the protesters on the grounds that the roads were totally inadequate to cope with the anticipated increase in traffic. The protests were in vain and it was proposed to provide substitute road services as from 1st

October 1937. It has already been mentioned in a previous chapter how a special funeral train was run to return victims of the Scottish fire to Achill. Resulting in part from this closure, all trains arriving and departing Westport in future used the up platform.

The Second World War led to a severe reduction in services as the result of the cutting off of coal supplies. Few alterations to the system were carried out during the war years, the two principal ones being at Claremorris and in and around the Broadstone. The village of Knock in County Mayo, some seven miles from Claremorris, had briefly hit the headlines in 1879 with claims of supernatural spiritual appearances, but it was not until August 1929 that the idea of organised pilgrimages to the Shrine was put forward. In the early 1930s, special trains were run to Ballyhaunis, later to Claremorris. In time, these specials were to run from the four corners of Ireland, putting a severe strain on resources and facilities at Claremorris.

Plans were therefore drawn up for alterations which were not finally completed until the early 1950s. In May 1941, a new central signal cabin with sixty-six levers was brought into use, allowing the closure of the three existing cabins – North and South Junctions and the Southern Yard, plus two Ground frames. In January 1942, a 55ft turntable replaced the 45ft one, enabling 'Woolwich' locomotives to be turned there. Later on, the Ballinrobe branch engine shed was demolished and the shed road extended to join the line coming in from the Southern (WL&W) yard; the branch platform was separated from the former down platform which thus became an island. In July 1944, the cabin at Broadstone was taken out of use, though it was not finally closed

until April 1947. During 1943, it had been announced by the Government that the entire transport system in the Irish Free State was to be reconstructed, a tribunal being set up to report. The Transport Bill giving effect to its proposals failed its second reading in the Dail, resulting in the resignation of De Valera and the calling of a general election. The Fianna Fail party was returned to power and the Bill in due course became law in November 1944. Effectively, a new company came into being on 1st January 1945, Coras Iompair Eireann was an amalgamation of the GSR and the Dublin United Transport Company and had a capital of £13.5 million.

Whilst services improved in 1946, this was shortlived as the winter of 1946-7 was the worst for many years. This resulted in severe coal shortages and by the beginning of February 1947 the only passenger train on the Midland was the night mail which ran only as far as Athlone. Goods trains ran on three days a week. Services slowly recovered with the importation of coal from the United States. Another problem causing severe difficulties was the seriously run-down state of both locomotive and rolling stock.

In July 1948, the Minister for Industry and Commerce commissioned a report on transport in Ireland. Headed by Sir James Milne, last general manager of the Great Western Railway, the report suggested that CIE and the Grand Canal should be amalgamated and brought under public ownership. The Bill passed through the Dail in 1949, the new nationalised CIE coming into being as from 1st June 1950 with the board being appointed by the Government. During 1950, the works at Broadstone resumed wagon building, one-hundred cattle wagons being turned out during the year. Also in that year, an additional passenger train to Galway was provided during the currency of the Summer timetable. This train was interesting in that it was provided by extending the 09.35 Kingsbridge to Portarlington on to Galway. It was to be the first use of the ex-GS&W Portarlington to Athlone route for a scheduled Galway train.

Also about this time, some difficulties were being encountered with the Whittaker staff exchanging apparatus, as a result of which these were replaced with Manson snatchers. The 1950s saw the beginning of the major dieselisation programme on CIE. Early 1953 saw the transfer of a number of diesel railcar sets on to the Midland for driver training. Some workings were taken over in the Summer 1953 timetable allowing savings in journey times of between twelve and twenty-one minutes. The first of the 'A' class diesel-electric locomotives arrived three years later, allowing substantial improvements: a 22% reduction in times to Westport and 18% to Galway. Shortly afterwards the new smaller 'C' class diesels were sent to the Ballina branch. During the Summer of 1954, the Grand Canal Street running shed was altered to service only diesel locomotives, all steam being transferred to Broadstone, a situation which lasted until 8th April 1961 when Broadstone shed was closed.

The Cavan branch closed on 1st January 1960, coincidental with the closure of the line from Cavan northwards to Monaghan; the Killeshandra branch had effectively been closed in 1944 but remained in situ until lifted in 1957. February 1963 witnessed the closure of the Ballaghadereen branch, Kilfree thus ceasing to be a junction and its cabin closed. Two months later, the Edenderry and Navan branches had their services terminated while in June a large number of stations and blockposts were closed. Athlone East cabin was closed in December and the junction points electrically operated from the West cabin; these points were recovered from Inny Junction. During November and December 1967, the Streamstown to Clara branch was lifted, there having been no regular service since 1947. Finally, the Loughrea branch closed in October 1975, the last of the truly rural branch lines to survive.

The year 1973 saw the transfer of the Galway and Westport trains to Heuston (Kingsbridge) and the Sligo trains to Connolly (Amiens Street), the latter trains continuing to use the Midland line from Glasnevin. In November 1981, a commuter service was instituted between Connolly and Maynooth, where a new cabin was opened. Additionally, the Sligo trains now stopped in Maynooth. It is heartening to note that a number of new suburban stations were opened in 1990. During recent years improvements have been made to many of the remaining stations on the Midland. The North Wall depot was converted as a container depot, a similar facility being provided at Ballinasloe. Athlone (Midland) was closed in 1985 and a new station opened on the site of the Southern yard utilising part of the old GS&W station. In connection with the introduction of CTC, Ballinasloe and Moate were made fringe boxes. The Mullingar to Athlone section is, at the time of writing, now mothballed although the track remains in place as an alternative route.

'D5' (ex 'A') class 4-4-0 No.548 at Amiens Street en route back to Broadstone shed in 1949. Originally built as No.126 *Atlantic* in April 1904 at Broadstone, she was rebuilt in 1925 with an 18 element superheater, piston valves, new frames raised above the driving wheels and Morton style cab. No.548 was withdrawn in June 1955. John Kennedy.

Chapter Twelve

SERVICES

FOR THE opening of the line to Enfield on Monday 28th June 1847, the company provided a service of four trains each way, leaving Broadstone at 06.00, 07.00, 12.00 and 17.00hrs. Departures from Enfield were at 08.30, 10.00, 15.00 and 17.00hrs. These trains operated on seven days per week with the exception of the first train in each direction which did not run on Sundays. Return tickets were to be available on Sundays. Details were also given of the passage boat arrangements on the Royal Canal in connection with the trains. Coaches and other conveyances also provided connections from such places as Athlone, Galway, Sligo, Edenderry, Trim, Athboy and Kells.

The line was extended to Kinnegad and Ballivor on 6th December 1847 which necessitated a slight recasting of the timetable. The 06.30 down now only went as far as Enfield with other down trains at 07.00, 11.00, 16.30 and 20.15, the latter being the mail train, carrying on to the new tempory terminus. The corresponding up mail left Kinnegad at 03.15. *Walsh's Guide* for June 1848 adds a few details. The 06.00 down (all three classes) stopped at Clonsilla (06.19), Maynooth (06.40), Kilcock (06.51), Enfield (07.10) and Kinnegad (07.30). The 08.15 (1st and 2nd class only) additionally stopped at Lucan, Louisa Bridge & Leixlip and Moyvalley. The 11.00 stopped at all stations thus serving additionally Blanchardstown and Ferns Lock, the journey taking two hours. Special cattle trains would be dispatched from Kinnegad on Wednesdays at 08.30 and 16.10, calling at Enfield, Kilcock and Maynooth. Cattle for these trains were to be at the stations one hour before departure and any cattle brought up by rail and remaining unsold could be sent back at half rates within 48 hours. Children unable to walk travelled free and those under the age of twelve were charged half fare.

October 1848 saw the line extended to Mullingar with four trains being provided on weekdays and three on Sundays. Within a month, it was announced in the *Westmeath Guardian* that an additional weekday train was being provided. At the same time, the passage boats on the Royal Canal were discontinued. Arrangements had been completed for the conveyance of light goods and cattle on the 15.00 down and 10.00 up trains with an extra cattle train leaving Mullingar on Wednesdays at 12.00. A board minute of 18th October 1850 ordered that fourth class carriages were in future to be attached to the mail trains, the fare to Mullingar to be 5s 0d.

Opening of the mainline throughout to Galway in August 1851 saw four trains each way, with additional short workings. Journey times varied from five and a quarter to five and three-quarter hours. There was also a goods train in each direction which carried fourth class passengers and required eight and a half hours. Correspondence appeared in *Saunders Newsletter* towards the end of 1851 regarding the unpunctuality of trains. One correspondent reported having joined a late train from Galway at Athlone, at which point it was already thirty minutes behind schedule. A further ten minutes was lost in the section to Moate and the journey came to a full stop at Enfield. After some delay, the passengers were informed that the engine, *Jupiter,* had sprung a leak, but a relief engine was being sent from Dublin. Before assistance came from this direction however, the up mail came on the scene at 04.20, the passengers eventually reaching Dublin at 06.15, more than ten hours late. In December, the down mail arrived twelve hours late due to the failure of the engine and also of the engine of a goods train sent to relieve it. This was of course during the period when the line was being operated under a haulage contract.

In January 1854, the down night goods leaving Broadstone at 22.00 took second and third class passengers onwards from Athlone, while in the up direction the goods left Galway at mid-day taking second, third and fourth class passengers. Opening of the branch to Longford on 8th November 1855 was for passenger traffic only and initially two trains were provided in each direction, a service which was to lead to complaints that the company would 'only condescend to favour the public with two trains, and they choose to start them during the cold wintry season in the dark of night'. Goods traffic commenced in December with an additional passenger train being provided from 1st January 1856, running in daylight hours.

The Cavan branch was opened on Tuesday, 8th July 1856 and once again there were two trains each way. In addition, a well-appointed four-horse coach was advertised to run daily from Cavan to Enniskillen. Various minor alterations were made in the service on the mainline in the years 1856 and 1857, with some reductions being made in May 1858. Short workings took place to Maynooth or Enfield from Dublin to allow the longer distance trains to run non-stop. For example, in August 1858 it was announced that the 10.30 to Galway would no longer call at stations from Blanchardstown to Ferns Lock. To serve these stations, an extra train would leave Broadstone at 09.45 stopping at all stations to Enfield, and returning from there at 11.15. *Wyer's Timetable* for July 1862 indicated down trains at 07.30 (to Enfield), 08.30 to Galway (arrival 13.30), 11.30, 14.45 (to Maynooth), 16.00, 17.00 (to Enfield) and the night mail at 19.30. There were two Sunday trains, at 09.00 and 19.30.

Following the opening of the line to Sligo, two trains were initially provided each way, from Dublin at 08.30 and 16.00, and at 06.45 and 15.45 from Sligo. Alterations to this service were made in February 1863, the afternoon departure from Sligo being substituted by a 12.00 to Dublin with a train at 16.30 running only as far as Longford, balanced by an 07.45 from Longford to Sligo. We have already seen in chapter four how difficulties arose over the Athlone to Galway extension in 1863, difficulties which led to a severe curtailment of services to and from Galway towards the end of the year. The board referred to the curtailment as an economic measure to reduce the loss-making situation, but one cannot escape the conclusion that the whole exercise was designed to teach a lesson to those west of the Shannon.

An advertisement appeared in the *Galway Vindicator* for 31st October 1863 advising that as from the following Monday, the 2nd November, both the 11.30 and 16.00 from Dublin would run only as far as Athlone. Passengers for Galway would in future be accommodated on a goods train leaving Athlone on the arrival of the 16.00 from Dublin. Similarly, the 07.00 and 16.00 up trains were discontinued as between Galway and Athlone, passengers being conveyed by the 05.30 up goods. The advertisement went further by stating that the company would not guarantee the arrival of and would not be responsible for delays to these goods trains. Predictably, the *Vindicator* had an editorial to the effect that the changes would not be accepted by the people of Galway. The board of directors, having guaranteed to them that any deficiency in the receipts of the line would be made up by baronial guarantee, had never attempted to manage that portion of the railway in a way to give public satisfaction. Furthermore, the proposed changes represented the worst they had ever made, these trains being the ones by which the greatest numbers travelled.

At the board meeting on 3rd December 1863, a complaint regarding the Galway service from the Galway Town Commissioners was read and discussed. In reply, they were advised that the reductions were made to reduce claims against the baronies and the board did not feel justified in altering the revised arrangements without the prior approval of the other baronies. The situation as far as Galway was concerned was that they were served by the 08.30 and 19.30 down and the 12.30 and 24.00 up plus a 10.40 Galway to Athenry only and the two Dublin to Athlone trains. Some improvements had been made by 1867 with a third train in each direction, 13.00 up and 11.45 down. In February 1874, the situation was reversed with the 13.00 now running only as

GSR No.544, the former MGWR No.11 *Erin go Bragh* 'C' class 4-4-0, reversing her train out of the arrivals platform at Broadstone in the early 1930s. No.11 was built in May 1915, rebuilt with larger boiler, superheater and piston valves in May 1926 and withdrawn from service in December 1935. Cattle wagons and vans make up the tail of the train. The late J Coughlan.

far as Athlone and the 16.00 running through to Galway.

In March 1878, a new service was advertised from Broadstone to North Wall in connection with the express boats to and from Holyhead. A train left Broadstone at 07.55 in connection with the 09.30 sailing with a similar connection into the evening sailing. In June 1885, alterations were proposed in services which would bring about a reduction in train mileage of 50,000 miles per annum. The plan was approved and was to lead to complaints from various quarters, including the Mullingar Town Commissioners who pointed out that Mullingar had no train between the 09.30 and 15.30 services. The directors agreed to put on an 08.00 up which would return about 14.00, but if this experiment proved unremunerative, it would be discontinued. Complaints also came from Boyle, Sligo, Castlebar and Westport, without success.

Following on a new agreement with the postal authorities for the faster conveyance of mails, a new limited mail service was introduced. In 1889, the limited mail left Broadstone at 07.40 with arrival in Galway at 11.30 and Sligo at 11.40. This represented a good improvement and was to remain unaltered until the advent of the new trains in 1902.

The Mayo Lines.
The Mayo lines encompass what was the GN&W radiating north-westwards from Athlone. The first section, which opened from Athlone to Roscommon on 13th February 1860, had three down and two up trains on weekdays and two each way on Sundays. Castlerea was reached on 15th November 1860 with three trains each way. This was the level of service which was to be provided as each subsequent section was opened with the exception of Westport which initially had only one train each way. A passenger service operated from Westport

to Westport Quay until 1st November 1889 with a summer only service for some years later.

As early as February 1863, complaints were being voiced in the *Mayo Constitution* regarding the irregularity of the trains. In February of the following year references were made to the Midland's resort to diverting the legitimate traffic of the GN&W. The fault did not lie with the able traffic manager, Mr Forbes, 'who is always anxious to develop traffic on the line, but is clearly traceable to the cramped, narrow-minded, yet arrogant mismanagement of the directory'. A traveller from Dublin to Castlebar in April 1869 mentioned a thirty-five minute wait at Athlone, where there was no first or second class waiting room. Arriving at Castlerea at about 21.00, he was told he would have to wait until 01.00 in a waiting room which 'had a miserable apology for a fire'. The journey onwards from there took four hours, and the correspondent commented that because it was basically a goods train, the passengers were treated 'with the same disregard as the cattle and horses in the wagons'.

The Meath Lines.
The Dublin and Meath Railway was opened for public traffic on 29th August 1862 with four trains each way between Dublin and Navan on weekdays and two on Sundays. On weekdays, trains left the Broadstone at 07.50, 10.50, 16.50 and 18.40 and Navan at 08.40, 11.40, 15.00 and 19.25. It will be recalled that the two companies entered a ten year agreement from 3rd April 1861 whereby the Midland was bound to provide a connection with the main line trains.

It was announced on 20th November 1862 in *Saunders Newsletter* that as from 1st December the company's trains would run daily to Kells, times and further particulars to be provided in future announcements. This came on 29th November, and was to

the effect that owing to the non-completion by the D&D of proper signals at Navan Junction, the trains advertised to be run to Kells were unavoidably postponed until further notice. Despite the clause in the D&D's original Act requiring it to concede running powers, it was obviously not happy on this score and was determined to be as obstructive as possible. The delay was short-lived but the D&D soon advertised 'quick, special trains' to Kells at reduced fares. The Midland in due course reduced its fares to a ridiculously low rate, which was fine for the travelling public but hardly conducive to profit making.

With the opening of the Athboy branch on 26th February 1863, two trains each way were provided, connecting with the Dublin trains. The Meath line working was taken over by the Midland in an agreement dated 10th February 1869, whereby the working company was required to run not less than two passenger trains each way on weekdays and one on Sundays. The Dublin & Meath line was subsequently leased to the Midland in 1875 and from that time onwards, complaints were continually made that the traffic was not being properly worked. The matter was referred to the railway commissioners in November 1879. As far as services were concerned the commissioners decided that a third train should be run each way, and so in the timetable for August 1880 we find down trains at 09.00, 13.15 and 17.15, with corresponding up workings.

The Midland was far from happy with the interference from the railway commissioners and did all in its powers to be relieved of operating the additional service, so much so that in June 1882 it served notice of an application to have the earlier order rescinded or else force the Meath company to pay the full

cost of the third train. The commissioners in fact refused to rescind the order so the third train remained until yet a further application was made in 1886 at which time the Midland was relieved of its obligation to run it.

Tuam and the smaller branches.

The A&T was worked by the Midland for a period of ten years from its opening on 27th September 1860. Two trains were provided in each direction on weekdays, leaving Tuam at 06.15 and 15.00, returning from Athenry at 12.15 and 20.35; journey time varied from 35 to 45 minutes. The service remained unaltered until 1st February 1866 when the evening working was discontinued. Up until this time, a Sunday service had been provided, but it was also discontinued at the end of the month. At the end of the ten year period the Midland handed the line back to the owning company which worked it itself for a further two years after which an alliance was forged with the W&L.

Services varied on the minor branches. For example, while there was an agreement to operate a minimum of two trains each way on weekdays on the Loughrea and Ballinrobe branches, the former had four each way at the opening, increased to five in 1895, while the latter had two each way increased in 1897 to four. The Ballaghaderreen and Killeshandra lines each had three trains each way.

The 1897 working timetable.

A copy of the working timetable on and from 1st May 1897 is still extant. This is a good point to review the company's services as the system had reached its greatest extent some two years earlier with the opening of the western branches.

Class 'J18' 0-6-0 No.588 is seen leaving Kilfree Junction. No.558 was built in 1895 by Sharp Stewart as MGW No.134 *Vulcan* of class 'Lm'. She received a GSR boiler in June 1927 and an X superheated boiler during 1940. The engine was withdrawn from service in November 1962. The original cost of No.134 was £2,630.00. The Lm class differed from the earlier L 0-6-0s in having steel frames and boilers as well as cast steel wheels. They also incorporated a new design of tender. The Atock designed locomotive is seen on a mixed freight on the Clifden branch in the early GSR period. Author's collection.

On the main line, the first departure was the limited mail at 07.00, timed to arrive in Galway at 10.51 with stops at Enfield, Mullingar, Athlone and all stations thence to Galway. It was followed by an 08.40, stopping at all stations to Enfield with the exception of Ferns Lock. This train stopped at Maynooth for eighty-eight minutes to allow two following trains to pass, so it must have taken few if any through passengers. The 09.15, with a connection from North Wall, made all stops to Galway, arriving at 14.04 with a through connection to Clifden (arriving 16.25). Next were two short workings, 11.50 to Mullingar and 15.20 to Athlone. Two further trains served Galway, the 16.30 and the 20.20 night mail which arrived at 01 15. The latter also operated on Sundays when it was the only train to Galway. The only other Sunday main line train was the 10.00 to Mullingar with a corresponding 19.00 up service. There were two goods trains in each direction on weekdays only, at midnight and 18.00 down and at 03.00 and 19.10 up, the 00.00 and 19.10 providing through Clifden connections.

There were corresponding up workings, the up night mail leaving Galway at midnight, arriving at Broadstone at 05.00 and North Wall at 05.30.

On the Sligo line, the connection out of the limited mail left Mullingar six minutes after the 08.23 arrival from Dublin and arrived in Sligo at 11.03. Three other down trains left Broadstone at 09.15, 16.30 and 20.20 with an additional short working from Longford at 07.00. These services operated only from Monday to Saturday with the exception of the night mail. The Sligo goods left North Wall at 22.30 and Sligo at 19.30. As regards the Mayo line, there were three trains each way daily as well as some short workings to and from Castlerea. On the remaining branches, a service of either three or four trains was provided, in connection with the mainline services.

As the result of the absorption of the WL&W into the GS&W system, the Midland was granted running powers between Athenry and Limerick. MGWR trains could also pick up passengers at intermediate stations. Some difficulties were encountered in this regard, although goods and livestock services began operating as from 9th January 1901 with one train in each direction at 03.30 from Athenry and 20.00 from Limerick. In April 1902, the Midland advised the GS&W of its intention to commence passenger services as from 1st June. This was shortlived, ceasing in 1906, but the goods service continued until January 1910 and occasional cattle trains ran until 1st December 1911.

With the introduction of new rolling stock and the larger 'A' class 4-4-0 locomotives, services on the mainline were accelerated. In the Summer of 1902, sixteen minutes were cut from the timing of the limited mail, with ten minutes also taken from the Sligo and Ballina connections. Breakfast cars were introduced for the first time on the down train and a luncheon and dining car on the corresponding 15.40 up from Galway. Then in 1903, a new tourist express was put on, leaving Dublin at 12.00 and arriving Galway at 15.10, Clifden at 17.00 and Achill at 17.30. The train was advertised in connection with the company's two hotels, at Recess and Mallaranny. A special platform was erected at the former hotel to provide easier interchange.

The new Broadstone built diner, No.3 was used on this train in the years 1904-6, the latter being the last year in which this service ran. As explained in the chapter on rolling stock, the three dining cars had only first and second class accommodation and prior to 1913, when third class corridor coaches first appeared, third class passengers could not avail of this facility with one exception. This was that on Monday mornings only, holders of third class commercial travellers' tickets

could avail of the second class diner between Dublin and Mullingar without extra charge. Even with the introduction of the third class corridor vehicles, they were not made welcome. The instruction was that they were to be admitted to the second class diner only when their meals were ready, when they were to be conducted to their seats. When they had completed their meals, they were at once to return to their carriage. Due to wartime shortages, it was found necessary in 1918 to withdraw the dining cars. A minimum service was however provided by putting van No.4 into the limited mail trains, and it was possible to obtain a breakfast as well as teas and light refreshments. The full service was reinstated in April 1919.

Early in 1903, a letter was received from the BoT enclosing copies of correspondence from a Mr Newlyn of Blanchardstown complaining about 'the general unpunctuality of the service and citing one particular case'. This was in fact the second such complaint as the matter had been raised in the House of Commons in May 1896. On both occasions, the company vigorously denied the charges levied against them. Two suggestions came from the traffic manager in 1904, one that the number of vehicles on the limited mails should be reduced. The second recommended that goods trains should be made up to sixty wagons with two brake vans when the new engines became available. This would enable a reduction in overall train mileage as it would dispense with one goods from Athlone and one from Mullingar to Dublin. This was readily agreed to, subject to the speed of these trains not exceeding 20 mph. The basic service as indicated in the 1897 timetable, with the accelerated timings introduced in 1902-3, was to remain in operation for the remaining life of the Midland, with some minor alterations.

Following on the conversion of two vehicles into slip carriages, we find two such operations in the summer 1911 timetable, from the 09.45 and 16.50 down Galway trains, both at Enfield in connection with the Edenderry branch. For the winter of 1911, only the evening train slipped and it was to remain at one per day thereafter right up to the GSR summer 1926 timetable, although the actual train varied – by 1920 it was the 12.00 down Sligo. One further slip working operated, it would appear only for the summer 1918 timetable, off the down Sligo at Inny Junction for the Cavan branch. It is difficult to understand the economics of such a slip as the timetable indicates that a light engine was sent from Mullingar to Inny Junction in advance of the passenger train.

A petrol railcar was introduced to the Westport to Achill service in November 1911. In the winter 1913 timetable, this railcar left Westport at 05.35, arriving in Achill at

07.25, with a return working at 18.20; additional stops were made in both directions at Carrowsallagh Bridge, Rossturk Crossing and at Tonragee 'for mail-bags only'. By 1916, the car had been withdrawn from this service as a directive of January 1916 states that it was in future to be used by the engineer for inspection purposes. The war years brought disruption of services as the result of coal shortages, control of all the Irish railways being taken over by the Government in December 1916. Some disruption resulted from the rising in Easter Week of 1916, the railway being put at the disposal of the military authorities. In April 1918, the Government called for an immediate reduction of 20% in coal consumption, thus bringing about a drastic reduction in services.

A much more serious disruption to train services resulted from the munitions strike of May 1920. By November 1920, there was only one passenger train on weekdays to Galway and Sligo, plus one to Kingscourt and one to Mullingar, the latter with a Cavan connection; Mayo was by now cut off from railway communication. Hardly had services been resumed than they were further disrupted by events of 1922 and 1923, described elsewhere. Achill was without a passenger train for a period of nine months until 16th April 1923, services returning to normal only after the cessation of hostilities in May of that year. By now there was barely eighteen months to go before the new Great Southern Railways came into being.

Excursion traffic.
Excursion traffic formed an important element in the Midland's revenue. Within days of the opening to Enfield, an advertisement appeared in *Saunders Newsletter* announcing that four special trains would run on Sunday 4th July to accommodate persons going to Mullingar fair on the following day. Even Ballinasloe, with its famous fair early in October, was catered for with four-horse coaches running from Enfield. By July 1853, excursions were being operated to Galway at a fare of 6s.0d for third class and 10s.0d for second class. The train left Broadstone at 08.00 on the Monday morning, returning at 18.00 on the next day; tickets were available for return only on this special train.

During the period when the Grand Canal dispute was at its height, excursions were made into GS&W territory as for example the operation of a steamer service from Athlone to Banagher in September 1854 in connection with the fair at the latter place. It was announced that wagons and horse-boxes would be available at Moate for those wishing to transport their purchases. Extremely low fares were advertised to Limerick via Athlone. In August 1857 an excursion train from Galway arrived in Dublin with 1,500 passengers in 50 carriages. Again, in

July 1859 a train of 25 carriages left Galway with 900 passengers, additional carriages being added at Mullingar from the Longford and Cavan branches, swelling the train to forty-four vehicles. Fares appeared to vary a great deal - on the latter excursion, the third class fare from Galway was 7s.6d but in June 1861 a similar trip cost 12s.6d. As a result only forty-nine people travelled from Galway with sixty-two on a similar train in July. In the opposite direction, an excursion from Dublin took almost 1,000 people to Galway. On arrival they were taken on a cruise on Lough Corrib on the steamer *Lioness* to Maam. This steamer operated a regular service on three days a week with car connections to Leenane and Letterfrack.

In October 1865, the *Loughrea Journal* praised the newly appointed traffic manager, Skipworth, 'who has done much to render himself popular as well as to increase revenue for the company'. The paper suggested however that he might go further by introducing cheaper fares as a means of inducing a large proportion of the population to enjoy the experience of a railway trip. It suggested running excursion trains for the Great Exhibition in Dublin at a fare of 5s.0d third class. Whether or not it was due to the newspaper's suggestion is unknown, but within a week cheap fares were being offered and close on 2,000 people travelled to Dublin.

An unusual special train was run on Tuesday, 27th April 1869 in connection with Mr Allan Pollock's Great Auction at Creggs near Donamon station. By 1877, circular excursions were being operated in conjunction with the GS&W. It was possible to travel from Kingsbridge via Limerick to either Foynes or Ennis and return via Galway and Broadstone; fares were 47s.6d and 37s.6d for first and second classes. In August 1880, the *Irish Banker* referred to a recent Sunday excursion from Cavan to Dublin, the first such in five years. It was particularly welcome as the Cavan people were disadvantaged in having no regular Sunday service. It was hoped therefore that the experiment might encourage the company to grant further concessions in this direction. At the half-yearly shareholders' meeting in the following month, a shareholder, Mr Hayes, protested against the running of Sunday excursions. The chairman in reply said he was sure that the majority of shareholders would be willing to leave the matter to the discretion of the directors who were always consulted by the manager.

Livestock specials.

It was inevitable with the line running through rich cattle rearing and fattening country that there would be an extensive traffic in this commodity. During the course of a House of Commons Select Committee on railway servants' working hours in 1892, Tatlow gave evidence to the effect that out of a total of 5,580 goods trains operated in the previous year, 1,723 were cattle specials, involving 835,018 head of livestock from 1,150 fairs. Largest of these by a considerable margin was the week long fair held at Ballinasloe at the beginning of October. The general arrangement was that empty wagon specials were worked from Dublin, Mullingar or Athlone on the day prior to the fair. Return trains would leave as soon as they were loaded, this generally being between 07.00 and 16.00, the earlier departures being worked by those drivers and guards who had the longest rest periods.

As already mentioned, Ballinasloe was the largest of these fairs. Its origins are lost in antiquity, long predating the coming of the railway or even the Grand Canal. The *Dublin University Magazine* of November 1853 stated that proceedings had been 'conducted for the last half-century with the utmost decorum and regularity'. It was the practice for many Dublin tradesmen to attend, dealing in jewellry, perfumery, haberdashery and even books. At the time of writing the article, it had been regrettably noted that the fair was being regularly attended by gamblers and pickpockets, marking the sign of the times. Persons attended not only from the whole of Connaught but also from the adjoining counties of Leinster and Munster. The first day was given over to a sheep show, held in the grounds of Garbally, liberally thrown open by the Earl of Clancarty. The second,

An 'A' class 4-4-0 with the down day mail at Athlone in the early years of the twentieth century. Both the locomotive and the TPO are in the then recently introduced blue livery. Athlone Public Library.

third and fourth days were respectively for sales of sheep, horses and horned cattle, while the last day was described as the 'poor man's fair', when all manner of ordinary country stock was brought to a common market. *Saunders Newsletter* in October 1861 quoted some figures in respect of Ballinasloe – 70,386 sheep in 1800, 94,764 in 1815, and 81,861 in 1860, while cattle in the same years totalled 7,749, 8,149 and 17,474 respectively.

Tatlow, in his autobiography, referred to Ballinasloe as being probably the largest assembly of cattle and sheep in the U.K. Within two months of opening to Galway, additional trains were run for passengers from Dublin and Galway, with two livestock trains laid on. In 1858, both the GS&W and the Midland advertised livestock trains, the former running via Parsonstown (Birr) with a special rate of 20s.0d per wagon. Six months earlier, the Midland had been charging a reduced rate of 35s.0d to Dublin. It was the practice during Cusack's chairmanship for himself and two or three other directors plus the Traffic Manager and Locomotive Superintendent to spend the week at Ballinasloe, so as to be able to entertain friends and customers. Guests were welcomed not only to dinner, but also to breakfast, lunch and light refreshments during the day. As Tatlow stated, 'it was not without advantage to the company . . . a good dinner solves many a difficulty, whilst the post-prandial cigar and a glass of grog, like faith, removes mountains'. By 1906, however the directors decided that the fair was so reduced in size and arrangements so satisfactory, that their attendance was no longer necessary. In October 1881, twelve specials were dispatched with a total of 446 wagons.

In connection with the Galway fair in June 1881, eight empty trains were run from Broadstone or Athlone, the Broad-stone trains stabling overnight at Athenry for disinfecting. This had become necessary as the result of a Government directive to try and reduce the incidence of foot and mouth disease. Nine specials were worked out of Galway between 06.50 and 15.15, eight to Dublin and one to Athlone. Loughrea fair in February 1881 produced four specials in each direction.

Mail services.

Hardly had the line been opened to Enfield when a letter was received from the Superintendent of mails enquiring into the carrying of the overnight mails to the west. The Secretary was instructed to check with the L&NW regarding charges made by them. Agreement on charges was not reached until the matter was referred to arbitration, the award being made in February 1849. In July 1860, Forbes was requested to report on

machinery for the catching of mailbags; why this was considered at this time is unknown as the first separate post office vans were not introduced on the Midland until 1873. and they were certainly not equipped with exchange apparatus, although it would appear small vans so fitted appeared on the GS&W in 1855.

As each new section of line was opened, the mail service was extended. In April 1884, the inspector of mails wrote to the company about a possible improvement in the mail service. He was informed that the company would be prepared to run trains from Dublin at 08.00 to Galway and Sligo running at a speed of 40mph, with return workings arriving in Dublin at 18.00 at a charge of 3s.0d per train per mile. This offer was declined but enquiry was made as to how much earlier the company would dispatch and accelerate the 09.00 departure. The company declined to alter this train, which was found most suitable for the general public; any earlier time would break the connection with the cross-channel steamers at North Wall.

The unsatisfactory nature of the west of Ireland mail service led to questions being raised in the House of Commons, it being suggested that the Post Master General arrange for a train leaving Dublin at 08.00 and reaching Galway in three and a half hours. Agreement was finally reached and incorporated in an indenture dated 29th February 1888. Payment was to be £29,030. 12s.6d per annum, in return for which the company was obliged to provide services as listed in the schedule to the indenture. Amongst other provisions was a requirement, if so requested by the postal authorities, for the company to provide at its own expense, separate post office vans. The down Galway mail now left at 07.40, arriving in Galway at 11.30. It was stipulated that if the English mails were late, the train could be delayed until 08.00 and should they reach Broadstone by that time, it could be further delayed while they were transferred.

In June 1894, the question of the west of Ireland mails came to the attention of the House of Lords in connection with the new loop line in Dublin. Up until then, the Kingstown mails were transferred across Dublin by road. This matter dragged on until April 1899 when agreement was finally reached with the DW&W enabling the running of through carriages. In January 1907, the company agreed to a request from the post office that the signalman at Kilcock should take charge of mailbags from the up night mail from 22.00 to 04.15, it being clearly understood that the company would in no way be responsible for their safety. The signalman was paid the large sum of 1s.0d per week for the additional trouble and responsibility.

Road services.

From its earliest years, the company was involved in subsidies for road car services. For example, in July 1847 it was agreed to allow a Mr Darling a sum of 3d per double mile for running a passenger car from Athboy via Trim and Summerhill to Kilcock. Also in July, a Mr Brogan was asked for proposals for a Castlepollard to Enfield service. In September, Darling advised that he was discontinuing his car service between Trim and Ferns Lock, this latter presumably replacing Kilcock. The service must have resumed later under another proprietor as an advertisement in *Saunders Newsletter* on 14th August 1850 refers to a coach leaving Athboy at 05.50 daily except Sunday to meet the 07.30 up and down trains, and returning on arrival of the 17.00 from Dublin. In March 1849, arrangements were made with Bianconi for a car service between Mullingar and Cavan via Granard with a fare of 3s.6d per passenger. With the opening of the Cavan branch in July 1856, a well-appointed car ran daily from Cavan to Enniskillen, thus bringing Londonderry within a day's journey from Dublin. Bianconi later operated a coach between Westport and Castlerea in connection with trains to and from Dublin, and in 1865 began running to Clifden. About this time a new service started between Clifden and Westport, a service subsidised for many years by the company – a subsidy of £20 was given to a Mr O'Brien on condition that the GN&W paid £10.

By 1876, O'Brien was receiving £200 for running this car during the tourist season; three years later an attempt was made to reduce this figure by 50%. O'Brien requested an additional £40 to operate a Recess to Letterfrack car in 1890 but was refused. By 1894, a Mr McKeown was running the Westport to Clifden car and this he continued to do until 1910 when the company expressed dissatisfaction. Perhaps the directors were confident of starting their own service, for they had been making enquiries into the purchase and running costs of motor cars for use at the hotels. In April 1911, Messrs Archers of Dublin agreed to supply vehicles. The three cars were registered IM179 to IM181 inclusive. They did not prove entirely successful, in part no doubt as the result of the treatment they were receiving from the Connemara roads. In January 1912, the manufacturers, the Commercial Car Company, agreed to provide larger cylinders and pistons and to uprate the engines to 25 hp. Their working life was short and references in the traffic minutes indicate that a new car was purchased from Cham-bers Motors for £380 in March 1914 while in April of the following year another car was ordered for the Recess Hotel. Only months before the demise of the company, in April 1924, it was decided to order three Karrier cars with large pneumatic tyres for the Clifden to Mallaranny service.

The company had an agreement with a Henry Hoey during 1907 and 1908 for an omnibus service from Broadstone to the city centre, while in 1911 discussions took place with the Dublin United Tramways Company for a possible tram service, although nothing came of this despite various meetings.

Fares.

The board discussed and approved a fares structure during April 1847. Shortly after the opening, it was agreed that return tickets would be made available to all three classes between any two stations at fare and a half, while in February 1849 fares for third class passengers in open carriages were fixed at ¾d per mile with no special return fares. Returns were not to be made available to third class covered passengers either. It was also agreed about this time that harvestmen would be brought from Mullingar to Dublin for 2s.0d, so long as they were in lots of twenty. In October 1849, the decision was taken to have fourth class carriages, actually wagons with seats, attached to the mail trains, fares to be 5s.0d to Mullingar with first class at 10s.0d. During the war with the GS&W, the fares to Limerick were systematically reduced to as low as 15s.0d first class and 6s.6d third class. The Limerick passenger travelled by rail to Athlone and from there by Shannon steamer. The correspond-

ing first class fare to Galway, a shorter distance, was £1 0s.0d. In an obvious attempt to attract additional passengers, advertisements stated that a stewardess attended the ladies' cabin on the steamer. Despite these low fares, the general fares structure was unlikely to attract other than the middle or upper classes. Commenting in October 1865, the *Roscommon Journal* was hopeful that with a new chairman at the helm, some serious efforts would be made to ensure that the company became of great public benefit. Everybody was agreed that fares and rates were too high and should be reduced so as to bring the railway within reach of all classes. The *Irish Times* had earlier in 1865 been trying to sell the same message to all Irish railway directors.

The Midland directors made a move in the right direction by announcing that as from 1st January 1866, third class passengers could obtain return tickets over the entire system and furthermore the time limits were extended. Drovers in charge of cattle were granted free passes and excursion tickets were to be more widely available at cheaper rates than on other lines. A new type of fare was introduced, for emigrants; through fares from Sligo, Galway, Westport and Castlebar were quoted to Liverpool, no charge being made for their luggage. It was however to be May 1872 before third class passengers were carried by all trains. The *Tuam Herald* commented that Mr Ward, the

efficient manager of the line, deserved much credit for this praiseworthy arrangement. Initially, the limited mails only carried first and second class passengers, but as from 1st June 1897 third class booked through from England were allowed to travel on the day mails.

In 1869, the company introduced a cheap system of parcels rates which proved successful. Towards the end of the 1870s, there was considerable distress in the western counties and two items of note occurred. The opening of the new cattle station at Liffey Junction was accompanied by a reduction of 15% in the rates for cattle and sheep. An even larger reduction, of 40%, was made in the rates for seed potatoes and oats from Dublin so as to alleviate distress. In January 1896, reductions were made in rates by passenger train for farm produce and fish to Dublin and the mainland, the *Railway Times* commenting favourably on the move. From 1911 onwards, consideration was given to the abolition of second class but it was not until September 1913 that it was finally agreed, the implementation date to be 4th May 1914.

The MGW bus photographed outside Broadstone in 1913, was one of three purchased for use between the two company hotels at Recess and Mallaranny. Courtesy John Kennedy.

WORKING TIMETABLES – 1ST JANUARY 1920

TABLE No. 1.

Main Line. DOWN TRAINS.

WEEK DAYS

Dist. N.C.	Stations	1 Westport Goods	2 Athlone Goods	3 RWR Goods	4 Pass. (Ex Loughrea)	5 Mullingar Goods	6 Meath Goods	7 Goods	8 Limited Mail	9 Cavan Pass.	10 Meath Pass.	11 Clara Mixed	12 Goods RWR	13 Sligo Pass.	14 Pass.	15 Meath Pass.	16 Pass.
—	KINGSTOWN PIER								6 5	6 5	6 5						
4 31	N. WALL L. & N.W.																
—	N. WALL M.G.W.	12 45	2 0								8 45			11 30	11 30		
—	Broadstone					3 30	5 0		7 25 / 7 30	9 0	9 25			1 10	1 30	1 50	3 0
1 33	Liffey Junc'n	1 0 / 1 15	2 15 / 2 30	3 15 / 3 30		3 45 / 4 0	5 15 / 6 0										
3 0	Ashtown									B	9 32 / 9 33					1 58 / 1 59	3 8 / 3 9
4 43	Blanchardstown									B	9 37 / 9 38					2 4 / 2 5	3 14 / 3 15
7 8	Clonsilla					4 25 / 4 40	6 20			B	9 44					2 12	3 22 / 3 24
8 72	Lucan									9 25 / 9 26							3 29 / 3 30
11 19	Leixlip									9 32 / 9 33							3 36 / 3 37
14 72	Maynooth		3 54 / 4 0			5 4 / 5 35				9 41 / 9 44							3 45
19 12	Kilcock					5 48 / 6 20				9 53 / 9 54							
20 75	Ferns Lock									9 59 / 10 0							
26 40	Enfield					6 42 / 7 15				10 11 / 10 14				1 55			
30 28	Moyvalley									10 21 / 10 22							
35 55	Hill of Down					7 42 / 8 30				10 32 / 10 35							
41 60	Killucan					8 48 / 9 20				10 46 / 10 50							
50 17	Mullingar	4 11 / 5 0	5 26 / 6 10	6 30 / 7 30		9 46			8 46 / 8 51	11 6		11 30		2 31	2 51 / 3 1		
58 22	Castletown		6 34 / 6 54									11 49 / 11 50			3 16 / 3 18		
61 56	Streamstown		7 5 / 7 25									11 58			3 25 / 3 27		
68 33	Moate		7 46 / 8 16						9 21 / 9 22						3 39 / 3 42		
78 5	Athlone	6 30	8 46	9 0				5 0	9 38 / 9 43				11 0		3 58 / 4 8		
85 0	Thomastown							5 45 / 6 30	10 6 / 10 8				11 45 / 12 15		4 21 / 4 22		
91 53	Ballinasloe							7 15 / 7 55	10 29 / 10 31				1 0 / 1 15		4 34 / 4 38		
101 40	Woodlawn							8 15 / 8 55	10 41 / 10 43				1 35 / 1 50		4 59 / 5 1		
107 15	Attymon Jn.				8 30			9 15 / 10 15	10 54 / 10 58				2 10 / 3 0		5 11 / 5 15		
113 36	Athenry				8 42 / 8 43			10 40 / 11 30	11 12 / 11 13				3 25 / 3 40		5 26 / 5 31		
121 26	Oranmore				8 57 / 8 59										5 45 / 5 46		
126 35	Galway				9 9			11 50	11 23				4 0		5 56		

No. 3.—RWR.—Runs when required.
No. 5.—Shunt at Hill of Down for Down Limited Mail to pass.
No. 7.—Cross 7.50 a.m. Up Passenger at Attymon Junction.
☞ ‖ Will call at Liffey Junction when required to take up Passengers ex Kingstown Pier.
B.—Stops when required to take up Passengers.

No. 12.—Cross Up Limited Mail at Athenry. RWR.—Runs when required.
S.C.—Slip Carriage for Enfield.—runs through to Edenderry and returns by 5.45 p.m. to Dublin.
Electric Train Staff Stations:—Ballinasloe, Woodlawn, Attymon Junc., Athenry (Ennis Junc.), and Oranmore.
☞ Restriction of Speed.—See page 2.
Agricultural College Siding between Athenry and Oranmore. for Working Arrangements see page 13.

WORKING TIMETABLES – 1ST JANUARY 1920

Main Line.
DOWN TRAINS.

TABLE No. 1.

Distance from Broadstone M.C.	STATIONS	17 Meath Pass.	18 Pass.	19 Clara Pass.	20 Mullingar Goods	21 Cavan-Castlerea Goods	22 Night Mail	23 Athlone and Ballina Goods	24 Galway Goods	25 Sligo Goods	26 Pass. (SUN)	27 Pass. (SUN)	28	29
	KINGSTN PIER													
	N. WALL L.&N.W.													
4 31	N. WALL M.G.W.													
	Broadstone	5 45	6 0		5 0		7 30	8 15	10 15	11 30	10 0	2 0		
1 33	Liffey Junction				5 15 / 6 15			8 30 / 8 45	10 30 / 10 45	11 45 / 12 0	10 9			
3 0	Ashtown		6 8 / 6 9								10 8			
4 43	Blanchardstown	(a)	6 14 / 6 15								10 14 / 10 15			
7 8	Clonsilla	(a)	6 22 / 6 24								10 22 / 10 24			
8 72	Lucan		6 29 / 6 30		6 40 / 6 55						10 29 / 10 30			
11 19	Leixlip		6 36 / 6 37		7 2 / 7 7						10 36 / 10 37			
14 72	Maynooth		6 46 / 6 48								10 46 / 10 48			
19 12	Kilcock		6 57 / 6 59		7 37						10 57 / 10 58			
20 75	Ferns Lock		7 4 / 7 5		8 20					1 24	11 3 / 11 4			
26 40	Enfield		7 16 / 7 21		8 45			10 9 / 10 19		1 34	11 15 / 11 18			
30 28	Moyvalley		7 30 / 7 31		9 5						11 25 / 11 26			
35 55	Hill of Down		7 42 / 7 44								11 36 / 11 39			
41 60	Killucan		7 56 / 8 1								11 49 / 11 54			
50 17	Mullingar		8 17	8 25	10 10	7 0	8 51 / 9 1	11 41 / 12 25	1 15	2 56	12 10	3 17 / 3 31		
58 22	Castletown			8 41 / 8 42		8 40	9 16 / 9 17							
61 56	Streamstown			8 49			9 24 / 9 25							
68 32	Moate						9 37 / 9 39					4 3 / 4 5		
78 5	Athlone						9 55 / 10 5	1 55	3 15 / 3 45			4 21 / 4 31		
85 0	Thomastown						10 18 / 10 19							
91 53	Ballinasloe						10 31 / 10 34					4 54 / 4 57		
101 40	Woodlawn						10 55 / 10 58					5 18 / 5 22		
107 15	Attymon Jn.						11 8 / 11 13		5 45					
113 36	Athenry						11 24 / 11 28		5 45			5 43 / 5 46		
121 26	Oranmore						11 42 / 11 46		6 5					
125 35	Galway						11 56		6 40			6 10		

WEEK DAYS (cols 17–25)   SUNDAYS (cols 26–29)

(a) Stops by signal to take up passengers.

No. 20.—Shunt at Kilcock for 7.30 p.m. Down Night Mail to pass.

No. 22.—Pass 5.45 p.m. Down Goods at Kilcock and cross 5.30 p.m. Up Goods at Ballinasloe and 9.35 p.m. Up Galway Goods at Attymon Junction.

Electric Train Staff Stations:—Ballinasloe, Woodlawn, Attymon Junc., Athenry (Ennis Junc.), and Oranmore.

☞ Restriction of Speed—See page 2.

Agricultural College Siding between Athenry and Oranmore for Working Arrangements see page 13.

WORKING TIMETABLES – 1ST JANUARY 1920

TABLE No. 14.

Sligo Branch.

DOWN TRAINS. — WEEK DAYS.

Distance from Broadstone (m.c.)	STATIONS	1 Cavan Goods ARR	DEP	2 Goods ARR	DEP	3 Goods ARR	DEP	4 Limited Mail ARR	DEP	5 Castlerea to Cavan Goods ARR	DEP	6 Cavan Pass. ARR	DEP	7 Goods R.W.R. ARR	DEP	8 Pass. ARR	DEP
	KINGSTN PIER							a.m.	6 5							a.m.	11 30
	N. Wall, L. & N. W		8 15		11 30				11 30								
	N. Wall, M.G.W.	1 27	2 0				11 30						9 0			p.m.	1 10
1 33	Broadstone	2 15							7 25								
	Liffey Junction																
60 17	Mullingar (arr)	11 41		a.m. 2 56		a.m. 2 56		8 46				11 6		12 0		2 31	
—	Mullingar (dep)		1 0		3mz45		5 0		9 0		9 15	11 20					2 41
56 28	Clonhugh												*				
57 36	Multyfarnham				7 45		9 15	9 14	9 15			11 33	11 34			2 57	2 58
60 69	Inny Junction					5 45	5 55				9 55	11 40				3 4	3 7
63 18	Street and Rathowen															3 13	3 14
67 42	Edgeworthstown			6 20	7 0	7 35		9 32	9 34					1 10	1 30	3 24	3 27
76 22	Longford	5 15	6 15					9 49	9 53					2 5	2 30	3 42	3 48
80 5	Newtownforbes					8 0	8 20									3 56	3 57
87 22	Dromod		6 55		7 45	8 45	9 0	10 13	10 14					3 6	3 35	4 10	4 12
93 0	Drumsna					9 20	9 45	10 26	10 27							4 24	4 25
97 62	Carrick	8 25	8 35	9 10	10 0	10 5	11	10 37	10 39					4 13	4 35	4 35	4 38
106 28	Boyle	9 10	10 0			11 35	11 40	10 55	10 59					5 10		4 54	4 57
112 40	Kilfree Junction			10 30	11 30			11 13	11 15							5 13	5 16
120 6	Ballymote					12 25	12 55	11 28	11 30							5 29	5 31
127 56	Collooney					1 15	1 55	11 44	11 45							5 45	5 46
—	Collooney Junction																
128 64	Carrignagat Junction																
129 56	Ballysodare					1 45	2 5	12 0								5 52	5 55
134 16	Sligo	12 30		12 30		2 20		12 0								6 5	

DOWN TRAINS.

STATIONS	9 Pass. ARR	DEP	10 Cavan Mixed ARR	DEP	11 Cavan Pass. ARR	DEP	12 ARR	DEP	13 Night Mail Pass. ARR	DEP	14 (Sun) Goods ARR	DEP	15 (Sun) Pass. ARR	DEP
KINGSTN PIER														
N. Wall, L. & N. W														
N. Wall, M.G.W.														
Broadstone						6 0				7 30				2 0
Liffey Junction														
Mullingar (arr)					8 17				8 51		a.m. 3 45		3 17	
Mullingar (dep)				1 20		8 30				9 5		3 45		3 35
Clonhugh						*				*				
Multyfarnham			1 50	1 51	8 44	8 45			9 20	9 21	*		*	
Inny Junction			2 10		8 53				9 27	9 34				
Street and Rathowen									9 40	9 41	*		*	
Edgeworthstown									9 51	9 54		4 11	4 10	
Longford									10 9	10 14	5 15	6 15	4 29	4 33
Newtownforbes									10 22	10 23			4 41	4 42
Dromod									10 36	10 39	6 55	7 45	4 56	4 57
Drumsna									10 51	10 52				
Carrick									11 2	11 5	8 25	8 35	5 19	5 21
Boyle									11 21	11 26	9 10	10 0	5 38	5 43
Kilfree Junction									11 40	11 43	10 30	11 30		
Ballymote									11 56	11 58	11 58		6 12	6 14
Collooney									12 12	12 13			6 28	6 29
Collooney Junction														
Carrignagat Junction														
Ballysodare									12 19	12 22	12 30		6 35	6 38
Sligo									12 32		12 30		6 50	

No. 2.—Cross 12 a.m. Up Goods at Longford, 7.5 a.m. Up Passenger at Carrick and shunt for Down Limited Mail at Kilfree Junction.
mz. Does not run on Mondays.
No. 3.—Cross 7.5 a.m. Up at Dromod and shunt for Down Limited Mail at Carrick.
No. 4.—Pass 5.0 a.m. Goods at Carrick and 3.45 a.m. Goods at Kilfree Junction.
No. 7.—Cross Up Limited Mail at Dromod. RWR runs when required and returns as may be arranged.

No. 13.—Cross 7.25 p.m. Up Goods at Boyle.
Electric Train Staff Stations—Carrignagat Junction, Collooney Junction, Collooney, Ballymote, Kilfree Junction, Boyle, Carrick, Drumsna, Dromod, Longford.
Banking Out of Passenger and Goods Trains for Sligo and Cavan Branches.—Drivers of above Trains are to be informed as to the loads they have on leaving Mullingar, and to be asked if they require assistance; if they do, arrangements must be made to bank out.

WORKING TIMETABLES – 1ST JANUARY 1920

Mayo Branch.—Down Trains.

TABLE No. 23.

STATIONS	Dist. from Broadstone M.C.	1 Ballina Fast Goods	2 Mixed	3 Westport Goods	4 Limited Mail E	5 Pass	6 Claremorris Goods	7 RWR	8 Cavan Castlerea Goods	9 Night Mail	SUNDAYS 10 Pass
		p.m.	a.m.	a.m.	a.m.	a.m.	p.m.	p.m.	p.m.	p.m.	p.m.
Kingstown Pier dep	—				6 5	11.30				7.30	2 0
N. Wall L.N.W. „	4 31										
N. Wall M.G.W. „	1 33			12 45	7 25	1.30				9 55	4 21
Broadstone „	78 5				9 38						
Liffey Junction „											
Athlone arr			a.m. 1 55	6.30		3.58					
Athlone dep	—	2 55		8 30	9 48	4 15				10 10	4 36
Killoom	83 66			9 25 / 9 35	9 59 / 10 0	4 26 / 4 27				10 42 / 10 46	
Knockcroghery	89 79			9 50	10 12 / 10 13	4 38 / 4 39	1 36 / 1 56		9 0	10 59 / 11 0	
Ballymurry	92 69			10 10	10 19 / 10 20	4 45 / 4 46				11 11 / 11 12	
Roscommon	96 19	3 50 / 4 0		10 28 / 11 25	10 27 / 10 9	4 53 / 4 57	2 15 / 3 15	4 15 / 5 15	9 55 / 10 10	10 27 / 10 43	5 12 / 5 15
Donamon	101 69				10 42 / 10 43	5 12	3 40	5 40	10 35	11 0 / 11 2	5 27 / 5 29
Ballymoe	107 49			11 49	10 54 / 10 55	5 22 / 5 24	4 20 / 4 40	6 10 / 6 30	11 35 / 11 50	11 11 / 11 12	5 40 / 5 42
Castlerea	112 53	5 0 / 5 30		2 32 / 2 37	11 5 / 11 9	5 34 / 5 53	4 58 / 5 15	7 18 / 8 15	12 0	11 22 / 11 26	5 52 / 5 55
Ballinlough	118 60	5 54			11 22 / 11 23	5 52 / 5 54	6 24	8 39		11 39 / 11 40	6 8
Ballyhaunis	124 2	6 19		p.m. 12 14	11 34 / 11 38	6 5 / 6 10	7 25 / 8 0	9 15 / 11 20		11 51 / 11 55	6 20 / 6 24
Bekan	128 58				11 48 / 11 49	6 20 / 6 21					
Claremorris	134 67	6 54 / 8 0		12 49 / 1 35	12 1 / 12 4	6 33 / 6 39	8.35	11.55		12 18 / 12 22	6 46 / 6 49
Balla	142 19	8 23		1 58 / 2 20	12 17 / 12 18	6 52				12 35 / 12 36	7 2 / 7 3
Manulla Junction	145 75	8 35		2 32 / 2 37	12 25 / 12 30	7 6 / 7 14				12 43 / 12 48	7 10 / 9 21
Castlebar	149 74			3 2 / 3 40	12 39 / 12 41	7 22 / 7 26				12 57 / 1 0	9 30
Islandeady	155 0				12 52 / 12 53	7 36 / 7 37					
Westport	160 74			4 15	1 4 / 1 9	7 47 / 7 57				1 23	
Newport	168 60		8 0 / 8 30		1 28 / 1 29	8 16 / 8 17					
Mallaranny	179 32		8 45 / 9 44		1 54 / 1 58	8 42 / 8 44					9 50
Achill arr	187 46		10 20		2 18	9 5					

No. 1.—Cross 2.0 a.m. Goods ex Castlerea at Roscommon. Cross 6.5 a.m. Up Passenger at Claremorris.
No. 2.—Stops at Carrowsallagh Crossing, 8.8; Rosturk Crossing, 8.11; Tonragee Crossing, 10.15. a.m.
No. 3.—Shunt at Castlerea for Down Limited Mail and Cross Up Limited Mail at Claremorris.
No. 4.—Pass Down Westport Goods at Castlerea. Cross Up Limited Mail at Castlebar.
No. 5.—Pass 1.0 p.m. Down Goods at Castlerea and Cross 5 p.m. Up Goods at Ballyhaunis. Cross Up Night Mail at Balla, and Up Westport Goods at Castlebar.
No. 6.—Cross Up Limited Mail at Roscommon. Shunt for 1.30 p.m. Down Passenger at Castlerea. Cross 5.0 p.m. Up Goods at Ballinlough.
No. 7.—RWR.—Runs when required and returns as may be arranged. Shunt for 1.30 p.m. Down Passenger at Roscommon. The 1.30 p.m. Down Passenger. Cross Up Night Mail at Balla.
No. 8.—Cross Up Claremorris Goods at Roscommon. Shunt for Down Night Mail at Donamon. Cross Up Westport Goods at Ballymoe.
No. 9.—Pass Cavan-Castlerea Goods at Donamon. Cross Up Westport Goods at Castlerea and Up Ballina Goods at Ballinlough.

☞ **CROSSING OF 1.30 P.M. DOWN PASSENGER AND UP NIGHT MAIL AT BALLA.**
The above Trains cross at Balla, and are to be accepted under the "Warning Arrangement." The 1.30 p.m. Down Passenger must be brought to a stand at the Down Home Signal and brought into the Cattle Bank Siding by a Green Hand Signal to be given by a man, who must stand at the Points and who will be responsible for seeing that they are properly made. After the departure of the Up Night Mail, the 1.30 p.m. Down Passenger is to be taken from the Cattle Bank Siding to the Passenger Platform. Station Master at Balla must personally see to the shunting, and have proper arrangements made. Cattle Bank Siding must be kept clear of wagons. It is most important that the carriages of the 1.30 p.m. Down should have the doors locked on the platform side at Claremorris before departure.

Mayo Branch.—Up Trains.

TABLE No. 24.

STATIONS	Dist. from Achill M.C.	11 Castlerea Cavan Goods	12 Pass	13 Lim. Mail E	14 Pass	15	16 Night Mail	17 Goods	18 Pass	19 Westport Goods	20 Ballina Goods	SUNDAYS 21 Pass
		a.m.	a.m.	a.m.			p.m.	p.m.	p.m.	p.m.	p.m.	a.m.
Achill dep	—			10 50								
Mallaranny arr/dep	8 14			11 11 / 11 15			3 30 / 3 59					10 0
Newport	18 62			11 42 / 11 44			4 14 / 4 58			6 30		10 22 / 10 24
Westport	26 32		6 5 / 6 17	12 12 / 12 15		Mixed	5 13 / 5 38			7 5 / 8 0	8 40 / 8 50	10 33 / 12 53
Islandeady			6 18 / 6 29	12 19 / 12 28			6 0 / 6 13					
Castlebar	37 32		6 31 / 6 50	12 45 / 12 59			6 24 / 6 46	5 0		9 5 / 9 35	9 10 / 9 35	1 2 / 1 5
Manulla Junc.	41 37		6 58 / 7 1	1 8 / 1 9			6 54 / 6 58					1 22 / 1 25
Balla	45 7	2 0	7 17 / 7 20	1 26 / 1 31			7 14 / 7 19			9 5 / 9 35	10 5 / 10 30	
Claremorris	52 39	2 23 / 2 38	7 32 / 7 33	1 44 / 1 45			7 31 / 7 32	5 0				1 48 / 1 50
Bekan	58 48	2 55 / 3 10	7 43 / 7 45	1 56 / 1 58			7 42 / 7 45	5 40 / 6 30		10 36	11 15 / 12 0	2 2 / 2 3
Ballyhaunis	63 24	3 35 / 4 0	7 56 / 7 57	2 10 / 2 11			7 56 / 7 57	6 55 / 7 28		10 38	12 25 / 12 40	2 2 / 2 3
Ballinlough	68 46		8 8 / 8 11	2 23 / 2 28			8 8 / 8 12	7 43 / 8 25		10 57 / 11 30	9 10	2 29 / 2 51
Castlerea	74 53	4 55	8 33 / 8 34	2 38 / 2 39			8 22 / 8 23	8 43 / 9 3		11 48	1 3 / 1 8	2 42 / 2 43
Ballymoe	79 57	6 0	8 44 / 8 47	2 50 / 2 51			8 34 / 8 35	9 25 / 9 45		12 35 / 12 40		2 54 / 2 56
Donamon	85 37		8 53 / 8 54	3 2 / 3 7			8 45 / 8 48	10 10 / 11 0				
Roscommon	91 7	12 25	9 0 / 9 1	3 13 / 3 14			8 54 / 8 55				2 13 / 2 16	
Ballymurry	94	2 30	9 13 / 9 14	3 20 / 3 21			9 1 / 9 2	11 20 / 11 40	6 22 / 6 24			
Knockcroghery	97 27			3 33 / 3 34			9 13 / 9 14		6 51 / 6 53	1 35		3 28
Killoom	103 40		9 45	3 45			9 25	12 15	7 15	2 45	3 13	3 51
Athlone arr	109 21	6 0		4 10			9 50				6 30	
Broadstone arr	187 46		12 25	6 20			12 15			7 35	1 0	6 7
N.Wall M.G.W. „	188 71			7 0								
N.Wall L.N.W. „			2 30	7 20								
Kingstown Pier „												

No. 11.—Cross Down Ballina Goods at Roscommon.
No. 12.—Cross Down Ballina Goods at Roscommon.
No. 13.—Cross Down Limited Mail at Castlebar, Down Westport Goods at Claremorris, and Down Claremorris Goods at Roscommon.
No. 16.—Cross 1.30 p.m. Down Passenger at Balla, Down Claremorris Goods at Ballyhaunis, and RWR Goods at Castlerea. Pass 5.0 p.m. Up Goods at Castlerea.
No. 17.—Cross 1.30 p.m. Down Passenger at Ballyhaunis. Cross 1.0 p.m. Down Goods at Ballinlough. Shunt for Up Night Mail at Castlerea. Cross Cavan-Castlerea Goods at Roscommon. Stops at Torrage Crossing, 5.41; Rosturk Crossing, 5.27; Carrowsallagh Crossing, 5.30 p.m.
No. 19.—Cross 1.30 p.m. Down Passenger at Castlebar, RWR Goods at Ballyhaunis, Down, Night Mail at Castlerea, and Cavan-Castlerea Goods at Ballymoe.
No. 20.—Cross Down, Night Mail at Ballyhaunis. **Reduction of Speed; see page 2.**
Engines Working Achill Branch.—Six-coupled engines must not work over this Branch.
Up Ballina Goods.—In future, should the Up Westport Goods run late and the Up Ballina Goods precede it from Manulla, then the Ballina Goods must take up the running of the Westport Goods as from Manulla, and the Westport Goods fall back to the schedule of the Ballina Goods.

Chapter Thirteen

ACCIDENTS

ONE OF the first accidents to come to the attention of the BoT occurred near Killucan on 17th September 1859 when an up troop special from Athlone was derailed at a section of line which had been removed by the permanent way gang. It transpired that the order for this train had been received by the traffic manager at about 16.30 on the previous evening after the departure of the afternoon train to Galway. No written notice could therefore be sent down the line until the 19.15 mail train, by which time the platelayers had gone home. They arrived for work the next morning not expecting an up train until 10.00 and proceeded to remove rails close to Milepost 39 for the purpose of replacing sleepers. Having said this, the man in charge of the gang was aware of the fact that specials were sometimes run without prior notice and took precautions for stopping such trains. The special left Athlone at 06.25 with a tender engine, seven carriages, a guard's van and a covered goods wagon; on board were 250 men of the 67th Regiment en route to Dublin.

Everything went normally as far as Mullingar which the train left at about 07.20. In the Killucan to Hill of Down section, the driver saw a platelayer displaying a red flag and almost immediately he passed over fog signals. Speed was reduced from an estimated 35mph to 3mph but before he could stop the train it was thrown off the line at the point where the rails had been removed and ran on for some 95 yards over the sleepers and ballast. It was fortunate that the train was derailed to the right on to the ballast rather than into the bog on the other side. In evidence given before Captain H W Tyler, it was clear that the man in charge had taken adequate precautions, sending the platelayer back 1,030 yards, where he put down five detonators, and he then went out a further 170 yards to display a flag. The driver of the special however had been a fireman for the past five years and had only driven occasionally during the two years previous to the accident. His fireman was a passed cleaner while the guard was only 20 years of age and had acted as such on only one previous occasion. All in all, Captain Tyler felt that these men 'would not have stopped the train as

readily as more experienced servants of the company'. He went on to say that he hoped that 'the present occurrence . . . will be the means of inducing the directors to adopt a more effective method of stopping their trains', a message which fell largely on deaf ears.

An accident on the newly opened Kells branch could have been avoided if the 24 hour clock had been in operation. A train broke through the gates at New Gate crossing, injuring the driver of a horse and cart. The Dublin & Meath had only commenced running trains over the branch two days previously and the gatekeeper misread the timetable supplied to him. To be fair, the train in question appeared in a listing of MGW main line trains and was confusing. The gatekeeper was arrested and brought before the local magistrate who sentenced him to one months imprisonment, the company promptly discharging him from its service. A memorial was in due course sent to the Lord Lieutenant seeking clemency on the man's behalf. The sentence was in fact altered to a fine of £5 but the board minutes do not indicate whether the company reinstated him.

An accident near Ballinasloe on 29th October 1864 had far reaching consequences at board level and has been referred to in that context in chapter five. The *Galway Vindicator* for 2nd November, under the headline 'Alarming accident on the Midland Railway', gave an extended description of the accident. The 13.00 down Galway train was derailed about two miles from Ballinasloe station at a point where the line traversed the bog of Clarara. A third class carriage behind the engine had become derailed and was propelled down the embankment, derailing the remainder of the train. The third class was 'smashed into fragments by the concussion' and two passengers were killed, another thirty-four being injured. Captain Rich attended on behalf of the BoT, his report being issued at the end of November. He found the accident had been due to excessive speed over a road of weak construction with defective timbers and poor drainage, and he recommended a reduction in the speed of trains until the line was relaid. In relation to the permanent way,

Rich described it as consisting of 75lb bridge rail tied transversely with cross-sleepers. The gauge was found to be between ⅜in and ½in wide, the method of securing the gauge by bolts through the longitudinal sleepers to the underside of the cross-sleepers being out of date.

Little reference appears in the board minutes to the accident. Thirteen months later, a minute of 7th December 1865 called Price's attention to the dangerous condition of the line between Woodlawn and Athenry, while a fortnight later the order was given for fifteen minutes to be added to the timings of all passenger trains. Despite the BoT's report, Ennis at the half-yearly shareholders' meeting in March 1865 said the accident was due to the saturation of the bog by heavy rains and the BoT requirement to interpose an empty carriage between the engine and the train proper. Furthermore, he believed the driver when he said his speed had only been 32mph. To be fair to the Midland, their track was probably no worse than that of other companies at the time. The Dublin, Wicklow & Wexford had two derailments, in 1865 and 1867, due to defective track. January 1871 saw another derailment due to 'sleepers being much decayed and the weak and bad system of cross-tying'.

On 7th October 1865 there was a collision at Kilcock between a goods train and a passenger train after wagons had been left insufficiently braked on a 1 in 100 falling gradient, resulting in twelve injuries. Some of these injuries resulted from passengers jumping out of the train after the driver whistled for the brakes. It was reported that the driver and fireman had also jumped off prior to the collision. Trap points were suggested to prevent a recurrence. A second collision occurred in September 1871 at Kilcock, this time when an engine hauling a disabled engine ran into the rear of an up goods train. The signalman had lowered the up distant and station signals, believing that the train was still outside the signal, whereas in fact only the last six wagons were, the driver having continued to draw up slowly. The driver of the light engine was aware that the goods had left Enfield 15 minutes ahead of him but saw the distant signal being lowered as he approached and assumed it was for him. Captain Rich suggested that the block telegraph might have prevented the accident and also recommended that the distant signal be moved further out.

1871 was not a good year for the MGWR. Another accident occurred on 23rd October at Galway, when four passengers were injured as a result of the 13.00 from Dublin colliding with some wagons which were in the course of being shunted to form the 19.10 up goods. The passenger train had run through the signal, the driver, 'an old and experienced servant', stating that the signal in question had been out of order for some time and had been left showing danger. The BoT report stated that the duties of some of the station staff at Galway appeared to have been done carelessly for some time. The station master was censured for not having the line clear for twenty minutes before the passenger train was due as required by the company's rule book. Four years later, Colonel Hutchinson investigated a collision at Castlebar between a down empty wagon special and the 02.00 down mixed train from Manulla Junction to Westport. Of the eight passengers on this train, one was killed and the remaining seven injured. Hutchinson found that not only had the crew of the special been on duty for $18\frac{1}{2}$ hours, but additionally they were unfamiliar with the road.

The next collision occurred at Killucan on 16th September 1876 when a goods train left standing on a 1 in 120 gradient ran away and collided with a down empty wagon special. On this occasion, there was suspicion that a drover travelling in the guard's van of the goods train might have tampered with the brakes; apart from this however, it was obvious that insufficient brakes had been applied to the train before the engine was uncoupled. It was lucky that the speed of the runaways was only about 10mph and that the following train had stopped at the distant signal, otherwise there would have been more than one person injured. The BoT recommended that drovers and others should not be permitted to travel in brake vans.

Before considering a series of collisions during the 1880s, three accidents with amusing or unusual aspects will be described. The first of these was on 29th August 1871 about 1¼ miles south of Cavan station involving a horse special from Mullingar to Cavan. The train, hauled by two locomotives, consisted of thirty-five wagons of horses, a brake van and a third class carriage for drovers. About a mile to the south of the accident site, the line falls towards Cavan on gradients of 1 in 81 to 1 in 62 for about half a mile, followed by quarter of a mile level and then rising to the point of the accident. The train was travelling at about 14mph when the driver of the second engine felt a jerk and on looking back saw a wagon off the road. The two engines and the first three wagons were stopped in about 170 yards and it was discovered that the rear of the third wagon was missing as was one of the horses which had been in it. The next five wagons had been derailed down the embankment and fourteen horses were dead. It was concluded that the accident occurred as the result of one of the horses kicking out the wagon end, falling out and derailing the next wagon.

The second accident occurred at Navan in April 1875 when a passenger endeavouring to board a moving train was pushed off by the guard, fell beneath the train and was killed. The third of this trio was on 26th December 1877 when a special from Dublin, consisting of engine, four empty cattle wagons and a brake van ran into the terminal station at Athboy, failed to stop, ran through a boundary wall and fell four feet into the street. The engine crossed the street and imbedded itself in a house occupied by one of the company's drivers. It was reported that the latter remained asleep in the room adjoining that demolished by the accident. It transpired that the guard of the train and a friend of the driver were on the footplate contrary to regulations. It is also quite likely that the crew may have been celebrating the season's festivities.

Three further accidents in 1877 showed that problems with the condition of the permanent way still persisted. A Meath line train was derailed at the facing points at Clonsilla Junction on the evening of 10th March 1877, resulting in injuries to five passengers. The vehicle first derailed was a 4-wheeled 29ft 2in first on a 14ft wheelbase marshalled between two 6-wheelers. There was no defect in the carriage and the cause was the lowness of the offside rail on the branch in the immediate vicinity of the facing points. It was recommended that a locking bar should be fitted. Following a derailment at Athlone in the following month a check rail was suggested on the junction curve at the west end of the station. A derailment at Castlerea in December resulted from a defective rail and the BoT report pointed out that the permanent way 'looked nearly worn out and would require a good deal of care and attention until thoroughly renewed'.

A number of accidents investigated by the BoT could have been avoided if interlocking had been provided or if block telegraph regulations had not been disobeyed. The first of these was a collision at Ballyhaunis on 11th June 1880 which resulted in four injuries. An up cattle special from Balla to Dublin consisting of a tender engine, 33 loaded cattle wagons and van was turned into the down loop where they came into collision with two third class carriages containing harvestmen. These carriages were intended to be attached to a harvest special. Ballyhaunis was a staff station worked by staff and ticket, the down loop was 330 yards long, although it was the up loop which was generally used by both up and down trains. The up home signal was visible from the distant, 350 yards away, but the driver's view of the loop was obscured by the water tank on the down platform and he first saw the carriages when only about 150 yards away. The driver of the cattle train said he had been unable to obtain water at Claremorris and therefore required to take some at Ballyhaunis and was thus expecting to run into the up platform road, both signals being off; if it was intended to put him into the loop it was normal to keep the signal at danger. He also alleged that the pointsman told him he had turned the train into the down loop on the Stationmaster's instructions. The latter, who had been at Ballyhaunis for the previous two and a half years said he had instructed the pointsman to caution the driver regarding the carriages in the loop. The pointsman had however no flags with him and relied on a hand signal. No blame was attached to the footplate crew, the main responsibility resting with the Stationmaster. It was most desirable that the points and signals be interlocked 'without unnecessary loss of time'.

Only a month later, a collision occurred at Mullingar station. On the morning of 15th July, the 09.00 up passenger from Galway came into collision with a portion of the 07.00 up Sligo which was being reversed along the platform to join it up to the Galway train. In error, the signalman turned the train through the crossover on to the down line, an unfortunate mistake by an experienced signalman – he had been in Mullingar cabin for the past 15 years. The accident would not have occurred had the points and signals been interlocked. Exactly a week later yet another collision occurred at Athlone when a GS&W train from Portarlington ran into the rear of a Midland passenger train standing at the down platform, injuring three passengers. Similar recommendations followed this accident.

Next we consider four accidents which would either have been prevented if block working had been in force or if block telegraph rules had not been disobeyed. An up Sligo passenger train over-ran the platform at Liffey Junction and came into violent collision with an empty coaching stock train which had just arrived from North Wall Fourteen passengers and four staff were injured. Absolute block working was in force between Ashtown and Broadstone; it was the practice to consider the up line clear when a train passed the junction signal which was 300 yards from the home signal, and the down line when a train passed the starting signal. The empty train was in course of crossing from the down to the up road to gain access to a siding at the back of the up platform when the Sligo train ran into it. A contributory factor was the failure of the tender brake on the latter train which was being attended to and doubtless distracted the footplate crew.

A collision took place on 5th January 1883 close to Lough Owel level crossing when the 08.45 up Sligo train was run into by the 06.00 goods from Cavan, injuring four cattle drovers in the rear vehicle of the Sligo train. The latter had stopped on the bank short of steam for some fifteen minutes despite the fact that a stop had already been made for the same purpose at Multyfarnham. A number of points were made by Colonel Hutchinson in his report. Had the guard of the Sligo train been more prompt in going back to protect his train, the collision could have been averted and the primary blame rested with him. The driver of the Sligo train was also negligent in allowing his train to run short of steam.

For the third of these accidents we must again return to Mullingar where on the early morning of 30th June 1886 an empty coaching stock train ran into the 22.00 down Sligo goods, injuring the driver of the former. The accident primarily resulted from the want of proper look-out on the part of the crew of the empty train. In fairness, the driver had been on duty for twenty-one hours. The mode of dealing with the Sligo goods was open to criticism as it had to set back along the mainline outside the junction home signal. The accident could have been avoided if absolute block working had been in force.

The last of this series of accidents was at Tuam Junction, Athenry on 2nd January 1884 when a W&L train coming off the Tuam branch collided with an up Galway train. Although the driver of the former train claimed that both the distant and home signals were clear, with the latter being put to danger as he approached it, the signalman strenuously denied that he had taken off his signal, his evidence being corroborated by a MGW ganger. It was obvious that the W&L driver had over-run his signals and that his speed had been too high approaching the junction.

The first decade of the present century saw a spate of accidents, the most serious of which involved the down night mail between Ballymoe and Castlerea in the early hours of the morning of 11th April 1903 as the result of a collision with a permanent way trolley on the line. One passenger was killed and a total of 15 people, including 4 employees, were injured. At one point, it was suggested that a goat tethered to one of the axles of the trolley might have dragged it on to the line. Colonel von Donop, the inspecting officer, doubted this and the more likely explanation was that the trolley

had been borrowed to return from a drinking session in town, although nothing was ever proved nor was the errant goat ever found.

Colonel von Donop investigated another accident some four months later, at Ballymote. A double-headed passenger train was diverted into the wrong road and collided with the up Sligo mail causing injuries to three passengers. In this instance the driver of the passenger train had been on duty for twenty hours. In evidence, he said that his train did not require a second engine, but that the 0-6-0 No.54 had been attached purely for the purpose of working it back to Sligo. The driver of the train engine, a 4-4-0, considered he was the driver of the train and therefore responsible for keeping a look-out for signals and he confirmed that both distant and home signals were off. The driver of the pilot also confirmed this, evidence contradicted by the signalman. In this instance, the latter's statement proved to be correct as the interlocking would not have allowed him to release the home signal. The colonel stated that Ballymote was unsuitable for the crossing of passenger trains and had never been accepted by the BoT as such. An additional factor was that the brake pipes between the pilot and train engines had not been connected, which meant that the driver of the pilot engine was unable to apply the brakes on the train.

Another signal over-run occurred on the night of 5th September 1910 when the down night mail collided with the engine of the 02.00 Manulla Junction to Westport which was shunting at the former point. Fifteen passengers on the mail were slightly injured, the driver of this train being found primarily responsible. His fireman was censured for not giving assistance while shunting arrangements at Manulla were found to be in need of alteration.

The final two accidents on the Midland occurred within a month of one another in 1919, the first of these on the evening of 21st October with a collision between the 13.30 down passenger and the up mail at Balla. Like Ballymote, some sixteen years earlier, Balla was not deemed suitable for the crossing of passenger trains although special instructions had been issued for the crossing of these two trains. This was to the effect that the down train was to be brought to a stand at the home signal, when it was then to be brought into the cattle bank siding by hand signal to be given by a man standing at the points and who was to be responsible for seeing that they were properly set. After the departure of the up mail, the down train was to be taken to the platform. On the evening in question, the down train was accepted under warning arrangements and a ticket handed to the driver with the staff. As soon as this train was accepted into the section, a

porter was sent to the south loop points to act as a hand signalman. Meanwhile, the up train arrived at the home signal which was lowered for the train to come in to the platform. Almost simultaneously the down train came through the loop points and a collision occurred. Whilst this latter approached the station at too high a speed, there was no doubt that the porter was largely responsible for the accident.

For our final accident, we move much further east to Moyvalley in the early morning of 18th November when a collision occurred between two goods trains. Due to a hard frost and fallen leaves on the rails, it had been found necessary to divide the 12.45 down goods about 1,000 yards from Moyvalley where a rising gradient of 1 in 108 had proved too much for the engine, 0-6-0 No.53. This engine – *see illustration on page 90* – was one of two fitted with the Cusack-Morton superheater and was always regarded as a particularly shy steamer as so rebuilt and this may have been a contributory factor although no mention of this is made in the BoT report. In any event, while the second half of the train was standing on the mainline, it was run into by the following 02.00 goods. There was a dispute between the signalmen at Enfield and Hill of Down as to whether the 12.45 had been cleared out of section. Colonel Pringle found that the entries in the Hill of Down signal cabin register had been altered and he was at a loss to understand the signalman's actions. Likewise, the guard of the 12.45 train should have had sufficient time to have gone back to protect his train.

One cannot escape the conclusion that many of these accidents could have been avoided but for the parsimony and slow response of the Midland directorate to change. It took the Ballinasloe accident to bring about a long overdue renewal of permanent way, although even then we find a BoT inspector calling attention to the poor condition of the track some thirteen years later. Similarly, lack of interlocking and block working were listed over a period of many years. As late as 1909, the company were being requested to explain to the BoT why many of the staff worked excessive hours. Even in that year, we find fifty-two cases of traffic crews exceeding thirteen hours, with at least two in excess of eighteen hours. There can be no excuse for this, other than an attempt to cut costs.

The accidents dealt with in this chapter were of the type which befell most of the railway companies of the British Isles from time to time. The MGWR had also to contend with many instances of malicious damage to its trains in the troubles of the 1920s. These are dealt with in Chapter Eleven and a full list of the locomotives to suffer malicious damage is given in Appendix D.

Chapter Fourteen

LOCOMOTIVES

DURING the course of researching the history of the MGWR, early contact was made with the one person who knew more about that company than anyone else, namely the late Bob Clements of Celbridge. Bob expressed a wish to see his lifetime's work of collating the company's locomotive history published, and to this the present writer readily agreed. The locomotives were not officially classified by the company until Atock's time. To make some sense and order out of the locomotive history of the Midland up to the Atock era, we have utilised Clements' system of classification for the engines which came before this time.

Fairbairns and Grendons.
The earliest locomotives, as was usual at this period, were ordered direct from manufacturers. The first reference in the board minutes is in January 1846 when a decision was taken to place advertisements seeking tenders for twenty locomotives. Messrs Fairbairn quickly responded, offering to supply ten, while in March Messrs J & R Mallett of the Seville Ironworks in Dublin proposed to supply five locomotives and tenders at £1,900 each, a figure accepted by the board. They were to be constructed according to the specifications of the company's engineer, Hemans, although it seems likely that these would have represented no more than broad outlines. Malletts obviously made a mistake in their calculations as by the end of March they had written stating that the price would be £2,030 each. The board saw no necessity for the increase and cancelled the order. On 16th April, Hemans was authorised to enter into a contract with Messrs Thomas Grendon & Company of the Drogheda Ironworks for five engines and tenders, if possible on terms more favourable than their offer of £2,260 each.

Towards the end of March, various parties were interviewed for the position of locomotive engineer, John Dewrance, late of the Liverpool & Manchester and the GS&W, being appointed at a salary of £300 per annum plus a company house on Cabra Road free of rent. Late deliveries from both manufacturers delayed the opening of the line. Though ordered after the Fairbairn

locomotives, the Grendon engines were the first into traffic. It would appear that the early engines were unnumbered as delivered, a situation altered by 1853, from which time until 1869 no names were allocated.

Class 1 consisted of five Grendon engines all 2-2-2s, named *Dunsandle, Vesta, Venus, Luna* and *Juno*, in due course Nos 7 to 11. They were delivered from April to December 1847, *Dunsandle* having the distinction of working the trial trips and the opening train. A lengthy description of her was included in an article on the first trial trip in the *Irish Railway Gazette*. She was described as inside-framed, with 14in x 18in cylinders and 5ft 7in wheels. There were 137 brass tubes, 10ft 6in long and 2in diameter with a copper firebox. She was coupled to a 6-wheeled tender holding 1,200 gallons of water and sufficient coke for 60 miles. The motion was referred to as being 'directly visible', probably indicating that it was partially visible through the frames rather than implying that it had outside gear for its inside cylinders. Two further engines to this design were added in 1852 and 1854, Nos 30 *Pallas* and 33 *Falcon*. No.11 *Juno* was sold to Edgeworth the contractor in September 1867 and was probably withdrawn about 1873. No.8 and either 9 or 10 were sold to the A&EJR, the remainder of this batch being withdrawn in 1869-71, Nos 30 and 33 lasting until 1875. They were of a standard Grendon design, some similar locomotives going to the D&D. A letter from Ramage, the locomotive superintendent, was read at the board meeting on 4th April 1866 suggesting that 'one of our light engines be altered to tank with an apartment to hold eight persons at a cost of £200'. This was approved and *Falcon* thus became a 2-2-4T and was used on Engineer's inspection duties.

There were six 2-2-2s in **Class 2** delivered from Fairbairn between June and December 1847. Named *Orion, Mars, Saturn, Mercury, Jupiter* and *Sirius*, later Nos 1 to 6. They had outside cylinders of 14in diameter, no other dimensions being known. A valuation of 1853 shows them to have very low average mileages, which suggests that they were not particularly successful. All were withdrawn in 1856 except for No.1 which had been rebuilt as a tank engine in 1852 and survived

until 1860. In fact the remaining five went to Grendons in part exchange for new locomotives, having been advertised for sale in May 1856. Ten engines were originally ordered, but only six were delivered. Fairbairn attended the board meeting on 19th August 1847, by which time the order had been reduced to six, and stated that materials for the others had been ordered.

In fact six more to a slightly altered design, were ordered, and these formed **Class 3**. They were Fairbairn singles, almost certainly to Dewrance's design and probably based on his 'Bird' class of 1841 for the L&M. Named *Heron, Condor, Petrel, Pelican, Cygnet* and *Ouzel* (Nos 12 to 17), these were inside cylinder engines and worked the main line trains until at least 1864, one of them being involved in the Ballinasloe accident. They were finally withdrawn in 1873-5.

The **Class 4** engines were three 2-2-2 well tanks from Fairbairn, ordered for the opening of the Galway extension in 1851: Nos 27 *Fairy*, 28 *Titania*, and 29 *Ariel*, were later renamed respectively *Bee, Elf* and *Fairy*. By this time the directors had decided to let out the working of their line to contract, a not uncommon turn of events in the early years of railway operations. In February 1849, Dewrance had been informed of this decision and he was allowed to go with three months salary. The line was worked by Dawson from March 1849 until August 1850 when he was replaced by Johnson & Kinder of the Bromsgrove Railway Carriage & Wagon Company. It would appear that the initial order was for four of the Class 4 locomotives but only three came to the MGW. The fourth engine appears to have ended up in Brazil in 1852, being used for the opening of that country's first railway. It is of interest to note that it is still in existence, having been preserved by the Brazilian authorities, and is thus the only locomotive with any Midland ancestry to survive. They were a standard Fairbairn design, similar to Nos 24 to 26 of the Belfast & Northern Counties Railway.

In June 1874, Atock was requested to obtain estimates for new boilers, Vulcans offering to rebuild them for £1,705 each, a figure which the MGW considered too high.

They therefore carried out the work themselves and they became saddle tanks. In their rebuilt form, they worked the Athboy, Edenderry and Kingscourt branches until displaced by the new 0-6-0 tanks introduced in 1891, after which they were employed on pilot duties at Broadstone. They were replaced in 1897 but survived on boiler wash-out duties until about 1906.

The **Class 5** engines represented a departure in that they were ordered from Messrs Longridge of Bedlington, although there is a theory that they were initially ordered from Hawthorns who subcontracted the job to Longridge. Nos 18 to 23 were 2-2-2s, named after stallions of the period – see Appendix C – and were delivered between November 1851 and February 1852. They were renumbered 88 to 93 in July 1873 and withdrawn about 1876, having in the interim been rebuilt as 2-4-0s.

Nos 25 and 26, the **Class 6** engines, came from Longridge and were the first coupled engines on the MGW, being 2-4-0s. They had inside frames and were apparently very successful, running up a large mileage despite the fact that they were goods engines. This could be explained by the fact that they most likely deputised for the less successful passenger classes. In fact, in 1876 this pair were working passenger traffic on the Mayo road. Both were gone by 1880.

Fairbairn 0-4-2 No.48, built in 1861, outside the Broadstone. This photograph is the earliest known of any MGW engine, the original being found in the GNR shed at Newry. As the engine is still to receive its nameplate – *Earl* – it was probably taken about 1861/2. No injectors appear in the photograph which seems to indicate that the class were fitted with pumps only. All six members of the class were withdrawn 1878/9. IRRS collection.

Class 7 consisted of a single 0-4-0 from Hawthorns. No.24 was named *Hawthorne* and delivered in 1852. She was ordered for the 'luggage train service', the first engine specifically for goods traffic. At the time this order was placed, Hawthorns were building eight similar engines for the Glasgow & South Western Railway, works Nos. 780 to 785 being allocated, No. 810 was allocated to the Midland engine, and 807 to a tenth, for the Monksland Railway. In the event, it was No.786 which came to Ireland and 810 went to Scotland. *Hawthorne* had a 4-wheeled tender holding 800 gallons of water. The name, differing in spelling from the manufacturers, may have been that of a race-horse. No.24 was scrapped sometime between 1873 and 1876, possibly having been renumbered 94 in the former year.

An order was placed with Fairbairn in 1852 for two **Class 8** 2-4-0 engines, with two more subsequently ordered although no trace of this latter order can be found. Nos. 31, 32, 34 and 35 were probably very similar to goods engines supplied to the W&L at this time. There is some doubt as to whether all four were goods engines, as there is some indication that at least one and perhaps two may have had larger wheels. No.31 worked passenger traffic on the Sligo road in later years, while 35 is known to have worked the Ballaghaderreen branch from the time of opening until she was scrapped in 1886.

In June 1853 it was resolved that the locomotive and civil engineering of the line should at the earliest possible period be placed under the superintendence of one competent resident engineer, an advertisement to this effect appearing in the *Railway Times* for 16th July. In due course, Edward Wilson of the York & North Midland Railway met with the approval of the board and was offered the position at a salary of £400 per annum. An identically worded advertise-

ment appeared in the same journal in August 1856 for a replacement. He left no stamp on the Midland's locomotive department and went to the Oxford, Worcester & Wolverhampton Railway, being presented with a service of plate on his departure from Broadstone. He was replaced by Joseph Cabry from the north of England.

Class 9 consisted of four engines ordered by Wilson from Grendons in 1854. It is unlikely that Wilson played any part in the design. In fact at the time, Stephensons had subcontracted work on an 0-6-0 to Grendons and it is quite possible that they were a Stephenson design. Two more of the class went to the Dundalk & Enniskillen. The four, Nos 36 to 39, arrived on the Midland between October 1855 and April 1856. They were long-boilered engines and capable of hauling 600 tons at 20mph. The boiler was constructed of Low Moor plates, ½in thick with a copper firebox. They had 168 of Greene's patent brass tubes. They do not appear to have been renumbered and were scrapped about 1880.

Class 10s were the last of the Grendons for the MGW. These were passenger 2-4-0s ordered in three batches. Nos 40 and 41 were delivered in August and September 1856 while Nos 2 to 6 came towards the end of 1857, being the engines supplied against the Fairbairns sent to Grendons. Finally, No.1 was ordered about March 1859, and delivered the next year. These engines finished their days on the Sligo line and were withdrawn between 1880 and 1884.

Class 11. About the time Nos 40 and 41 were being delivered, an order was placed with Messrs Stephenson for a single 2-4-0. It is generally believed that this engine, which was delivered almost immediately, was taken from an order for the South Australian Government Railways, one of which was illustrated in the *Railway Magazine* for

September 1944. Four very similar engines were built about the same time for the Birkenhead Railway. No.42, named *Ouzel,* when the practice of giving names to locomotives was resumed in the late 1860s, was either scrapped before 1875 or retained her original number to a later date.

Class 12. The Grendon/Fairbairn era came to a close with the delivery in 1861 of the last of six 0-4-2s from Fairbairns, Nos 43 to 48. Later renumbered 49-54, they survived until 1879/80 although by this time were in poor condition and had been removed from the

goods to finish out their days on ballast and pilot work. The earliest known photograph of any MGWR engine is of No.48 of this class.

Cabry ran into difficulties with the board in 1862, being accused of corruption in connection with the letting of contracts for rolling stock and permanent way materials without obtaining competitive tenders. As a consequence, he resigned and was replaced by Robert Ramage who had been Chief Draughtsman under Ben Connor at the St. Rollox works of the Caledonian Railway. At this time, the locomotive and civil engineering departments were separated. Before Cabry's departure however, orders had been placed for six passenger engines from Hawthorn and six goods engines from Neilsons.

Class 13. The Hawthorns, Nos. 49 to 54, arrived in 1862 and had double sandwich frames, outside springs, a polished brass dome on the second ring of the boiler and a safety valve on the firebox. They were the last singles built for the Midland and had the largest driving wheels (6ft 6in) of any on the line. Believed to be to the manufacturer's design, they were obtained for the main line express services. Renumbered 43 to 48 in 1873, they were relegated to branch line services about this time and were scrapped between 1883 and 1887.

Class 14. The six Neilsons of 1863 were destined to be the forerunners of a total of thirty-six to come from that source. Nos 55 to 60 were 0-4-2s, later named after rivers or lakes and were probably similar to the 1860

Above: **2-2-2WT** *Elf* **in use as a stationary boiler at Broadstone around 1900. Three engines of this type were introduced in 1851, being heavily rebuilt in 1874/5 and nominally withdrawn in 1897. They remained in use as stationary boilers until about 1906.** The late H Fayle, courtesy IRRS.

Below left: **Joseph Cabry, Locomotive Superintendent from 1856 to 1862. He left in 1862 following accusations of corruption in the letting of contracts for rolling stock and permanent way materials.** Author's collection.

Fairbairns, having raised fireboxes. All were scrapped in 1885.

Class 15. A second batch, Nos 61 to 66 arrived in the following year and were named after wild animals. Withdrawn between 1887 and 1889, it is possible that some parts were used in new 0-6-0s built at Broadstone.

Class 16. Ramage favoured the 0-4-2 type and a further six came from the Glasgow firm of Dübs & Company in 1867. Nos 67 to 72 were eventually named after towns served by the Midland.

Ramage submitted a report on the locomotive stock situation to the board early in 1867, following which he was requested to immediately prepare plans and specifications for six or eight passenger engines. Despite the apparent urgency, the order for the six engines was postponed until after March 1868, at which time it was decided that engines be named as well as numbered.

In fact it was not until the board meeting of 30th December 1868 that it was decided to seek tenders for four passenger engines, two to be delivered by 30th June and two by December 1869.

Class 17. This 2-4-0 was originally supplied by Fossick & Hackworth to the D&M in 1862, where it was No.7 and known as the 'drag-all', presumably because she was more powerful than any of their other locomotives. She does not appear to have been particularly successful on the Midland. No.11 *Meath* was later renumbered 85 and was withdrawn in 1886.

Class 18. Avonside's tender of £2,200 each was accepted in January 1869 for four 2-4-0s. A further two were ordered later in the year. Midland numbers were 8, 9, 10, 73, 74 and 75, the latter three becoming 7, 11 and 12 in July 1873. Few dimensions are known of these engines and no photographs or drawings are believed to exist. We do know that the tenders were of typical Caledonian design as used by Ramage at this time. Whilst active on the main line throughout their working lives, they do not appear to have worked on the Limited Mails. They were scrapped in 1889/90.

An interesting item appears in the board minutes for 17th March 1869, when Ramage was ordered to prepare drawings for a 7ft 0in outside cylinder engine. The drawings were prepared and duly approved as in October it was announced that the outside cylinder passenger engine would be built in the works at a cost estimated at £2,500. This order was not carried out and it is difficult to see how such a locomotive could have been constructed at the Broadstone in 1869/70, bearing in mind the inadequate and cramped state of the works. Its construction would have predated the earliest known construction there by almost ten years, and even that only followed on the 1877 extensions to the works. Further research into this locomotive shows that the proposed design bore strong similarities to the Caledonian 8ft Singles designed by Ben Connor.

Class 19. The last of the classes to appear under the Ramage era, these were a further batch of 0-4-2 engines from Neilson. Nos 7 and 76 to 86 differed from the earlier ones in having modified frames and boilers, the latter being 3½in larger in diameter and with three rings instead of four. After 1887 they were relegated from main line goods work to piloting and ballast duties.

The Atock era.
Ramage was replaced by Martin Atock from the Waterford & Limerick. He was in a sense unusual in that he started his career in England, but spent most of his working life in Ireland. Other locomotive engineers, notably Aspinall and Ivatt of the GS&WR, came to Ireland early in their careers before moving on to the bigger English railway companies, having established their reputations in Ireland. Atock was born in Preston in 1836 but moved shortly afterwards to Stratford where his father George was to become Carriage & Wagon Superintendent of the Eastern Counties Railway. Martin himself joined the Great Eastern Railway, becoming a draughtsman. He married in 1859 and moved to Limerick two years later on his appointment as Locomotive Superintendent to the W&L. He was to remain with the Midland for twenty-eight years until his retirement in April 1900. He died in November 1901 shortly after returning from a visit to London. During his time at the Broadstone, considerable improvements were made in the locomotives and rolling stock and the company's workshops were extended.

Immediately following his appointment, Atock was instructed to prepare a report on the condition of the rolling stock. During Ramage's ten year tenure, additions to stock had consisted almost entirely of 0-4-2s apart from the six Avonside 2-4-0s. There were many complaints in regard to time-keeping and it was therefore necessary to bring about some urgent changes. In the meantime, the last six of the Class 19 locomotives were delivered by Neilsons. These included some to the design alterations being made by Atock. At this time a new locomotive classification system was introduced, details of which have survived.

Class D. Also known as the '13-24' class after the road numbers, all were delivered during 1873 from Neilsons of Glasgow. Some rather inappropriate names were chosen for this class, as for example *Rapid, Racer, Speedy* and *Swift,* none of which could possibly have applied to these engines. In general, the design, with larger cylinders and boilers remained the standard passenger engine down to the turn of the century. Parts of these engines found their way into their Broadstone-built replacements. A basically similar class of five engines was ordered from Dübs in June 1875, Nos 30 to 34 being delivered in 1876. Two further batches were added, six from Beyer Peacock in 1880/1 and sixteen more between 1883 and 1887. Of the latter group, twelve were built at Broadstone and four came from Kitsons. All were basically similar. No.36, one of the Beyer engines, was named *Empress of Austria* after the Empress Elizabeth who came to Meath to hunt at the time of its introduction. It is interesting to note that no known photograph exists of this engine despite its imperial associations.

These engines were to be found on all but the heaviest passenger duties, working the Sligo and Mayo portions of the Limited Mail. The Beyer engines were in due course rebuilt into the first bogie engines on the

Martin Atock, Locomotive Superintendent from 1872 to 1900, began his railway career on the Great Eastern Railway before moving to the Waterford & Limerick. Atock brought a considerable degree of standardisation to Broadstone and instituted a policy of replacing locomotives and rolling stock at 20 year intervals.
Author's collection.

Midland and will be separately dealt with as such. The Kitson and Broadstone group were rebuilt between 1902 and 1908 with new boilers and the last of them was withdrawn in 1923. A later group of 2-4-0s introduced in 1889/90 were sufficiently different to warrant separate treatment.

An entry in the traffic minutes for 14th July 1870 refers to an order to the company solicitor to report on whether the engine *Hawk* may be disposed of, a further entry in June 1873 ordering Mr. Connolly to remove same. Research indicates that this was not in fact a Midland engine, but a Sharp 2-2-2 built in 1839 for the Ulster Railway and originally named *Spitfire*. It was purchased from the U.R. by Dargan for use on the Belfast & Ballymena Railway in 1847. In March 1864, among plant advertised for sale at Trim on completion of the Athboy branch was this engine. The purchaser was apparently a Mr French, who had the engine repaired by the Midland, but did not pay for the work. Although sold to Charles Connolly, a Dublin ironfounder, it appears to have remained at Broadstone until at least June 1873.

Class L. In September 1875, seven 0-6-0s were ordered from Stephensons at £2,777 each, three to be delivered in March 1876 and four in April. Three further engines were ordered in February 1876 and the delivery of all ten was completed by August. Nos 86 to 95 were the first of the standard Midland goods engines to Atock's design. The Midland engine was considerably larger than the GS&W '101' class which was a Beyer Peacock design, although the latter was nominally more powerful. The MGW boiler at 4ft 3in was 3in larger in diameter and 1½in shorter. A further fifty-seven examples were added to stock in later years, making them the most numerous class on the line. They were designed to handle forty-five wagon goods trains, and despite their wheel diameter of 5ft3in (5ft1½in on the 'Ln' class), were seldom used on passenger services, unlike the GS&WR 0-6-0s.

Towards the end of 1876, consideration was given to the inadequacy of the works at the Broadstone for carrying out repairs to engines. As a consequence, Price was ordered to make recommendations for new locomotive fitting shops. Mr Wilkinson, the architect, submitted plans in March 1877 and work proceeded to such effect that Cusack was able to report completion of building work by September 1878, only the machinery requiring delivery. This extension to the works meant that the company were now in a position to construct their own locomotives. The first of these were six of the standard goods engines. These included parts from the recently withdrawn Fairbairn 0-4-2s, including the old driving

wheels of 5ft 1½in. This led to them being given the designation 'Ln' class. One important alteration from the earlier 'L's was the provision of a steam brake. Nos 50, 51, 52, and 54 were scrapped without receiving GSR numbers. No.53 was rebuilt in 1919 with the Cusack-Morton superheater and again in 1925 with a Robinson superheater and piston valves. She was withdrawn in 1950 as CIE No.567.

A much larger group of these engines was introduced between 1885 and 1889 as Class L, followed by yet more in 1891-5. Some of this second group, designated Class Lm, came from Sharp Stewart, others from Kitson, the remainder being built at Broadstone. These three groups represented a departure from the earlier locomotives in that steel frameplates replaced iron and they had steel boilers, the sliding firehole doors being replaced by a door with a flap. Another difference was the provision of larger tenders carrying 2,100 gallons of water and 4½ tons of coal. Following on Atock's retirement in 1900, work began on the rebuilding of the 'L' class, Belpaire boilers being fitted. After the formation of the GSR, a standard Inchicore 'X' boiler was fitted to the 'L' and 'Lm' classes - the 'X' was in fact identical to the 'Z' as fitted to the former GS&WR '101' class except for the barrel and firebox lengths. Three of the engines were Civil War victims, twenty were withdrawn between 1923 and 1928 largely due to the introduction of the much larger 'F' and 'D2' classes. None was withdrawn from 1928 until 1954.

Class H. While the 'Ln' class were being built, Messrs Avonside wrote offering four

A contrast in MGWR motive power. 'L' class 0-6-0 No.67 *Dublin* in front of a 'B' class 0-6-0. In the background is 'P' class 0-6-0T No.615 (ex-101).
The late H Fayle, courtesy IRRS.

locomotives recently built and suitable for heavy goods traffic. The asking price was £1,800 each, plus carriage. These engines had been ordered by the Waterford, Dungarvan & Lismore Railway who had refused them due to late delivery. They had already been offered to both the W&L and the DW&W who were not interested due to weight problems. The Midland made an offer of £1,500 each, later increased to £1,600 which was accepted. Nos 96 to 99 arrived in January 1880. Due to their small boilers and fireboxes, they were initially restricted on the main line, being used mainly for banking at the North Wall. They were heavily rebuilt in 1906-8 with high-pitched boilers similar to that fitted to the 'A' and 'B' classes, but with sloping grates to accommodate the rear axles.

They were extremely powerful as rebuilt, capable of hauling fifty-five wagons on the main line. In 1914, No.99 was chosen as a guinea-pig for trials with the new Cusack-Morton superheater. The header was located in a heating chamber above the firebox, which communicated with the latter by means of a small number of vertical smoke or fire tubes. The entire unit was capable of removal by withdrawing eight bolts. Tests were carried out on the 22.15 down Mullingar goods, and while some economies were shown, the equipment was removed in 1918. She was withdrawn in 1945 as No.622. Her sisters, after being fitted with Robinson superheaters in 1919 were withdrawn in 1949 as GSR Class J6.

Class P. During 1880, the Broadstone turned out four 0-6-0 tanks, Nos 100 to 103, for banking out of the North Wall goods yard. As built, they had 18in x 24in cylinders, 4ft 6in wheels and 14ft 11in wheelbase and heating surface of 1,053 square feet. Known as the 'heavy' tanks, they were one of only two classes of tank engine introduced on the Midland after 1880. The class was rebuilt in 1900-3 with Belpaire boilers, the weight being slightly increased from 43 to 44½ tons. They became GSR Nos 614 to 617 and were fitted with GS 'X' boilers and extended smokeboxes. A further engine, No.105, was added in 1890. One of these engines, No.102, was fitted with armour-plating in 1922 and unofficially named *King Tutankamen*.

Class 7-12. By 1889, it had become necessary to replace the six Avonside 2-4-0s of 1869. They were superseded by six Broadstone built 2-4-0s carrying the same numbers and names as the earlier engines. The boilers were identical to those on the standard goods engines but surprisingly they had iron rather than steel frame plates. The Armagh accident of June 1889 led to the BoT requiring the provision of automatic brakes, with which these engines were fitted.

Class E. In connection with the western extensions, Atock designed a class of 'light tank', so called to distinguish it from the slightly heavier 'P' class already mentioned. As the Broadstone works were already fully engaged with the standards, the order went to Sharp Stewart and Kitsons. In all, twelve of the class were built, three by Sharp Stewart in 1890, six by Kitson in 1891 with a further three coming from the latter firm in 1893. As built, these engines had tall cast-iron chimneys which gave them a rather handsome appearance, being in some respects like the Brighton 'Terriers'. The Sharp engines had 500 gallon tanks against 580 in the Kitsons, both having 1¾ tons coal capacity, their weights varying from 35 tons to 35t 16cwt. They were rebuilt in the period 1911 to 1924 with greater water capacity and a bunker reduced to 1¼ tons capacity. Initially, these engines were used on the newly opened Achill and Clifden branches. After the amalgamation, some found their way onto the former Dublin & South Eastern line's suburban services, while a few were sent to the isolated Waterford & Tramore section to replace that line's ageing singles where they remained until displaced by diesel railcars in the 1950s.

Class K. Whilst the last batch of the standard goods engines was in the course of construction, the Broadstone undertook the renewal of the Neilson and Dübs 2-4-0s of the 1873-6 period. Between 1893 and 1898 a total of twenty engines emerged from the Broadstone, numbered 13 to 24 and 27 to 34. These were Atock's last passenger type. They spent the early part of their lives on the Limited Mails and on the 09.15 down, a very heavy train with Galway, Sligo and Achill portions. This latter train frequently necessitated double-heading with two of the class as far as Mullingar. The introduction of the much larger 'A' class 4-4-0s in 1902 saw their downgrading and their appearance all over the system. In 1918 No.24 received a superheated boiler and 'D' valves, following which she was tested on the Sligo portion of the Limited Mail along with No.16 which had received a new saturated boiler in 1916. These tests showed a fuel saving of almost 20% by the former as a result of which a further eleven were so rebuilt by 1925.

All but one of the class, a Civil War victim, passed to the Great Southern and the first withdrawals did not take place until 1954. They remained on the Sligo and Mayo roads until about 1926 when they were replaced by the 'C' and 'F' classes. Beginning in 1937 they reappeared on the Sligo line and remained on passenger workings until displaced by the diesel railcars in the 1950s. In fact they even made a brief re-appearance on the Galway night mail during the period 1948 to 1950. They were amongst the last remaining 2-4-0 type engines working in the

'L' class 0-6-0 No.56 *Liffey* was built at Broadstone in 1885. The locomotive went through various rebuildings in the course of its long life, including the fitting of a Belpaire boiler in March 1902 and superheating in 1934. As CIE No.595 the engine was withdrawn in December 1957.
The late H Fayle, courtesy IRRS.

world at the time of their withdrawal and were certainly the only superheated engines of this wheel arrangement. The K class were regarded by many as the best engines on the Midland and were a great tribute to Atock.

As already mentioned, Atock retired in 1900 and was replaced by the Chairman's son, Edward Cusack, who had been Atock's assistant since March 1890. Atock is perhaps best remembered for his unusual fly-away cabs, but he was the man who brought some measure of standardisation to the locomotive stock of the Midland. During his tenure, it became the practice to renew engines after twenty years. He could never have anticipated that some of his engines would last to the end of steam in the 1960s.

Cusack and Morton.
The remaining years of the Midland were characterised by the introduction of larger and more powerful engines which left the company with an excellent fleet. Cusack had spent four years as an apprentice at Kitsons followed by two years at Crewe as an improver. It is clear that much of the practical work at the Broadstone was left to the Chief Draughtsman, Walter H Morton, who had also spent time at Kitsons where he became assistant works manager before moving to the MGW in 1900. Cusack resigned in March 1915, and after a period of uncertainty Morton was appointed Locomotive Engineer six months later with D C Urie as his assistant.

Class D-bogie. Though Atock had an aversion to bogies, this class of 4-4-0s was first introduced in March 1900, followed by five more. They were in fact rebuilds of the earlier Beyer-Peacock 2-4-0s although generally referred to as new engines. The drawings for these engines are dated August

1899 so the design must be attributed to Atock. Only one, No.36, had an Atock cab, the remainder having the new square cabs. As built, the class had small cylinders measuring 16in x 22in, and boiler pressure of 150lbs per square inch. They spent most of their working lives west of Mullingar, seldom working through to Dublin and were known as the 'Mayo Bogies'. Further rebuilding took place in 1918/9 when Nos 2 and 3 were superheated, their cylinders being increased to 17in x 24in. Three further engines were rebuilt under the Great Southern.

Class W. While Cusack was settling in, Messrs Kitson approached the company in October 1900 offering to supply two locomotives built for the WL&W and not now required by them following their absorption into the GS&W. They were initially offered at a price of £3,200, a figure declined at first. Nos 141/2 were 0-6-0s designed by J G Robinson of the WL&W and were identical to that company's No.2. They were the first engines on the Midland with Belpaire fireboxes and after the amalgamation were renumbered with the ex-WL&W engines, as Nos 233 and 234.

Class A. Nos 124 to 149 represented a considerable advance on previous Midland standards and they were, at the time of their introduction, the largest 4-4-0s in Ireland. They were specifically built to haul the much accelerated main line express traffic and in particular the Limited Mail for which new bogie rolling stock was constructed. Initially, they were employed only between Dublin and Mullingar, pending the strengthening of the Shannon bridge at Athlone. A notable departure from previous practice was the livery of the new engines – they were painted royal blue, lined yellow with red

Class 7-12, 2-4-0 No.9 *Emerald Isle,* was one of six built in 1889/90 as replacements for the Avonside Mail engines of 1869/70. They had steel boilers and incorporated redesigned motion with four slidebars and, were reported to be very economical in terms of coal consumption. No.9 was withdrawn around 1912.
The late H Fayle, courtesy IRRS.

lines around the funnel rim. Buffers and buffer beams were bright red and there was brass beading around the splashers together with a brass safety valve casing. Between 1916 and 1919, four members of the class were rebuilt with superheaters, piston valves and extended smokeboxes. The first of these was No.124 *Mercuric.* Superheating consisted of a Schmidt 18-element unit. As built, they received new and enlarged 3,000 gallon tenders but difficulties were frequently encountered with hot boxes and when they were rebuilt the decision was taken to couple them to 'C' class tenders, the originals being transferred to the Avonsides. On rebuilding, they also lost their distinctive blue livery, being painted black with red numbers and nameplates.

No.124 was tried out on the Limited Mail against saturated members of the class and also against No.11 which had also been superheated. No.124 acquitted herself well enough to warrant the rebuilding of further members of the class. She was seriously damaged in the malicious Streamstown derailment of February 1923 and was heavily rebuilt in 1924, almost to the point of being a new locomotive with shortened and strengthened frames and a new Morton cab. Nos 126 and 128, were later similarly treated. They were recognisable by the raised footplating over the driving wheels.

Class B. While the 'A' class were in course of construction, tenders were sought for additional goods engines, the contract going to the North British Locomotive Company who agreed to supply four 0-6-0s at £3,445 each less 2.5%, for delivery early in 1904. The boilers and tenders were similar to the 'A' class. They were rebuilt during the war years with larger cylinders, piston valves and superheating, but due to a surplus of goods engines on the Midland section, they had comparatively short lives and all had gone by 1939.

Class C. This was a class of smaller 4-4-0s suitable for express work on all parts of the system. Complete sets of parts were obtained from Kitsons for six engines, a further three being constructed from the older '7-12' class. All working parts were similar to the 'A' class, but they were 8 tons lighter. Two rebuilds occurred, five receiving Robinson superheaters, piston valves and high pitched boilers with extended smokeboxes. The other four, whilst superheated, did not have raised boilers or extended smokeboxes, and retained slide valves. No.10 had Holden oil-burning equipment installed for a short time in 1910-2.

These were the last engines nominally built to Cusack's designs, although plans were drawn up in 1912 for a proposed 'pilot tank' based on the B class goods engine. This would have been an 0-6-2 tank with 19in x 26in cylinders, 4ft 6in wheels and a weight of 65 tons. Water and coal capacity were to be 1,800 gallons and 2½ tons respectively. The outline drawing shows it to have

been similar in appearance to the 'P' class.

The first world war took a heavy toll on locomotive repairs and renewals and in November 1917 Morton presented a report to the board making various recommendations. Mention is made of a 2-6-0 design, five of which were to be built. Nothing further is known of this design and only two references appear in the traffic minutes.

The subject of coal consumption was raised in March 1918 in the context of proposed savings. The General Manager reported that 62,716 tons of coal had been used in 1917, 35,602 on goods and 23,231 tons on passenger trains, the balance on shunting and other duties. A 20% reduction was sought and to give effect to this would involve drastic cuts in passenger services. As it was, consumption had been reduced by 9% compared with 1913. A further report from Morton in 1919 drew attention to the serious state of the locomotive stock. He referred to the average age of the goods engines, little knowing that some of them would be in service for a further 40 odd years.

Class F. Thus in June 1919 we find the board considering tenders for additional engines from Armstrong Whitworth at £10,765 each, Morton strongly urging acceptance as increases in steel prices of 20% were in the offing with the withdrawal of Government subsidies. Five came from Armstrongs and a further eighteen emerged from the Broadstone. These were mixed-traffic 0-6-0s with 5ft 8in wheels, and were superheated with 8in piston valves, the last

nine having raised footplates. As built, they had steam heating apparatus, making them suitable for passenger work which they frequently undertook, although they were known as the 'cattle engines'.

Class D2. The final class was not a Midland design at all. After the war, the Government sought to find peacetime work for the munitions factories and a 2-6-0 design based on Maunsell's locomotives on the South Eastern & Chatham Railway was contracted to Woolwich Arsenal. Morton, with an eye for a bargain, persuaded the board to purchase twelve sets of parts, only one of which was constructed before the amalgamation. The remainder were constructed at the Broadstone under the Great Southern, while a further fifteen sets were assembled at Inchicore. Six of the later GSR engines had 6ft wheels.

The Railmotor. In November 1911 a petrol railcar entered service on the Achill branch. Purchased from Charles Price & Sons of Manchester at a cost of £446, it had a four cylinder, 27hp engine and could be driven from either end. Maximum speed was quoted as 53mph. The body had reversible seats for eleven third class passengers with lockers at either end for luggage and mailbags. It received a new engine in 1914, and

No.99 *Cambria,* as built by Avonside in 1880 for the Waterford, Dungarvan & Lismore Railway which refused delivery. In this form they were underpowered and were rebuilt in 1906/8 with larger boilers.
The late H Fayle, courtesy IRRS.

Walter H Morton, the Last locomotive Superintendent of the MGWR, succeeded Edward Cusack in 1915. Although Cusack was nominally in charge from 1900, there is considerable evidence to suggest that much of the design work was carried out by Morton. Both had served their time at Kitsons, Morton rising to become Assistant Works Manager there. Author's collection.

by 1916 had been relegated to use by the Civil Engineer. It was still at Inchicore in 1935 in Midland livery.

So we come to the end of the Midland locomotive history. At the amalgamation, 140 locomotives were nominally renumbered into Great Southern stock, although a number of these were scrapped fairly quickly and probably never carried their new numbers. All lost their nameplates and the last to retain MGW livery was No.79 *Mayo*.

Nothing is known of the earliest livery, but by 1889 emerald green was being used with black and white lining. Cusack's blue has already been referred to, this being applied to the passenger engines, at which time the tenders were lettered MGWR in small sans-serif gold lettering. Goods engines were unlined blue. This livery was not very serviceable and by 1905 a grass green was being applied. This lasted until 1913 when black became the standard colour.

No.99 as fitted with a Cusack-Morton superheater over the firebox. The design does not appear to have been a success due to leakages past the joints on top of the firebox. The equipment was later fitted to No.53 which was involved in an accident near Moyvalley in 1919. Although no reference is made in the official report, poor steaming may have been a contributory factor in the accident. This photograph was taken around 1916.
The late H Fayle, courtesy IRRS.

The drawing shows how the superheater elements were on top of and connected to the firebox in the Cusack-Morton system. Drawing by Padraig O'Cuimin.

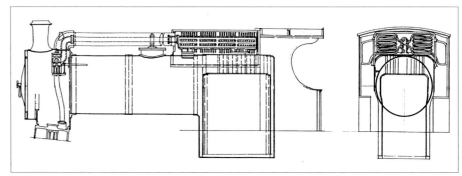

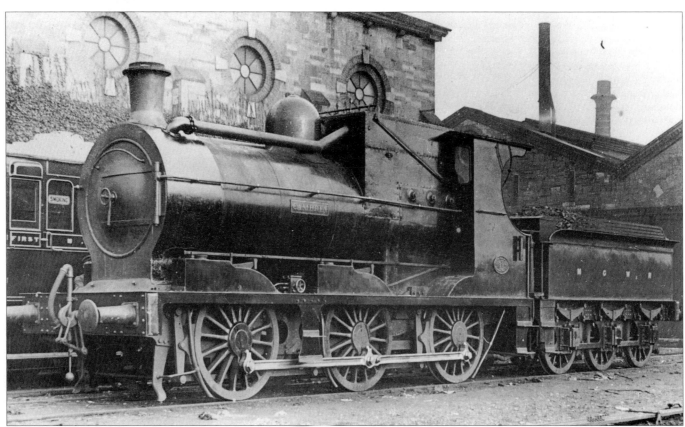

Chapter Fifteen

ROLLING STOCK

THE EARLY HISTORY of the company's rolling stock is vague and largely lacking in details. We are fortunate that a Rolling Stock register giving details of stock from Atock's time onwards is still extant. The earliest reference is an advertisement placed in February 1846 calling on coachbuilders to tender for several first, second and third class carriages along with luggage vans, carriage trucks, horse boxes, goods, cattle and ballast wagons, amounting in all to 100 in number. At least two firms tendered as Hemans was requested to consider Dawson's letter and to name a price for the composite carriages 'according to the scale we are paying Messrs Adams'. In July 1847, Hemans expressed satisfaction with Mr. Fagan's horse boxes, two being ordered at £120 exclusive of varnishing, wheels and springs. These boxes were already manufactured as they were to be delivered within ten days, and an order with Adams was cancelled. Twelve months later the Land & Works Committee recommended that a contract for three luggage vans should go to the Irish Engineering Company.

At the half-yearly shareholders' meeting in March 1849 it was reported that there were 178 carriages and wagons in service, but no details are quoted. About this time, Hemans was authorised to have seats put into eight cattle wagons. These were obviously the fourth class carriages which it was ordered in October were to be attached to each mail train in future. Prior to this, fourth class passengers had to stand or sit on the floor of these wagons. A report in *Saunders Newsletter* for 1st July 1851 shows that not all of these vehicles were fitted with seats. An inquest was held into the death of one Thomas Burke, a reaper coming up to the city in company with about twenty-five 'other persons of the same class' in one of the cattle wagons. The guard of the train deposed that the reapers were in the habit of climbing up on top of the cattle wagons. The deceased had been warned during the Mullingar stop but apparently ignored this as he was struck by an overbridge near Maynooth. The coroner said it would be very desirable if seats were to be placed in such wagons. The company protested that it would be very inconvenient when they might be used next time for the carriage of cattle, necessitating the removal of the seats!

Repairs were carried out during 1849 to a large percentage of the rolling stock as Hemans reported in July on Dawson's account for repairs to 105 carriages, obviously including wagons, amounting to £421.8s.11d, and offering to complete the remainder for £140, both figures being accepted. In December 1849 there had been complaints regarding delays to trains and it was ordered that for the future not more than 12 cattle wagons should be attached to passenger trains unless a special engine was provided. Complaints were also received of insufficient room in the first class compartments. This was addressed by the conversion of a second class carriage, built by another Dublin coachbuilder Hutton, to a composite. Messrs Adams were asked to prepare drawings and estimates for composites to hold 90 and 120 passengers – it is little wonder that there were complaints regarding overcrowding. An interesting item appears in the board minutes in February 1850 when Messrs Wilson & Company's tender for an iron mail train carriage at £470 was approved. Nothing further is known of this vehicle although Mr Bob Clements was of the opinion that it was probably an experiment in metallic coach construction. It remained in service as a coach until July 1869 when Ramage was asked to report on how it could be utilised for traffic and it was decided to convert it into a drover's van.

As we have already seen, a haulage contract was entered into in August 1850 with Messrs Johnson & Kinder and it was decided to order the following additional stock: five firsts at £480, six seconds at £400, six thirds at £300, ten horse boxes at £140, six carriage trucks at £100 and three parcels vans at £290. Two additional composites, two thirds, ten horse boxes and a van were all that were found necessary in connection with the opening of the Galway extension in August 1851.

A good description of the company's first class carriages of this period is given in Sir Francis Head's book entitled A *Fortnight in Ireland,* published in 1852:

'The coupé was so large and so high, that with the greatest ease I could pace from one side to another with my hat on; and then resuming my seat, it was really quite delightful to find myself in a quiet study with large plate glass windows – I began to examine the little chamber in which I was receiving so much placid enjoyment. My attention to it was attracted by an unusual looking object immediately before me, which proved to be a blue cloth covered table, suspended at a convenient level by a pair of small hinges, which enabled one, with the assistance of a small contrivance beneath, to raise and fix it.

I next discovered a sliding door by which the coupé could be divided into two chambers, and on continuing my search, I observed several trifling indications of another hidden luxury, which, on unbuttoning a hasp, proved to my great astonishment, to be two comfortable beds and hair mattresses, in which two couples, closing the intermediate door, might separately sleep as comfortably and as innocently as if they were at home'.

On an earlier journey to Maynooth, Sir Francis travelled second class. The train was painted a rich dark blue, and both the first and second classes had four seats covered with glossy Morocco leather. The carriage roofs were painted white and had two round black iron ventilators about nine inches high. Both classes had linen curtains on the windows, with Venetian shutters above them, painted in two shades of light blue.

In June 1854, Dargan approached the board requesting a loan of one second and three third class carriages for use on the D&W until 1st October, a request which was duly granted. The D&W had ordered a number of coaches in May 1853 but these had proved insufficient, hence the loan from the MGW. By June 1855 the rolling stock returns show a total of ninety-five coaching vehicles comprising eight firsts, thirteen seconds, thirteen composites, twenty-one thirds, one state carriage, sixteen carriage trucks and twenty-three horse boxes. The state carriage had been presented to the company by Dargan and is referred to in more detail later in the chapter. In connection with the opening of the Longford and Cavan branches, it was necessary to order six further composites, six thirds, six brakevans, four carriage trucks and five horse boxes. These were all

4-wheeled, the composites having the second class compartments at each end.

There is little reference to rolling stock during the next ten years, but by the end of this period carriages and wagons were being constructed in the company's own workshops at the Broadstone. By now, the first class had been reduced to three vehicles, partly due to conversion to composites. In September 1868, attention was drawn to a letter from the BoT requiring the provision of smoking compartments on all passenger trains with effect from 1st October. In October, the board ordered that the third class carriages should for the future be painted in a more economical manner, an order which was also to apply to horse boxes and carriage trucks. Apart from the provision of smoking compartments, the BoT were now also talking of requiring a means of communication between the driver and guard. In this context, Price was sent over to York to attend a demonstration, but he was unable to recommend any of the methods tried, and instead suggested that the company could avoid having to so equip their trains if they did not run more than 20 miles without stopping. Further consideration of

Top: **Brake third No.11M was built for branch line use in 1883 at a cost of £446. It seated twenty-four passengers and was in service until March 1954.** D Coakham.

Above: **A number of coaches went through various rebuildings and reclassifications. This one was saloon No.182M, a composite which was originally an all First when built in 1893. The vehicle lasted as late as 1960.** D Coakham.

the matter was postponed until the Railway Clearing House reported their views. Some twelve months later, in January 1871, it was decided to equip one train on an experimental basis.

A dangerous practice was referred to in January 1870 by the BoT, namely the carrying of rails on the footboards of passenger carriages which should be discontinued. The engineer was ordered to desist from the practice and in future, rails were to be carried in the tender Presumably they were carried on the off-side of trains but it is surprising that no accidents resulted from this practice, the new solution being no better. The painting of carriages was again referred to in June when it was decided that it should

be done by contract, with preference being given to men in the company's employment.

In June 1872, Martin Atock was appointed Locomotive Superintendent. He began to introduce new standard types of rolling stock from about 1879 onwards. It became the policy to renew rolling stock at about twenty year intervals and this was to remain the pattern up to 1925. From this time onwards, we can trace the history of the carriage and wagon stock with some degree of certainty due to the existence of a register started in 1890 and which is still extant. Before beginning a description of this stock under the various classes, we will first of all consider factors common to all Atock stock.

The main feature of his designs was that right up until just before his retirement he built 6-wheelers, of which there were three basic underframe lengths – 28ft 11in, 29ft 11in and 30ft 11in, corresponding respectively to 29ft, 30ft and 31ft body lengths, all with a common wheelbase of 20ft, equally divided. In a paper read in January 1891 to the Institute of Civil Engineers in Ireland, Atock explained that he had given a good deal of thought to the ratio of wheelbase to carriage length. Buffing gear was of the long-spindle type, taken to rubber shock absorbers, and up until 1905 side chains were fitted, some 2ft 8in apart and centred on the drawhook. Between 1879 and 1910, all carriages had Mansell wooden block wheels of 3ft 7½in diameter. The bodywork of all the Atock 6-wheelers was 9ft in overall width turning under to 8ft 6in. Roof radius was 12ft and height from rail to roof apex was 11ft 4in. Internal width was 8ft 6in and the height from floor to ceiling was 7ft.

The windows were a distinctive feature of the Atock carriages with the top corners rounded and the bottom ones square. Sizes varied according to class and compartment size. Roof fittings varied as means of lighting were changed, while syphon type ventilators gave way to the torpedo type from about 1890 onwards. The standard oil lamp of J Defries & Sons' design was in use in later years, electric lighting first appearing on an experimental basis in July 1895. Some conversion work was done between that date and the outbreak of war in 1914, the latter interrupting the work. During the civil war, damage caused to stock necessitated the fitting of additional electrical equipment. By July 1923 there remained twenty 6-wheelers still using oil with a further twenty-two wired for electricity but lacking dynamos or batteries. A brief experiment with paraffin lighting was tried out in 1887 but as there is no further mention, it appears to have been a one-off conversion. An interesting point in relation to lighting is that Midland carriages did not have steps for access to the roof, so attention to the roof lamps had to be by means of step ladders.

Prior to 1912 the heating of carriages was by means of footwarmers. In February of that year, Cusack was requested to report on the best method of steam heating with an estimate of the costs involved. This latter was estimated at £35 per coach as against £33 per annum for footwarmers as there were no wages involved, the persons who filled them being engaged in other duties. Authority for the conversion was given in 1913 and seven years later it was discovered that Midland fittings were not compatible with the GN and GS&W carriages. Outside communication cords were in use almost up to the end of the Midland, consideration being given to the use of internal cords as late as 1917 only after difficulties had been encountered in obtaining cords.

The final item of general interest concerns the livery of the coaching stock. In the early days, both blue and green are referred to and reference has been made to the order in 1868 for a more economical style of painting. Ahrons in his *Locomotive and Train Working in the Latter Part of the Nineteenth Century* states the carriages were painted 'brown of a shade not unlike that of the old Great Eastern stock, but the titles and numbering were in very small letters and figures'. Atock as we know had connections with the Great Eastern. On 6th February 1901, it was stated that the proposed new style for painting of carriages had been approved; this was the blue livery introduced for the new Limited Mail stock. The upper panels were white with blue beading, the lower panels and ends being blue; lining was in black and straw. These colours did not weather well and on 21st February 1905 the directors ordered that all passenger carriages and vans were to be repainted brown as they came in for repairs, though excluded from this order were the dining cars, the Royal saloon and the long bogie coaches and their attendant vehicles. About August 1917, a number of carriages were painted in various colours with a view to a further livery change and in October 1918 it was decided to adopt dark lake with vermilion lining. Lettering was painted or transferred on the waist panels in sans-serif with back-shading. Letters and vehicle numbers were 3in high, the carriage classes being printed in full in letters 2½ inches high.

First class carriages.

Excluding those vehicles later reclassified to first class, six separate groups of firsts were introduced between 1879 and 1924, in addition to which three older 4-wheelers built by the Bristol Wagon Company survived until 1893. The first of the new vehicles, numbered 10 to 15 were built at the Broadstone in 1879 with four compartments. Nos 12, 13 and 15 were withdrawn in 1903, the remaining two surviving into CIE days, one as a

Top: **Atock's five compartment design, of which No.40M was one, was probably the best known of the Midland 6-wheelers. Atock windows were distinctive with curved corners at the top and square ones at the bottom. The suffix M was added to the numbers of the ex MGWR stock by the GSR to indicate its origin. CIE continued to use the M suffix.** D Coakham.

Above: **This Cusack designed 6-wheeled four compartment first with two lavatories, was built at Broadstone in 1906 at a cost of £600. The roof profile of Cusack's vehicles was quite distinctive.** D Coakham.

parcels van, the other as the Sligo accident van. The second batch were virtually identical, coming out of the Broadstone between 1880 and 1889. In 1893, the earliest lavatory firsts appeared, having only three compartments and a coupé, the latter with large end windows. The two lavatory compartments were in the centre of the coach, the end compartments not having access to them; seating was reduced from 32 to 26. There were eight of these vehicles, three from Broadstone, the remainder from Ashbury. Three of them were Civil War victims, the

remainder surviving into CIE days. Only three more 6-wheelers were built, No.20 of 1905 being a 30ft vehicle, while Nos. 11 and 14 dating from 1906, were 31ft long. They had the new Cusack roof contour matching the bogie stock. No.20 had four compartments with 32 seats and weighed 14½ tons, while the other two were 26 seaters with two lavatories, access to which was available from all four compartments.

As the new Limited Mail bogie stock will be dealt with separately there only remains one further first class type to be mentioned, the two bogie vehicles numbered 35 and 36 introduced in 1914. These were 54ft, seven compartment, side corridor vehicles with a seating capacity of 56 and a tare weight of nearly 28½ tons. Again, they had the Cusack roof, but interestingly had Atock style windows. Following on the abolition of second class in 1914, a further seventeen vehicles were upgraded to firsts, a situation which resulted in a surplus of first class seats.

Second class.

Three Bristol-built 4-wheeled seconds from 1873 survived until 1892, to be replaced by Broadstone built 6-wheelers. All second

Top: **Cusack bogie second No.26 was built in 1902 for the Limited Mail set by the Lancaster Carriage & Wagon Company at a cost of £1,880. As built, accommodation was provided in two compartments and a saloon. The coach had two lavatories. It was converted to a first, seating 46 passengers and renumbered 33 in April 1914. It was finally withdrawn in 1955/56.** IRRS collection.

Centre: **Corridor bogie coach No.163M was photographed in CIE livery. Built in 1903 as a composite it was converted to an all-first class vehicle in 1930. Latterly used as an ambulance coach to convey the infirm to Claremorris, the railhead for the pilgrimage traffic to the religious shrine at Knock, No.163M was withdrawn in 1961.** Courtesy John Kennedy.

Bottom: **Van No.59M was built for the Limited Mail Set in 1903. There were two double doors and lookouts on either side. No side windows were provided except for the droplights in the doors.** R N Clements.

class stock introduced after 1879 was 6-wheeled with the exception of the Limited Mail stock, and were 30ft in length. The first of the Atock vehicles, a batch of five built at Broadstone in 1880, apparently had five compartments, the centre one being for luggage. Three of these were replaced in 1903, the remaining two becoming thirds in 1914. Nos 6 and 7 of 1884 and 9 to 14 of 1890 seated 40 passengers in four compartments, again with a centre luggage compartment. Nos 9 and 12 had this latter compartment replaced by two lavatories in 1906, access being restricted to the adjoining compartments only. These became firsts in 1914, the remainder being downgraded to thirds; all but two of these subsequently received lavatories with seating increased to 48. The first of the new lavatory seconds, a 38-seater, appeared from the Broadstone in 1892, becoming firsts in 1914. Finally, five coaches to the same design were built by Ashbury in 1894 for the western extensions. One compartment was reserved for ladies, and one for smokers. These also became firsts in 1914.

Third class.
The first of the 6-wheeled thirds did not appear until 1881 and in the interim a number of 4-wheelers were introduced. A total of twenty such had been introduced by Ramage between 1864 and 1869, all of which survived to be replaced between 1890 and 1892; little is known about them except that they had five compartments. A further forty-four were introduced by Atock with the design of the bodywork being similar to the later 6-wheelers, but they differed from the Ramage coaches in having two compartments with longitudinal seating. The majority were replaced between 1893 and 1901, although one was rebuilt in 1906 as a composite saloon for the Paymaster while another was converted to Mortuary van No.58. Older than any of these were the 6-wheelers, Nos 67 and 68, built by Joseph Wright & Sons in 1862 for the opening of the D&M. They were 28ft in length on a 14ft 6in wheelbase, with wheels of 3ft 3in diameter and five compartments. Both were withdrawn in 1890.

The first of the Atock 6-wheelers appeared in 1881 and had six compartments on a 31ft body, a layout which proved to be rather cramped, although there were seventy-three similar vehicles on the GS&W. Various conversions were carried out on the Midland vehicles, some to brake thirds, others had lavatories fitted, while two more became sleeping carriages for the permanent way department. The year 1890 saw the introduction of what undoubtedly were the best known of the Midland 6-wheelers, the five compartment thirds, a total of seventy-seven such vehicles being built at the Broadstone.

They were 30ft long, weighed 12tons 11cwt and had seating for 60 passengers. All had a half-back between two of the compartments at one end, and one 'Ladies Only' compartment, the latter no doubt a concession to the BoT's wishes. Thirteen of these were victims of the civil war. No less than sixty of them came into GSR stock and the last of them was not finally withdrawn until 1961. At least one of them was rebuilt with two lavatories and upholstered seats were provided from 1914 onwards. Prior to that, third class seats comprised no more than a flush-finished bench contoured to support the back.

Apart from the Limited Mail stock, there were two more groups of thirds, both bogie types. In 1916, two vehicles were outshopped, Nos 108 and 109, quite different in appearance and layout. No.108 had originally been dining car No.3 built in 1904 and was rebuilt with a centre corridor to accommodate 78 in two inter-connected saloons. One source states that she was first converted in April 1915 with a seating capacity of 64, the seating being later altered to reversible tramway type, increasing capacity to 78. There were two doors on each side of the coach which was fitted with vestibule connections. Unlike the other two diners which had clerestory roofs, No.3 had a high roof with domed ends. It was in later years used as a concert car in excursion trains and was destroyed in a fire at Athlone on 8th July 1942. At the time of rebuilding, the 6-wheeled bogies were transferred to the Royal saloon in replacement for the latter's four wheel bogies which went under No.108. No.109 was a side corridor vehicle with eight compartments and two lavatories and was the last 54ft vehicle built; seating capacity was 80. Vestibuled, she had round-top windows on the corridor side reminiscent of the Atock era, while the compartment side had a door and two windows to each compartment. There were four doors on the corridor side.

Finally in 1923, three 60ft bogie coaches on Belgian underframes came out of the Broadstone. They had a high elliptical roof and were wider than other coaches at 9ft 6in. Side corridor vestibuled vehicles, they had nine compartments seating ninety passengers plus a lavatory at each end. On the compartment side were nine doors, four on the corridor side.

Composites.
The oldest vehicle on the composite list in 1890 was the 6-wheeled saloon built by Dawson in 1847 at a cost of £579. Little is known of this vehicle in its original condition except that it had three compartments in a 25ft body. It was rebuilt in 1891 as a 4-wheeled inspection saloon, probably the directors' saloon. Next was No.10 built at the Broadstone in 1866, a note in the regis-

ter stating it was 'all of mahogany'. So to 1879 when two family saloon coaches were built by Metropolitan at a cost of £1,347. Nos.29 and 30 had a first class saloon in the centre, furnished with couches and armchairs upholstered in maroon velvet with woodwork of Moulmein teak. The walls and ceilings were panelled with sycamore bordered with tulip wood. One of these saloons was used by the Empress of Austria during her Irish visits. At one end was a retiring room and a spacious compartment for the family luggage, while at the other end was a small second class compartment for the family servants. The saloon had large windows.

A letter in the *Roscommon Journal* for 12th September 1879 from the MGW's Traffic Manager, Mr Ward, drew attention to an advertisement regarding 'our new family carriages which ought to be convenient to the gentry and are available on application'. Fares equivalent in amount to not less than four first and two second class single tickets were charged; when more than seven first class tickets were taken, servants were allowed to travel second class at third class rates. In 1914 they were re-numbered 37 and 38, the former remaining in service until 1953 when it became service vehicle 309A. No.38 was destroyed in the Athlone fire in 1942.

Between 1872 and 1886, the number of composites had gradually been reduced from fifty-one to thirty. To compensate for this reduction, thirty-seven new coaches were introduced between 1885 and 1887, eight from the Midland Carriage & Wagon Company, the remainder from the Broadstone. They had four compartments, two firsts in the middle and two seconds. Body length was 29ft, tare weight 14 tons 1cwt 3qtr, and accommodation was for 16 first and 20 second class passengers. On the abolition of second class, they became first and third class. The first bogie coaches on the Midland were the four tricomposites designed in 1897 by Atock and introduced in 1900. Built by Metropolitan at a cost of £1,550 each, they had the Atock windows but the roof was higher and rounded at the sides. They were 53ft long, 9ft wide and had two compartments of each class arranged symmetrically about a central luggage compartment. The Limited Mail sets did not have composites built for them, although three more were built in 1903-4. Nos 44 to 46 were seven compartment, side corridor vehicles on 54ft underframes, weighing 28 tons. Two lavatories were fitted at the ends and they had 24 first and 32 second class seats. There were four doors on the corridor side, seven on the compartment side. They became all-first in 1914, with 56 seats, and reverted to composites in 1930-1.

Finally in 1924, four 60ft coaches were built on Belgian underframes with three first (18 seats) and five third class (50 seats) com-

Above: **Bogie third No.108 was formerly diner No.3. As built, she was fitted with 6-wheeled bogies which were later transferred to the Royal Saloon. The coach was destroyed by fire at Athlone in July 1942.** Courtesy John Kennedy.

Left: **The Royal Saloon of 1903 and probably the most luxurious vehicle to run on an Irish Railway. Extensive use was made of exotic and expensive woods and it boasted such refinements as electric bells and cigar lighters. It is to be regretted that this magnificent vehicle was not preserved.** Courtesy CIE.

partments. Once again, they were vestibuled, side corridor coaches with a tare weight of 33 tons. These coaches appeared from the Broadstone in December 1924 right at the end of the Midland era, and a further five in various stages of completion were turned out by the GSR as 46M to 50M, although with inferior GSR third class seating. Before leaving the composites, mention should be made of the Midland's two slip coaches. In April 1903, the board considered a proposal from Cusack that two composites should be suitably altered as slip carriages to run on the Limited Mails for the convenience of passengers for Edenderry. This was approved and one vehicle was put into service in that year, with a second in 1908. Nos 35 and 36 were rebuilds of 1886 coaches and had three compartments and a van accommodating 8

first and 24 second class passengers. The Enfield slip was to remain a feature of the Midland timetable up to the end. Additionally, for at least one season, a slip was made for the Cavan branch, at Inny Junction.

Limited Mail stock.
A decision was taken in September 1900 to modernise the Limited Mail service, as the result of which Cusack was requested to prepare drawings and specifications for two first, second and third class carriages and two brake vans. Consideration was postponed on the question of a dining car. Tenders were considered at the board meeting on 8th May 1901, the contract being awarded to the Lancaster Carriage & Wagon Company at £15,060 for two trains to be ready by 1st May 1902. By January 1902 how-

ever, it was obvious that deliveries would be late, due to the Leeds Forge Company not having delivered the bogies. The reason put forward was that delays had been incurred due to the commandeering of the works by the War Department for war provisions for South Africa. A nominal penalty of £10 per vehicle was suggested, with the company finally agreeing to a total of £124.

An account was rendered in August but consideration was postponed pending a resolution of the penalty for late delivery. The makers issued a writ in September for recovery of the balance of the monies due following payment of £12,189.11s.1d, but it was not until January 1903 that agreement was reached. The Lancaster vehicles were delivered in July 1902 while two thirds were built at the Broadstone in 1901 followed by two more in 1902. The first class had a 28ft centre saloon with a 7ft compartment at each end, one for ladies and one for smokers; total seating capacity was only 26. Numbered 26 and 27, the former received a clerestory roof in 1918 and became a composite in 1934 with 46 seats. No.27 was converted to all-third 193M in 1955 and was withdrawn in 1960/61. No.26 was similarly converted in 1954 as 196M. The second class were identical in layout with 30 seats in the saloon and eight in each end compartment. They became firsts Nos 33 and 34 in

1914 and remained in service until 1956 and 1960 respectively. The thirds were 79 and 83 (1901) and 94 and 95 (1902) and had eight compartments and two lavatories; there were one ladies and two smoking compartments. Finally, the brake vans 59 and 60 had two double doors on each side with side lookouts, but no side windows apart from the droplights in the doors; vestibules were fitted in 1924.

Dining cars and state carriages.

Diners 1 and 2 constructed for the Limited Mail were 54ft vehicles on two 6-wheeled bogies with accommodation for 12 first and 12 second class passengers. The initial cost was £2,220 each. The kitchens occupied the centre of the cars and were full width, with first class on one side and second on the other with no intercommunication. Cooking was done on coal ranges, lighting was electric and both had full steam heating. They had clerestory roofs, weighed 37 tons and as built had large fixed windows with an early form of air conditioning by means of electric fans. This was not a success and they later acquired small opening lights over the main windows which still did not entirely solve the ventilation problem. Later alterations included conversion to first and third class in April 1914. In 1926, the seats were removed from No.2 and replaced by GSR style armchairs. No.1 was maliciously damaged at Streamstown on 17th February 1923 and in 1946 had a corridor included around the kitchen, while both were converted to gas cooking in June 1949.

Diner No.3 was something of a mystery vehicle. Built at the Broadstone in 1904 at a cost of £2,250, she was also 54ft long, ran on 6-wheeled bogies and accommodated 24 passengers. She apparently differed considerably from other Midland vehicles but no diagram and few photographs exist of her in original condition. The roof contour was nearly elliptical and there were doors at the end and in the middle, windows having ventilators, no doubt intended as a remedy for the poor ventilation in the earlier vehicles. The kitchen was probably in the middle. In April 1915, No.3 was converted to third class coach No.108, at which time her bogies were given to the Royal Saloon.

Until 1904 the role of State carriage was undertaken by the 6-wheeled vehicle known as the Dargan Saloon. Originally built for William Dargan in 1847 by Dawson of Phibsborough in Dublin, it was presented to the Midland on completion of the Galway contract in 1851. Tatlow in his autobiography briefly described it as follows - 'the panels were modelled on the old stage coach design with a great bow window adorning each end. In the 70s and 80s it enjoyed the distinction of being the favourite coach on the MGWR of the Empress of Austria in her hunting days in Meath'. One source refers to a new underframe being fitted in 1886 when it received vacuum brakes and was re-upholstered by Fay & Company.

Obviously mindful of the Dargan saloon's age, consideration was given at the board meeting of 31st December 1902 to the provision of a carriage for the use of the Lord Lieutenant on his periodic visits to Rockingham and indeed the King should he choose to travel over the Midland. The design was approved and work commenced at the Broadstone on 19th February 1903, being completed on 29th June. Messrs Millar & Beatty's tender for panelling and interior decoration at £465 was approved. Built on a 54ft underframe, she had 4-wheel bogies and was undoubtedly the most luxurious and comfortable vehicle ever to run on the Midland, if not on the entire Irish rail system. It consisted of a 6ft 6in long observation saloon and smoking room at one end, opening on to the main saloon 18ft 11in long; additionally it had a dining room, kitchen and dressing room. The main hall had double entrance doors and was handsomely panelled in wainscot oak in polished teak framing with a parquet floor. The main reception saloon was panelled in satinwood, again with teak framing and with pencilled cedar mouldings. From the floor and between each window and at the doors were fluted cedar Corinthian columns with curved satinwood capitals supporting heavy cornices. It was furnished with a specially woven Donegal carpet, and had numerous settees and armchairs, finished in sage green

brocade. The dining area had two round dining tables with curved oak dining chairs finished in green leather. The kitchen, the end of which had a vestibule connection, was very well appointed. The coach was electrically lit and sported such refinements as electric bells from all rooms to the kitchen and electric cigar lighters in the smoking room.

As built, it was painted Royal blue with white panels above the centre line, the whole picked out in gold lining with the company's crest and the Royal coat of arms. When diner No.3 was rebuilt in 1915, her 6-wheel bogies were put under the saloon. She was repainted dark lake in 1924 and green in CIE days, becoming No.346 under the GSR.

TPO vans.

The first of these vehicles were combined luggage, brake and post office vans, four of which were ordered from Bristol in June 1872, plus two more in October of the following year. These were three compartment 6-wheelers. All were withdrawn in 1900 when they were replaced by Broadstone built vehicles. Four more generally similar vans were added to stock in 1885 from Brown Marshall. The new mail contract of 1886 required the company to provide special Post Office vehicles and four such vans were built at the Broadstone, two in 1887 and two in 1888. They were 30ft long without brake compartments. Complaints reached the board in January 1889 of damage to doors and the net apparatus of the new vans caused by the neglect or carelessness of the Post Office officials in not lowering and taking up the apparatus at the proper time.

Two of the 1900 batch of vans were maliciously destroyed, No.2 at Streamstown and No.28 at Achill on 12th January 1923. In 1908, the secretary of the G.P.O. wrote requesting that the TPOs on the Mullingar to

TPO No.27M, built at Broadstone in May 1909 at a cost of £350 in replacement for an earlier vehicle of 1885. Lavatory fitted at the request of the postal authorities in July 1944, it was reported out of stock in 1957/8. H Richards collection.

Sligo service be lighted. In June 1923, when consideration was being given to the replacement of maliciously damaged vehicles, it was decided to build a bogie Post Office van on the understanding that the night mail would be reinstated. The new van had a 41ft sorting compartment and entered service in 1925; in GSR livery. It had the distinction to be the last new coaching vehicle turned out of the Broadstone.

Brake vans.
Excluding those vehicles which provided postal accommodation, a batch of eighteen vans with two third class compartments was introduced between 1887 and 1890, built on the standard 29ft 11in underframe and having raised lookouts on the roof. A basically similar class appeared between 1888 and 1890 but without passenger accommodation. Cusack introduced more in 1907-10, one of which was fitted with a pantry in 1914 for serving teas, necessitating the fitting of gangways. Ten more vans were built in 1924. Included under the heading of brake vans were two conversions of earlier 4-wheeled thirds to mortuary vans in 1893 and 1896. These became Nos 56M and 58M in GSR days when they were used as fish vans.

Other coaching stock.
Included under the heading of coaching stock were horse-boxes, carriage trucks, fish vans and the one-off motor car van. The Midland horse box was a distinctive type of vehicle with its sloping dog box at one end. Numbers reached fifty-six by 1891 and remained so until December 1892 when there were sixty in traffic, a figure which was to remain unaltered until 1923 when one was destroyed at Streamstown. Twelve boxes were ordered from Metropolitan at £169 each in November 1870. A Metro drawing of 1871 shows them to have had a groom's compartment at one end. Their length was 15ft on a 9ft wheelbase. The remainder were built at the Broadstone, the 1889 version having three compartments, a groom's compartment, a three-stall box and the dog box. The groom's accommodation was rather primitive, having only a bench seat with no back support or artificial lighting. The final version appeared in 1906, the characteristic dog box replaced by a full height harness room with standard door and droplight.

Carriage truck numbers rose from sixteen in 1852 through twenty-two in 1872 to twenty-four by 1897, all from 1868 onwards being built at the Broadstone. Some of these vehicles remained in service until the 1950s. In 1873, six 'meat and fish' vans were ordered from Metropolitan at £200.10s.0d each, delivery being made in the following year. They had outside framed bodies with horizontal sheeting and double roofs; double centre doors were provided with horizontal louvres on all sides. Ten more followed in 1877 and four in 1878. Finally under this classification, ten came from the Midland Railway Carriage & Wagon Company in 1883. The carriage register shows all thirty to have been renewed as cattle boxes between 1894 and 1898. Under the latter heading, fifty-five vehicles are listed in 1898; in December of that year this number reduced to forty-nine with six fish vans, a process which continued until June 1899 when the numbers were totally reversed. The motor car van was a conversion of a six-compartment carriage. Photographs show it to have been a straight sided vehicle with Atock style windows. It was maliciously destroyed at Kingsbridge in 1921, rebuilt and then destroyed again at Streamstown in 1923, but survived to become parcels van No.63M in 1929.

An Officers' Conference minute of 20th March 1923 lists a total of forty-five coaching vehicles destroyed in the Civil War, namely one bogie first, four 6-wheel firsts, three

Top left: **Wagon No.937 built in 1906 and broken up in 1935 had a capacity of 7 tons.** Author's collection.

Left: **Horse box No.55M in GSR livery. The Midland horse box with its dog box at one end was a very distinctive vehicle. The groom's compartment had very little in the way of comfort.** IRRS collection.

Above: **12 ton locomotive coal wagon No.1704 was built at Broadstone in 1913.** Author's collection.

Above right: **20 ton brake van No.21 was built in October 1924 at a cost of £600 specially for the North Wall to Broadstone coal trains as indicated by the plate in the bottom left hand corner. It was broken up at Mullingar in 1954-5.** IRRS collection.

Right: **No.1229 was a 7 ton 3-plank locomotive coal wagon with a single brake; one of twenty built at Broadstone in 1881 at a cost of £65 each. It was scrapped at Cork on 21st August 1955. To its right is another coal wagon, similar to No.1704 above, while the left hand wagon is of GS&W origin.** W H Butler collection.

composites, sixteen thirds, eleven passenger brake vans, a horse box, seven fish vans, a carriage truck and a post office van. It was recommended that the twenty-three 6-wheel passenger coaches be replaced by twelve bogie coaches.

Wagon stock.

As with the coaching stock, few details have survived of the early Midland goods stock. Various firms are mentioned in the early days in connection with wagon construction for the company, including at least three Irish firms – Messrs Dawson, Fagan and the Irish Engineering Company. The company built wagons at the Broadstone during the 1860s with the former goods store being converted to a wagon shop in 1870. Following Atock's appointment, he reported to the board recommending that wagon renewal be increased to 100 per year. As with the coaching stock, there were features common to all goods stock which resulted in a typical 'Midland' vehicle. All wagons built between 1872 and 1921 were 6ft 9in wide between solebars. Wheels had eight spokes and a 3ft 3in diameter. Body sheeting consisted of 1in tongued and grooved timber with planks 6½in wide. Grease axle boxes were fitted up to 1914 after which they began to be superseded by

oil boxes. Until 1885, brake gear consisted of a single wooden block operated by a lever. Between 1885 and 1906, two cast-iron blocks were used on a single pair of wheels, but following a BoT directive a change was made to either-side brakes.

Standard covered goods wagons.

Numerically these were the largest class of wagon throughout the period under review, with 972 in service in 1872, rising to over 1,700 in 1914. Rated at 7 tons capacity, they were used for both goods and cattle traffic, due in no small measure to an insufficiency of cattle wagons. The initial batch was ordered from Metropolitan in 1872 to a drawing dated 23rd February 1872. In 1893, a slightly larger version was brought out, while in 1912 the decision was taken to renew all open cattle wagons as covered goods vehicles and some further design alterations are evident at this time. A diagonal brace was incorporated from the horizontal to the top of the door pillar.

Cattle wagons.

These fall under two headings, open and covered, the latter first introduced in 1899. Cattle wagons built in 1885 were similar in design to the 1872 series of covered wagons, some minor design improvements being

incorporated in a batch of 100 from the Ashbury Carriage & Wagon Company in 1890 and a further 100 from the Birmingham Carriage & Wagon Company in the following year.

Drawings were prepared in 1898 for a covered cattle wagon, thirty being supplied by Metropolitan in 1899. As delivered, they were piped, later being fitted with full vacuum gear. By 1912, there were 430 covered cattle wagons in stock.

Open box wagons.

Includes traffic and locomotive coal wagons. Fifty of 8 tons capacity came from Metropolitan in 1876 followed by twenty more 3-plank wagons with a single brake, built at the Broadstone in 1881. A further eighty for locomotive coal were introduced between 1882 and 1888. In the following year a new drawing was prepared incorporating alterations including double brakes. In 1907, a new 4-plank wagon of 10 tons capacity was designed, the top plank being continuous with a 3-plank cupboard type door below on each side. Five years later, a 12 ton design was introduced, still with a 4-plank body, but with higher sides and curved ends and full door. The last Midland design was on a 16ft 11in underframe to the new Irish standard specification, capacity being 10 tons.

Hopper wagons.

Used for the transport of locomotive coal and permanent way materials, twenty were delivered from Metropolitan in 1873 of 10 tons capacity. They were of wooden construction with sheet-iron lining to the hopper and doors. In 1905, twenty-four hoppers of 12 tons capacity came from the Leeds Forge Company for the use of the PW Department with a further twenty-four being delivered in 1910. Ten of the former and five of the latter were sold to the D&SER in 1922 for £4,131.16s.6d, the price including a plough van. In March 1922 seventeen 20 ton wagons of Belgian manufacture were purchased for £3,900. They were bilateral discharge wagons apparently originally built for the Norte Railway in Spain. Two of them were unusual in having the typical continental arrangement of a brakeman's shelter at one end. Two more, for the PW Department were purchased in 1923.

Butter, creosote and timber wagons.

The remaining goods stock, excluding brake vans will be considered under this heading. Butter wagons were first introduced in 1901 when four were built at the Broadstone followed by six more the following year. A traffic minute of 2nd May 1905 confirmed that four of these wagons were to be fitted with ice refrigeration for that season's traffic from Limerick. The basic underframe was similar to the standard covered wagon, the body being double sheeted with louvre vents all round at floor and roof level for ventilation; they were piped for running in passenger trains.

In 1915 a new design of covered goods wagon was introduced for Guinness traffic.

These were 16ft 8in long on a 9ft 6in wheelbase. Also in 1915, two tank wagons 18ft long and of 12 tons capacity were built by Charles Roberts of Wakefield for creosote traffic, replacing two earlier such vehicles. As early as 1854, consideration was being given to the carriage of ammunition. In May of that year, Wilson reported that he could not satisfactorily alter two existing wagons and two new ones were ordered. To replace these wagons, Nos.179 and 405 were built respectively in 1898 and 1899. They had outside sheeting of 12swg steel plate, the joins being covered by 2in mild steel plates while the interior was lined with 1in sheeting, the floor with 6lb lead sheet as were the walls to a height of 1ft 10½inch. Timber trucks were built from 1873 onwards, being twin wagons normally used in pairs for the carriage of round timbers and other long loads.

During the period 1872 to 1924, six boiler and furniture vans entered service, two from Ashbury in 1877 of 7 tons capacity, two more to the same design in 1892 but 6in longer at 20ft 6in. Finally in 1908 a 20 ton low loader was introduced. No.3003 cost £229.9s.0d, had an all steel body and underframe on six wheels. Twelve heavy wagons remain to be mentioned, the 35 ton bogie well wagon and the eleven 40 ton bogie rail wagons. The former, No.3409, acquired in 1924, was a

This locomotive coal wagon, one of seventeen 20 ton vehicles purchased in March 1922. Of Belgian manufacture, they were originally intended for the Norte Railway in Spain. Two of them had the a typically continental brakeman's shelter at one end. IRRS collection.

Belgian-built vehicle, 60ft 6in long, and 9ft 6in wide, running on two 4-wheel bogies at 49ft centres. The four bogie rail wagons obtained in 1921 at a cost of £11,000, were numbered 1106 to 1109, and were most likely war surplus. The others, Nos 3401 to 3407, came from Metropolitan and formed part of the relaying train.

Goods brake vans.

These were numbered in their own list, but included ballast vans, plough and Locomotive Department sleeping vans. Eight vans were built in the works in 1874 which included a birdcage lookout in the guard's compartment, next to which was a passenger or drover's compartment. There was a veranda at the rear. They were rated at 8 tons, later increased to 11 tons. A new design emerged for the western extensions in 1892. Nos 50 to 55 had two passenger and one luggage compartment. They had no veranda but did have a birdcage. The passenger compartments were at the ends with the guard in the middle. In 1912, two 20 ton 6-wheel vans, with steel underframes appeared. In the last year of the company's independent existence, a redesigned 4-wheeled van appeared with two verandas, no birdcage or ducket, but with one welcome refinement – a stove. Six of the twenty-four were completed by the Midland, the remainder by the GSR.

Finally there were the incline vans specially built for the Liffey, Westport Quay and Sligo Quay lines. Two were introduced in 1873 followed by one in 1875 and two more in 1877. There were four ballast and four separate ballast plough vans. As regards the sleeping vans, there were three in all, No.47 of 1876, No.49 of 1890 and a new No.47 in 1909, when the original was broken up.

Bretland tracklayer.

The years of neglect from 1914 onwards saw the permanent way in dire need of replacement. The methods then in use were no longer practicable, partially due to the large increase in wages, and so the Chief Engineer, Arthur Bretland, turned his attentions to the design of a mechanical tracklaying system. The basis of the design was the prior assembly of new track in lengths and their transport to the relaying site where the old lengths would be lifted out complete, to be returned to the central depot for dismantling.

Mullingar was chosen as the location for the central prefabrication of track lengths, a portion of the extensive storage sidings being allocated for this purpose. An overhead 65ft span gantry was erected with a total travelling length of 500ft, enabling long trains of flats to be handled. Electricity was the motive power and in full operation the plant could unload 240 tons of rails or 1,500

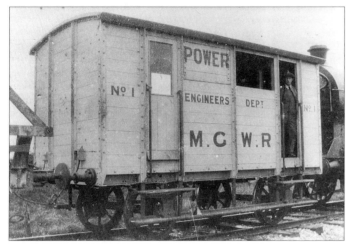

Top: **The Bretland tracklayer train in action. It could handle 900 yards of track in an 8 hour shift. The train consisted of a locomotive, power van, a series of flat bogie trucks, the crane and associated runner trucks under the cantilever, plus brake van. Its main drawback was that it could not deal with staggered rail joints.** Courtesy John Kennedy.

Above left: **Power van No.1 was an integral part of the tracklaying train. Steam was supplied by means of a special take-off from the engine which thus had to be modified to work with the train. The van provided electric current at 100 volts, thus enabling work to be carried out at night.** Courtesy John Kennedy.

Above right: **The site of the Bretland track fabrication plant was at Mullingar. These sidings were in later years used for the storage and scrapping of locomotives and rolling stock. In more recent times the area has been cleaned up and is now in use for the dismantling of track panels from the Sligo line.** The late J P O'Dea, courtesy of the National Library of Ireland.

sleepers per hour. A new mechanical track-laying train was constructed, central to which was the relaying crane supported on two bogies, one 4-wheeled and one 6-wheeled, the latter under the main load. The centre of the crane was in the form of a portal to the dimensions of the loading gauge through which the truck complete with sleepers could pass.

To the rear of the crane were the bogie wagons on which ran the conveyor, an inverted U-shaped structure. The conveyor could propel itself along tracks on the wagons by means of a motor, another motor hoisting the lengths of track. The locomotive which accompanied the relaying train had a special take-off from the dome to supply steam to the train's power van, which in turn supplied electricity for powering the electric motors and lighting for night time use. Sad to relate, the tracklayer was to see very limited service following the amalgamation, apart from the singling of the Midland. It was said to have been unsuitable for dealing with staggered rail joints which predominated on the GS&W. The relaying crane ended its days as the chassis for wagon No.3408. A variation to the design was used on the London & North Eastern Railway.

Breakdown cranes.
Two 10 ton travelling cranes were purchased in 1861 for £320 each from Messrs Bray & Waddington. No.2 was rebuilt in 1902, No.1 in 1908. The latter was broken up in October 1924, the scrapping date for No.2 is unknown. In July 1896, Cowan & Sheldon tendered for a 15 ton accident steam crane at £800. The boiler was 4ft 5in diameter, stood 7ft 3in high and drove two 8in x 14in cylinders. The crane, No.133A, ended its career on the Bandon section based at Rocksavage, unsuccessful attempts having been made to sell it in June 1923 when an advertisement appeared in the *Irish Times*. It was involved in a derailment on the Sligo line in November 1909, reportedly due to insufficient brakes.

In 1923, two new 20 ton cranes were supplied by Cowan & Sheldon. These had makers' numbers 4111 and 4112 and were part of a production run of four built to a Ministry of Munitions order dated 17th November 1919. The maker's drawing shows them to have been built to a gauge of 5ft, a probable indication that they were intended for Russia. The disposal of the other two is unknown. The boilers, of the cross-tube type, were 4ft 3in diameter, and 6ft 3in high with a pressure of 100 lb/in² driving two 8in x 12in cylinders. Overall length was 26ft 10in with a 16ft wheelbase. Lifting capacity was 20 tons at 19ft and 10 tons at 33ft radius.

Livery.
The standard wagon livery was a dark slate grey, with locomotive and traffic department coal wagons being black. Permanent way vehicles were sand-beige while passenger train wagons and brake vans were brown.

Chapter Sixteen

THE COURSE OF THE LINE

Bearing in mind that the company operated a route mileage of 538 miles it will not be possible to provide a very detailed description of every feature of the system. The first part of the chapter will outline the facilities provided at various locations, the remainder dealing in brief with such aspects as permanent way, bridges and signalling. Distances quoted are in miles and chains as used by the MGWR. The present tense has been used to describe the features on lines and facilities currently open, the past tense for those now closed. Station closure dates can be found in Appendix B.

For the opening of the line there was probably little more than the platforms at the Broadstone. Later in the year the 475ft long and 120ft wide two-span roof, was erected over the two platforms and the four carriage roads. At the time of its erection, it was regarded as one of the wonders of Dublin and it is said to have been copied, albeit on a larger scale, for the roof of Lime Street station in Liverpool. The main building was completed in 1850 to the design of the company's architect, J S Mulvany. Dr Maurice Craig regarded it as a superior building to Kingsbridge and went on to say 'its lonely grandeur is emphasised now by its disuse as a terminus and the melancholy quarter of high and dry hotels beside it'.

An Ordnance Survey map of 1847 indicates that there was a four road carriage shed behind the up platform and entered by means of two small turntables at the outer end. A siding connected Dawson's Railway Carriage factory, which was later purchased by the company and incorporated into the works as it expanded. On the down side opposite to the centre of the platforms was a ten-road roundhouse. The carriage shed was partly converted into a goods shed in 1850 and was completely given over to goods by 1864 when the next O.S. map was prepared. Also by this date the roundhouse had been reduced to a semicircle with a second, larger, turntable between it and the station buildings. A new roundhouse and engine shed were provided in 1873, these being the buildings remaining to the end of steam. The distinctive clock tower was erected in 1874.

Following on the closure and filling in of the canal basin, the site was occupied as permanent way and wagon shops together with a sawmill. This latter was dispensed with when a mill was erected at Liffey Junction. Working out from the main building, the others were occupied in later years as follows: a small building at right angles was occupied as a parcels office; the carriage shop was separated from a larger building divided in three – at the front was the carriage paint shop, behind which were the boiler shop and smithy. This block was in turn separated from the next large building with a traverser in between providing access. This final building was a fitting shop, machine shop and engine paint shop.

Leaving the Broadstone, the line climbed through a deep cutting and passed under the North Circular Road. At Liffey Junction (01.33) the Liffey branch from the North Wall trailed in on the up side behind the signal cabin. At this point, the line meets up with the Royal Canal, alongside which it runs for most of the way to Mullingar. There are up and down island platforms and a long cattle loading bank on the down side although the station is no longer used. The only passenger services were certain connections from the North Wall. If the boats were late, the Limited Mail was stopped to enable boat passengers to join the train. Just before the junction were the coke ovens on the up side and just beyond, the company's creosote works.

Under Broome Bridge, the line then passes Reilly's Crossing, site of a short-lived station in 1847. Ashtown (03.08) was not opened until August 1902 and then only for race traffic; it opened fully in 1905 and was closed in 1934. There were two platforms with a 10-lever cabin at the Galway end on the up side. A siding was installed on the down side in 1882 to serve the adjoining Todd's Mill. Blanchardstown (04.43) had two platforms with the main buildings on the up side. At one time there was a crossover to enable the banking engines to return to North Wall; this was removed to the top of the bank at Coolmines Crossing (05.60) where a signal cabin existed until 1906. There was also a siding on the up side and on the Galway side of the road bridge.

Clonsilla (07.08) became the junction for the Meath line in 1862 with the actual point of junction just beyond the station on the up side, where the remains of a locomotive shed can still be seen in the undergrowth. The station building and cabin are on the up side, the latter at the Dublin end beside the crossing, beyond which were sidings and a cattle bank. Lucan North (08.72), so called to distinguish it from the GS&W station, was originally referred to as Coldblow for Lucan and had a goods store and siding on the down side in connection with Shackleton's Mill. The siding only connected with the down line which necessitated the goods returning wrong road to Clonsilla, signalled as a ballast train working in the section.

Leixlip (11.20) was originally known as Louisa Bridge for Leixlip. Maynooth (14.72) was and is the terminus for suburban services and thus had a turntable on the down side at the Galway end, where there were also goods sidings and cattle banks on both sides. Kilcock (19.12) was one of only two Midland stations with staggered platforms, the other being at Float on the Cavan branch. The station, opened in 1850, replaced an earlier one beside the town. The latter was closed as it was on a 1 in 100 gradient which caused problems for trains restarting from the station.

Ferns Lock (20.75), more correctly Ferrans Lock, was a former block post with two platforms with an 11-lever cabin on the up side. Kilbrook (23.45) was a block post and site of a ballast pit siding on the down side by a facing junction. Enfield (26.40), more correctly Innfield, was the first terminus of the line. There are up and down platforms, the cabin originally on the down platform at the Dublin end, is now on the up side. The main buildings have been demolished and there were extensive goods and cattle facilities. Enfield became the exchange point for the Edenderry branch in 1877, the actual point of junction being a mile further west. When the main line was singled in 1931, the junction was dispensed with and the branch slewed onto the down line which was retained into Enfield.

Nesbitt Junction (27.62), where there was never a station, had the branch diverging by a facing junction on the down side with a

15-lever cabin. Moyvalley (30.28), a former block post, had the main building and cabin on the down platform, behind which was Moyvalley House, a one time hotel on the Royal Canal. One of a number of intermediate block posts brought into use in 1891 for shortening long sections was 34 Mile Cabin; others were at 39, 46, 73 and 85 miles. Hill of Down (35.55), known initially as Kinnegad & Ballivor, was a temporary terminus from December 1847 until the line was opened to Mullingar in October 1848. Killucan (41.60) had the station buildings and a goods store with sidings on the up side, the 23-lever cabin being on the down side.

Mullingar (50.17), terminus from October 1848 until August 1851, became a junction in 1855 with the opening of the Longford branch. The present station dates from 1857 and had five platforms, two on the main line plus two and a bay on the Sligo side, the line into the latter now lifted. A refreshment room and Mullingar No.1 cabin were situated between the up Galway and down Sligo platforms. A short double line section existed out to No.2 cabin beside the locomotive shed on the down side on the Galway line. Goods facilities and a store existed at the Galway end of the up main platform. Further out on the main line was the site of the Bretland tracklaying depot, later used for the storage of old locomotives and rolling stock awaiting breaking up. Newbrook (51.40) had two platforms on the down side with stands in between used in connection with the adjoining racecourse. There was a 24-lever cabin on the up side.

Castletown (58.22), a former block post with goods sidings on both sides was followed by Streamstown (61.56), junction for the Clara branch which diverged by a facing junction at the Galway end of the island platform on the down side. The main buildings were on the down platform with a goods store at the Dublin end of the up platform. Moate (68.33) was a block post and is now a fringe box to the Centralised Traffic Control. It had goods and cattle sidings. Athlone (78.05) was an important junction station. Coming in from the east, the GS&W branch from Portarlington trails in on the down side at the East Junction. The GS&W had its own station which was closed in 1927, but reopened in a modernised form in 1985 following the closure of the Midland station. After the East Junction, the main line crosses the Shannon by a 542ft long bridge with a central opening span and ran into the Midland station which had two platforms with a bay behind the down one used by Mayo line trains. The main buildings which included refreshment rooms were on the up side with a goods store and siding on either side at the Galway end. The west cabin was on the up side just before West Junction where the Mayo line diverges on the up side.

In Midland days, there was a locomotive shed and turntable in the 'V' of the junction.

Monksland (79.14) was a former block post closed in 1928 which controlled entry to the ballast pit, the siding for which diverged on the up side. The pit was open from 1877 to 1928 although little used after the opening of Lecarrow in 1910. Carrowduff (84.71), so named by the GSR in 1925, was opened as Thomastown in 1912 and before that was an intermediate block post known as 85 Mile Cabin. Ballinasloe (91.53) was a very important livestock centre noted for its annual fair described elsewhere. There are two passenger platforms with the cabin at the Dublin end on the down side. Extensive sidings existed at the Galway end on both sides. Between Ballinasloe and Woodlawn, at 98 miles, a temporary permanent way siding existed for loading sleepers. Woodlawn (101.31) was a block post with a passenger platform on the up side, opposite which was a goods platform and cattle bank served by a loop. Attymon (107.20) was the junction for the Loughrea branch which diverged by a facing junction on the down

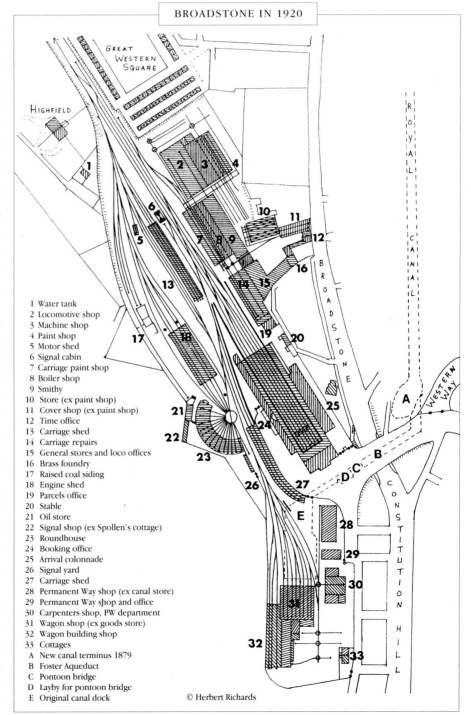

BROADSTONE IN 1920

1 Water tank
2 Locomotive shop
3 Machine shop
4 Paint shop
5 Motor shed
6 Signal cabin
7 Carriage paint shop
8 Boiler shop
9 Smithy
10 Store (ex paint shop)
11 Cover shop (ex paint shop)
12 Time office
13 Carriage shed
14 Carriage repairs
15 General stores and loco offices
16 Brass foundry
17 Raised coal siding
18 Engine shed
19 Parcels office
20 Stable
21 Oil store
22 Signal shop (ex Spollen's cottage)
23 Roundhouse
24 Booking office
25 Arrival colonnade
26 Signal yard
27 Carriage shed
28 Permanent Way shop (ex canal store)
29 Permanent Way shop and office
30 Carpenters shop, PW department
31 Wagon shop (ex goods store)
32 Wagon building shop
33 Cottages
A New canal terminus 1879
B Foster Aqueduct
C Pontoon bridge
D Layby for pontoon bridge
E Original canal dock

© Herbert Richards

side. Branch trains terminated at their own platform just before the junction. The station signal cabin was located on the down main line platform. There was a second platform and goods facilities on the up side.

Athenry (113.36) was also an important junction, the line from Claremorris coming in on the up side before the station. The main buildings are on the down platform which had a nameboard reading 'Athenry & Ennis Junction', that on the up side reading 'Athenry & Tuam Junction'. There were goods facilities beyond the level crossing at the Galway end followed by Ennis Junction where the line to Ennis and Limerick diverges by a facing junction on the down side. About two miles west of Athenry was a siding for the nearby Agricultural College; special instructions for its use appeared in the working timetables. Oranmore (121.32) was a former block post with two platforms, the cabin being on the down side beside the level crossing at the Dublin end.

The approach to Galway (126.53) offers splendid views of Galway Bay, with the line crossing Lough Atalia, an inlet of the sea, on

a fine viaduct. Originally there were two platforms under the overall roof but the down one was closed by the GSR, walled off and used as a road freight depot. The signal cabin of 42 levers is on the down side immediately across the viaduct followed by the goods yard from which the Docks branch curved sharply away. The Clifden branch diverged on the up side by a trailing junction, necessitating branch trains reversing to and from the station. A new platform was constructed by CIE in 1961 at the back of the old up platform, and beyond this is the diesel locomotive shed and turntable. Immediately beyond the buffer stops at the end of the main platform is the railway hotel.

Mullingar to Sligo.

Just outside Mullingar station beyond Canal crossing were Canal Bridge sidings (50.61). On the down side there was a cattle loading bank. Levington Crossing (52.33) was a former block post from 1929 to 1963 where there was a down loop. The crossing is situated on a dangerous bend on the main Sligo road. Passing alongside Lough Owel which feeds the Royal Canal, the line reaches Clonhugh (56.28) which had two platforms with the station building on the up side. This station was the scene of an extended dispute

Top: **The locomotive shed at Broadstone with a varied selection of Midland engines. On the left of the photographer was the turntable and roundhouse, the latter with its distinctive clock tower erected in 1877. This area is now surfaced with tarmacadam and used as a parking area for Bus Eireann vehicles, all the buildings having been demolished.** K A Murray collection.

Left: **A 'C' class 4-4-0 No.5 *Croagh Patrick* is receiving attention in the erecting shops at Broadstone. One of her pistons is in the foreground. The two boy apprentices were probably paid about 10s.0d per week. Although still named and carrying her Midland crest and maker's plate, she appears to have her GSR number 539 on the buffer beam. This dates the picture to the period just after the 1925 amalgamation.** Courtesy John Kennedy.

with the local landowner, Lord Greville, who insisted on trains stopping there for him in accordance with an earlier agreement. Multyfarnham (57.36), situated on a 3 mile falling gradient varying from 1 in 150 to 1 in 80, is a former block post, the cabin being still in existence to protect the adjoining level crossing. Inny Junction (60.69), another former block post, was the junction for the Cavan branch which diverged on the up side. There were three platforms and the remains of a locomotive shed can be seen on the up side; all platforms and the station buildings have been demolished. Street & Rathowen (63.18) had a single platform on the up side since the singling of the line, prior to which there was also a down one.

Mostrim (67.52), previously known as Edgeworthstown which is in fact the name of the adjoining village, has two platforms with the cabin still showing the old name at the Sligo end on the down side. It had the distinction of having two MGW enamel nameboards, presumably of the same date, but with different spellings, one reading Edgworthstown. Immediately beyond the station begins a climb at 1 in 150 to the summit two miles away from which point the line falls, first at 1 in 80 easing to 1 in 150, almost into Longford six miles away.

Longford (76.16) was the terminus of the line from 1855 to 1862; it was also the end of the double line section from Mullingar. There were the usual two platforms and goods facilities, the main goods store being on the up side at the Sligo end. The goods yard on the down side behind the platform has in recent years been converted to handle container traffic. There was originally a locomotive shed and turntable on the site of this yard. Leaving the station, the line crosses the former Longford branch of the Royal Canal by a swing bridge which has since been removed.

Newtownforbes (80.05) had a single platform on the up side with a siding on the down side serving a goods store. Dromod (87.25), once the interchange point for the narrow gauge Cavan & Leitrim Railway, has two platforms and the usual goods facilities. The cabin, on the down side, controlled opening bridges in both of its sections, the Canal bridge at Longford and the Shannon bridge at Drumsna. Shannon Bridge (92.00) had an opening span and was the only telescopic bridge on the Midland, the opening span being drawn back instead of the more usual turning method. The principle involved was described in an illustrated article in *The Engineer* in May 1869. Drumsna (93.00) had the usual facilities and is followed by Carrick-on-Shannon (97.60) whose station is still open. Boyle (106.33) was an important station with two platforms and goods facilities, including those to enable grain to be loaded. It is still open for passenger traffic.

Kilfree Junction (112.40) was just beyond the summit of a climb almost all the way from Boyle with some stretches at 1 in 100. This was the junction for the Ballaghaderreen branch which trailed in on the down side. There were two platforms, that on the down side being an island. Today there is little evidence of there having been a station here. There was a refreshment room here prior to the First World War. The line now falls for nearly two miles at 1 in 100, easing to 1 in 125 and 250 before levelling off into Ballymote (120.36). It was a block post with two platforms with the main building on the up side and goods accommodation beyond the platforms. The line then runs in a cutting on a rising gradient, avoiding the Ox Mountains which lie ahead.

Collooney (127.56) ceased to be a block post in 1930, the abandoned up platform still being in existence. There were goods facilities at the Dublin end. Leaving the station, the line passes over the site of the connecting line from the GS&W station to that of the SL&NC and immediately beyond the former's track from Claremorris trailed in on the down side. Shortly afterwards comes the site of Carrignagat Junction (128.60) where the SL&NC joined on the up side. From here to Ballysodare (129.61) the SL&NC trains ran over the former MGW up road. Ballysodare had two platforms with the goods shed and station building on the down side. Just beyond the station, a half-mile long siding came in from the flour mills of Pollexfen & Company. The line again falls, at 1 in 80, towards Sligo (134.16), the last half-mile being double track.

The station is reached on a curve past the

site of the engine shed and turntable, the latter retained to turn the single cab '121' class diesel locomotives which have worked Sligo line trains for a number of years. The present cabin is in the 'V' where the Quay branch diverges on the down side. The station has two platforms with two intermediate sidings. It was burned down during the Civil War and was rebuilt in much the same style although the overall roof was not replaced. When it was being rebuilt, the decision was taken to build a hotel which was not however completed until the GSR had taken over.

The Quay branch has always been worked as a goods only line and is on a steep falling gradient of 1 in 70. One track was extended on to the quay itself beyond the goods station, the extension being the property of the Sligo Harbour Commissioners. It included a loop and fanned out into three sidings at its extremity.

Athlone to Westport and Ballina.

The Mayo branch, as it was always known, was in reality a secondary main line, today single track throughout although double in Midland days as far as Roscommon. It diverges from the main line to the west of Athlone with the first station at Kiltoom (84.00) which was opened in 1879 as a block post. It had two platforms but no sidings. Nine Mile Bridge (87.00) was the site of platforms used annually on 24th June by a special train from Athlone in connection with the nearby St John's Well pilgrimage. Just beyond was Lecarrow (88.20) with its large ballast quarry on the up side, one of two supplying permanent way materials for CIE. There was a long siding with a loop passing under the stone crusher; entry was

by means of a ground frame and subsidiary ETS instrument.

Knockcroghery (90.00) is now the first block post on the branch; there are two platforms with the cabin on the up side at the Dublin end beside the crossing and there was a goods store at the Westport end on the down side. Ballymurry (92.71) also had two platforms but no goods accommodation. The line falls at 1 in 150 to Roscommon (96.20), an important station with the station buildings on the up side and a tall cabin on the down platform. There is a large goods store on the up side and a cattle loading bank. Leaving Roscommon, the line climbs for two miles and reaches Donamon (101.73), a former block post with a single platform with a cabin, both on the down side. There was a loop on the up side serving a cattle bank and a siding to the goods store.

Ballymoe (107.55) was a picturesque station situated some miles from the village, it being basically a block post although livestock traffic was dealt with there. There were two platforms, with a goods store, sidings and cabin, all on the down side; there was an old water tower beside the goods store. Frenchlawn crossing (109.01) was the scene of the 1903 accident which was alleged to have been caused by a goat. The next station, Castlerea (112.60) was the last of the handsome GN&W stations as finances were depleted at this point, leading to inferior buildings at such places as Westport and Ballina. It was an important station with goods facilities and it at one time boasted a locomotive shed and turntable. The 26-lever cabin is on the up side at the Westport end beside the crossing. A long siding extends from the up loop off which is the goods store and a cattle bank.

Lough Atalia Bridge was perhaps unique in that, whilst it included an opening span as built, it is believed to only have been opened once in connection with the Board of Trade inspection before the line was opened. Prior to its construction, local interests had vigorously campaigned for an opening span. This undated photograph was probably taken in the closing years of the nineteenth century. Author's collection.

Leaving Castlerea, the line crosses the River Suck and begins climbing at 1 in 94 past the site of ballast pits long out of use, to a summit more than three miles away. Ballinlough (118.60) was opened as a single platform station in 1880, that on the up side being added in 1902 when a loop was installed. A long siding served a cattle bank and goods store on the down side. Another long siding extended towards Westport to another ballast pit. The line climbs for nearly two miles at 1 in 102 and 270 before reaching Ballyhaunis (124.12) which had a loading bank, goods store and sidings at the Dublin end on the up side. Next was Bekan (128.58), a small station with only an up platform. From here the line climbs at 1 in 100 for a short distance before falling at 1 in 100 for more than a mile into Claremorris.

Claremorris (135.00) was the most important station on the Mayo branch and was a terminus for seven months in 1862. It was and is the station for the pilgrimage traffic to Knock. Prior to the opening of the Ballinrobe branch in 1892 it was similar to many of the other GN&W stations on the line. A branch platform, engine shed and sidings were located on the down side, but it achieved greater significance with the opening of the Athenry & Tuam Extension to Claremorris Light Railway in 1895 and its extension northwards to Collooney. The line from Tuam approached from the down side and entered the down main platform, running parallel to the Westport line and then diverging across the latter at North Junction. There were originally three signal cabins at Claremorris, at North and South Junctions as well as one for the Ballinrobe branch. The present 66-lever cabin was brought into use in May 1941. Major alterations were completed during 1952 in connection with the Knock pilgrimage traffic.

On leaving Claremorris, the line swings left and runs through boggy country. There is a long fall of almost six miles, some of it at 1 in 94 through Balla station (142.35) which has one platform and goods and cattle facilities. The Balla cattle fair was an important one in the Midland calendar. Next is Manulla Junction (145.71) where the Ballina branch diverges on the up side. The station here was fairly substantial with the main buildings on an island platform on the up side; there was a separate platform on the down side serving Westport trains. The signal cabin at the Dublin end was destroyed during the Civil War and was replaced by a new one at the Westport end. The station was closed in 1963, ceasing to be a block post in June 1964, the branch points being remotely operated from Balla. Then in November 1988 a new portacabin type signal cabin was brought into use on the island platform, at which time the cabins at Balla and Castlebar were closed. Castlebar

(149.74) located on a reverse curve necessitating a speed restriction, is probably the busiest station on the line. It has two platforms with the main buildings on the up side as is the goods yard which includes a container gantry.

The small single platform station at Islandeady (155.39) was the last to be opened by the MGW, in 1914, and is followed by a falling grade of 1 in 100 and then a short rise at the same figure before levelling out on the approach to Westport (160.74). Here there are two passenger platforms, the station buildings being on the up side. Two lines branched off at Westport, namely those to Westport Quay and Achill. The goods store is on the up side just beyond the Quay end of the platform and immediately beyond is the junction for the Achill branch which is now a short spur used in later years as a siding. Opposite the junction, on the down side are the two-road engine shed and turntable.

The Westport Quay line leaves the station on the level, climbs briefly at 1 in 200 and then falls nominally at 1 in 65 for almost a mile to reach sea level at the Quay station (162.67). Here there was a passenger platform as well as one for goods, the former served by a siding on the down side. There was also a siding to serve Messrs Rank's store. Formerly, the line continued across the public road out on to the quay itself.

Retracing our steps to Manulla Junction we must take a brief look at the Ballina branch. The branch curves sharply away to the right from the main line to the first station at Ballyvary (150.30) with its single platform on the up side and goods store reached by a trailing siding. There was a signal cabin at Ballyvary until 1940. The River Moy is crossed some six miles further on, before Foxford (157.14) with its two platforms and signal cabin on the down side beside the level crossing, is reached. There was a goods store on the up side served by a trailing siding and a cattle bank on a siding behind the up platform. Ballina is now the terminus of the line following the closure of the Killala extension and has the main passenger platform on the up side. Access to a locomotive shed and turntable were from a loop on the down side. Extensive alterations were carried out at Ballina in the 1970s and it now handles a lot of traffic in connection with the Asahi chemical factory at Killala. Apart from this, Ballina served a large area of north Mayo and always dealt with a good deal of freight traffic. Beyond the station, the Killala line passed through a level crossing and here a short stub of the branch was retained as a goods sidings.

The Meath road.
The branch diverged on the up side of the main line to the west of Clonsilla station and

crossed the Royal Canal which runs beside the main line at this point. The first eleven miles from the junction as far as Drumree were at one time double track. The first station was Dunboyne (10.32) which had two platforms with a short spur from the down line to a cattle bank and goods yard. Fairyhouse (12.54) was opened by the Midland shortly after it took over the working of the Meath line in connection with traffic to the nearby race-course. Originally there was only one platform, a second one being added in 1882. On race days Fairyhouse handled as many as thirteen special trains. It was used by regular passenger services for a four year period from July 1926. Batterstown (15.72) was a fine station with two platforms and a cabin on the up side. There were goods and cattle facilities at the Drumree end on the up side. Following the singling of the line some alterations were carried out, including the provision of a new cabin.

Drumree (18.73) was the end of the double line section, singled in 1919 as far as Dunboyne and from there to Clonsilla in 1925. There was a 20-lever cabin on the down platform, two spurs on the down side giving access to cattle banks. There was no goods store in MGW days, this being provided in 1927. Kilmessan Junction (24.20), was where the Athboy branch diverged, its trains using the island platform on the down side. The platform on the up side was the site of the main buildings. There was a goods yard and cattle bank as well as an engine shed and turntable of 45ft diameter. Kilmessan was the locomotive headquarters of the old Dublin & Meath.

Bective (27.25) had a down side platform as well as a goods siding and cattle bank, with a 5-lever ground frame worked with a key on the Navan Junction – Kilmessan staff. Navan Junction (30.42) was a fine station with four platforms, two MGW and two GNR. All the usual facilities were provided at Navan. Proudstown Park (33.00) was another platform provided specifically for race traffic but only lasted for a short period. Gibbstown (34.32) had one platform on the down side with a cabin at the Kingscourt end and a loop on the up side used in connection with stock specials. Wilkinstown (37.00) also had only one platform which had a double armed signal. On the up side was a run around loop and cattle bank, this being lengthened in GSR days to enable trains to cross.

Between Wilkinstown and Nobber, a halt was opened in 1928 at Castletown-Kilpatrick (39.70) but it only remained in use until 1935. Nobber (43.23) had a single, up side, platform with a goods store behind and there was a long siding on the down side capable of holding thirty wagons. Kilmainhamwood (46.12) had a passenger platform on the up side and a loop on the down side with a trailing siding into a cattle bank. Between here and Kingscourt was the Gypsum Siding installed in 1939 and worked by a 2-lever ground frame off the staff. Kingscourt (50.45), terminus of the line, had but one platform on the down side with sidings giving access to timber and goods banks. On the up side were a locomotive shed and 45ft turntable while beyond the level crossing at the Dublin end was Thompson's siding on the up side. A drawing of the station in 1893 shows two signal cabins, one on the platform with six levers and the second on the down side opposite Thompson's siding with five levers, this latter cabin being dispensed with about 1910. Just outside the station was the brick factory which provided heavy traffic, special instructions being in operation for wagons which were dealt with on the running line.

The Cavan line.

Inny Junction has already been described in the section on the Sligo line but it was unusual in having no proper road access although it is still possible to go by a bad track across the bog to the site of the station. Gradients on the first part of the branch were easy although there was a stretch of half a mile at 1 in 150 against down trains. Float (64.75) was on a falling 1 in 150 and had two platforms with the buildings on the up side as was the goods store; the cabin was on the down side beside the crossing. The second, staggered, platform was installed in 1905 enabling trains to be crossed. Ballywillan (70.09) had a platform on the up side with a separate goods platform and two goods stores. A platform on the down side was disused from 1900. A change of name was suggested in 1896 as it was frequently confused with the DW&W station of Ballywilliam. About 1½ miles south of Ballywillan station a siding diverged on the up side and ran for about a mile into Ballywillan ballast pit, in use until about 1915.

Between here and the next station at Drumhowna (76.15), opened in 1913, was Carnagh crossing. At the latter were sidings in connection with Ritchie's mining operations. Briefly, a Mr Ritchie operated iron mines at Cleenragh, near the village of Aghnacliff on the west side of Lough Gowna. The ore was transported by cart to the lake, taken across the lake in boats and then by road to Crossdoney. The company agreed to provide rails for a narrow gauge tramway from the lake to Carnagh where tranship sidings were laid on the down side; these were removed in 1877. Drumhowna (76.15) was situated on a sharp 1 in 80 climb as a result of which there were special instructions for shunting. The single platform was on the down side with a goods siding and store behind. It was forbidden for trains with passenger vehicles to shunt here. There were

A typical MGWR signal cabin at Float on the Cavan line, photographed shortly before the branch closed. Although this cabin has external steps many had the steps placed internally for added security. Also typical are the Midland pattern crossing gates. Author's collection.

further steep gradients with a long fall at 1 in 80 before levelling off into Crossdoney (81.34), junction for the Killeshandra branch which trailed in on the down side.

There were both up and down platforms, with the 28-lever cabin at the Mullingar end of the up platform. The buildings were on the down side with a goods siding and shed at the Cavan end of the down platform. Between Crossdoney and Cavan, the line passed through Tunnel Cutting, so called because the original plans were for a tunnel. At Cavan (85.47) the MGW made an end-on junction with the GNR line from Clones. There were two platforms, that on the down side being an island, the down face of which provided the through connection. The buildings were on the up platform which was in two sections ending at buffers one side for Midland trains and the other for those of the

GNR. The cabin was in the middle of this platform between the station building and the goods store. There was an engine shed and turn-table on the down side.

North Wall or Liffey branch

The branch diverged from the main line on the up side at Liffey Junction and crossed the Royal Canal. Between here and Glasnevin Junction, three quarters of a mile away, the long siding to the North City Mills ran beside the branch before diverging into the mills on the down side. There are in fact two double Junctions at Glasnevin, both controlled from West Road signal cabin. The GS&W line from Islandbridge joined on the up side with the Drumcondra line diverging immediately beyond. Originally the junction faced the opposite way allowing GS&W traffic access to their own line and the MGW line while MGW trains could only gain access to their own line. To enable Midland trains to run to Amiens Street via the Drumcondra link-line, alterations were made to the layout in the 1930s.

The double-tracked North Wall branch drops on a steep gradient under Cross Guns bridge and the main Belfast road to Newcomen Junction, site of the famous battle

Midland mileposts as described above.
From top to bottom are: **full mile, quarter mile, half mile and three-quarter mile.**
Author's collection.

concerning the CofDJR. The short curve to Amiens Street station diverges on the up side just before the branch passes under the GNR line out of Amiens Street. West Road cabin is on the down side and controlled both lines from Glasnevin Junction. The Midland line runs into the goods terminus on the up side, other lines running on to the L&NW and GS&W termini.

Engineering and Permanent Way.
Bridge rails weighing 75lb per yard were used in the early days. These were laid on longitudinal sleepers maintained to gauge by cross-sleepers beneath. Iron tie-rods were later used in addition to the cross-sleepers. Flange rails were used on the first section of line opened as far as Enfield. Following the Ballinasloe accident of 1864, extensive relaying was carried out with 76lb iron flat bottom rail being used in conjunction with steel points and crossings. Steel rail began to make an appearance in 1870 and was used in 23ft lengths. The western branches were laid with lighter rail of 65 lb. In 1897 the MGW introduced a heavy rail of 94lb in 60ft lengths. This was unusual for the time as only a year before, the L&NWR had rolled the first 60ft rails at Crewe. Whilst the weight remained at 94 lb, the length was reduced to 45ft around the turn of the century and this became the standard for the remainder of the MGW's existence.

Much of the ballast used came from the company's quarry at Lecarrow, although at different times a large number of quarries existed around the system. The main line followed the Esker Riada, a glacial ridge of gravel running across the country; on the main line alone, there were at least seven separate quarries or ballast pits.

Midland mile posts were unusual, fractions of miles being indicated by the shape of the plate. Full miles were on square plates, quarter miles on square plates one-quarter full size placed diagonally. Half mile plates were triangular, while the three-quarter miles were the same size as the mileposts, placed diagonally and with the top quarter removed, thus producing a 'V' shape. The Midland did not use gradient boards except on the Meath and Longford branches.

Bridges and tunnels.
There were few significant engineering features on the Midland. There were two major bridges on the main line, the crossing of the River Shannon at Athlone and Lough Atalia

on the approach to Galway. The Shannon bridge was supplied by Fox, Henderson & Company, its components being shipped in through Limerick. It was of five spans, with the two longest at 166ft 6in each and a centre opening span of 120ft. Lough Atalia was also a swing bridge, the opening span being of 157ft on either side of 40ft fixed spans. It had the distinction of never having been opened apart from the initial test carried out in 1851. On the Sligo line, the Drumsna bridge has already been alluded to and the only other bridge of note was the Canal crossing at Longford, while on the Mayo lines there was the crossing of the River Moy near Foxford.

On the Liffey branch, a swivel bridge was installed at the canal crossing at Newcomen Junction when Spencer Dock was built. The bridge carrying Sherriff Street over the Spencer Dock was an unusual floating swivel bridge invented by the company's engineer, James Price. The bridge was supported on a buoy floating in a well formed in one of the abutments, the turning of the bridge being effected by turning the buoy. Leaving Galway, the Clifden branch crossed the Corrib on a lattice girder bridge of three 150ft spans, with an opening section.

There were few tunnels on the Midland. On the Liffey branch there was one of 292 yards, another of 89 yards on the Clifden branch just outside Galway at Prospect Hill and two at Newport on the Achill branch. The second and shorter of these was opened in February 1896 when a 12 chain radius curve around a hill was abandoned.

Signalling.
Little is known of the early signalling, one of the first references to the subject followed a collision in 1888 on the Sligo road, when it was mentioned that a disc signal was turned to danger.

Early semaphores were 3-position double-arm signals on the station platforms. A sample of this type lasted until the closure of the Ballaghaderreen branch and it is a great shame that this was not preserved. Distant signals on the Midland were generally referred to as 'back signals'.

Interlocking began to appear about 1875 and permissive block replaced time interval working. Following the Armagh accident, the BoT required the installation of absolute block working on all lines. This required the provision of additional block cabins. Staff working appears to have been extended to all single lines about 1866 but it was of a type not acceptable to the BoT. The first Webb & Thompson electric train staff instruments date from 1890. Staffs came in different shapes; the round headed ones were coloured red, triangular shaped staffs were blue and the square headed staffs used on branch lines were coloured green.

Chapter Seventeen

PERSONNEL

THE *Railway Times* for 13th March 1847 included an advertisement for various positions in the new company, including that of Locomotive Superintendent, Carriage Superintendent, Superintendent of Police, Station Superintendent at Dublin, ticket issuers at the termini and intermediate stations, parcels office clerk, railway guards and porters. At the board meeting on 26th March, various salaries were approved by the board - an Assistant Superintendent at £1.5s.0d per week, ticket clerk at £1.10s.0d, parcels clerk at £1.0s.0d, ticket issuer at £1.5s.0d, two first class Stationmasters at £5 per month plus house, four second class at £4 plus house, twenty-five policemen at 13s.0d plus clothes, twenty-five porters at 12s.0d plus clothes, four guards at 16s.0d plus clothes and ten night watchmen at 10s.6d plus coat and capes. Charles Wade was appointed Police Superintendent, no mention being made of his salary. It was stipulated that no person over forty was to be appointed, nor was anybody 'subject to any bodily infirmity or defect'.

In May, the following additional staff were appointed, a head porter at Broadstone at 16s.0d plus clothes, and five porters at 12s.0d. The ticket issuer at Enfield was also to act as parcels porter with assistance from a porter. A Mr Nugent was appointed cashier at Broadstone and Mr Murray, clerk at the Canal office was to be the chief ticket issuer. Peter Poe was given the position of ticket issuer at Broadstone. Apparently he must have proved very satisfactory as within a month he was being considered for the position of Station Superintendent. By January 1849 he was put in charge of all stations. with the proviso that he was to visit one or more of them daily.

Lord Dunsandle, who had been the company's first Chairman, died of fever on 7th August 1847 and was replaced by the Deputy-Chairman, John Ennis. Within six months, it was ordered that staff numbers be reduced at stations, while in June 1848 porters' wages were reduced from 12s.6d to 10s.0d and those of policemen from 13s.0d to 11s.6d. Stationmasters' salaries were also reduced. Those at the first class stations, which were Maynooth, Kilcock, Enfield and Hill of Down, to £4 per month and second class to £3, each with an allowance for coal and candles between 1st October and 1st April annually. The Kilcock Stationmaster was to have his lodging money reduced from 7s.0d to 5s.0d while the head porter at Broadstone was ordered to pay 1s.6d per week for his house.

In the context of staff reductions, Dewrance confirmed in August that he had dispensed with a foreman, a coke clerk, a night timekeeper, a fitter, a millwright, a joiner, four labourers, four engine turners, a fireman and a brakeman. At this time further reductions were made in wages. In February 1849, the board took the decision to work the locomotive department by contract, a popular move at this time amongst railway directors. Dewrance was informed that his services would not be required after 5th March, his salary for the following quarter being paid in lieu of notice. With the opening to Galway in August 1851, it was of course necessary to appoint additional staff. Stationmasters at Athlone, Ballinasloe and Galway were to receive £60 per annum, those at Castletown, Woodlawn and Athenry £40, those at Streamstown and Oranmore £36. As most of the stations on the extension were not ready for habitation, the directors agreed to allow 10s.0d per week toward lodgings.

At the time of the Railway Commission in 1868, the MGW returned details of staff as follows; fifty-two stationmasters, thirty-two guards, 402 porters, one Locomotive Superintendent, seventy-four drivers and firemen, 245 fitters, 122 cleaners, one permanent way engineer, 118 inspectors and gangers and 563 platelayers, a total of 1,717. These figures included the operational staffs of the A&T and the GN&W, but not the D&M who had a further 495 men. Wages were by now improving under the chairmanship of Ralph Cusack. In November 1871, the locomotive superintendent, Robert Ramage, who had replaced Cabry in October 1862, was informed that the directors were not happy with the manner in which his department was being operated as there were frequent complaints as to the late running of trains and irregularity of drivers. If more experienced drivers were required, Ramage should obtain their services, although for the future, no person was to be given charge of an engine until his name, age and length of service were submitted to the board and their prior approval obtained.

The locomotive department came to the attention of the board in January 1875 when the first recorded strike occurred amongst the company's staff. A special board meeting was held on 12th February to consider the position from which it is clear that the dispute centred around overtime payments. On 1st January the rule regarding these payments had been changed to bring Midland practice into line with that pertaining on the GS&WR. These differed from the MGWR's previous model, the L&NWR at Crewe. The company now decided to revert to the earlier procedures. The company had in the interim dismissed and replaced the strikers, but agreed to re-employ any for whom vacancies existed, priority being given to those with the longest service.

Strikes occurred at various times over the ensuing years. In December 1897, the main line passenger guards sent a memorial to the directors seeking a revision of their pay scales, and payments and allowances for Sunday work. The board agreed to consider the matter, and in the meantime the Meath line guards sought an increase. In September of the following year, the goods guards complained of the uncomfortable nature of their vans. It was reported that thirty-eight of the fifty-two vans in service were the subject of the complaint, having been put into service twenty-five years previously.

The locomotive department was in the news in May 1902 when Cusack reported that he had received seven days strike notice from the fitters and boilermakers. The company adopted a hard line, demanding that the men be given notice to quit the company's houses and Cusack was requested to confer with his opposite numbers on the DW&W and the GS&W as to engaging as many men as might be required to maintain a service. This apparently did not produce an adequate response. The strike commenced on 22nd May and dragged on until early November when it was stated that of the sixty men who had struck, fifty-one had returned on the company's terms, namely at their old rate of pay with no increase and piece work to be at the discretion of Cusack. Of the nine who had not returned, three had been in breach of the law, one was deceased, one was in hospital following a serious accident, one had only been a temporary, two had emigrated and only one was employed elsewhere.

Another strike, of short duration, occurred in March 1909 when sixteen men involved in breaking up old wagons at Broadstone refused to work on a Saturday afternoon. The men obviously quickly realised the weakness of their position and worked the following Saturday. Further disputes occurred in 1911, 1913 and 1915, the latter in respect of a war bonus which was being paid to railway servants on British lines. Following various meetings, it was agreed that they should receive bonuses of between 1s.0d and 1s.6d, payable on a monthly basis.

Up until the outbreak of war in Europe in 1914, prices remained relatively stable, but by 1916 the cost of living was beginning to rise substantially. The railways in Britain were placed under Government control at the beginning of the war, but this was delayed in Ireland until December 1916 when the Irish Railway Executive Committee was set up. As far as railway staff were concerned, one of the first acts of the executive was the payment of a bonus of 7s.0d, the first of a number to be paid during the ensuing three years. Far from leaving the men better off, they barely maintained their position, with the cost of living increasing by 125%. Government control ceased on 15th August 1921, leaving all of the companies much worse off financially than they had been in 1913. A boilermakers' strike in 1921 led to locomotives being loaned by both the GS&W and the GNR to enable services to be maintained.

Working conditions.
Ramage reported in January 1872 that the driver and fireman of the ballast train had been on continuous duty for 50 hours. As a result, the civil engineer was ordered to see that this did not occur again. The standard working week in the shops at Broadstone was 54 hours, reduced to 40 in 1879 due to the great depression in trade and the consequent fall off in traffic. By the end of the 1880s it had become obvious that railway employees in general were working excessive hours in many cases. To enable consideration to be given further to the matter, a select committee was set up in 1891. In relation to the Midland, an example was cited of the 20.00 down Athlone goods. This train was due in Athlone at 00.45, where the crew remained for 4½ hours before returning to Dublin where they were due at 10.00. During the Athlone stopover, anything up to

2½ hours was involved in shunting so they had little time for rest, and in all were on duty for 16½ hours.

Evidence from Joseph Tatlow indicated that in March 1888, 31.8% of days worked by drivers exceeded 12 hours, with 20.73% exceeding 13 hours. By March 1890 these figures had dropped respectively to 21.7 and 10.51%. Hours worked by passenger guards varied from 40 hours on the main line to a maximum of 76½ hours on the Cavan branch. At this time there were 168 drivers and firemen, forty-one passenger and twenty-five goods guards, 124 signalmen and twenty-eight shunters. Tatlow stated that all staff were liberally treated and were most satisfied with their conditions of employment. Work was of a much lighter character than in England, with fewer trains. By this time, most of the men could avail of a week's paid leave of absence. The company owned 465 houses, exclusive of Stationmasters' houses, those in Dublin being occupied by drivers, firemen, guards and porters at a rent of 1s.0d per week. Gatekeepers occupied their houses free of charge.

Some further information was given in relation to pay. Prior to 1889, there was no regular scale of wages for foremen, guards, checkers, signalmen or porters. In July of that year, the company voluntarily increased signalmen's wages from 17s.0d per week to 22s.6d, with a further increase to 23s.8d in April 1890. Firemen started at 3s.0d per day for shunting work to a maximum of 4s.0d for a limited number of men passed for driving. Drivers' pay varied from 5s.0d to 7s.6d per day. Those staff who were away from home overnight received 1s.6d for the first night, 4s.0d for the second and 2s.6d for the third night. Staff at Dublin were paid weekly, those at country locations fortnightly.

In July 1898, the BoT had reason to write urging the company to prevent excessive hours of duty on the Sligo line goods, having received a report of the footplate crew being on duty for 14½ hours in the previous March. Ten years later, a further letter from the BoT referred to the crew of a ballast train being on duty for up to 16 hours per day for five consecutive days.

The appendix to the report of the Select Committee on Railwaymen's Hours of Work gave details of uniforms supplied to various staff. As early as June 1847, a Mr Ireland was requested to produce guards' suits with caps but excluding top coats, at a cost of £4.2s.0d, and complete porters' suits at £1.13s.6d each. Greatcoats were ordered for the footplate crews in December 1848 at £2.8s.0d each, a very necessary requisite in those days when the only protection provided was a weatherboard at the front of the footplate. In March 1866, it was ordered that blue caps with the initial letters of the company be issued to Stationmasters. Five months later, the Stationmaster at Edgeworthstown was told that all Stationmasters were required to wear caps and if he refused to do so, he would receive a month's notice.

As an example of the stability of prices, it is noteworthy that enginemens' top-coats were ordered in October 1873 at the same price as those obtained in 1848. Four years later, it was decided to replace the top-coats with jacket and trousers at an additional 4s.0d each. November 1895 saw a memorial from the signalmen in Dublin for a change of uniform from corduroy to cloth. Comparisons were made with the GN and the GS&W, the latter providing better quality cloth suits at an additional 10s.0d per suit. The GNR signalman's clothing was similar to that of the Midland men and the directors decided not to make a change.

A regular feature of Midland life was the annual excursion for the workmen in the locomotive shops at the Broadstone. In July 1881 they went to Navan, while in 1894, 675 expressed an interest in going to Cavan; the company agreed to lay on a train for 500 men, necessitating the provision of a revised list. By June 1917 the men wished to go further afield, requesting an outing to Warrenpoint. They were informed that such excursions had been abolished on the GN and the GS&W, but the Directors agreed to run an excursion so long as it was restricted to the company's own system. Two years later, a similar request was refused on the basis that the Irish Railways Executive Committee did not approve.

A group of station officials at an unknown location. At one time, Stationmasters were threatened with dismissal for not wearing uniform caps. Author's collection.

Running shed staff at Ballina in 1924.
Seated left to right: **Drivers P Dawson and P McNamee, foreman W A Smyth, drivers J McGill and J Berry.** Standing are: **Cleaner Mulvanny, fireman Bligh and cleaner Timlin.** Author's collection.

Discipline.

With the line barely opened, a driver was dismissed in December 1847 for being drunk in charge of a train and causing a delay of almost three hours. In July 1850 Driver Ashton was reprimanded for displaying party colours on his engine on the 'twelfth'. Three members of staff were in trouble in January 1867 – Driver Proudfoot was fined 10s.0d for being asleep on his engine at North Wall, his fireman 5s.0d for being absent and a shunter 2s.6d for driving the engine. This type of incident could well be related to the excessively long hours worked at that time. A case of missing goods at Ballyhaunis in September 1869 led to the entire station staff being discharged and given fourteen days pay. Theft of brandy at Westport two years later saw a driver and fireman similarly discharged as they were believed to have been implicated. On the other hand, when the INW complained of shortages in their accounts at Cavan, the Midland decided to take no action on the grounds that their accounts were in order.

When engine No.63 *Lion* failed at Maynooth in November 1878, the driver telegraphed for a relief engine, causing considerable delay to traffic while another engine was sent from the Broadstone. Subsequently, when it was discovered that the defect could have been remedied within half an hour, the driver's Christmas gratuity was reduced by 10s.0d. These bonuses appear to have been paid from an early date. The withholding of all or a portion of the gratuity was a common punishment for misdemeanours. Two further cases of sleeping crews came to light in 1879 and 1881. In the former, the driver and guard of the up Meath goods were found asleep in the latter's van at Nobber, causing 60 minutes delay. In the second instance, the delay was only 40 minutes but on this occasion the crew falsified the departure time. Similar offences appear to have attracted quite different punishments. A fireman who took colza oil from a signal lamp at Castlerea in August 1882 was dismissed while his driver forfeited his Christmas gratuity for having allowed him.

In December 1889, a train overran Street station, leaving two passengers behind, one of whom was struck by a hamper thrown out by the guard. The crew were brought before the board and the driver, who pleaded forgetfulness, was fined 2s.0d from each of ten pays; the guard was reduced by 1s.0d for each of ten pays. In June 1894 it was reported that the down Sligo goods had been worked from Ballysodare to Sligo by the fireman and a porter as the driver was drunk. A fight between a driver and his fireman on the North Wall shunter in September 1902 led to blood being spilt and both men being discharged. The driver stated that before going on duty, he had requested a different fireman, a request declined by the shedman, who was reprimanded and fined.

The dangers of going outside the cab to carry out oiling operations was drawn to the attention of all footplate staff in 1903 following the death of a fireman who had been struck by the iron frame of the net for catching mailbags at Hill of Down. The engine concerned was one of the new 'A' class which suffered problems with hot boxes on the tender when new. Although the company endeavoured to evade liability on the grounds that the apparatus was the responsibility of the post office, a judge awarded £40 to each of the man's parents.

Although some of the punishments handed down at times might appear harsh, the Midland looked after its employees reasonably well. The company operated a benefit society which was partly a sick fund, partly a pension fund, and which applied to all wages staff. A safety committee was set up at the Broadstone to look after the interests of the men there.

Chapter Eighteen

HOTELS AND CATERING SERVICES

THE MIDLAND directors took a decision at an early stage to become involved in the hotel business and so on 23rd January 1851, we find a contract being awarded to William Dargan for the construction of an hotel adjoining the new terminal station at Galway. It will be recalled from Chapter Two that the Midland had received a Government loan of £500,000 for the completion of the line to Galway. Some of this loan was diverted into the hotel, an action which was to cause dissent amongst the baronies who were to guarantee the loan. Obviously, in an attempt to justify its actions, John Ennis advised at the half-yearly shareholders' meeting in August 1852 that the hotel had been opened and was felt to be of great public advantage. Indeed, the Directors felt convinced that the very superior accommodation it provided was generally acknowledged by all who had visited it to be productive of the most beneficial effects on the railway traffic.

The *Railway Times,* reporting early in September, made reference to the Government loan, but pointed out that the Government auditor had agreed that the company could not have done better with the money than by placing it in Galway, where tourists and many others might be accommodated and thereby add 'in a vast degree' to the line's traffic. The journal's correspondent found the hotel full to capacity on the occasion of his visit. The 1849 Act giving effect to the loan referred to the baronies contributing towards the payment of any monies borrowed to complete the line. This did indeed appear to indicate an intention that the monies should be used for completing the railway. Hardly surprising then, that the baronies objected. The board minutes remain remarkably silent on this issue but it is clear that the matter was pursued energetically, so much so that the MGWR (Baronies Contribution) Act was passed in April 1854.

The following extract from the preamble to the Act puts the matter very succinctly - 'inasmuch as it is apprehended that certain of the said monies so expended, though beneficial generally to the Public and to the said Railway Company, may not have been in all cases expended in Works by which the said Baronies . . . may be considered to derive direct advantage'. Under the provisions of the Act, the capital as far as the baronies were concerned was reduced to £470,000. Correspondence between the Company Secretary, Beausire, and the Secretary of the Loan Commissioners in 1853 shows that a figure of £24,960.1s.10d had been expended on the hotel.

The hotel building, commanding a fine view over Eyre Square, was designed by Mulvany and communicated directly with the station behind it. One description indicated that it had forty-four bedrooms, eight sitting and three coffee rooms. An advertisement was placed in December 1851 for a proprietor as the company had decided not to run it themselves. Nothing is known of the first tenant, but in February 1853 it was rented for one year to a Mr Birchenough for £300. He had previously been with the Royal Hotel in Liverpool. This contract was later renewed for two years at the same rent, and additionally it was agreed that hotel goods could be conveyed free. It was stipulated that no porters from other hotels were to be permitted on to the arrivals platform. Some dispute apparently arose between Birchenough and the company, as when the lease came due for renewal in May 1856, orders were given that Mr Maclean, a house agent, be employed to take up possession of the furniture and the premises. Proceedings were threatened on behalf of the tenant, who claimed the company had illegally taken possession a day early. This was denied, but Birchenough was given possession until 25th March 1857.

Once again, the position for the next twelve months is unclear. A Mr Kilmurray declined to take the hotel in October, so in December it was advertised to let in whole or in part. In the following February a Mr Dean was to be put in possession as soon as the necessary deeds were completed. James Dean had previously been steward and manager of the Royal Western Yacht Club of Ireland. The *Galway Vindicator* in reporting his move, described the hotel as a splendid establishment 'which as regards apartments or means of accommodation is second to none in the Kingdom'. It reported the opening of the hotel for guests from 1st March. The culinary department could rightly be regarded as one of primary importance and would receive Mr Dean's special attention, while with respect to wines, he pledged himself to supply his customers and friends with the same class and quality which he previously imported direct from the first houses in the trade. Finally, it was reported that hot and cold baths were always ready. Mr Dean remained in occupation until October 1865, when he announced that he was moving to Clifden to take over an hotel lately occupied by Mr Hunt. The *Galway Vindicator* advised that the hotel would be closed for some months until an enterprising tenant could be found.

In December, a Mr Odlum was requested to furnish the board with an estimate of the probable cost of plate, house-linen, hardware, delph, china and other articles preliminary to opening the hotel, Mr Dean being given permission to remove a clock and other articles belonging to him. Two weeks later, it was confirmed that Odlum was to be granted the hotel rent free for one year, while in February, Messrs Millar & Beatty's £154.10s.0d tender for new carpets was accepted. Despite this apparently generous offer on the part of the Directors, Odlum's stay was a short one for on 16th May, the *Vindicator* announced that Mr Bergin, late of the Prince of Wales Hotel in Athlone, wished to advise the nobility, gentry and the public in general that the Railway Hotel was open for the reception of visitors. It was announced that the hotel had recently undergone a thorough renewal and could now be regarded as one of the best appointed in Ireland. As for Bergin himself, he had had long experience as a first class hotel keeper.

The annual rent was agreed at £250, payable monthly; Bergin was to pay for the licence, the company paying all rates and taxes and expending £300 on necessary repairs. Despite the glowing terms of the announcement, at least one tourist complained that Bergin, 'whilst an obliging man, had more than he could manage in the hotel'. This tourist complained of the property being 'sadly out of repair' and called on the Directors to put it right. John Bergin remained in charge until 1871, when it was reported that he had refused permission to one of the company's representatives to carry out an inspection of the hotel furniture. Shortly afterwards, Bergin departed and the hotel was let to Colonel and Mrs Hackett, who were to remain in occupation until 1924.

The Hacketts later operated the various refreshment rooms and restaurant car services. In April 1884, Mrs Hackett wrote saying that if the company was not disposed to lay out money in improving the hotel, she would be prepared to expend a sum of £1,000 for that purpose if granted a 31 year lease, all rates and taxes to be paid by the company. This offer was initially declined, but two weeks later a further proposal was accepted. This stipulated that Mrs Hackett would purchase the furniture in the hotel for £1,000, she would take a 31 year lease, keeping the property as an hotel. During that period, Mrs Hackett would not sell, sublet or assign the premises. The rent was agreed at £120 per annum, payable twice yearly in May and November. The company agreed to maintain the roof but all other repairs would be the tenant's responsibility. Finally, the tenant was to be granted a first class pass, the manager a second class, while servants for the hotel would receive up to fifty-two passes a year for the down journey only.

With the approaching expiry of the lease, the Hacketts approached the board in July 1914 requesting a renewal. An increase of £50 per year was offered for the rent, the board deciding to defer a decision pending an inspection. This was carried out by the entire board on Saturday, 26th September, following which a 21 year lease was agreed from 1st May 1915 with an option on either side to review every three years. In December 1921, complaints were made of over-charging, poor food and want of cleanliness. A new manager was appointed who obviously had the desired effect as in November 1922 the hotel was described as being most comfortable and clean. It was suggested that the board might consider taking over the hotel when a suitable opportunity arose, and in fact it was managed by the company as from 10th March 1924, Miss McCarthy, late of the Recess Hotel, being appointed manageress.

Western Hotels.

No further advances were made into the hotel business until the closing years of the nineteenth century, although during the intervening years a number of establishments were offered to the company. At the half-yearly meeting in August 1894, one of the shareholders enquired as to the company's intentions in relation to hotels, particularly bearing in mind the extension of the company's system into the tourist areas of Connemara and Mayo. In reply, Sir Ralph Cusack said that the board had conferred with the Directors of three other railway companies and as a result a decision had been taken in principle to construct hotels.

At that stage it had not been decided how many there would be or even where, although the Chairman was of the view that there should be one each on the Achill and Clifden branches. So, some two months later, the well known firm of Sir Thomas Deane & Son were appointed architects for the hotels to be erected by the company. Sir Thomas Deane reported back to the board meeting on 29th October on his visit to Achill Sound, Mallaranny and Recess as possible sites, the latter two being in due course chosen.

Mallaranny.

Early in November 1894, it was reported that about twenty acres of land attached to Ennell Lodge between the railway and the road which had been let to the company on a long lease at £50 per annum, would revert to Mr Stoney. Negotiations were entered into and early in the new year the Stoney Estate agreed to accept £1,500 for immediate possession and inheritance of fifty-four acres of land, houses and premises. This led to a visit to the area by the newly appointed hotels committee in March when a suitable site was chosen for an hotel. It would seem that plans had already been drawn up for the hotel at Recess, as consideration was given to whether these plans could be utilised at Mallaranny. It was decided not to utilise them directly but to alter them somewhat to provide less sleeping accommodation thus entailing less expenditure. It was also reported that there was no well on the grounds at Mallaranny, water for the station being taken from a lake about half a mile away, and whilst dark coloured, it was used for drinking purposes by the people of the village.

As a result of this decision, Sir Thomas was instructed to prepare plans based on twelve guest rooms and four sitting rooms; drawing and dining rooms were to be sufficient to allow for later extensions in accommodation. The public rooms were to be 13ft from floor to ceiling and the bedrooms 10ft. The building itself was to be of a plain, substantial, character with no unnecessary ornamentations, the entire cost not to exceed £5,000. Tenders were received in July 1895, that of Collen Brothers at £7,498 15s.11d being accepted on the understanding that work would be completed by 1st June 1896. In October, the contractors requested permission to take possession of Ennell Lodge for the use of their foreman, a request which was refused. The company later relented to the extent of agreeing to let the ground floor rooms at a rent of 5s.0d per week at the pleasure of the directors.

With work proceeding, the hotels committee was instructed in February 1896 to ascertain what plate, cutlery, glass, furniture and carpets would be required and to this end consulted Mr Holden, Managing Director of the Gresham Hotel in Dublin. The planned completion date passed with quite an amount of work still outstanding. On 8th May of the following year, the *Railway Times* was able to announce that the hotel was about to open, while later in the same month a good description was given following a visit from representatives of the English press. The hotel was described as a magnificent building in a picturesque situation, with the waters of Clew Bay lying directly beneath it. A superb suite of rooms promised every comfort to visitors, while the scenery provided a varied and attractive panorama of land and seascapes. The building itself was described as spacious, commodious and perfectly equipped with all modern conveniences, including electric light. A Miss Gorton from London was appointed manageress at a salary of £80 per annum plus washing.

In March 1898 it was decided to issue combined rail and hotel tickets from both Galway and Athenry which included first class return travel. These tickets were subsequently offered from other stations. Also about this time, the engineer was requested to prepare plans for enlarging the hotel which was frequently found to be full. These plans were submitted to the board and approved in July 1898, when it was also suggested that hot and cold water baths would be of great advantage to the guests and should not cost more than £550. The estimated cost of the extra accommodation was £6,164.0s.0d. Mr C J Fergusson visited and inspected the extension works on behalf of the board in May 1900, reporting that they were substantially complete. By now, Miss Gorton had moved on and been replaced by Miss Kilsby. In July she reported that the company's boat for the use of hotel patrons required an anchor and rope; these were ordered and a charge of 1s.0d per hour levied for its use.

It was also decided to provide a golf links on land adjoining the hotel, work on which was also completed in 1900. It was found necessary to provide a pavilion, the engineer estimating its cost at £200. Always on the lookout for bargains, it was realised that the company's cricket club pavilion at Liffey Junction was now little used and could be transferred to and erected at Mallaranny for no more than £25. Four sets of clubs, two each for ladies and gentlemen, were provided in a stand in the hall of the hotel.

Cheap day return tickets were issued from Westport, Newport and Castlebar which included a charge for the use of the links. A golf man was in due course appointed and was ordered to wear a cap with the words 'Golf Links' clearly visible. He was allowed 5% on all monies paid by the players.

During the course of a Directors' inspection in August 1902, Miss Kilsby reported that many complaints had been received regarding the quality of the claret; instructions were given regarding the importance of providing wines of the best quality. Serious losses were reported during the Winter 1903 season and the board gave Miss Kilsby a month's notice in September 1904. To be fair, it is difficult to imagine many people visiting West Mayo during the winter months. Sixty-seven applications were received for the vacant position, Miss Stevenson being appointed on 14th February 1905. Her stay was short as on 2nd January 1906 she announced her intention of leaving at the end of the following month and she was replaced by the hotel's bookkeeper, Miss S Burke.

Miss Burke in turn resigned in February 1909. In February 1912, the Directors decided to purchase a 5-seater car for use at the hotel, Messrs R & W Archer of Dublin quoting accordingly. Another facility for the hotel patrons were bathing boxes, which had apparently been provided for some years. In 1912 however, the residents of Cushlehka refused to allow them on the beach unless a payment of £1 per box was made, which led to their withdrawal. Closing the two western hotels during the winter months was considered on a number of occasions during the war years but it was not until October 1921 that this idea was put into practice.

Recess.

There had been a hotel located at Recess since at least July 1852 when an advertisement in the *Galway Vindicator* called the attention of its readers to the excellent salmon and trout fishing in the area. William Inglis of the Ballynahinch Estate Office wrote to the company in January 1895 drawing attention to the very desirable new building within a mile of Recess station which was to be let as a hotel – this was Finnisklin Lodge on the road to Leenane. The Directors replied that they were not in a position to form an opinion as to its suitability or otherwise as a hotel. Plans were drawn up for a hotel at Recess early in 1895, plans which were opposed by the local landowner, Mr Berridge, who said, through his solicitor, that he hoped the company would abandon its intention of erecting a hotel. A petition was sent to the company on behalf of the hotel keepers and merchants of the area. In November, Colonel Whittle wrote offering to transfer to the company his inter-

est in the lease of the Recess Hotel and property for £850, a figure which was accepted.

Early in February 1896, the hotels committee arranged an interview with Miss Mullarkey, tenant of the hotel, to ascertain whether she would be prepared to give up possession at once and become manageress for the company up to 1st November. She declined the offer, preferring to remain on as a tenant. She was given notice to quit as from 1st November, an action which led to a memorial from the Reverend Canon Lynskey and residents of Clifden suggesting that compensation be paid, a request which was declined. Mr O'Neill's plans estimated at £4,060 were approved. These included raising a portion of the old building to the level of the main wing. As work neared completion, Mrs Hackett approached the board with a proposal to become its tenant, but she was advised that the company had decided to run the hotel themselves.

An advertisement in the *Galway Vindicator* early in June stated that the hotel occupied a picturesque situation in the midst of Connemara's Lake District close to the celebrated Ballynahinch Salmon Fishery. It also stated that a special platform had been provided opposite the hotel for visitors arriving by rail, There were thirty-four bedrooms and by the end of May, the hotel was reported to be full. The area about the hotel was ideally suited for both fishing and shooting and it was not long before Lieutenant Beresford approached the board offering the fishing rights on three small lakes plus three boats at £25 per annum; £10 was offered but declined. Many years later, a question was asked at a board meeting as to charges for shooting both at Recess and Mallaranny. It was agreed that visitors to the hotels be charged 1s.0d per grouse or hare, everything else to be free. Various minor alterations were carried out over the years. In October 1903, plans and estimates were requested to provide rooms for visitors' servants, but it is not clear whether this was carried out.

In August 1907 it was agreed that a small shed should be provided for empties and some trees should be cut down; the ever careful directors ordered that the stumps should be used as seating in the grounds. By 1916, the photographic dark room was not receiving sufficient use and it was accordingly converted into a housemaid's pantry, which was much needed. It was necessary to supply a window and surprisingly a water supply – one would have thought the latter would be an essential requirement for a dark room. At the height of the civil war, the end came for the Recess Hotel when it was burned to the ground on 8th October 1922. It is said to have been destroyed following the occupation of Oughterard by the Nationalist forces to prevent the Irregulars from

making it a barracks. A malicious damages claim for £50,000 was in due course lodged with the Government.

Other hotel projects.

At the time when the company was in correspondence with the Board of Works regarding the Achill extension, one of its requirements was the provision of sufficient land at Achill Sound for the building of a hotel. In January 1895, plans and estimates were submitted for a small hotel and refreshment room which were not proceeded with. The Railway Hotel at Westport was put up for sale at various times between 1895 and 1906, being offered to the company on each occasion. Likewise, Mr Sheridan, proprietor of the Slievemore Hotel in Dugort requested assistance from the company in 1905 in connection with a proposed enlargement of the hotel, either by way of a loan or by contribution. The reply was in the negative.

The company became involved in a plan to construct an hotel at Rosses Point near Sligo, when an offer of £700 was made for the lands required, later increased to £1,000, possession being taken in March 1914. Tenders for construction were placed before the board on 23rd June, that of Campbell & Son of Belfast at £15,490 being accepted; work to be completed in seventy-eight weeks. The contractors agreed to bring in all materials by rail to Sligo via Cavan. Some initial works were carried out but then postponed due to the outbreak of war. At one point in 1915, it was suggested that the GS&W might be approached to see whether it might be interested in taking it over. Some half-hearted ideas about resuming work were floated in 1920 and 1923, but there the matter rested. The last hotel project with which the MGWR became involved, followed the burning down of Sligo station, was when plans were drawn up for an hotel beside the new station. This was not completed until after the demise of the Midland and was opened by the GSR as one of the Great Southern hotels.

Catering.

From the beginning, the Directors decided that catering should be an essential part of the company's service to the public, so it is hardly surprising to find plans for a refreshment room at Mullingar being agreed within days of the line opening to that point. Similar accommodation was also provided in 1858 both at Athlone and Broadstone. In the early days, additional time was provided at Athlone and Mullingar to enable long-distance passengers to leave their trains and partake of food. August 1877 saw Messrs Stafford's tender for £27 for the erection of a refreshment room at Cavan being accepted, with another one being opened at Cavan Junction two months later. This latter does not appear to have remained in use for very long although the Stationmaster was up before the board for having beer on the premises, it having been part of his agreement that no alcoholic liquor would be sold. Colonel and Mrs Hackett signed a tenancy agreement for Cavan in June 1888 on the basis of a rent of 19s.3d per week until 7th April 1892 and 23s.1d per week for a further year. It was renewed in 1893 at £60 per annum and became part of an overall agreement in 1901.

A complaint from a Mr Concannon of London reached the board in July 1897 in relation to the refreshment room at Athlone. During the course of a journey from Galway to Dublin, Concannon had telegraphed forward from Athenry requesting a hot luncheon. On arrival however, he had been given a cold meal. The matter was referred to Mrs Hackett for her observations, with the comment that she should each day have a sufficient supply of chops and steaks on hand, complaints of this nature bringing no credit either to the refreshment service or to the company. The excuse given was that there were difficulties in storing meat without a larder or cold store. There was no response to this from the board and certainly no offer of assistance.

A refreshment room was opened at Claremorris early in 1898, an agreement similar to that at Cavan being entered into by the Hacketts. In March 1900, Mrs Hackett requested accommodation for her attendants there, and it was agreed to convert the lamp room. Finally, in 1902 consideration was given to refreshment facilities at Sligo which were, in due course provided. An agreement signed with the Hacketts in December 1901 for the tenancy of the Midland's refreshment rooms shows them to have been at Broadstone, Mullingar, Athlone, Claremorris, Cavan and Sligo. The tenants were to 'well and sufficiently supply all railway passengers and other persons with all proper and necessary food, drink and other materials of best quality'. These goods were to be retailed and sold at moderate and reasonable prices, the annual rent was to be £1,000.

Before and after the introduction of dining car facilities, it was possible to obtain luncheon baskets on many trains, as witnessed by a typical advertisement in the summer 1911 timetable. Five refreshment rooms were listed, Sligo having been closed. On offer were breakfast baskets for 2s.6d, luncheon baskets for 3s.0d with a reduction of 6d being made when neither beer nor wine were taken. In the restaurants themselves, breakfasts and hot luncheons were available at 2s.0d and 2s.6d respectively.

With the impending introduction of the dining cars to the Limited Mail trains in the Summer of 1902, Mrs. Hackett submitted sample menus and wine lists, with the company providing uniforms for the cars' attendants. The dining cars were later included in the tourist expresses to Clifden and Achill. In the early years, the dining cars were restricted to first and second class passengers only. In July 1909 it was agreed that as a trial, third class passengers should be allowed to use the second class dining cars without extra charge, as was then done on the GS&W and the Northern Counties Committee. Up to that time, passengers were charged the difference between the second and third class fares for the time they occupied the dining car.

Wartime coal shortages resulted in a decision at a special board meeting in April 1918 to suspend restaurant car services for the duration of the conflict. In fact, whilst the cars themselves were withdrawn, the company continued to provide a limited service by serving teas and light refreshments from van No.4 included in the limited mail set. It was agreed in April 1919 that the full service be reinstated as soon as possible, the service remaining virtually unaltered until the amalgamation.

This pair of handbills were issued by M F Keogh, General Manager at Broadstone in March 1922. They were printed in black ink on pale green MF stock (left) and buff (right) by Browne & Nolan Ltd of Dublin.

Midland Great Western Railway.

RAILWAY CO.'S HOTEL AT
RECESS (Connemara)
Combined Rail and Hotel Tickets
ARE ISSUED AS UNDER FROM 1st APRIL TILL 30th SEPTEMBER.

FROM	FIRST CLASS			THIRD CLASS		
	(a) Weekly Tickets (7 days)	(b) Three-day Tickets	(c) Two-day Tickets	(a) Weekly Tickets (7 days)	(b) Three-day Tickets	(c) Two-day Tickets
	£ s. d.	£ s. d.	£ s. d.	£ s. d.	£ s. d.	£ s. d.
BROADSTONE	7 7 0	4 11 0	3 14 0	6 18 0	3 17 0	3 2 0
MULLINGAR ...	7 6 0	3 16 0	3 1 0	6 15 0	3 7 0	2 12 0
ATHLONE	6 15 0	3 8 0	2 13 0	6 7 0	3 2 0	2 7 0
BALLINASLOE	6 11 0	3 4 0	2 9 0	6 4 0	2 19 0	2 4 0
ATHENRY ...	6 2 0	2 18 0	2 4 0	5 17 0	2 13 0	2 2 0
GALWAY	5 18 0	2 15 0	2 4 0	5 12 0	2 12 0	1 19 0
LOUGHREA ...	6 7 0	3 2 0	2 7 0	6 1 0	2 17 0	2 2 0
LONGFORD	7 7 0	4 3 0	3 8 0	6 18 0	3 13 0	2 18 0
CAVAN	7 7 0	4 6 0	3 11 0	6 18 0	3 13 0	3 0 0
EDENDERRY ...	7 7 0	4 5 0	3 10 0	6 18 0	3 13 0	2 19 0
ROSCOMMON ...	7 2 0	3 13 0	2 18 0	6 13 0	3 6 0	2 11 0

(a) Hotel Accommodation, viz.:—Dinner on day of issue; Breakfast, Lunch, and Dinner on six following days, and Breakfast and Lunch on eighth day; Attendance and Bedroom on seven nights.

(b) Hotel Accommodation, viz.:—Dinner on day of issue; Breakfast, Lunch, and Dinner on two following days; Breakfast and Lunch on third following day; Attendance and Bedroom on three nights.

(c) Hotel Accommodation, viz.:—Dinner on day of issue; Breakfast, Lunch, and Dinner on following day; Breakfast and Lunch on second following day; Bedroom and Attendance on two nights.

Holders of these Tickets must show the Hotel Coupon on entering the Hotel. Free Fishing in connection with above Hotel. Also Fishing on famous Inagh Lough at moderate rates.

Motor Cars attached to Hotel Garage.

For further particulars apply to the Manageress, Railway Hotel, Recess, Connemara; to Station Masters at the various Stations; or to Traffic Manager, Broadstone, Dublin.

M. F. KEOGH,
General Manager.

BROADSTONE, DUBLIN,
March, 1922.

Browne & Nolan, Ltd., Printers, Dublin.

Midland Great Western Railway.

RAILWAY CO.'S HOTEL AT
MALLARANNY (ACHILL)
Combined Rail and Hotel Tickets
ARE ISSUED AS UNDER FROM 1st APRIL TILL 30th SEPTEMBER.

FROM	FIRST CLASS			THIRD CLASS		
	(a) Weekly Tickets (7 days)	(b) Three-day Tickets	(c) Two-day Tickets	(a) Weekly Tickets (7 days)	(b) Three-day Tickets	(c) Two-day Tickets
	£ s. d.	£ s. d.	£ s. d.	£ s. d.	£ s. d.	£ s. d.
BROADSTONE ...	7 7 0	4 17 0	4 2 0	6 18 0	4 0 0	3 5 0
MULLINGAR	7 7 0	4 10 0	3 6 0	6 18 0	3 11 0	2 16 0
ATHLONE	7 3 0	3 13 0	2 18 0	6 13 0	3 6 0	2 11 0
ATHENRY ...	7 7 0	4 3 0	3 8 0	6 18 0	3 12 0	2 17 0
GALWAY	7 7 0	4 7 0	3 12 0	6 18 0	3 15 0	3 0 0
ROSCOMMON ...	6 16 0	3 9 0	2 14 0	6 7 0	3 2 0	2 7 0
CASTLEREA ...	6 10 0	3 4 0	2 9 0	6 3 0	2 19 0	2 4 0
BALLYHAUNIS	6 7 0	3 1 0	2 6 0	5 19 0	2 16 0	2 2 0
CLAREMORRIS	6 2 0	2 18 0	2 3 0	5 17 0	2 13 0	2 2 0
CASTLEBAR ...	5 16 0	2 14 0	2 6 0	5 11 0	2 9 0	1 17 0
WESTPORT	5 12 0	2 10 0	2 2 0	5 7 0	2 5 0	1 17 0
BALLINA	6 5 0	3 1 0	2 6 0	6 0 0	2 16 0	2 2 0
CAVAN	7 7 0	4 17 0			6 18 0	4 0 0

(a) Hotel Accommodation, viz.:—Dinner on day of issue; Breakfast, Lunch, and Dinner on six following days; Breakfast and Lunch on eighth day; Attendance and Bedroom on seven nights.

(b) Hotel Accommodation, viz.:—Dinner on day of issue; Breakfast, Lunch, and Dinner on two following days; Breakfast and Lunch on third following day; Attendance and Bedroom on three nights.

(c) Hotel Accommodation, viz.:—Dinner on day of issue; Breakfast, Lunch, and Dinner on following day; Breakfast and Lunch on second following day; Bedroom and Attendance on two nights.

Holders of these Tickets must show the Hotel Coupon on entering the Hotel. Free Fishing, Golfing and Shooting in connection with above Hotel.

Motor Cars attached to Hotel Garage.

For further particulars apply to the Manageress, Railway Hotel, Mallaranny, Co. Mayo; to Station Masters at the various Stations; or to Traffic Manager, Broadstone, Dublin.

M. F. KEOGH,
General Manager.

BROADSTONE, DUBLIN,
March, 1922.

Browne & Nolan, Ltd., Printers, Dublin.

Chapter Nineteen

ROYAL CANAL & SHANNON STEAMER SERVICES

THE FULL history of the Royal Canal has been told elsewhere (*The Canals of the South of Ireland* by V T H Delany, David & Charles, 1966), but a brief pocket history would not perhaps go amiss since the canal was owned by the MGW throughout the entire existence of the railway company. The Royal is believed to have been born in the course of a disagreement in the Grand Canal boardroom which led to the resignation of one of its directors, who vowed to 'start a rival canal and carry all the traffic'. Whether or not this is true, the Royal Canal company was incorporated in 1789 to construct a canal from the River Liffey to the River Shannon at Tarmonbarry, north of Lough Ree. A similar line had been proposed as early as February 1756 but the Grand Canal project was decided upon at that time.

Parliament surprisingly agreed to the rival scheme but stipulated that it should not come within four miles of the Grand Canal in the course of the first fourteen miles from Dublin. A grant of £66,000 in 4% debentures was given, a further £134,000 being promised by subscribers, who included the Duke of Leinster, Viscount Ranelagh, Lord Longford and James Connolly. An Act of 1792 granted a further £23,000 to enable the company to construct docks at the canal's Liffey terminus. These were never built by the canal company, being eventually completed by the MGW in 1873. Work began in 1789 but was severely delayed due to the inadequacy of surveys. The main line in the meantime reached Kilcock by 1796 when further financial assistance had to be obtained from Parliament. The Broadstone branch was completed in 1801. Much criticism of the canal's course through Maynooth was made on the grounds that a more northerly route would have avoided both the Deep Sinkings at Clonsilla and the Ryewater Aqueduct, both of which were very expensive. It is believed the course of the canal was decided at the request of the Duke of Leinster, who lived at Carton House, and wished the canal to pass by his town of Maynooth rather than further north.

Further difficulties were encountered in crossing Cappa bog and the canal had only reached Enfield by 1800. Further financial assistance was sought in 1801 and a grant of £78,856 was given only on the understanding that no further assistance would be forthcoming until Mullingar was reached. It was in fact opened to Killucan in 1805 and Mullingar in the following year. By 1810, although still not completed, the canal was beginning to attract a good deal of traffic. 52,643 tons of goods were carried in that year although this must be compared with 205,443 tons on the Grand.

Further financial problems led to a reorganisation of the Royal Canal company in 1812, when the Directors General for Inland Navigation took over its affairs. The canal was finally opened throughout to the Shannon on 26th May 1817, and had cost a total of £1,421,954 to construct. A new company, the New Royal Canal Company was formed in 1818; with the canal now complete and clear of debt, it was enabled to make a profit, although this was always modest in comparison to its rival. The main canal was 90 miles 30 chains in length, more than eleven miles longer than its rival. There were a total of forty-six locks, twelve of which (mostly double) were in the first 6½ miles from Dublin. The climb out of the city was followed by 7½ miles of level, two of which passed through the Deep Sinkings at Clonsilla, where the towpath was up to 20ft above water level in places. The summit, 324ft above mean sea level, was reached beyond Killucan, 45 miles from Dublin.

Apart from the locks, there were thirty-eight bridges, three aqueducts and several harbours, as well as two hotels – at Broadstone and Moyvalley. The principal cargos eastbound were corn and potatoes from Longford, Roscommon, Mayo and Sligo, pigs and cattle from Mullingar, Ballymahon and Longford and turf from the midland bogs. In the reverse direction, coal and general merchandise were the main products. There was little through traffic, the majority being between towns on the canal. Freight traffic was up to 80,000 tons by the 1830s, peaking at 112,000 tons in 1847, after which it declined to 30,000 by the 1880s and 10,000 tons by the 1920s, one-third of the latter being Guinness traffic. By 1946 there were only two trading boats left and the last of these stopped in 1951.

At their peak passenger numbers around 40,000 per annum, again representing rather less than half that of its rival, the Grand Canal. Speeds were low, Dublin to Mullingar (53 miles) taking 13½ hours. In 1845, two boats left Broadstone daily at 09.00 and 14.00. Some twenty years earlier, the *Sligo Journal* advertised a boat leaving Dublin at 15.00, arriving at Tenlie (39th lock) at 09.00 the next morning, from whence a 'comfortable caravan' travelled to Boyle, arriving there for an overnight stop at 17.00. The journey was completed the next morning, the through fare being 16s.0d.

Details of the negotiations with the railway company leading to the canal's purchase have already been recounted in Chapter One and will not therefore be repeated here. The MGW had a statutory obligation to maintain the navigation to the satisfaction of the Board of Control, but inevitably after the opening of the railway, the number of traders declined and passenger traffic was withdrawn after a few years. A branch off the main canal to Longford had been opened on 19th January 1830 but plans for a similar extension to Roscommon were shelved due to the likely expense. The Longford branch was 5.2 miles long and had no locks.

The MGW decided to operate its own carrying trade in 1871 and this lasted until 1886. Horse drawn boats were used until 1875 when steamers were purchased. The completion of the Spencer Docks in 1873, whilst providing the company with a good and profitable distribution centre for goods arriving by sea, contributed a very little traffic to the canal – 4,864 tons in 1922 out of a total of 179,198 tons. Two serious accidents occurred on the canal, both in 1845, one involving the capsizing of a packet-boat load of emigrants in Longford Harbour, twelve people being drowned. The second was in November of the same year when a packet-boat struck a rock in the Deep Sinkings, resulting in sixteen deaths.

In August 1870 the company obtained an estimate of £970 from Grendons for the supply of a cargo steamer suitable for use on the canal and, after seeking the opinion of the shareholders as to trading on the canal, proceeded to order two vessels. By August of the following year, one of them was disabled and Ramage's report was sent to Grendons who replied that there was no reason for supposing any defects existed either in design, imperfect materials or workmanship. In March 1872 orders were given for the engine of the disabled steamer to be put in proper working order and, whilst two lower estimates were obtained, that of Courtney Stephens of Dublin at £1,850 for two boilers was accepted; an allowance of £300 was made for the old machinery and the order was to be completed by 1st May 1873 subject to a penalty of £10 per week. Steamer No.1 was reported disabled in March 1874 with a broken main shaft.

August 1876 saw Mr Hayes of Stoney Stratford offering to supply a tug for £830. This offer was accepted and in the following February, Hayes applied for payment due for *Pioneer*. Six months later, he offered a second tug for £985, the company offering £1,000 if he substituted brass for iron tubes; this tug was apparently named *Mermaid* and was ready for inspection and trials in May 1878. A third tug *Rambler* came from the same source. It is not clear how many vessels were owned and operated by the company, but the names *Rattler* and *Dauntless* also appear in the traffic minutes, the former in connection with a request from a Mr Lefroy for terms for letting. She was offered in March 1890 for 30s.0d per week on condition that he carried out any repairs and agreed to return her at once should the company require her. *Dauntless* appears much later in January 1908 when a Mr Claridge agreed to accept £80 for her. In 1916, Morton raised the question of scrapping the two old steamers lying at the Royal Canal Dockyard, an offer subsequently made by the Hammond Lane Foundry being accepted.

There would appear to have been a third steamer extant at this time as in April 1920 Morton suggested that the engine and machinery of the remaining canal steamer should be sold and the hull converted for carrying out repair work on the canal. One of these three may have been *Conqueror* which was hired to a Mr Powderly in March 1892 for £3 per week.

The company obtained powers in 1877 to close about 150 yards of the Broadstone branch and to fill the canal harbour there. This work was necessitated in order to provide a new approach road to the station. The old canal stores were incorporated into the wagon building shops. In November 1897, a letter was received from Sir Charles Cameron MD, suggesting the advisability of filling up the canal from Phibsborough to the Broadstone basin as the water was stagnant and might well be the cause of an outbreak of typhoid in the area. The company's reply was that it would require Parliamentary sanction to fill in any portion

of the canal, but there appears to have been no offer to obtain the necessary powers.

Six months later, the engineer reported on pollution arising from the drowning of dogs in the canal. The Dublin Corporation law agents took the matter in hand in November 1899 again enquiring about the closure of the branch, the only response being to ask the engineer to use every exertion to keep it free of all offensive matter. Unsatisfied, the law agents stated that the Corporation had powers to take over the canal and enquired if the company would facilitate them. The Directors had no objection but suggested the corporation should hand back the filled-in section. Needless to say, the Corporation refused to sanction the expenditure of public money unless the land could be handed over for the benefit of the public. This matter dragged on until powers were obtained under the company's Act in 1909 to enable it to close this section.

Little of note happened as regards the canal in the twentieth century. There was a brief revival of the turf trade during the second world war. The last trader, Leech of Killucan, ceased to trade in 1951. The canal was officially closed to navigation on 9th April 1961 and a dam was placed across the canal west of Mullingar, cutting off its water supply from Lough Owel. Local authorities were then allowed to erect low culvert bridges across the cut, thus effectively preventing further use. In 1978, the decision was taken to transfer the two main canals from CIE to the Office of Public Works, who were already responsible for the Shannon navigation system. Meanwhile in 1974, the Royal Canal Amenity Group was set up with the aim of saving the canal and since then a number of new lock gates have been made with the co-operation of Anco, the industrial training authority. It is interesting to report that some 70 miles of the canal have now been rewatered and its future appears to be assured.

Some brief statistical data concludes this account of the Royal Canal. The tidal lock into the River Liffey measures 174ft by 24½ft. The smallest lock on the canal was No.18 at Thomastown Bridge near Killucan and was 75ft by 13ft 3in. Broome Bridge, beside Liffey Junction, is notable in that Sir William Rowan Hamilton, the mathematician and astronomer, came on the fundamental formula for quanternian multiplication while crossing over this bridge on his way home from Dunsink observatory.

Shannon steamer services.

At the height of the war with the GS&W during the 1850s, the directors turned their thoughts to the operation of a service to Limerick, utilising the River Shannon for part of the journey. The first reference to this came in July 1852 when the company

'resolved to put steamboats on to convey passengers and goods arriving by railway to and from different stations in County Clare'. The first steam vessel to operate on the Shannon had arrived in 1825 and by 1845, the CofDSP company had eight steamers plying on the river. In February 1857, a board minute records that Captain Mills, late of the British & Irish Steampacket Company, was requested to proceed to London to ascertain whether steamers cannot be procured suitable for service between Athlone and Dromineer on the river Shannon. A month later it was reported that the trial of a steamer purchased in Glasgow for £1,850 had been satisfactory and the decision was taken to name the vessel *Midland*. She was advertised to operate between Athlone and Lough Derg in the summer of 1857, but nothing further is known of her.

What we do know is that two vessels were purchased in Glasgow in 1857, the *Duchess of Argyle* and the *Artizan*. Both were paddle steamers, the former having been built at Dumbarton in 1848, the latter at Rutherglen in 1856. They were steamed to Limerick where they were cut up into sections, floated up the Shannon to Athlone and reassembled there. The *Duchess* was reported to have been an iron boat of light draught with high-pressure engines, comfortably and handsomely fitted up. She was capable of 16 knots and could complete the 58 mile journey from Killaloe to Athlone in 4½ hours; her sister boat was apparently slower, taking a little under six hours. The *Duchess* struck a submerged rock in 1857 in fog and was abandoned, but was later refloated and sold to the GS&W under the terms of the arbitration award between the two companies and she operated until 1862.

The service as operated by the Midland in 1858 saw passengers from Dublin arrive at Athlone at about 11.15, where they boarded the steamer for Killaloe, at which point they transferred to a horse bus which arrived in Limerick at 18.45, 9½ hours after leaving Dublin. The fare was 12s.6d first and 6s.0d third class as against 23s.9d and 10s.9d by the GS&W. On the other hand, rail passengers on the GS&W completed the journey in six hours. *Artizan* was also transferred to the GS&W in 1862 and along with the *Duchess of Argyle* ended its days at Killaloe. A fourth vessel, the *Lord Lorton*, was built in 1855 at Greenwich and occasionally carried passengers. As late as 1880 the MGW advertised combined rail and steamer tickets from the south of Ireland to Ballyhaunis in County Mayo in connection with Knock pilgrimage traffic. So came to an end the Midland's excursion into water borne operations. As far as the Shannon was concerned, it was short-lived but it had the effect of putting the CofDSP company off the river.

Appendix A

ABBREVIATIONS

A&EJR	Athenry & Ennis Junction Railway.	D&SER	Dublin & South Eastern Railway.	INWR	Irish North Western Railway.
A&TR.	Athenry & Tuam Railway.	D&WR	Dublin & Wicklow Railway.	K&KJR	Kingstown & Kingsbridge Junction
ARSN Co.	Atlantic Royal Steam Navigation	DP&DB	Dublin Port & Docks Board.		Railway.
	Company.	DTCR	Dublin Trunk Connecting Railway.	L&CR	Limerick & Castleconnell Railway.
B&NCR	Belfast & Northern Counties Railway.	DUTC	Dublin United Tramways Company.	L&NWR	London & North Western Railway.
BoT	Board of Trade.	DW&WR	Dublin,Wicklow & Wexford Railway.	LM&SR	London Midland & Scottish Railway.
BoW	Board of Works.	GCIR	Great Central Irish Railway.	MGWR	Midland Great Western Railway.
C&HR	Chester & Holyhead Railway.	GJR	Grand Junction Railway.	N&KR	Navan & Kingscourt Railway.
C&LR	Cavan & Leitrim Railway.	GN&WR	Great Northern & Western Railway.	NWR	North Western Railway.
CDB	Congested Districts Board.	GN&WT	Great Northern & Western Trunk	PWLC	Public Works Loan Commissioners.
CI Co.	Consett Iron Company.		Railway.	S&BJR	Sligo & Ballaghaderreen Jct. Railway.
CIR	Central Ireland Railway.	GNR	Great Northern Railway.	SL&NCR	Sligo Leitrim & Northern Counties
CofDJR	City of Dublin Junction Railways.	GPJR	Galway Pier & Junction Railway.		Railway.
CofDSP	City of Dublin Steam Packet Company.	GS&WR	Great Southern & Western Railway.	UR	Ulster Railway.
D&BJR	Dublin & Belfast Junction Railway.	GSR	Great Southern Railways.	W&CIR	Waterford & Central Ireland Railway.
D&DR	Dublin & Drogheda Railway.	GWR	Great Western Railway (of England).	W&KR	Waterford & Kilkenny Railway.
D&ER	Dublin & Enniskillen Railway.	IGWR	Irish Great Western Railway.	W&LR	Waterford & Limerick Railway.
D&MR	Dublin & Meath Railway.	INMR	Irish North Midland Railway.	WL&WR	Waterford,Limerick & Western Railway.

Appendix B

LIST OF STATIONS & INTERMEDIATE BLOCK POSTS

DUBLIN - GALWAY

Miles	Station	Open	Closed	Remarks
00.00	Broadstone	1847	1937	
01.33	Liffey Jct	1864	1937	
01.67	Broombridge	1990	Open	
02.06	Reilly's Bridge	1847	1847	
03.08	Ashtown	1902	1934	Reopened 1982
04.43	Blanchardstown	1847	1934	Reopened 1990
04.50	Castleknock	1990	Open	
05.60	Coolmines	1891	1906	Block post
05.61	Coolmines	1990	Open	
07.08	Clonsilla Jct	1847	1963	Reopened 1981
08.72	Lucan	1847	1941	
10.20	Leixlip Confey	1990	Open	
11.20	Leixlip	1847	1963	Reopened 1981
14.72	Maynooth	1847	1963	Reopened 1981
18.40	Kilcock	1847	1848	
19.12	Kilcock	1848	1963	
20.75	Ferns Lock	1848	1963	Correct name Ferrans Lock
23.45	Kilbrook	1891	1906	Block Post and Ballast Pit
26.40	Enfield	1847	1963	Reopened 1988
27.62	Nesbitt Jct	1877	1930	
30.28	Moyvalley	1847	1963	
33.05	34 Mile Box	1891	c1912	Block Post
35.55	Hill of Down	1847	1963	
38.00	39 Mile Box	1891	c1912	Block Post
41.60	Killucan	1848	1963	Open as Block Post
45.52	46 Mile Box	1891	1977	
50.17	Mullingar	1848	Open	
51.40	Newbrook	1902	1929	
58.22	Castletown	1851	1963	
61.56	Streamstown Jct	1851	1963	Open as jct.1863
68.33	Moate	1851	1987	
72.08	73 Mile Box	1891	1962	
78.05	Athlone (MGWR)	1851	1985	
79.14	Monksland	1877	1928	Ballast Pit
84.71	Thomastown	1912	1925	Block Post from 1891
84.71	Carrowduff	1925	1963	GSR name for Thomastown
91.53	Ballinasloe	1851	Open	
101.31	Woodlawn	1851	Open	
107.20	Attymon Jct	1890	Open	
113.36	Athenry	1851	Open	
121.32	Oranmore	1851	1963	
126.53	Galway	1851	Open	

LIFFEY JCT - NORTH WALL

00.00	Liffey Jct	1864	1927	Signal cabin closed 1991.
01.30	North City Mills	1866	1977	Siding
02.78	North Wall	1864	Open	Freight only

MULLINGAR - SLIGO

Miles	Station	Open	Closed	Remarks
50.17	Mullingar	1848	Open	
52.33	Levington	1929	1963*	Level Crossing & Block Post*
56.20	Clonhugh	1855	1947	
57.36	Multyfarnham	1855	1963	
60.69	Inny Jct	1856	1931	Cavan Jct until 1878
63.18	Street & Rathowen	1877	1963	
67.52	Edgeworthstown	1855	Open	Renamed Mostrim by GSR
76.22	Longford	1855	Open	
80.05	Newtownforbes	1863	1963	
87.25	Dromod	1862	Open	
93.00	Drumsna	1863	1963	
97.62	Carrick-on-Shannon	1862	Open	
106.33	Boyle	1862	Open	
112.40	Kilfree Jct	1874	1963	
120.15	Ballymote	1862	Open	
127.56	Collooney	1862	Open	
128.03	Collooney Jct	1895	1976	
128.60	Carrignagat Jct	1875	1930	
129.61	Ballysodare	1862	1963	
134.16	Sligo	1862	Open	
134.50	Sligo Goods	1862	Open	Goods only
135.09	Sligo Quay	1900	Open	

ATHLONE - WESTPORT

Miles	Station	Open	Closed	Remarks
78.05	Athlone	1851	1985	services trans. to GS&WR sta.
84.00	Kiltoom	1880	1963	
87.25	Nine Mile Bridge	?	?	Pilgrimage traffic only
88.20	Lecarrow	1910	1989	Ballast Pit Sidings
90.00	Knockcroghery	1860	1963	
92.71	Ballymurry	1860	1963	
96.19	Roscommon	1860	Open	
101.73	Donamon	1860	1963	
107.55	Ballymoe	1861	1963	
112.53	Castlerea	1860	Open	
118.60	Ballinlough	1880	1963	
124.02	Ballyhaunis	1861	Open	
128.58	Bekan	1909	1963	
134.67	Claremorris	1862	Open	
142.35	Balla	1862	1963	
145.71	Manulla Jct	1868	Open	Closed 1963-1988
149.74	Castlebar	1862	Open	
155.39	Islandeady	1914	1963	
160.74	Westport	1866	Open	
162.67	Westport Quay	1874	?	

CLONSILLA - KINGSCOURT

Miles	Station	Open	Closed	Remarks
07.08	Clonsilla Jct	1862*	Open	* as a junction
10.32	Dunboyne	1862	1947/1963	
12.52	Fairyhouse Bridge	1881	1931	
15.72	Batterstown	1862	1947/1963	
18.73	Drumree	1862	1947/1963	
24.20	Kilmessan Jct	1862	1947/1963	
27.25	Bective	1862	1947/1963	
30.42	Navan Jct	1862	1947/1963	
33.00	Proudstown Park	1914	1939	
34.32	Gibbstown	1872	1947/1963	
37.00	Wilkinstown	1872	1947/1963	
39.70	Castletown Kil.	1927	1935	
43.23	Nobber	1872	1947/1963	
46.12	Kilmainham Wood	1872	1948/1963	
50.45	Kingscourt	1875	1947/Open via ex-GNR line from Drogheda for Gypsum traffic.	

KILMESSAN - ATHBOY

Miles	Station	Open	Closed	Remarks
24.20	Kilmessan Jct	1864	1963	
29.61	Trim	1864	1953	
36.32	Athboy	1864	1953	

NESBITT JCT - EDENDERRY

Miles	Station	Open	Closed	Remarks
27.62	Nesbitt Jct	1877	1930	
33.60	Carbury	1877	1931/1963	
37.20	Edenderry	1877	1931/1963	

STREAMSTOWN JCT - CLARA (MGW)

Miles	Station	Open	Closed	Remarks
61.56	Streamstown Jct	1863	1963	
64.58	Horseleap	1875	1947	
69.09	Clara (MGW)	1863	1925	

ATTYMON JCT - LOUGHREA

Miles	Station	Open	Closed	Remarks
107.20	Attymon Jct	1890	1975	
111.26	Dunsandle	1890	1975	
116.15	Loughrea	1890	1975	

INNY JCT - CAVAN

Miles	Station	Open	Closed	Remarks
60.69	Inny Jct	1856	1931	
64.75	Float	1856	1947/1960	
70.09	Ballywillan	1856	1947/1960	
76.15	Drumhowna	1913	1947/1960	
81.34	Crossdoney Jct	1856	1947/1960	
85.47	Cavan	1856	1947/1960	

CROSSDONEY JCT - KILLESHANDRA

Miles	Station	Open	Closed	Remarks
81.34	Crossdoney Jct	1886	1947	
83.70	Arva Road	1886	1947	
88.35	Killeshandra	1886	1947	

KILFREE JCT - BALLAGHADERREEN

Miles	Station	Open	Closed	Remarks
112.40	Kilfree Jct	1874	1963	
117.28	Island Road	1909	1963	
119.15	Edmondstown	1874	1963	
122.03	Ballaghaderreen	1874	1963	

MANULLA JCT - KILLALA

Miles	Station	Open	Closed	Remarks
145.75	Manulla Jct	1868	1963	Re-opened 1988
150.30	Ballyvary	1894	1963	
157.01	Foxford	1868	1963	Re-opened 1988
166.21	Ballina	1873	Open	
174.30	Killala	1893	1931/1934	

GALWAY - CLIFDEN

Miles	Station	Open	Closed	Remarks
126.53	Galway	1851	Open	
134.28	Moycullen	1895	1935	
138.61	Ross	1895	1935	
143.20	Oughterard	1895	1935	
153.36	Maam Cross	1896	1935	
160.55	Hotel Platform	1902	1922	
162.67	Recess	1895	1935	
168.16	Ballynahinch	1895	1935	
175.46	Clifden	1895	1935	

CLAREMORRIS - BALLINROBE

Miles	Station	Open	Closed	Remarks
134.67	Claremorris	1892	1960	
142.05	Hollymount	1892	1960	
147.31	Ballinrobe	1892	1960	

WESTPORT - ACHILL

Miles	Station	Open	Closed	Remarks
160.74	Westport	1866	Open	
168.69	Newport	1894	1937	
179.32	Mallaranny	1894	1937	
187.46	Achill	1895	1937	

Note: Where two closure dates are indicated, the first refers to passenger traffic, the second to goods traffic.

A SELECTION OF
MGWR STATION DRAWINGS

MOATE

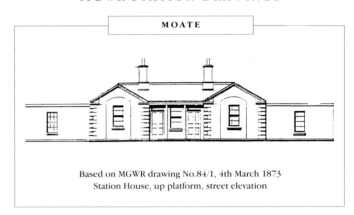

Based on MGWR drawing No.84/1, 4th March 1873
Station House, up platform, street elevation

ATHENRY

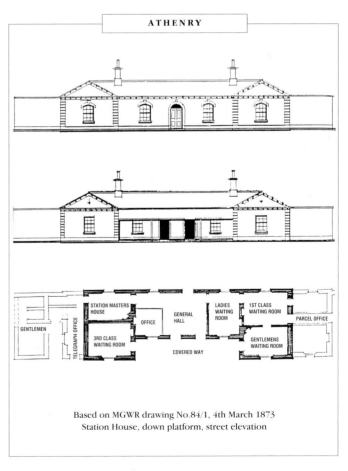

Based on MGWR drawing No.84/1, 4th March 1873
Station House, down platform, street elevation

LUCAN NORTH

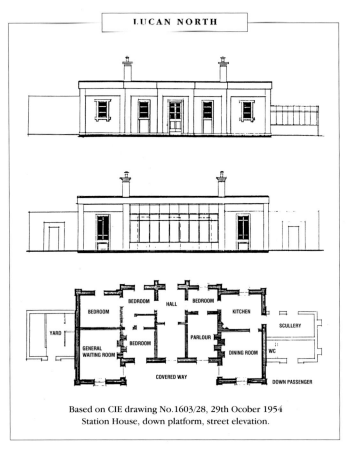

Based on CIE drawing No.1603/28, 29th Ocober 1954
Station House, down platform, street elevation.

LEIXLIP

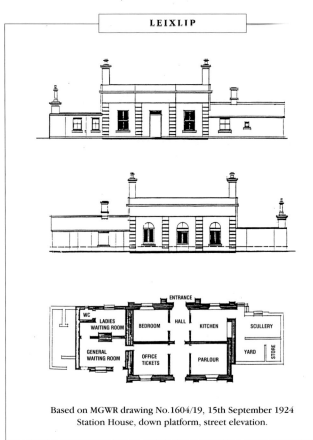

Based on MGWR drawing No.1604/19, 15th September 1924
Station House, down platform, street elevation.

KILCOCK

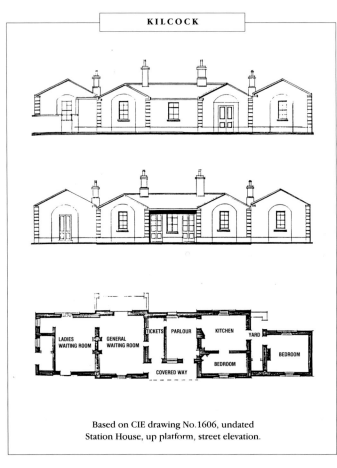

Based on CIE drawing No.1606, undated
Station House, up platform, street elevation.

MOYVALLEY

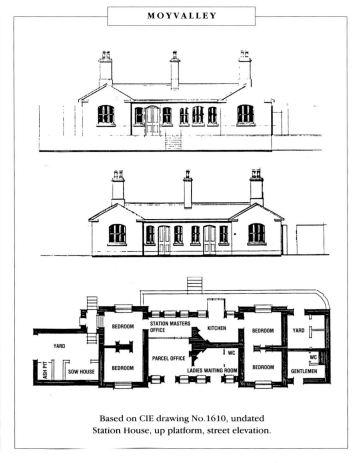

Based on CIE drawing No.1610, undated
Station House, up platform, street elevation.

ATHLONE

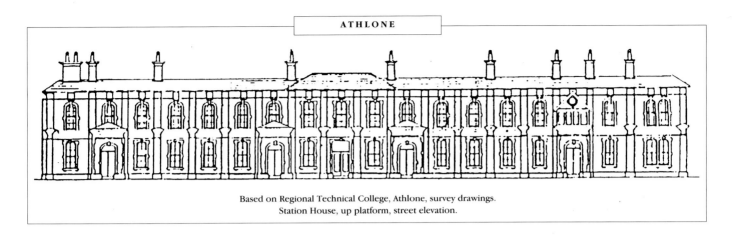

Based on Regional Technical College, Athlone, survey drawings.
Station House, up platform, street elevation.

ROSS

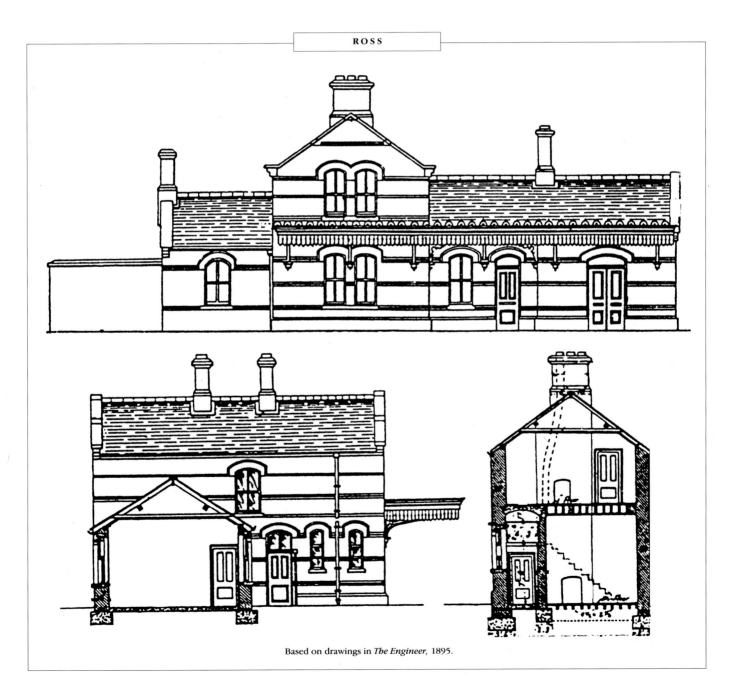

Based on drawings in *The Engineer,* 1895.

Class A No.124 *Mercuric* of 1905 after her first rebuild in June 1916 with a superheater and piston valves and an unusual form of extended smokebox. No.124 was severely damaged in a malicious derailment at Streamstown in 1923, following which she was heavily rebuilt. The locomotive was withdrawn as CIE No.550 in March 1957.
Author's collection.

'G2' 2-4-0 No.656, the former MGWR No.30 *Active*, was built at Broadstone in April 1898, incorporating parts from the old 'D' class of 1873/6. Regarded by many as Atock's finest design, No.656 lasted until March 1957 having been superheated in 1926. They were believed to be the only superheated 2-4-0s in the world and possibly the last working 2-4-0s anywhere on main line duties.
The late H Fayle, courtesy IRRS.

'P' class 0-6-0T No.105 *Hercules* was built at Broadstone in 1890 for use on the North Wall pilot duties. The class remained on these duties throughout their working lives, apart from an occasional trip to Amiens Street on the boat trains. It was withdrawn in 1949 as CIE No.618.
The late H Fayle, courtesy IRRS.

Appendix C

LOCOMOTIVES

Class	No.	Name	Maker/No.	Intr.	Wdn.	GSR No.	GSR Cl.
1	7	Dunsandle	G	1847	1871		
1	8	Vesta	G	1847	1870		
1	9	Venus	G	1847	1869		
1	10	Luna	G	1847	1869		
1	11	Juno	G	1847	1867		
1	30	Pallas	G	1847	1875		
1	33	Falco	G	1847	1875		
2	1	Orion	F	1847	1860		
2	2	Mars	F	1847	1856		
2	3	Saturn	F	1847	1856		
2	4	Mercury	F	1847	1856		
2	5	Jupiter	F	1847	1856		
2	6	Sirius	F	1847	1856		
3	12	Heron	F	1848	1873		
3	13	Condor	F	1848	1873		
3	14	Petrel	F	1848	1875		
3	15	Pelican	F	1848	1873		
3	16	Cygnet	F	1848	1873		
3	17	Ouzel/Snipe	F	1848	1875		
4	27	Fairy/Bee	F	1851	1897		
4	28	Titania/Elf	F	1851	1897		
4	29	Ariel/Fairy	F	1851	1897		
5	18	Eclipse	L	1851	1880		
5	19	Childers	L	1851	1872		
5	20	Arabian	L	1851	1873		
5	21	Voltigeur	L	1851	1873		
5	22	Harkaway	L	1852	1873		
5	23	Birdcatcher	L	1852	1873		
6	25	Cyclops	L	1852	1880		
6	26	Vulcan	L	1852	1880		
7	24	Hawthorne	H/786	1852	1873		
8	31		F	1853	1880		
8	32		F	1853	1880		
8	34		F	1854	1880		
8	35	Wren	F	1854	1885		
9	36	Stockwell	G	1885	1881		
9	37	Voltigeur	G	1855	1881		
9	38	Birdcatcher	G	1856	1881		
9	39	Harkaway	G	1856	1881		
10	1	Orion	G	1860	1882/4		
10	2	Jupiter	G	1857	1880		
10	3	Juno	G	1857	1880		
10	4	Venus	G	1857	1882/4		
10	5	Mars	G	1857	1882/4		
10	6	Vesta	G	1857	1880/4		
10	40	Emperor	G	1856	1880		
10	41	Regal	G	1856	1880/3		
11	42	Ouzel	St/1048	1856	1880		
12	43	Regent	F	1860	1879		
12	44	Duke	F	1860	1879		
12	45	Marquis	F	1860	1879		
12	46	Baron	F	1860	1879		
12	47	Viscount	F	1860	1879		
12	48	Earl	F	1860	1879		
13	49	Queen	H/1170	1862	1880/5		
13	50	Viceroy	H/1171	1862	1884/7		
13	51	Leinster	H/1172	1862	1886		
13	52	Munster	H/1173	1862	1884/7		
13	53	Ulster	H/1174	1862	1886/7		
13	54	Connaught	H/1175	1862	1887		
14	55	Inny	N/937	1863	1885		
14	56	Liffey	N/938	1863	1885		
14	57	Lough Corrib	N/939	1863	1885		
14	58	Lough Gill	N/940	1863	1885		
14	59	Shannon	N/941	1863	1885		
14	60	Lough Owel	N/942	1863	1885		
15	61	Lynx	N/1042	1864	1887		
15	62	Tiger	N/1043	1864	1888		
15	63	Lion	N/1044	1864	1888		
15	64	Leopard	N/1045	1864	1888		
15	65	Wolf	N/1046	1864	1888		
15	66	Elephant	N/1047	1864	1889		
16	67	Dublin	D/185	1867	1888		
16	68	Mullingar	D/186	1867	1887		
16	69	Athlone	D/187	1867	1889		
16	70	Ballinasloe	D/188	1867	1888		
16	71	Galway	D/189	1867	1887		
16	72	Sligo	D/190	1867	1888		
17	85	Meath	F&H	1864	1885		
18	7	Connemara	A/779	1869	1889		
18	8	St.Patrick	A/803	1870	1890		
18	9	Emerald Isle	A/778	1869	1890		
18	10	Faugh a Ballagh	A/777	1869	1889		
18	11	Erin go Bragh	A/780	1869	1890		
18	12	Shamrock	A/802	1870	1890		
19	73	Comet	N/1575	1871	1892		
19	74	Luna	N/1579	1871	1892		
19	75	Hector	N/1580	1871	1892		
19	76	Lightning	N/1576	1871	1892		
19	77	Star	N/1577	1871	1891		
19	78	Planet	N/1578	1871	1891		
19	79	Mayo	N/1579	1872	1892		
19	80	Dunsandle	N/1722	1872	1891		
19	81	Clancarty	N/1717	1872	1892		
19	82	Clonbrock	N/1718	1872	1892		
19	83	Lucan	N/1719	1872	1891		
19	84	Dunkellen	N/1720	1872	1891		
D	13	Rapid	N/1784	1873	1893		
D	14	Racer	N/1785	1873	1893		
D	15	Rover	N/1786	1873	1895		
D	16	Rob Roy	N/1787	1873	1895		
D	17	Reindeer	N/1788	1873	1894		
D	18	Ranger	N/1789	1873	1893		
D	19	Spencer	N/1790	1873	1894		
D	20	Speedy	N/1791	1873	1894		
D	21	Swift	N/1792	1873	1896		
D	22	Samson	N/1793	1873	1896		
D	23	Sylph	N/1794	1873	1896		
D	24	Sprite	N/1795	1873	1896		
D	30	Active	D/905	1876	1897		
D	31	Alert	D/906	1876	1897		
D	32	Ariel	D/907	1876	1897		
D	33	Arrow	D/908	1876	1898		
D	34	Aurora	D/909	1876	1898		
L*	86	Bullfinch	St/2284	1876	1928	577	J18
L*	87	Buzzard	St/2285	1876	1925		
L*	88	Buffalo	St/2286	1876	1925		
L*	89	Bison	St/2287	1876	1925		
L*	90	Beaver	St/2288	1876	1925		
L*	91	Bear	St/2289	1876	1928	579	J18
L*	92	Bittern	St/2290	1876	1957	575	J18
L*	93	Butterfly	St/2305	1876	1923		
L*	94	Badger	St/2306	1876	1923		
L*	95	Bulldog	St/2307	1876	1927	(573)	J18

N.B. * These locomotives were later rebuilt as Class Lm. Continued on page 130

Above: **Class A 4-4-0 No.127** *Titanic* **as built in 1903. At the time of their introduction they were the largest 4-4-0s in Ireland. Never noted for their speed due to the use of crossed rods, they were nevertheless strong pullers. Rebuilt in 1920 with a superheater and piston valves, this engine was withdrawn, as CIE No.545, in June 1955.** The late H Fayle, courtesy IRRS.

Top: **'D-bogie' 4-4-0 No.37** *Wolf Dog,* **was turned out of Broadstone in September 1900. Officially described as new engines, they incorporated many parts from the '7-12' class. No.37 was renumbered 35 in 1922 and 6 in 1924. Superheated in August 1935, it became GSR No.533 and was withdrawn in July 1953.** The late H Fayle, courtesy IRRS.

Left: **Class C 4-4-0 No.544 at Inchicore, being prepared to work the 'Claddagh Express' to Galway; one of two such engines normally reserved for this duty. They were introduced as a lighter version of the 'A' class to provide greater route availability.** John Kennedy.

Above: **Class D5 (ex-'A') No.550 (ex-124) as finally rebuilt in June 1924 with raised footplating and Morton style cab. Three of the six members of the class were so rebuilt. No.550 was withdrawn in March 1957.** The late H Fayle, courtesy IRRS.

Below: **An IRRS outing at Clara on 21st July 1954 when a coach was attached to the branch goods train at Streamstown. The engine is an ex-MGWR 2-4-0.** John Kennedy.

Class J5 0-6-0 No.635 seen here at Inchicore, was built at Broadstone in 1921 as 'Fa' No.41. Others came from Armstrong Whitworth in 1924 and a further batch, Nos 86-95 (Fb) distinguishable by the platforms being raised clear of the side rods, was built at Broadstone in 1924. No.635 was withdrawn in 1957.
John Kennedy.

Class B No.143 *Canada*, built in 1904 by the North British Locomotive Company. As far as possible, parts were interchangeable with the 'A' class. No.143 was fitted with a superheated boiler from No.124 in 1916. The class had a short working life, probably due to the introduction of the 'Woolwich' Moguls in 1925.
Courtesy John Kennedy.

No.619 (ex 96) as rebuilt in 1907 with a new 'A' class boiler. She received a superheater and piston valves in 1921. In this form they were the strongest goods engines on the Midland, taking turns on the main line goods with the 'B' class. No.619 was withdrawn in 1949.
The late H Fayle, courtesy IRRS.

Above: **The Royal Train at Broadstone in 1907 with No.129 *Celtic*. The bogie van is No.59. The third vehicle is the Royal saloon, at that time running with 4-wheeled bogies.** Des McGlynn collection.

Right: **'Woolwich' 2-6-0 No.385 built at Inchicore in 1927 and withdrawn in May 1960. In their original condition these engines were similar in appearance to the Southern Railway (England) 'N' class.** The late H Fayle, courtesy IRRS.

Below: **Class D6 4-4-0 No.541 outside Broadstone shed in 1936. Originally No.8 *St Patrick* she was turned out of Broadstone in June 1913. Rebuilt in November 1917 with larger boiler, superheater and piston valves, No.541 remained in service until October 1959. This photograph clearly illustrates the Morton extended smokebox which was designed to accommodate the superheater.** The late H Fayle, courtesy IRRS.

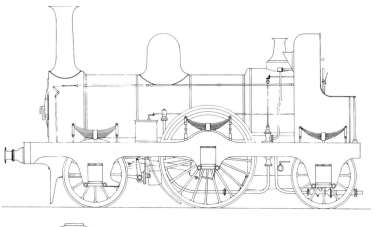

Hawthorn-Single (Class 13) 2-2-2

Built by Hawthorn, introduced in 1862
Distance from buffer beam to
tender drawbar: 23ft 9½in

Scale 4mm to 1ft

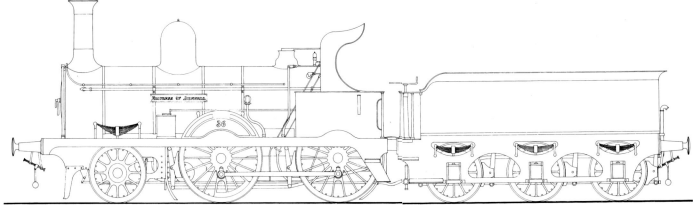

Class D 2-4-0 No.36 *Empress of Austria*

Built by Beyer Peacock & Company, 1881
Length over buffers including tender: 46ft 4in
Length over frames including tender: 42ft 4in
Width over footplate: 7ft 7in

Livery 1881: emerald green, lined black and
white, no company initials on tender, dome
polished brass, name plate brass letters with
vermillion background.

Scale 4mm to 1ft

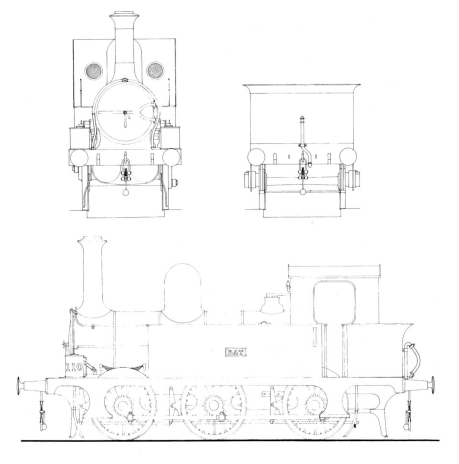

Class E 0-6-0 No.110 *Bat*

Built by Sharp Stewart & Company, 1891
Length over buffers: 28ft 7½in
Length over frames: 24ft 7½in
Width over footplate: 7ft 7in

Livery 1905: blue, lined black and white.

Scale 4mm to 1ft

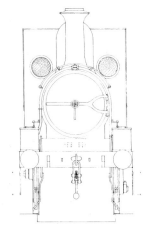 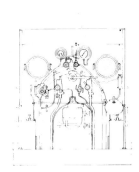 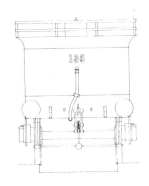

Class Lm 0-6-0 No.135 *Arran Isles*

Built by Kitson & Company, Leeds, 1891
Length over buffers including tender: 46ft 0in
Length over frames including tender: 42ft 0in
Width over footplate: 7ft 7in

Livery 1915: unlined black, company initials on tender.

Scale 4mm to 1ft

'D-bogie' 4-4-0 No.2 *Jupiter*. Sometimes regarded as rebuilds of the Beyer 2-4-0s of 1880/1, the six engines of this class were in effect new engines – the first bogie engines on the MGWR. No.2 was out-shopped from Broadstone in March 1900 and superheated in June 1920. As GSR/CIE 'D16' No.534, she received an 'X' class superheater Belpaire boiler in November 1932 and was eventually withdrawn in 1949. Author's collection.

Class	No.	Name	Maker/No.	Intr.	Wdn.	GSR No.	GSR Cl.
Ln	49	Marquis	B	1879	1928	(563)	J16
Ln	50	Viscount	B	1879	1925	(564)	J16
Ln	51	Regent/Baron§	B	1880	1926	(565)	J16
Ln	52	Baron/Regent§	B	1880	1927	(566)	J16
Ln	53	Duke	B	1880	1950	567	J16
Ln	54	Earl	B	1880	1925	(568)	J16
H	96	Avonside	A/1211	1878	1949	619	J6
H	97	Hibernia	A/1214 ††	1878	1949	620	J6
H	98	Caledonia	A/1212 ††	1878	1949	621	J6
H	99	Cambria	A/1213	1878	1945	622	J6
D	1	Orion	B	1884	1922		
D†	2	Jupiter	BP/1960	1880	1949	534	D16
D†	3	Juno	BP/1961	1880	1949	535	D16
D	4	Venus	B	1884	1910		
D	5	Mars	B	1884	1910		
D	6	Vesta	B	1884	1916		
D†	25	Cyclops	BP/1962	1880	1945	531	D16
D†	26	Britannia	BP/1963	1880	1949	532	D16
D	35	Airedale	K/2901	1886	1922		
D†	36	Empress of Austria	BP/1964	1881	1949	530	D16
D†	37	Wolf Dog	BP/1965	1881	1953	533	D16
D	38	Eagle	K/2902	1886	1923		
D	39	Hawk	K/2903	1886	1922		
D	40	Lily	K/2904	1886	1922		
D	41	Regal	B	1883	1915		
D	42	Ouzel	B	1883	1921		
D	43	Leinster	B	1887	1916		
D	44	Ulster	B	1887	1911		
D	45	Queen	B	1886	1916		
D	46	Munster	B	1887	1921		
D	47	Viceroy	B	1886	1921		
D	48	Connaught	B	1887	1922		
P	100	Giantess	B	1881	1955	614	J10
P	101	Giant	B	1881	1951	615	J10
P	102	Pilot	B	1881	1950	616	J10
P	103	Pioneer	B	1881	1959	617	J10
P	105	Hercules	B	1891	1949	618	J10
7-12	7	Connemara	B	1889	1909		
7-12	8	St Patrick	B	1890	1914		
7-12	9	Emerald Isle	B	1890	1912		
7-12	10	Faugh a Ballagh	B	1889	1910		
7-12	11	Erin go Bragh	B	1890	1922		
7-12	12	Shamrock	B	1890	1910		
L	55	Inny	B	1885	1961	594	J19
L	56	Liffey	B	1885	1957	595	J19
L	57	Lough Corrib	B	1885	1959	596	J19
L	58	Lough Gill	B	1885	1959	597	J19
L	59	Shannon	B	1885	1963	598	J19
L	60	Lough Owel	B	1885	1963	599	J19
L	61	Lynx	B	1888	1957	600	J19
L	62	Tiger	B	1888	1959	601	J19
L	63	Lion	B	1888	1959	602	J19
L	64	Leopard	B	1888	1923		
L	65	Wolf	B	1888	1965	603	J19
L	66	Elephant	B	1889	1961	604	J19
L	67	Dublin	B	1888	1957	605	J19
L	68	Mullingar	B	1887	1962	606	J19
L	69	Athlone	B	1889	1961	607	J19
L	70	Ballinasloe	B	1888	1959	608	J19
L	71	Galway	B	1887	1954	609	J19
L	72	Sligo	B	1888	1963	610	J19
L	85	Meath	B	1886	1924		
L	140	Wren	B	1886	1925	(611)	J19
E	106	Lark	K/3370	1891	1954	551	J26
E	107	Robin	K/3371	1891	1963	552	J26
E	108	Swallow	K/3372	1891	1955	553	J26
E	109	Fly	SS/3693	1891	1955	554	J26
E	110	Bat	SS/3694	1891	1955	555	J26
E	111	Wasp	SS/3695	1891	1956	556	J26
E	112	Hornet	K/3380	1892	1959	557	J26
E	113	Gnat	K/3381	1892	1960	558	J26
E	114	Stork	K/3382	1892	1960	559	J26
E	115	Achill	K/3527	1894	1963	560	J26
E	116	Cong	K/3528	1894	1959	561	J26
E	117	Moy	K/3529	1894	1963	562	J26
Lm	73	Comet	B	1892	1959	582	J18
Lm	74	Luna	B	1891	1957	576	J18
Lm	75	Hector	B	1891	1961	612	J19
Lm	76	Lightning	B	1892	1925	(569)	J18
Lm	77	Star	B	1892	1963	589	J18
Lm	78	Planet	B	1893	1925	(570)	J18
Lm	79	Mayo	B	1892	1927	(578)	J18
Lm	80	Dunsandle	B	1891	1963	574	J18
Lm	81	Clancarty	B	1893	1963	613	J18
Lm	82	Clonbrock	B	1892	1963	583	J18
Lm	83	Lucan	B	1892	1925	(571)	J18
Lm	84	Dunkellen	B	1891	1925	(572)	J18
Lm	130	Ajax	SS/4057	1895	1955	584	J18
Lm	131	Atlas	SS/4058	1895	1960	585	J18
Lm	132	Pluto	SS/4059	1895	1957	586	J18
Lm	133	Titan	SS/4060	1895	1961	587	J18
Lm	134	Vulcan	SS/4061	1895	1963	588	J18
Lm	135	Arran Isles	K/3584	1895	1923		
Lm	136	Cavan	K/3585	1895	1961	590	J18
Lm	137	Maynooth	K/3586	1895	1959	591	J18
Lm	138	Nephin	K/3599	1895	1962	592	J18
Lm	139	Tara	K/3600	1895	1965	593	J18
K	13	Rapid	B	1893	1961	659	G2
K	14	Racer	B	1893	1959	650	G2
K	15	Rover	B	1895	1959	660	G2
K	16	Rob Roy	B	1895	1959	651	G2
K	17	Reindeer	B	1894	1959	661	G2
K	18	Ranger	B	1893	1954	652	G2
K	19	Spencer	B	1894	1963	653	G2
K	20	Speedy	B	1896	1923		
K	21	Swift	B	1896	1955	662	G2
K	22	Samson	B	1896	1959	663	G2
K	23	Sylph	B	1896	1961	664	G2
K	24	Sprite	B	1897	1959	665	G2
K	27	Clifden	B	1897	1957	666	G2
K	28	Clara	B	1897	1963	654	G2
K	29	Clonsilla	B	1897	1961	655	G2
K	30	Active	B	1898	1957	656	G2
K	31	Alert	B	1897	1957	667	G2
K	32	Ariel	B	1898	1959	668	G2
K	33	Arrow	B	1898	1961	657	G2
K	34	Aurora	B	1898	1954	658	G2
W	141	Limerick	K/3974	1901	1929	(233)	J17
W	142	Athenry	K/3975	1901	1950	234	J17
A	124	Mercuric	B	1905	1957	550	D5
A	125	Britannic	B	1905	1954	547	D5
A	126	Atlantic	B	1904	1955	548	D5
A	127	Titanic	B	1903	1955	545	D5
A	128	Majestic	B	1902	1931	549	D5
A	129	Celtic	B	1902	1959	546	D5
B	143	Canada	NBL/16128	1904	1933	646	J2
B	144	Australia	NBL/16129	1904	1930	647	J2
B	145	India	NBL/16130	1904	1934	648	J2
B	146	Africa	NBL/16131	1904	1934	649	J2
C	4	Ballynahinch	B	1910	1950	538	D7
C	5	Croagh Patrick	B	1910	1952	539	D7
C	6	Kylemore	B	1911	1959	542	D6
C	7	Connemara	B	1909	1953	540	D6
C	8	St Patrick	B	1913	1959	541	D6
C	9	Emerald Isle	B	1912	1953	537	D7
C	10	Faugh a Ballagh	B	1909	1959	543	D6
C	11	Erin go Bragh	B	1915	1955	544	D6
C	12	Shamrock	B	1913	1951	536	D7
Fa	36		B	1922	1959	636	J5
Fa	37		B	1922	1963	637	J5
Fa	38		B	1922	1963	638	J5
Fa	39		B	1921	1957	633	J5
Fa	40		B	1921	1959	634	J5
Fa	41		B	1921	1957	635	J5
Fa	42		B	1922	1962	639	J5
Fa	43		B	1923	1960	640	J5
Fa	44		AW/175	1922	1959	641	J5
Fa	45		AW/176	1922	1961	642	J5
Fa	46		AW/177	1922	1955	643	J5
Fa	47		AW/178	1923	1957	644	J5
Fa	48		AW/179	1923	1955	645	J5

† = Rebuilt as 'D-bogie' engines 1900-1.

Class	No.	Name	Maker/No.	Intr.	Wdn.	GSR No.	GSR Cl.
Fb	86		B	1924	1957	623	J5
Fb	87		B	1924	1965	624	J5
Fb	88		B	1924	1961	625	J5
Fb	89		B	1924	1961	626	J5
Fb	90		B	1924	1961	627	J5
Fb	91		B	1924	1954	628	J5
Fb	92		B	1924	1954	629	J5
Fb	93		B	1924	1959	630	J5
Fb	94		B	1924	1954	631	J5
Fb	95		B	1924	1959	632	J5
D2	49		W/B	1925	1960	372	K1
Railmotor			C Price	1911	1933		

§ = Names transposed when both engines in works for overhaul.
†† = Actual numbers not clear to which applied.
GSR numbers in brackets were allocated but not applied.

LOCOMOTIVE BUILDERS

A	Avonside Engine Co., Bristol.	H	R&W Hawthorn, Leith.
AW	Armstrong Whitworth.	K	Kitson & Co., Leeds.
B	Broadstone Works of the MGW.	L	R B Longridge & Co., Bedlington.
BP	Beyer Peacock & Co., Manchester.	N	Neilson & Co., Glasgow.
D	Dübs & Co., Glasgow.	NBL	North British Locomotive Co., Glasgow.
F	William Fairbairn & Sons, Manchester.	SS	Sharp Stewart & Co., Glasgow.
F&H	Fossick & Hackworth	St.	R Stephenson & Co.
G	Thomas Grendon & Co., Drogheda.	W/B	Woolwich Arsenal, assembled at Broadstone from parts.

Appendix D

LOCOMOTIVES MALICIOUSLY DAMAGED 1922/23

No	Name	Date	Remarks
3	Juno	1 March 1923	84mp, Mayo branch
13	Rapid	4 January 1923	Kingscourt
14	Racer	10 January 1923	Achill branch
15	Rover	10 January 1923	Achill branch
20	Speedy	3 February 1923	Killala (destroyed)
21	Swift	25 January 1923	Islandeady
25	Cyclops	7 February 1923	154mp Mayo branch
27	Clifden	14 December 1922	Sligo
		30 January 1923	123mp, Sligo branch
28	Clara	10 January 1923	Sligo
36	Empress of Austria	22 January 1923	Location unknown
37	Wolf Dog	12 December 1922	Achill
		10 January 1923	Achill branch
40		10 January 1923	Sligo
43		17 February 1923	Streamstown
44		16 January 1923	Mayo branch
52	Regent	13 January 1923	Streamstown
64	Leopard	16 January 1923	Streamstown (destroyed)
66	Elephant	17 February 1923	Streamstown
71	Galway	27 March 1923	133mp, Sligo branch
73	Comet	18 December 1922	Thomastown
79	Mayo	20 April 1923	Ballymoe
80	Dunsandle	7 July 1922	95mp
81	Clancarty	20 January 1923	85mp, Mayo branch
		11 December 1922	Manulla
86	Bullfinch	16 January 1923	Monksland Pit
89	Bison	8 November 1922	Manulla
90	Beaver	6 December 1922	74mp
92	Bittern	16 August 1922	Kiltoom
		21 September 1922	Athlone
93	Butterfly	10 January 1923	Sligo (destroyed)
96	Avonside	7 November 1922	North Wall
97	Hibernia	4 January 1923	Kingscourt
116	Cong	5 September 1922	Ballinrobe
124	Mercuric	17 February 1923	Streamstown
130	Ajax	10 April 1923	20mp, Meath branch
135	Arran Isles	13 January 1923	Streamstown
138	Nephin	27 February 1923	Athlone

Appendix E

PRINCIPAL LOCOMOTIVE DIMENSIONS

Class	Wheels	Cylinders	Boiler pressure	Driving wheels	Heating surface	Grate area	Weight
			(lbs/in^2)		(sq/ft)	(sq/ft)	(tons/cwt)
1	2-2-2	14"x18"		5'7¾"			
2	2-2-2	14"x		5'6"?			
3	2-2-2	14"x20"		5'7¾"			19.19
4	2-2-2WT	11"x15"		5'1"			
5	2-2-2	15"x20		5'7½"			
6	2-4-0	16"x20"		5'1"			
7	0-4-0	15"x20"		5'0"			
8	2-4-0	16"x21"		5'1½"			
9	0-6-0	16"x24"		5'1"			28.00
10	2-4-0	15"x20"		5'6¾"			
11	2-4-0	14"x20"		5'6"	68+760	11.25	
12	0-4-2	16"x24		5'1½"			
13	2-2-2	15"x22"		6'6"	83+916	14.1	30.05
14	0-4-2	16"x24"	120	5'0"	88+1054	14.75	
15	0-4-2	17"x24"		5'2"	87+1246	14.7	
16	0-4-2	17"x24"		5'2"	95+1246	15.1	32.12
17	2-4-0	16"x22"		5'1½"			
18	2-4-0	16"x22"		6'3"			
19	0-4-2	17"x24"	130	5'2"	87+1149	15.4	31.11
A	4-4-0	18"x26"	175	6'3"	150+1213	20	53.08
B	0-6-0	18"x26"	175	5'5"	150+842+170	20	50.11
C	4-4-0	18"x26"	175	6'3"	126+778+170	15.75	46.13
D	4-4-0	16"x22"	150	5'8"	95+984	16	40.00
E	0-6-0T	15"x22"	150	4'6"	72+668	13	33.12
F	0-6-0	19"x26"	175	5'8"	126+808+165	17.5	49.00
H	0-6-0	18"x24"	175	4'9"	116+832+172	20	46.03
K	2-4-0	17"x24"	150	5'8"	95+1020	15.5	37.10
L	0-6-0	18"x24"	150	5'3"	95+1020	15.5	40.04
Lm	0-6-0	18"x24"	150	5'3"	114+939	15.5	40.19
Ln	0-6-0	18"x24"	150	5'1½"	114+939	15.5	49.54
P	0-6-0T	18"x24"	150	4'6"	115+938	16	44.16
W	0-6-0	18"x24"	150	5'2"	108+875	18	41.04
D2	2-6-0	19"x28"	200	5'6"	135+1391+285	25	62.04

Appendix F

ROLLING STOCK RETURNS

	1860	1870	1880	1890	1900	1910	1920	1924
Engines	42	75	100	105	127	139	139	139
Carr-1st.class	5	5	18	20	25	24		
Carr-2nd.class	13	14	14	20	25	24		
Carr-3rd.class	30	69	88	81	93	95	147*	155*
Composites	31	51	39	38	42	47		
State carriages	1	1	1	1	1	2	2	2
Dining Cars						3	2	2
Carriage Trucks	20	22	22	22	24	24	24	23
Horse Boxes	28	44	56	56	60	60	60	59
Fish Vans		6	20	30	55	55		
Luggage Vans	23	26	30	48	57	63		
P.O.Sorting Vans				4	4	4	4	3
Open Box Wagons	5	117	151	201	201	286	459	532
Covered Goods	261	922	1483	1331	1581	1646		
Cattle Trucks	295	308	103	405	635	735	505	459
Timber Trucks	30	30	42	42	48	75	73	73
Boiler Trucks			2	2	4			
Powder Vans	1	2	2	2	2	2		
Ballast Wagons	32	80	102	102	102	138	136	115
Coal Trucks			90	90	140	140	140	139
Travelling Cranes		3	2	2	3	3	3	2
Brake Vans		14	38	49	55	65	63	54
Trav.Water Tanks		1						
Coke Trucks	6							

*Method of recording vehicle numbers altered at this period. This figure relates to carriages of uniform class. Wagon stock likewise was grouped differently at this period also, making it difficult to compare with earlier statistics.

COVERED GOODS WAGON 1893 CLASS

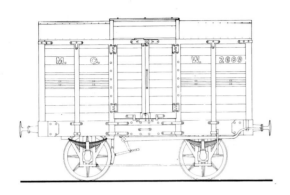

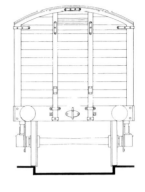

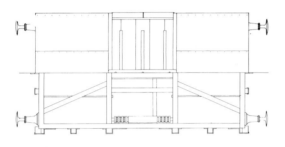

Wheel diameter: 3ft 3½in
Length over headstocks: 14ft 2in
Width over solebars: 7ft 5⅛in
Width over framing: 8ft 1⅛in

Livery 1890-1924: black, lettering white.

Scale 4mm to 1ft

7 TON OPEN BOX WAGON 1889 CLASS

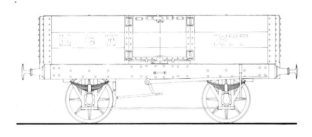

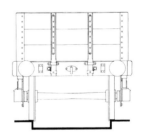

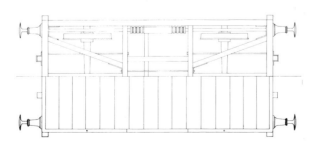

Wheel diameter: 3ft 3½in
Length over headstocks: 16ft 0in
Width over body: 7ft 7⅛in

Livery 1890-1924: black, lettering white

Scale 4mm to 1ft

HORSEBOX 1889 CLASS

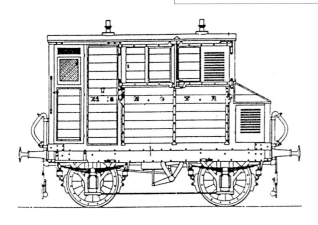

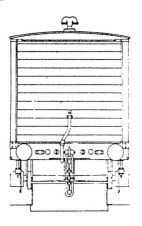

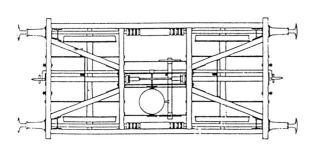

Length over headstocks: 15ft 0in
Width over solebars: 7ft 5⅛ in
Width over body: 8ft 1in
Wheel base: 9ft 0in
Wheel diameter on tread: 3ft 7½ in
Livery 1918-1924: body dark lake,
lining straw, shaded black.

Scale 4mm = 1ft

GOODS BRAKE VAN 1874 CLASS

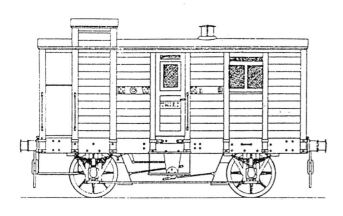

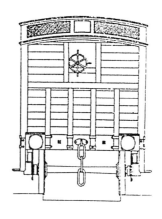

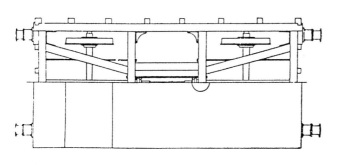

Length over headstocks: 17ft 6in
Width over solebars: 7ft 9⅛ in
Width over framing: 8ft 5⅛ in
Wheel base: 10ft 6 in
Wheel diameter on tread: 3ft 3½ in
Rating: 1924 (11 tons), 1874 (8 tons)
Livery 1924: mid green, lettering white,
ironwork black.

Scale 4mm = 1ft

Appendix G

PASSENGER ROLLING STOCK

FIRST CLASS

No.	Length	Compts	Wheels	Maker	Intr.	Wdn.	Remarks
1	30'	4	6	MGWR	1882	1941	32 seats. To 200A, 1940
2	30'	4	6	MGWR	1883	1941	32 seats
3	30'	4	6	MGWR	1883		32 seats
4	30'	4	6	MGWR	1889		To 178M Third, 1931
5	30'	4	6	MGWR	1889		To 164M Third, 1930
6		4	4	Bris	1873	1893	Cost £409
6	31' coupé	4	6	MGWR	1893		To 181M Compo, 1939
7		4	4	Bris	1873	1893	
7	31' coupé	4	6	MGWR	1893	1923	Destr. Achill 20-1-23
8		4	4	Bris	1873	1893	
8	31' coupé	4	6	MGWR	1893		To 182M Compo, 1939
9	30'	4	6	MGWR	1884		To 170M Third, 1930
10	30'	4	6	MGWR	1879		To 172M Third, 1930
11	30'	4	6	MGWR	1879	1907	To 61M Parcels Van 1907
11	31'	4	6	MGWR	1906		26 seats, 2 lav.
12	30'	4	6	MGWR	1879	1894	
12	30'	6	6	Ash	1914	1963	Ex 21 Second, Jan 1914
13	30'	4	6	MGWR	1879	1903	
13	30'	6	6	Ash	1914	1954	Ex 24 Second, Feb 1914; M.D. Islandeady 24-1-23
14	30'	4	6	MGWR	1879	1906	R/b as Sligo Ax van
14	31'	4	6	MGWR	1906	1959	M.D. Kingscourt, 4-1-23
15	34'	4	6	MGWR	1879	1903	
15	30'	5	6	MGWR	1914	1964	Ex 16 Second, Feb 1914
16	30'	4	6	MGWR	1880		To 169M Third, 1930; M.D. 154mp, Mayo line, 7-2-23
17	30'	4	6	MGWR	1884	1956	32 seats
18	30'	4	6	MGWR	1884		To 167M Third, 1930
19	30'	4	6	MGWR	1884		To 165M Third, 1930
20	30'	4	6	MGWR	1884	1905	32 seats
20	30'	4	6	MGWR	1905	1954	
21	31' coupé	6	6	Ash	1894	1923	Destr. Killala, 3-2-23
22	31' coupé	6	6	Ash	1894	1923	Destr. Drumree, 24-1-23
23	31' coupé	6	6	Ash	1894	1949	To Stores Van 306A
24	31' coupé	6	6	Ash	1894		26 seats, lav.
25	31' coupé	6	6	Ash	1894		To 184M Compo, 1939; M.D. Streamstown, 17-2-23
26	54'	2+S	8	Lanc	1902		To 26M Compo, 1934; 46 seats fr 1946, 2 lav, clersty
27	54'	2+S	8	Lanc	1902		To 193M Third, Jan 1955
28	54'	7	8	MGWR	1914		Ex 46 Compo, Jan 1914 To 166M Compo, 1930; S.C.
29	54'	7	8	MGWR	1914		Ex 45 Compo, Apr 1914, To 175M Compo, 1931
30	54'	7	8	MGWR	1914		Ex 44 Compo, Apr 1914, To 163M Compo, 1930; 56 seats
31	53'	11	8	Metr	1914		Ex 41 Compo; To 31 Compo, Jan 1920
31	25'		4	MGWR	1920	1948	Ex 5 Compo
32	53'	11	8	Metr	1914		Ex 42 Compo; To 1 Third,
33	54'	2+S	8	Lanc	1914	1956	Ex 46 Second, Apr 1914
34	54'	2+S	8	Lanc	1914	1960	Ex 27 Second, Apr 1914
35	54'	7	8	MGWR	1914		To 162M Compo, 1930; 46 seats, 2 lav, S.C.
36	54'	7	8	MGWR	1914	1923	Destr. Sligo, 10-1-23
37	30'	4	6	Metr	1914	1953	Ex 30 Compo Family Sal
38	30'	4	6	Metr	1914	1942	Ex 29 do; Destr by fire Athlone, 8-7-42
39	30'	6	6	Ash	1914	1962	Ex 25 Second, Mar 1914
40	30'	5	6	MGWR	1914	1949	Ex 15 Second, Mar 1914; M.D. Kiltoom, 23-1-23
41	30'	6	6	Ash	1914	1961	Ex 22 Second, Mar 1914
42	30'	5	6	MGWR	1914	1959	Ex 17 Second, Apr 1914
43	30'	5	6	MGWR	1914		Ex 12 Second, Apr 1914
44	30'	5	6	MGWR	1914	1923	Ex 9 Second, Apr 1914 Destr. Achill, 12-1-23
45	30'	6	6	Ash	1914	1959	Ex 23 Second, Apr 1914 To 183M Compo, 1939
46	22' 6"	4	4	MGWR	1924	1930	Ex 79 Third & 43 Compo. Conv. to service veh. & sold
47	31' 3"	3	6	Daws	1924		Old State coach; R/b 1904 To Belfast Museum in 1964
165M	30'	4	6	MGWR	1944		Ex Third 165M, 1944
178M	29'	4	6	MGWR	1943	1959	Ex Third 178M, 1943

SECOND CLASS

No.	Length	Compts	Wheels	Maker	Intr.	Wdn.	Remarks
1	30'	5	6	MGWR	1880		To 62 Parcels Van
2	30'	5	6	MGWR	1880	1903	
3	30'	5	6	MGWR	1880		To 107 Third, Apr 1914
4	30'	5	6	MGWR	1880		To 105 Third, Mar 1914
5	30'	5	6	MGWR	1880	1903	
6	30'	5	6	MGWR	1884		To 103 Third, Mar 1914
7	30'	5	6	MGWR	1884		To 99 Third, Jan 1914
8	30'	5	6	MGWR	1885		To 101 Third, Feb 1914
9	30'	5	6	MGWR	1890		To 44 First, Apr 1914
10	30'	5	6	MGWR	1890		To 96 Third, Jan 1914
11	30'	5	6	MGWR	1890		To 104 Third, Mar 1914
12	30'	5	6	MGWR	1890		To 43 First, Apr 1914
13	30'	5	6	MGWR	1890		To 97 Third, Jan 1914
14	30'	5	6	MGWR	1890		To 100 Third, Jan 1914
15		4	4	Bris	1873	1892	
15	30'	5	6	MGWR	1892		To 40 First, Mar 1914
16		4	4	Bris	1873	1892	
16	30'	5	6	MGWR	1892		To 15 First, Feb 1914
17		4	4	Bris	1873	1892	
17	30'	5	6	MGWR	1892		To 42 First, Apr 1914
18	30'	5	6	MGWR	1885		To 102 Third, Mar 1914
19	30'	5	6	MGWR	1885		To 98 Third, Jan 1914
20	30'	5	6	MGWR	1885		To 106 Third, Mar 1914
21	30'	6	6	Ash	1894		To 12 First, Jan 1914
22	30'	6	6	Ash	1894		To 41 First, Mar 1914
23	30'	6	6	Ash	1894		To 45 First, Apr 1914
24	30'	6	6	Ash	1894		To 13 First, Apr 1914
25	30'	6	6	Ash	1894		To 39 First, Mar 1914
26	54'	2+S	8	Lanc	1902		To 33 First, Apr 1914
27	54'	2+S	8	Lanc	1902		To 34 First, Apr 1914

THIRD CLASS

No.	Length	Compts	Wheels	Maker	Intr.	Wdn.	Remarks
1	31'	6	6	MGWR	1881	1914	
1	53'	4	8	Metr	1922	1958	Ex 32 First, Dec 1922
2	22' 6"	2	4	MGWR	1875	1893	
2	30'	5	6	MGWR	1893	1956	M.D. Manulla 8-11-22
3		5	4	MGWR	1869	1891	
3	30'	5	6	MGWR	1891		60 seats. R/n 509A 1985
4	22' 6"	2	4	MGWR	1876	1894	
4	30'	5	6	MGWR	1894	1954	
5	22' 6"	2	4	MGWR	1876	1894	
5	30'	5	6	MGWR	1894	1956	
6	22' 6"	2	4	MGWR	1877	1896	
6	30'	5	6	MGWR	1896	1923	Destr. Achill, 12-1-23
7	22' 6"	2	4	MGWR	1875	1894	
7	30'	5	6	MGWR	1894	1923	Destr. Drumree, 24-1-23
8	22' 6"	2	4	MGWR	1875	1895	
8	30'	5	6	MGWR	1895	1924	To P.W. power van, 1924
9	22' 6"	5	4	MGWR	1869	1891	
9	30'	5	6	MGWR	1891	1964	60 seats
10	22' 6"	2	4	MGWR	1876	1894	
10	30'	5	6	MGWR	1894	1956	
11	31'	6	6	MGWR	1883	1911	2 compts conv to brake compt.
11	31'	4	6	MGWR	1911		R/b as 3rd.brake 70M
12	22' 6"	2	4	MGWR	1876	1895	
12	30'	5	6	MGWR	1895	1923	Destr. Achill, 20-1-23
13	22' 6"	2	4	MGWR	1875	1893	
13	30'	5	6	MGWR	1893		†M.D. Streamstown,16-1-23
14	31'	6	6	MGWR	1883	1911	
14	31'	5	6	MGWR	1911		R/b as C.C. & 2 lav.
15	22' 6"	2	4	MGWR	1876	1894	
15	30'	5	6	MGWR	1894	1949	
16	22' 6"	2	4	MGWR	1877	1895	
16	30'	5	6	MGWR	1895	1949	M.D. Streamstown,16-1-23
17	22' 6"	2	4	MGWR	1876	1895	
17	30'	5	6	MGWR	1895	1949	
18	22' 6"	2	4	MGWR	1876	1894	
18	30'	5	6	MGWR	1894	1954	
19	22' 6"	2	4	MGWR	1877	1896	
19	30'	5	6	MGWR	1896	1956	M.D. Streamstown,17-2-23
20	22' 6"	2	4	MGWR	1877	1896	

THIRD CLASS

No.	Length	Compts	Wheels	Maker	Intr.	Wdn.	Remarks
20	30'	5	6	MGWR	1896	1923	Destroyed Sligo,10-1-23
21	31'	6	6	MGWR	1881	1909	2 compts.conv to brake
21	30'	5	6	MGWR	1910		
22	22'6"	2	4	MGWR	1878	1897	
22	30'	5	6	MGWR	1897		
23	22'6"	2	4	MGWR	1875	1894	
23	30'	5	6	MGWR	1894	1959	
24	31'	6	6	MGWR	1882	1915	To Sleeping van no.1
24	31'	5	6	MGWR	1912	1923	Destroyed Sligo, 10-1-23
25	22'6"	2	4	MGWR	1878	1897	
25	30'	5	6	MGWR	1897	1956	60 seats
26	31'	6	6	MGWR	1883	1913	To Motor van no.1,1913
26	31'	5	6	MGWR	1912	1960	C.C. 2 lav
27	31'	6	6	MGWR	1882	1911	
27	31'	5	6	MGWR	1911	1954	C.C. 44 seats
28	22'6"	2	4	MGWR	1878	1897	
28	30'	5	6	MGWR	1897	1949	M.D. Mayo line,7-2-23
29	22'6"	2	4	MGWR	1875	1893	
29	30'	5	6	MGWR	1893	1959	60 seats
30	22'6"	2	4	MGWR	1876	1895	
30	30'	5	6	MGWR	1895		60 seats, E.L.1935
31	31'	6	6	MGWR	1881		
31	31'	5	6	MGWR	1911	1923	Destroyed Sligo, 10-1-23
32	22'6"	2	4	MGWR	1877	1896	
32	30'	5	6	MGWR	1896	1923	Destr. Kiltoom, 23-1-23; new van 28 built on u/f
33	31'	6	6	MGWR	1881		
34	31'	6	6	MGWR	1883	1920	To Mess van with loco breakdown train
35	22'6"	2	4	MGWR	1876	1894	
35	30'	5	6	MGWR	1894	1959	
36	22'6"	2	4	MGWR	1878	1897	
36	30'	5	6	MGWR	1897	1961	
37	31'	6	6	MGWR	1882	1915	To Sleeping van no.2
37	31'	5	6	MGWR	1912	1960	44 seats
38	22'6"	2	4	MGWR	1877	1896	
38	30'	5	6	MGWR	1896	1954	60 seats
39	22'6"	2	4	MGWR	1877	1896	
39	30'	5	6	MGWR	1896		
40	22'6"	2	4	MGWR	1878	1898	
40	30'	5	6	MGWR	1898	1954	
41	22'6"	5	4	MGWR	1864		
41	30'	5	6	MGWR	1890	1954	M.D. Streamstown, 17-2-23
42	22'6"	5	4	MGWR	1864		
42	30'	5	6	MGWR	1890		60 seats
43	22'6"	5	4	MGWR	1864		
43	30'	5	6	MGWR	1890	1923	Destr. Streamstown, 17-2-23
44	22'6"	5	4	MGWR	1864		
44	30'	5	6	MGWR	1890	1923	Destr. Kingscourt, 4-1-23
45	22'6"	5	4	MGWR	1864		
45	30'	5	6	MGWR	1891		
46	22'6"	5	4	MGWR	1864		
46	30'	5	6	MGWR	1891	1956	
47	22'6"	5	4	MGWR	1865		
47	30'	5	6	MGWR	1891	1961	M.D. Liffey Jct 8-12-22
48	22'6"	5	4	MGWR	1865		
48	30'	5	6	MGWR	1891	1960	
49	22'6"	5	4	MGWR	1865		
49	30'	5	6	MGWR	1891		
50	22'6"	5	4	MGWR	1865		
50	30'	5	6	MGWR	1891	1923	Destroyed Sligo,10-1-23
51	22'6"	5	4	MGWR	1866		
51	30'	5	6	MGWR	1891	1924	U/f used for new van
52	22'6"	5	4	MGWR	1866		
52	30'	5	6	MGWR	1891	1959	
53	22'6"	5	4	MGWR	1867		
53	30'	5	6	MGWR	1892		
54	22'6"	5	4	MGWR	1867		
54	30'	5	6	MGWR	1892	1961	
55	22'6"	5	4	MGWR	1867		
55	30'	5	6	MGWR	1892	1942	M.D. Kiltoom, 1-3-23 Destroyed Athlone,8-7-42
56	22'6"	5	4	MGWR	1867		
56	30'	5	6	MGWR	1891		
57	22'6"	5	4	MGWR	1868		
57	30'	5	6	MGWR	1891		
58	22'6"	5	4	MGWR	1868		
58	30'	5	6	MGWR	1892	1954	Gas-lighting
59	22'6"	5	4	MGWR	1878		
59	30'	5	6	MGWR	1899	1954	
60	30'	5	6	MGWR	1892	1956	
61	22'6"	2	4	MGWR	1876	1895	
61	31'	5	6	MGWR	1895	1923	Destroyed Drumree, 24-1-23

THIRD CLASS

No.	Length	Compts	Wheels	Maker	Intr.	Wdn.	Remarks
62	30'	5	6	Ash	1892		60 seats
63	30'	5	6	Ash	1892	1924	
64	30'	5	6	Ash	1892	1949	E.L.1936
65	30'	5	6	Ash	1892	1959	
66	30'	5	6	Ash	1892	1954	
67		5	6	Wr	1862		Ex D&M
67	30'	5	6	MGWR	1890	1956	
68		5	6	Wr	1862		Ex D&M
68	30'	5	6	MGWR	1890	1923	M.D. Kingscourt, 4-1-23
69				Wr	1869	1889	Ex D&M
69	30'	5	6	Ash	1892	1959	
70	22'6"	2	4	MGWR	1878	1898	
70	30'	5	6	MGWR	1898	1954	
71	31'	6	6	MGWR	1882	1912	To Broadstone breakdown van
71	31'	5	6	MGWR	1912	1952	44 seats, 2 lav
72	31'	6	6	MGWR	1882		
72	31'	5	6	MGWR	1911	1954	
73	22'6"	2	4	MGWR	1877	1893	
73	30'	5	6	MGWR	1893	1949	To Workmens' train, 299A
74	31'	6	6	MGWR	1881		2 compts conv to brake
74	31'	4	6	MGWR	1911	1922	Destr. Ballywillan by fire, 5-12-22
75	22'6"	2	4	MGWR	1878	1899	
75	30'	5	6	MGWR	1899	1961	M.D. Islandeady, 25-1-23
76	31'	6	6	MGWR	1881	1925	R/n 76A on 29-2-1916
77	22'6"	2	4	Metr	1878	1899	
77	30'	5	6	MGWR	1899	1949	M.D. Manulla Jct 8-11-22 To P.W. sleeping van 307A
78	22'6"	2	4	Metr	1878	1899	
78	30'	5	6	MGWR	1899	1923	Destr. Achill, 12-1-23
79	22'6"	2	4	Metr	1878		Conv Inspection Coach, to 43 Compo 1901
79	54'	8	8	MGWR	1901	1963	
80	22'6"	2	4	Metr	1878	1898	
80	30'	5	6	MGWR	1898	1949	Destr. Sligo, 10-1-23 *

* The Carriage & Wagon Register states that this coach was destroyed at Sligo, but a pencilled note indicates that it went through shops for routine repair and returned to traffic on 28th June 1924, not having been maliciously damaged. Engineer was to be written to for an explanation.

No.	Length	Compts	Wheels	Maker	Intr.	Wdn.	Remarks
81	22'6"	2	4	Metr	1878	1898	
81	30'	5	6	MGWR	1898	1959	60 seats
82	22'6"	2	4	Metr	1878	1900	
82	30'	5	6	MGWR	1900	1923	Destroyed Sligo, 10-1-23
83	22'6"	2	4	Metr	1878	1896	To Mortuary van 58
83	54'	8	8	MGWR	1901	1958	
84	22'6"	2	4	Metr	1878	1897	
84	30'	5	6	MGWR	1897		
85	22'6"	2	4	Metr	1878	1899	
85	30'	5	6	MGWR	1899		
86	22'6"	2	4	Metr	1878	1899	
86	30'	5	6	MGWR	1899	1956	
87	22'6"	2	4	Metr	1878	1900	
87	30'	5	6	MGWR	1900	1960	M.D. Liffey Jct
88	22'6"	2	4	Metr	1878	1897	
88	30'	5	6	MGWR	1897	1956	
89	30'	5	6	Ash	1892	1954	
90	30'	5	6	Ash	1892	1923	Destroyed Sligo,10-1-23
91	30'	5	6	Ash	1892	1959	
92	30'	5	6	Ash	1892	1949	
93	30'	5	6	Ash	1892	1924	U/f used in Brake van 12
94	54'	8	8	MGWR	1902	1952	Conv. to Ambulance coach-16 stretchers
95	54'	8	8	MGWR	1902	1961	64 seats, 2 lav
96	30'	5	6	MGWR	1914	1954	Ex 10 Second
97	30'	5	6	MGWR	1914	1925	Ex 13 Second
98	30'	5	6	MGWR	1914	1952	Ex 19 Second
99	30'	5	6	MGWR	1914	1956	Ex 7 Second
100	30'	5	6	MGWR	1914	1956	Ex 14 Second
101	30'	5	6	MGWR	1914	1954	Ex 8 Second
102	30'	5	6	MGWR	1914	1924	Ex 18 Second; To Ballast Mess van 43
103	30'	5	6	MGWR	1914	1949	Ex 6 Second; 48 seats
104	30'	5	6	MGWR	1914	1961	Ex 11 Second
105	30'	5	6	MGWR	1914	1923	Ex 4 Second; M.D. at Killala, 3-2-23
106	30'	5	6	MGWR	1914	1964	Ex 20 Second; 36 seats
107	30'	5	6	MGWR	1914		Ex 3 Second; 42 seats
108	54'	2	12	MGWR	1915	1942	Ex Diner 3, 30-4-1915; destroyed by fire 8-7-42
109	54'	9	8	MGWR	1916	1956	78 seats,2 lav
110	60'	9	8	MGWR	1923	1961	90 seats; weight 33T; s.c.
111	60'	9	8	MGWR	1923	1959	90 seats; weight 33T; s.c.
112	60'	9	8	MGWR	1923	1960	90 seats; weight 33T; s.c.
113	60'	9	8	MGWR	1924	1962	90 seats; weight 33T; SC

Continued on page 138

6-WHEEL THIRD 1890 CLASS

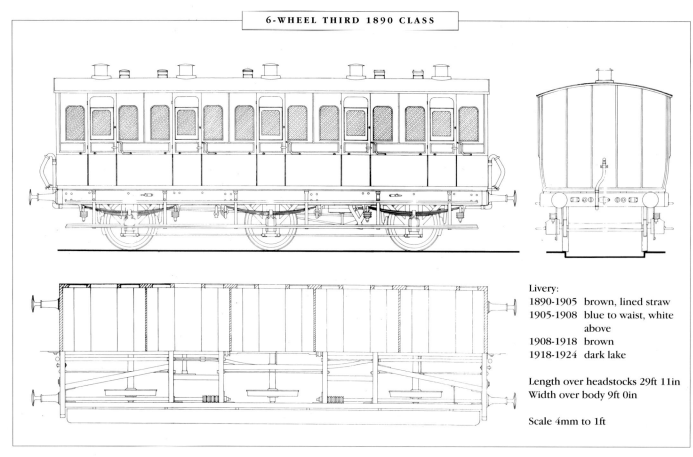

Livery:
1890-1905 brown, lined straw
1905-1908 blue to waist, white
            above
1908-1918 brown
1918-1924 dark lake

Length over headstocks 29ft 11in
Width over body 9ft 0in

Scale 4mm to 1ft

6-WHEEL LAVATORY SECOND

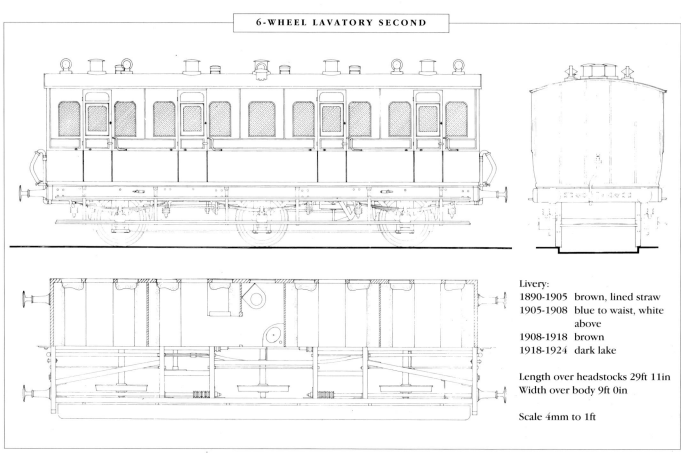

Livery:
1890-1905 brown, lined straw
1905-1908 blue to waist, white
            above
1908-1918 brown
1918-1924 dark lake

Length over headstocks 29ft 11in
Width over body 9ft 0in

Scale 4mm to 1ft

6-WHEEL BRAKE THIRD (BRANCH LINE) 1887 CLASS

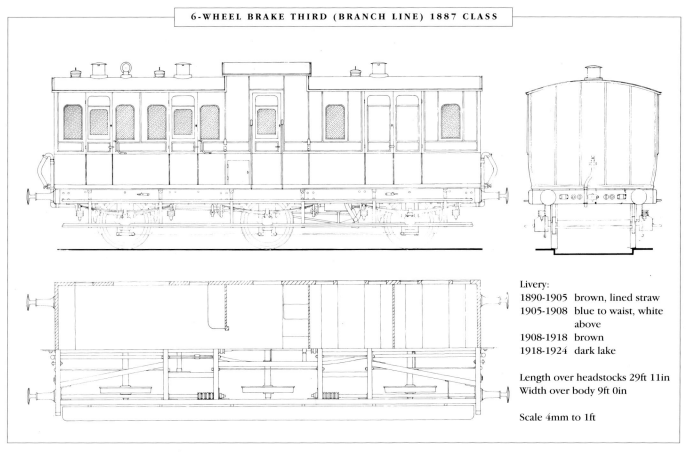

Livery:
1890-1905 brown, lined straw
1905-1908 blue to waist, white
above
1908-1918 brown
1918-1924 dark lake

Length over headstocks 29ft 11in
Width over body 9ft 0in

Scale 4mm to 1ft

4-WHEEL THIRD CARRIAGE

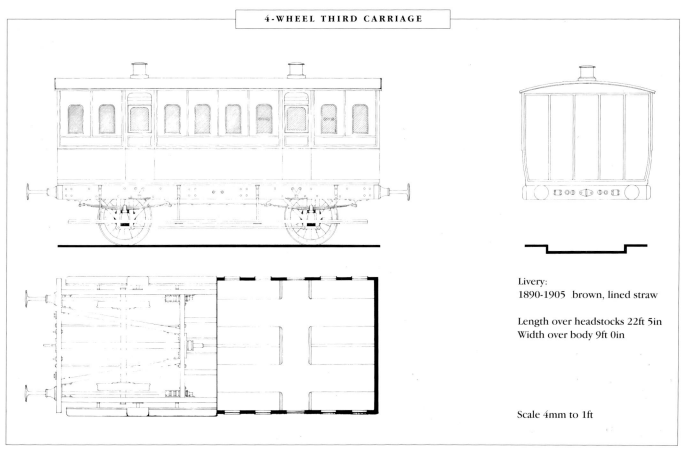

Livery:
1890-1905 brown, lined straw

Length over headstocks 22ft 5in
Width over body 9ft 0in

Scale 4mm to 1ft

THIRD CLASS

No.	Length	Compts	Wheels	Maker	Intr.	Wdn.	Remarks
150M	29'	4	6	MGWR	1929	1962	Ex 17M Compo, 1929
151M	29'	4	6	MGWR	1929		Ex 28M Compo, 1929
152M	29'	4	6	MGWR	1929	1956	Ex 8M Compo, 1929
153M	29'	4	6	MGWR	1929	1953	Ex 3M Compo, 1929
154M	29'	4	6	MGWR	1929	1949	Ex 24M Compo, 1929
155M	29'	4	6	MGWR	1929	1949	Ex 26M Compo, 1929
156M	29'	4	6	MGWR	1929	1954	Ex 9M Compo, 1929
157M	29'	4	6	MGWR	1929	1961	Ex 11M Compo, 1929
158M	29'	4	6	MGWR	1929	1959	Ex 22M Compo, 1929
159M	29'	4	6	MGWR	1929		Ex 25M Compo, 1929
160M	53'	7	8	Metr	1930		Ex 40M Compo, 1930; reconv to 40M in 1932
161M	53'	7	8	Metr	1930		Ex 31M Compo, 1930; reconv to 31M in 1932
162M	54'	7	8	MGWR	1930		Ex 35M First, to Compo 162M 1930 & to 3rd 1955
164M	30'	4	6	MGWR	1930		Ex 5M First, 1930
165M	30'	4	6	MGWR	1930		Ex 19M First, 1930
166M	54'	7	8	MGWR	1930	1962	Ex 28M First & 166M
167M	30'	4	6	MGWR	1930	1956	Ex 18M First, 1930
168M	29'	4	6	MGWR	1930	1954	Ex 13M Compo, 1930
169M	30'	4	6	MGWR	1930		Ex 16M First, 1930
170M	30'	4	6	MGWR	1930	1960	Ex 9M First, 1930
171M	29'	4	6	MGWR	1931		Ex 16M Compo, 1931
172M	30'	4	6	MGWR	1930	1959	Ex 10M First, 1930
173M	30'	4	6	MGWR	1931	1949	Ex 18M Compo, 1931
174M	29'	4	6	MGWR	1931	1953	Ex 15M Compo, 1931
175M	54'	7	8	MGWR	1931	1960	Ex 29M First & Compo
177M	29'	4	6	MGWR	1931		Ex 19M Compo, 1931
178M	29'	4	6	MGWR	1931		Ex 4M First, 1931 & reverted to 1st. 1943
180M	29'	4	6	MGWR	1931	1956	Ex 14M Compo, 1931
193M	54'	3	8	Lanc	1955	1961	Ex 27M First, 1955
196M	54'	3	8	Lanc	1954	1962	Ex 26M Compo, 1954

COMPOSITES

No.	Length	Compts	Wheels	Maker	Intr.	Wdn.	Remarks
1	29'	5	6	MGWR	1885	1954	
2	29'	5	6	MGWR	1885	1956	
3	29'	4	6	MGWR	1885		To 153M Third, 1929
4	29'	4	6	MGWR	1885	1949	
5	25'	3	6	Daws	1844		To 31 First, 1920
6	29'	4	6	MGWR	1885	1923	Destr. Drumree, 24-1-23
7	29'	4	6	MGWR	1885	1956	
8	29'	4	6	MGWR	1885		To 152M Third, 1929
9	29'	4	6	MGWR	1885		To 156M Third, 1929
10		4	4	MGWR	1866	1893	'All of mahogany'
10	29'	4	6	MGWR	1893	1925	
11	29'	4	6	MGWR	1885		To 157M Third, 1929
12	29'	4	6	MGWR	1885	1961	Seats - 16+24
13	29'	4	6	MGWR	1886		To 168M Third, 1930
14	29'	4	6	MGWR	1886		To 180M Third, 1931; M.D. Streamstown, 16-1-23
15	29'	4	6	MGWR	1886		To 174M Third, 1931
16	29'	4	6	MGWR	1886		To 171M Third, 1931
17	29'	4	6	MGWR	1886		To 150M Third, 1929
18	29'	4	6	MGWR	1886		To 173M Third, 1931
19	29'	4	6	MGWR	1886		To 177M Third, 1931
20	29'	4	6	MGWR	1886		
21	29'	4	6	MGWR	1886		
22	29'	4	6	MGWR	1886		To 158M Third, 1929
23	29'	4	6	MGWR	1886	1960	
24	29'	4	6	MGWR	1886		To 154M Third, 1929
25	29'	4	6	MGWR	1887		To 159M Third, 1929
26	29'	4	6	MGWR	1887		To 155M Third, 1929
26	54'	2+S	8	Lanc	1934		Ex 26M First, to 196M Third, 1954
27	29'	4	6	MGWR	1887	1960	
28	29'	4	6	MGWR	1887		To 151M Third, 1929
29	30'	4	6	MGWR	1891		To 38 First, April 1914
30	30'	4	6	MGWR	1891		To 37 First, April 1914
31	29'	4	6	Midl	1896	1954	
31	53'	11	8	Metr	1920		Ex 31 First. to 161M Third; 1932 1960 Reconvtd to 31M 1932
	29'	4	6	MGWR	1886	1956	
33	29'	4	6	MGWR	1886	1923	Destr. Drumree 24-1-23
34	29'	4	6	MGWR	1886	1923	Destr. Sligo 10-1-23
35	29'	4	6	Midl	1886	1903	
35	29'	3	6	MGWR	1903	1959	Slip Carriage; conv.to Trial train van 245A
36	29'	4	6	MGWR	1886	1908	
36	29'	3	6	MGWR	1905		Slip Carriage
37	29'	4	6	MGWR	1886	1960	
38	29'	4	6	MGWR	1886	1954	
39	53'	11	8	Metr	1900	1962	Orig. tri-compo till '14
40	53'	11	8	Metr	1900		To 160M Third, 1930
41	53'	11	8	Metr	1900		To 31 full First, 1914

COMPOSITES

No.	Length	Compts	Wheels	Maker	Intr.	Wdn.	Remarks
41	29'	4	6	Midl	1886		
42	53'	11	8	Metr	1900		To 32 First, 1914
43	22' 6"	2	4	MGWR	1901		Ex 79 Third, to Inspection carriage; to 46 First, 1924
43	60'	8	8	MGWR	1924	1961	
44	54'	7	8	MGWR	1903		To 30 First, 1914
45	54'	7	8	MGWR	1903		
46	54'	7	8	MGWR	1904		To 28 First, 1914
47	31' 3"	3	6	Daws	1904		Old State Coach, R/b 1904; To 47 First in 1924
48M	60'	8	8	GSR	1925	1956?	33 tons; 18-1st & 50-3rd.
49M	60'	8	8	GSR	1926	1962	
50M	60'	8	8	GSR	1926	1961	
52	30'	4	6	Metr	1879		Ex 1 Saloon c1882; To 29 Compo c1891
53	30'	4	6	Metr	1879		Ex 2 Saloon c1882; To 30 Compo c1891
162M	54'	7	8	MGWR	1930		Ex 35M First, 1930
163M	54'	7	8	MGWR	1930		Ex 30M First, 1930;to Ambulance coach
175M	54'	7	8	MGWR	1931		Ex 29M First
181M	31'	4	6	MGWR	1893	1954	Ex 6M First, 1939
182M	31'	4	6	MGWR	1893	1960	Ex 8M First, 1939
183M	30'	6	6	Ash	1894	1959	Ex 45M First, 1939
184M	30'	6	6	Ash	1894	1956	Ex 25M First, 1939
185M	30'	6	6	Ash	1894		Ex 41M First, 1940
186M	30'	6	6	Ash	1894	1954	Ex 24M First, 1940
187M	30'	6	6	MGWR	1892		Ex 15M First, 1940
188M	30'	6	6	MGWR	1892	1949	Ex 40M First, 1940
189M	31'	6	6	MGWR	1906	1961	Ex 11M First, 1940
190M	30'	6	6	Ash	1894		Ex 12M First, 1940
191M	30'	6	6	Ash	1894	1954	Ex 13M First, 1940
192M	30'	6	6	MGWR	1890	1954	Ex 43M First, 1940

STATE CARRIAGES AND DINING CARS

No.	Length	Compts	Wheels	Maker	Intr.	Wdn.	Remarks
		3	6	Daws	1844		To Compo 47
(346)	55'6"	4	12	MGWR	1903		25 seats*
1	54'	2	12	Lanc	1902	1958	24 seats; To 1st/3rd Apr 1914
2	54'	2	12	Lanc	1902	1958	To 1st/3rd, 1914
3	54'	12	12	MGWR	1904		To 108 Third, Apr 1915

MAKERS

Ash	Ashbury Carriage & Wagon Co.	Lanc	Lancaster Carriage & Wagon Co
Bris	Bristol Wagon Works	Metr	Metropolitan Carriage & Wagon Co
Daws	Dawson of Phibsborough	Midl	Midland Carriage & Wagon Co
GSR	Great Southern Railways	MGWR	Midland Great Western Railway

NOTES: CC - Centre Corridor; R/b - Rebuilt; U/F - underframe; Ax - Accident; MD - Maliciously damaged; † - Still extant at Mullingar in the care of RPSI; S - Saloon; SC - Side Corridor; R/n - renumbered.
* Number allocated by GSR - not numbered by MGWR. Coaches with M suffix are ex MGWR vehicles, either reclassified or renumbered post 1925, by the GSR.

Appendix H

CHAIRMEN & PRINCIPAL OFFICERS

CHAIRMEN	SECRETARIES	ENGINEERS
1845 Lord Dunsandle	1845 Henry Beausire	1845 Sir John Macneill
1847 John Ennis	1876 G W Greene	1846 George W Hemans
1865 George Maunsell	1902 R L Badham	1853 Edward Wilson
1865 Ralph Cusack	1910 Percy Hay	1856 Joseph Cabry
1904 Hon R Nugent	1924 Edward Taylor	1862 James Price
1912 Major H C Cusack	(Acting)	1878 Robert Greene
		1882 G W Kelly
MANAGERS	**LOCOMOTIVE**	1890 A H Smythe
1849 Peter Roe	**SUPERINTENDENTS**	1894 W P O'Neill
1855 William Forbes	1847 John Dewrance	1919 Arthur Bretland
1865 William Skipworth	1849 Contract	
1869 John Ward	1853 Edward Wilson	
1890 Joseph Tatlow	1856 Joseph Cabry	
1913 Michael Keogh	1862 Robert Ramage	
	1872 Martin Atock	
	1900 Edward Cusack	
	1915 Walter H Morton	

Appendix I

PRINCIPAL ACCIDENTS

Date	Location	Pass. K	Inj	Staff K	Inj	Comments	Date	Location	Pass. K	Inj	Staff K	Inj	Comments
17-9-59	Killucan	-	-	-	-	Rails removed by PWD.	22-7-80	Athlone	-	3	-	-	Collision
17-12-62	Kells branch	-	-	-	-	Ran through crossing gate.	9-10-81	Liffey Jct	-	14	-	4	Collision.
29-10-64	Ballinasloe	2	34	-	-	Excess speed on poor PW.	5-1-83	Lough Owel	-	4	-	-	Collision.
7-10-65	Kilcock	-	5	-	7	Collision - goods ran away.	2-1-84	Athenry	-	3	-	2	Collision - overran signals.
21-11-70	Athlone	-	-	2	-	Shunting accident.	30-6-86	Mullingar	-	-	-	1	Collision.
3-1-71	Oranmore	-	-	-	-	Derail, due bad PW.	14-6-89	Ballyhaunis	1	-	-	-	Overcrowding.
29-8-71	nr Cavan	-	-	-	2	Horse kicked end of wagon.	30-9-89	Carrick	-	-	-	-	Collision - crew 12 hrs on duty.
27-9-71	Kilcock	-	11	-	1	Collision.	6-1-94	Moate	-	1	-	2	Collision - signal frozen.
23-10-71	Galway	-	4	-	-	Collision - bad station work.	11-4-03	Ballymoe	1	11	-	4	Hit obstruction on line.
27-4-75	Navan	1	-	-	-	Guard pushed passenger out.	2-8-03	Ballymote	-	3	-	-	Collision - road incorrectly set.
30-10-75	Castlebar	1	7	-	-	Collision - crew 18hrs on duty.	14-1-05	73 Mile box	-	2	-	1	Collision - overran signals.
16-9-76	Killucan	-	1	-	-	Collision - goods ran away.	29-6-06	Broadstone	-	-	-	1	Shunting.
10-3-77	Clonsilla	-	5	-	-	Derail - no locking bar.	27-7-06	Hill of Down	-	-	1	-	Ganger asleep and hit by train.
23-4-77	Athlone	-	-	-	-	Derail - no check rail.	13-3-08	Maynooth	-	2	1	-	Collision - wgn fouled rng line.
4-12-77	Castlerea	-	8	-	-	Derail - defective rail.	9-3-09	Athlone	-	-	-	1	Shunting - different couplings.
26-12-77	Athboy	-	-	-	1	Overran station.	5-9-10	Manulla Jct	-	15	-	-	Collision - overran signals.
11-6-80	Ballyhaunis	-	4	-	-	Collision - no interlocking.	21-10-19	Balla	-	-	-	-	Collision.
15-7-80	Mullingar	-	-	-	-	Collision - no interlocking.	18-11-19	Moyvalley	-	-	-	-	Collision.

Appendix J

TICKETS

Tickets can be divided into the following categories:

1 Limited Mail, all classes
2 First class,
    not available by Limited Mail
3 Second class,
    not available by Limited Mail
4a Third class,
    not available by Limited Mail
4b Third class Parliamentary
5 Child and Special issues
6 Dog and Bicycle tickets
7 Through tickets to the U.K.

Four different company titles were used, viz M.G.W.R., Midland Great Western Railway, M.G.W.Ry and Midland Great Western Ry. As regards size, they were standard Edmonson card tickets as used by LM&SR etc.

1. Limited Mails.
All had the words 'Limited Mail' printed on them and a special colour scheme was employed. Both pre-printed destinations and blank cards were used. First class singles were brick red, returns red with a central white horizontal band, the return half having a yellow background instead of pure white. Later versions had a skeleton 'R' in black.

Second singles were lilac with faint white diagonals, while returns had green outward halves with three white bands, and three vertical white bands. Third singles were green, returns outward green and inward buff. There was a thin blue horizontal line and one thin vertical blue line on each half. The skeleton 'R' was later used and final issues had both halves green.

2. First class.
Singles were white with fare in bottom right corner although later versions show 'Revised fare' just below the conditions and above the issuing station. Variants existed from Sligo and Athenry to non-MGW stations which had the words 'by GS&W train'. Returns had white outward, yellow return with 'R' on later issues. Final issues were all white with 'Revised fare'. Variants included 'Tourist' below the class; these had a thin horizontal green line. Excursions were white with two vertical pink bands on outward half and a very thick green band on return. Saturday to Monday tickets had a thick pink band (outward) and thick blue (return). Market tickets were yellow throughout with a thick horizontal red band on both halves and 'R' on return half. Later types were white overprinted 'M' on return half.

3. Second class.
Singles came in various shades of blue. The outward half of returns were blue, return half red. Weekend tickets had blue and white outward, return pink and white, while Excursion outward halves were white with two vertical yellow bars, returns white with a central pink stripe. Privilege tickets were similar to ordinary seconds.

4a. Third class.
Singles were straw/buff. Variations similar to first class existed for non-MGW stations. There were special Emigrant tickets with the legend 'Emigrants Third Class'; an example was Ballymote to Southampton via North Wall, Chester, Crewe, Willesden and Kensington. Harvestmens' tickets were 'available on Fridays and by 3rd class trains only' and were white with a horizontal blue band. Return tickets had buff outward and green return halves, some with skeleton 'R'. Excursion tickets were white, outward half having two large vertical mauve stripes and return one thick vertical green band.

Market tickets were green with a horizontal red band, although later issues were buff with 'M'. Soldiers-on-leave tickets were buff outward and green return half, and were valid for two months. There were special excursion tickets for such organisations as the Irish National Foresters and the Gaelic League, and presumably others existed for similar bodies.

4b. Parliamentary.

Only single versions of these have been seen and were buff with three vertical black lines.

5. Child and Special issues.

No special child tickets are known to exist. It is likely that adult tickets were used with the repeated name of the destination station removed with a special cutter. These pieces were pasted on a sheet of paper and sent to Audit at the end of each month. Dublin, North Wall issued tickets for Broadstone, and although in MGW colours, they were pure L&NW tickets even to the extent of hav-ing the L&NW audit number 446 on them. Special paper tickets were issued to first and second class passengers travelling to stay in the Midland hotels. Special tickets were also issued from Castlebar and Westport to Mallaranny for golfers, which included admission to the company's golf links.

6. Dog and Bicycle tickets.

The former were yellow and were all blank cards to handwritten destinations, while early bicycle tickets were red, white and yellow. Issues in the 1920s were pink. White returns also exist.

7. Through tickets to U.K. destinations.

First and saloon had three routes: B&I North Wall to Liverpool, Kingstown and L&NW to Holyhead and GWR via Holyhead and Chester. Third and saloon were similar, the GWR tickets being green and the L&NW buff, both overprinted with a skeleton 'S'. Third and deck were buff and were not overprinted.

Finally, both the D&M and the GN&W are known to have issued their own tickets in the early days, but these are extremely rare nowadays.

The author's sincere thanks go to the late Charles R. Gordon Stewart and to Eugene Field for the foregoing information.

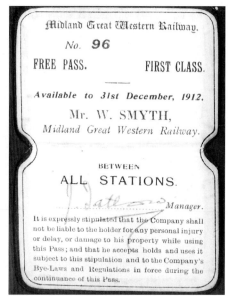

INDEX

Further related titles from Midland Publishing Limited

Irish Railways in Colour From Steam to Diesel 1955-1967
by Tom Ferris
Includes over 200 colour illustrations
ISBN 1 85780 000 1

The Irish Narrow Gauge Volume One: From Cork to Cavan
by Tom Ferris
Includes over 200 b/w illustrations
ISBN 1 85780 010 9

The Irish Narrow Gauge Volume Two: The Ulster Lines
by Tom Ferris
Includes 287 b/w illustrations
ISBN 1 85780 017 6

Midland/OnLine Video Programmes

Irish Railways Volume 1
Running time 55 minutes

Irish Railways Volume 2 The Swansong of Steam in Ulster - 1962-64
Running time 63 minutes

Irish Railways Volume 3 The Irish Narrow Gauge: Colour Films 1939-1959
Running time 50 minutes

For price and availability contact
Midland Publishing Limited
24 The Hollow, Earl Shilton
Leicester, LE9 7NA
Tel: 0455 233 747; Fax 0455 841 805

The visitor will not fail to observe
the singular yet graceful railway bridge over
which the Dublin line is carried
across the Shannon,
'being a construction on the bowstring
and lattice principle.
It is entirely of iron, supported by twelve cylindrical piers,
and is 560 feet in extreme length, including two spans
over roads on either side of the river.
It consists of two spans of 175 and two of forty feet each, the
latter separated by a pier, formed by four cylinders,
supporting a swivel, which admits of the navigation
of the adjacent opens'.

Reproduced from
The Official Illustrated Guide
to the Midland Great Western, Dublin & Drogheda,
Great Southern & Western Railways
by George S Measom